# Stage Blood:
## Vampires of the
## 19th-Century Stage

# Roxana Stuart

Bowling Green State University Popular Press
Bowling Green, OH 43403

Library of Congress Catalog Card Number: 94-72404

ISBN: 0-87972-659-8 Clothbound
0-87972-660-1 Paperback

Cover design and type by Laura Darnell-Dumm

# Contents

# List of Illustrations

# Acknowledgments

Thanks to Dr. Daniel Gerould, Dr. Marvin Carlson, Dr. Miriam D'Aponte, Leonard Wolf, Rona Ostrow, Dr. Eva Friedman, Dr. Edward Dee, Ann Dobbs, and Eric Stenshoel for their assistance and encouragement, and especially to Scott, Bertram, and Miranda for their love and support.

# Introduction

In tombs of gold and lapis lazuli
Bodies of holy men and women exude
Miraculous oil, odour of violet.

But under heavy loads of trampled clay
Lie bodies of the vampires full of blood;
Their shrouds are bloody and their lips are wet.
      —W.B. Yeats, "Oil and Blood"

When we go to the theatre, we want to be delighted and instructed, certainly, but we want much more: to fall in love, to have the limits of our imagination stretched, to undergo terrible ordeals vicariously and gain our heart's desire, to defy the hostile stars as we go down to death even as we triumph over it.[1] One special pleasure that the theatre offers—with great intensity because of the physical presence of the actor—is to thrill us by scaring us out of our wits. Ever since Aeschylus's Furies caused people in the audience to die of fear and women to miscarry, this tradition has been part of theatre. Terror is one of the two essential elements of Aristotelian catharsis. As Eric Bentley writes in *The Life of the Drama*:

In the theatre, phenomena like...Dracula are not eccentricities but prototypes.... There is no comparison...between the potency of the novel and acted play. Physical presence on the stage makes an essential difference here. It is not in the quiet of libraries, bedrooms or kitchens that devotees of...bloodsucking swoon. It is in the theatre. (176)

Vampires are dangerous and attractive: they kill, or confer immortality, depending on their whim. They perfectly embody the revulsion and the attraction to the erotic that lie at the heart of human experience, the simultaneous longing for—and terror of—being devoured. They are a nightmarish projection of irrational attitudes toward sex and death that are hidden from the waking

**1**

mind. In *On the Nightmare* Ernest Jones theorizes on the subconscious sexual basis of the vampire superstition:

Complex and...fundamental emotions are at work in the construction and maintenance of the vampire superstition. It is...[a] product of the deepest conflicts that determine human development and fate—those concerned with the earliest relationships to the parents...repressed desires and hatreds derived from early incest conflicts. (129)

Human sexuality certainly did not disappear in the Victorian age because of strict obscenity laws, censorship, and the prudery of the queen. It manifested itself in literature in many symbolic forms, and in society as a kind of mass hypocrisy—for example, the pretended idealization of woman while the reality was often contempt and exploitation. The surface of prudery, and the "dirty secret" beneath the appearance, is one form of social decadence. Nineteenth-century English and French writers, unless they went underground, could not write graphically about sex: it had to be camouflaged as something else. The vampire's unique ability to commit sexual violation without involving the genitals ideally suited him for this role. Since dead persons do not literally engage in sexual intercourse, there is nothing specifically prurient with which to reproach the writer. When a vampire drinks blood, he is engaging in a sex act without the embarrassments of nudity, pregnancy, or various other unmentionables; thus, in an age when Flaubert and Baudelaire were tried for obscenity, the writer of vampire stories or plays could revel in any number of taboo subjects with impunity.

From the Romanticists to the Symbolists, the vampire is an important 19th-century archetype—he reflects changing social attitudes toward sex, women, eating, foreigners, disease, and death. The vampire of western culture originates in East European folklore as a kind of beast or a walking corpse; is transformed by German *Sturm und Drang* writers such as Goethe and Bürger and by the English Romantic poets into an outcast wanderer, a destroyer of women who is tortured by remorse (1770-1820); by the French writers of melodrama into a sexual polygamist and suave serial killer (1820-60); by the English dramatists and later gothic novelists such as James Malcolm Rymer and Bram Stoker into a sophisticated, continental sexual deviate, seducer of women, and spreader of contagion (1860-1900).

Beginning in 1820, the 19th century produced a steady stream of plays about vampires, originating in France and quickly "cannibalized" by the English and Americans. Many important figures of 19th-century English, French, and American theatre were involved in the production of these plays. Approximately 35 in number, the vampire plays are evenly distributed through the century, so that a study of each production in sequence provides a useful look at theatre practices, as well as social and psychological insight into the age and into popular taste as reflected in the changing personality of this icon of popular culture, the vampire, who has continued to resurface in one form or another for the last 250 years.

In June of 1820 *Le Vampire*, by Charles Nodier, Pierre Carmouche, and Achille Jouffrey, was produced in Paris, based on a short story by John Polidori which in turn was based on an unfinished work of Lord Byron. Parodies of the play were written by Eugène Scribe and Mélesville, and by Nicholas Brazier, Auguste Rousseau, Marc Antoine Désaugiers, and others. Within two months James Robinson Planché had adapted the play into English in London. The vampire was played by Thomas Potter Cooke, who became the leading English actor of melodrama in the mid-19th century.

The success of the play in England was such that a rival version quickly appeared by W.T. Moncrieff, and the interest in vampires inspired dramatizations of Robert Southey's *Thalaba the Destroyer* in 1823 and Ludvig Tieck's short story "Wake Not the Dead," which was the basis for George Blink's play, *The Vampire Bride* (c. 1834). In 1828 an opera, *Der Vampyr* by Heinrich Marschner had long runs in Leipzig and, with English libretto by Planché, in London.

In 1851 in Paris, Alexandre Dumas père contributed a fairy extravaganza, *Le Vampire*, with masque and ballet. Dion Boucicault adapted Dumas's play into English and acted the title role, appearing for the first time under his own name in *The Vampire* in 1852 at the Princess Theatre in London. He then shortened the play and retitled it *The Phantom*, acting in it in a number of American cities. Boucicault's version was burlesqued in 1872 by R. Reece's *The Vampire* at the Royal Strand. Gilbert and Sullivan's *Ruddygore* (1887) in the original version satirizes gothic melodrama in general, and in particular parodies Boucicault's *The Vampire*.

In 1897 Henry Irving's manager Bram Stoker wrote *Dracula*. Although Stoker himself never stated so specifically, many of his biographers believe he modeled his vampire on Irving, whom he vainly hoped would play the role. Hamilton Deane dramatized the novel in 1924, and in 1927 he co-wrote with John Balderston the American version of *Dracula* which starred Bela Lugosi. Since then there have been many imitations and adaptations of *Dracula*, especially in film, including, among many sequels and takeoffs, a few genuine works of art such as F.W. Murnau's *Nosferatu* (1922).

The plays were money-makers, usually without literary pretensions. "Vampire" in a play's title could bring in a certain audience, whose gratification was an unacknowledged, if not quite respectable, sexual titillation which carried with it undertones of sado-masochism, misogyny, violence, and even devil-worship.

Like many other manifestations of popular culture, vampire melodramas exploited the dark side of sexual fantasy while pretending to condemn it, superficially sugar-coating the real content with platitudinous moralizing and a correct ending, with the vampire defeated (but never quite destroyed). Yet as Peter Brooks notes in his study of the theatres of the "Boulevard du Crime" in Paris, where the first vampire plays originated, "It was the moment of reigning evil which fascinated" [C'était l'instant du mal regnant qui fascinait] (348).

Christopher Prendergast in *Balzac, Fiction and Melodrama* perceptively points out that there is a dark side to melodrama that was largely unacknowledged:

It is precisely here that the moral and emotional confusion of melodrama, its naively ambiguous manipulation of fantasy, is most acutely felt. For it is here, in the operations of nemesis, that the "dark" taste for violence and the "respectable" desire for order are simultaneously and indissociably met..... This oscillation between the claims of order and the excitements of disorder, between the genuflection to virtue and the complicity in the demonic, defines one of the central patterns of the melodramatic mode and demonstrates, despite its outward simplicity of design, its fundamental emotional and moral incoherence; in melodrama we simultaneously pay homage to the idea of moral order and yet secretly enjoy the violence which threatens it. Emotionally and morally incoherent, melodrama is also blind. The tension between its overt moral ideology and its subterranean feelings goes wholly unexamined. (12, 11)

The vampire melodramas vividly illustrate this observation.

This book is to be a study of the vampire on stage, and I hope to able to demonstrate the following patterns:

1. The cycles of vampire plays usually come at periods of social stress. They also seem to follow the death of a monarch or prominent figure in the public consciousness. The major cluster-periods are: Paris and London in the 1820s; Paris, London, and America in the 1850s; and London and America in the 1890s. The Parisian vampire craze of the 1820s may reveal the ambivalent feelings of love and hate toward Napoleon; in England, the vampire plays may be a ventilation of the long-buried anxieties toward the just-deceased mad king George III. Both the French and English had an obsessive love-hate relationship with the personality of Lord Byron, whose public image became intertwined with the vampire in the popular imagination.

This supposition is supported by Ernest Jones's theory, which he propounds in *On the Nightmare*, of the vampire superstition being rooted at its deepest level with incest fantasy; father-killing; fear, hatred, and desire toward the all-powerful father figure, whom we long to have return from the dead and resume his power over us, yet simultaneously fear the possibility (105). Mad kings, emperors, notorious poets—these were father-figures which were both admired and loathed. Like the vampire, Napoleon returned from the brink of annihilation a number of times. George III may have suffered from porphyria, a disease whose symptoms were often taken for signs of vampirism. The political turmoil in mid-century France, and the maelstrom of new ideas in the 1890s which threatened traditionally held conventions and beliefs, brought the vampire back again, a kind of sublimated nightmare of personal vulnerability to mysterious forces which seemed beyond any individual's control.

2. The two major characteristics of vampires are revenance and blood-drinking. As the century progresses, the emphasis moves from the former to the latter. The plays display an accelerating degree of cruelty and violence, and in the last cycle, emphasize the guilt and complicity of the female victims in their own sexual degradation and murder. This leads to the third point:

3. According to Noël Carroll in *The Philosophy of Horror, or Paradoxes of the Heart*, the pattern of the horror genre is either 1) reactionary: violated norms restored—terrifying monster is destroyed; or 2) emancipatory: valorization of oppositional sentiments—sympathetic monster meets tragic end, or survives (205). The vampire plays move from the emancipatory mode, with the vampire figure emerging out of the Romantic anti-hero, to

reactionary, with *Dracula* as probably the major document emerging from the conservatism and xenophobia of the late Victorian era.

Although *Dracula* was written in 1897 and is quintessentially Victorian, it was not dramatized (except for one staged reading at the Lyceum in 1897) until 1924. I feel it is such an important example of the genre and such a seminal work that it cannot be omitted. Therefore, the book will be divided into two parts: Part One, the main body of my study, will examine 19th-century melodrama; Part Two, functioning as a kind of epilogue, will examine 20th-century developments of the Dracula theme and the major Dracula plays and films. The Conclusion will compare the two vampire archetypes, Ruthven and Dracula, and discuss the influence of 19th-century theatrical structures and conventions on this 20th-century art form, film.

Part One will begin with a survey of early vampire literature, broken into five categories: origin in antiquity, East European folklore, German *Sturm und Drang*, gothic novels, and English Romantic poetry, for the purpose of providing a background for the origin of the vampire prototype. The main focus of my work will be the analysis and comparison of a selection of French and English melodramas to discover what elements they possess in common, and more important, how they differ; in other words, how the vampire myth takes on varying characteristics as it shifts from genre to genre and from place to place.

I have limited the selection of plays to those that deal with literal vampires, since metaphorical vampirism is the theme of hundreds of plays, including great ones such as *The Master Builder* and *The Ghost Sonata*, and the study would be swamped. Since there is such an abundance of material even within this limitation, only the most important examples can receive full attention. The major plays, in terms of influence and merit, in my opinion, are those by Nodier, Planché, Marschner, Blink, Dumas, the two by Boucicault, and the various *Draculas*. Many of the others, which may be mentioned only in passing, are satires or imitations of these plays.

Because of the overwhelmingly dominant position of *Dracula* among vampire plays and films since it was written in 1897, much of the earlier material has been obscured. Many of the texts are not readily available; indeed, Boucicault's *The Vampire* (1851), a very important play in this study, was not published and exists only in manuscript form. St. John Dorset's *The Vampire* (1821), on the other hand, was published but not produced.

Because so much of the material is inaccessible, and therefore unfamiliar to scholarly as well as general readers, I feel it is necessary to supply background material and illustrative passages from the plays. However, since much of the historical material is not directly related to the thesis, the following material will be presented in appendices:

A. Catalogue of plays with production data
B. Plot summaries and excerpted scenes
C. Biographical information
D. Cast lists
E. Selected filmography

In my study of 19th-century vampire plays, I hope to show an evolving pattern: from the relative innocence and romanticism of the 1820s to the sadism, misogyny, and preoccupation with perversion of the late 19th century; from simplicity and moral clarity to doubt, ambiguity, and uncertainty; from horror at the spectacle of evil, to fantasies of complicity in sexual violence, vicarious cruelty and destruction, and fascination with the demonic.

My second objective is to act as re-discoverer and advocate for a few of these forgotten plays, to bring them back to the attention of scholars, theatre practitioners, and general readers as worthy of attention by reason of their exotic interest or intrinsic worth. My study is to be an account of these plays and their life onstage; the search for pattern is to be secondary to that.

Before proceeding to the body of the work, I think it will be useful to make a brief survey of the state of scholarship on the subject of vampires and literature, a field which has attracted much interest in the last 30 years. There are at least four levels of criticism in modern vampire studies: 1) ethnographic and anthropological explorations of the subject which take a scientific approach; 2) scholarly literary studies; 3) books on vampire lore and literature intended for popular consumption; and 4) "pop-trash" guidebooks for consumers and connoisseurs of horror fiction, comics, television, and movies. There are excellent and useful books of all four types, and they include a wide range of approaches within these categories.

While many authors touch on theatrical vampires tangentially, I have not found any book entirely devoted to the subject. Useful articles dealing with comparisons between particular plays include Ronald McFarland's "The Vampire on Stage: A Study in Adaptations" (*Comparative Drama*, 1987) which compares Nodier and Planché, Richard Switzer's "Lord Ruthven and the Vampires" (*French Review*, 1955), and A. Owen Aldridge's "The Vampire Theme: Dumas pére and the English Stage" (*Revue des Langues Vivants*, 1973-74).

A problem for any scholar working with vampires in literature is posed by Montague Summers,[2] whose books, *The Vampire: His Kith and Kin* (1928) and *The Vampire in Europe* (1929), are still considered by many writers and readers of vampire lore to be definitive. Summers based his work in part on Abbé Calmet's *Traité sur les Apparitions des Esprits, et sur les Vampires...* (1746), interspersed with literally hundreds of references to Greek, Roman, Egyptian, Assyrian, and biblical texts. His organization is erratic: he skips around chronologically and geographically, abruptly veering off into modern case studies in the midst of the classical sections. The second book rehashes the first, is more anecdotal, and argues the actual existence of vampires. However most recent studies rely on Summers as the prime source for vampire history and folklore, including Douglas Hill's *The History of Ghosts, Vampires and Werewolves* (1973), Basil Cooper's *The Vampire in Legend, Fact, and Art* (1974), Anthony Masters's *The Natural History of the Vampire* (1974), and Donald Glut's *The Dracula Book* (1975).

Summers's scholarship is impugned by Ernest Jones in the first edition of *On the Nightmare*: "Montague Summers' [work] is a learned, though not comprehensive, study which unfortunately is written from the point of view of occultism and so contributes nothing directly to the psychology of the belief" (130). In his recent *Vampyres: Lord Ruthven to Count Dracula*, Christopher Frayling writes that Summers's books are "unreliable, and have for too long been treated as gospel" (424). He recommends as more authoritative Tony Faivre's *Les Vampires* (1962), Sturm and Volker's *Von denen Vampiren oder Menschensaugern* (1973), and Ornella Volta's *Il Vampiro* (1962).

Since my study is concerned not with vampires per se but as figures of theatrical literature, the most useful works for me have been the literary studies: Mario Praz's *The Romantic Agony* (1930), Eino Railo's *The Haunted Castle: A Study of the Elements of English Romanticism* (1927), and Bram Dijkstra's *Idols of Perversity: Fantasies of Evil in Fin-de-Siècle Culture* (1986), and especially Carol Senf's *The Vampire in Nineteenth-Century Literature* (1988), and James B. Twitchell's *The Living Dead: A Study of the Vampire in Romantic Literature* (1981). Nina

Auerbach has written with great originality on this subject in *Woman and the Demon: The Life of a Victorian Myth* (1982) and *Private Theatricals: The Lives of the Victorians* (1980). Her particular interest is female vampires. America's leading writer on vampires is Leonard Wolf, of whom Frayling writes, "Of the spate of books...recently published, by far the best are the work of Leonard Wolf (*A Dream of Dracula*, 1972; *The Annotated Dracula*, 1975). Wolf's reading of *Dracula* is extremely subtle, and I am indebted to it (even if our conclusions differ)" (428).

Relevant works which have bearing on the broader sociological implications of the vampire belief, examining its manifestation in art or custom in the context of popular culture, include two anthropological studies: Philippe Ariès's *The Hour of Our Death* (1982) and Paul Barber's *Vampires, Burial and Death: Folklore and Reality* (1990); and two analyses of the horror genre in mass entertainment: Walter Kendrick's *The Thrill of Fear: 250 Years of Scary Entertainment* (1991), and Noël Carroll's *The Philosophy of Horror: Paradoxes of the Heart* (1991).

In summary, I am making a thematic study investigating the distinguishing features of 19th-century plays concerning vampires; primarily a literary study but backed up by production history and cultural context. I believe the more distant a play is from us in time, the more it must be studied in its social and historical context to be understood. I hope also that the study will provide insight into the evolving taste of the theatre audience as the basic vampire theme is metamorphosed in succeeding eras, and treated in various theatre genres—melodrama, burletta, tragedy, opera, ballet, satire, burlesque, operetta, and film.

# Part One

# Ruthven

# Chapter 1

# Origins

He is known everywhere that men have been. In old Greece, in old
Rome; he flourish in Germany all over, in France, in India, even in the
Chernesese; and in China, so far from us in all ways, there even he is,
and the peoples fear him at this day. He have follow the wake of the
berserker Icelander, the devil-begotten Hun, the Slav, the Saxon, the
Magyar.

—Bram Stoker, *Dracula*

In his introduction to the first 20th-century edition of *Varney the
Vampire* (c. 1847), "The Vampire in Legend, Lore, and Literature,"
Devendra P. Varma links the vampire myth to the folklore of India,
Nepal, Tibet, Mongolia, and China, suggesting that the legend was
carried to the West along trade routes from the Orient.[1] Varma
detects vampire qualities in the fang-like teeth of the carved images
of the Nepalese Lord of Death, the Tibetan devil Yama, the
Mongolian God of Time who floats in a sea of blood, and Kali, the
Hindu mother goddess and avid blood-drinker, often pictured with
a crown of skulls and a necklace of human hands.

Stories of these weird gods who subsisted by drinking the blood of
sleeping persons originated with the Hindus of ancient India. And Tibetan
manuscripts concerning vampires were held in such high regard that they
were embalmed to increase their sanctity.... The vampire motif is an
anthropomorphic theme, a human-animal, life-death configuration. The
vampire kills and re-creates. He is the Destroyer and the Preserver, for the
passive vampires of life turn into active ones after death. Westerners have
viewed vampire lore as a fascinating but unsolved enigma, but the origins
of this myth lie in the mystery cults of Oriental civilizations. (14)

Tony Faivre in *Les Vampires* refers to vampire-like beings in ancient
Chinese folklore called *kiang-se*, and to the Vetâls of Indian folklore;
both myths concern corpses returning to life after being fed with

**13**

with blood (111-14). Fangs are also a common motif on the images of blood-drinking gods of the civilizations of Mexico.

Montague Summers, with massive documentation in both *The Vampire—His Kith and Kin* and *The Vampire in Europe*, traces the origin to Babylonia, Assyria, and coastal Egypt. Of the dozens of classical references with which he buttresses his argument, I will mention two examples from Greek and Roman texts which were sources for the Romantic poets. The *empusa*, a shape-shifting demon of Greek mythology, appears in *The Life of Apollonius of Tyana* (217 A.D., IV: 25) by Philostratus. This tale of a female vampire who became the lover of Menippus, but is unmasked by Apollonius in time to save the young man's life, was the source for Keats's *Lamia* (1820). A Roman vampire story appears in *Fragmenta Historicorum Graecorum* (A.D. 117-38), a fragment by Phlegon of Tralles, a freed slave of Hadrian's. The original source for Goethe's "Die Braut von Korinth" (1797), it tells of a dead girl, Philinion, who leaves her grave in physical form to sleep with her fiancé, thus linking the ancient version of the vampire to the more modern Slavic version, with the important living-dead characteristic. A vampire by this definition is an animated corpse, not a ghost; this characteric of physicality becomes unique to the vampire as it evolves from its early connection with ghouls (monsters who devour dead bodies), werewolves (shape-changers), and wraiths (grave-haunting spirits).

Concluding the anthropological section of his study, Summers states:

The vampiric idea was present among well-nigh all ancient peoples, with one great difference...whereas the true vampire is a dead body, the vampires of older superstitions were generally ghosts or spectres, but ghosts that were sometimes tangible and spectres who could do very material harm to living people by exhausting their vitality and draining their blood. (*Europe* 64)

Examples of vampires in later cultures include the night-walking monster Grendel in *Beowulf*, a view argued by Nicholas Kiessling in an article in *Modern Philology*. He points out that Grendel attacks by night, sleeps underground by day, has superhuman strength, sucks the blood of his victims, has a "she-wolf" for a mother, and can be destroyed only by decapitation. An 11th-century Anglo-Saxon epic, *A Vampire of the Fens*, contains echoes of *Beowulf* and develops these themes. In the 12th century William of Newbury relates several episodes concerning vampires—including the vampire of Alnwick Castle, an animated corpse that was the source of plague in the district. In ancient Ireland there was a mythical demon, "Dearg-dul" (cf. Irishman Bram Stoker's "Dracula"), meaning "red blood-sucker" in Gaelic (Jones 121). The various strands of superstition and myth came together in 16th-century Romania, Hungary, Poland, and Moravia, a region which was the meeting place of eastern and western religions after the fall of Constantinople in 1453. Ernest Jones makes the interesting argument that the superstition grew in this region as a result of rival religious dogmas:

The Greek Orthodox Church—it is said in a spirit of opposition to the Roman Catholic pronouncement that the bodies of saints do not decompose—supported the dogma that it is the bodies of the wicked, unholy, and especially excommunicated, persons which do not decompose. Just as the Roman Catholic Church taught that heretics could be turned into werewolves, the Greek Orthodox Church taught that heretics became vampires after death. (103)

The superstition spread westward in the 18th century when Serbia and Wallachia were acquired by Austria through the Treaty of Passarowitz in 1718. Occupying Austrian soldiers filed reports of the local practice of exhuming corpses and staking them. These eye-witness accounts made their way westward and educated Europeans became aware of them. The question of the existence of vampires received a great deal of attention at German universities, and literally dozens of treatises were produced, fourteen in 1732 alone, including John Heinrich Zopfius's *Dissertatio de Uampiris Seruiensibus* (Halle, 1733) and John Christian Harenberg's *Von Vampyren* (Leipzig, 1739). From Germany, the subject passed to England and France. The word "vampire" first appeared in English in 1734 according to the *Oxford English Dictionary*: "These vampyres are supposed to be the Bodies of deceased Persons, animated by evil Spirits, which come out of the Grave, in the Night-time, Suck the blood of many of the Living, and thereby destroy them" (*Trav., three English Gent.* in *Harl. Misc.* 1745).

Dom Augustin Calmet's *Traité sur les Apparitions des Esprits, et sur les Vampires ou les Revenants de Hongrie, de Moravie et de Selésie* appeared in Paris in 1746, and was quickly translated into other languages. It appeared in English as *The Phantom World* in 1749. Calmet was the Benedictine Abbot of Senones, and the most widely respected biblical scholar in Europe. The *Traité*, which cites more than 500 "documented" cases, lent credence to the reality of vampires and kindled scholarly interest. Calmet's definition ran:

The Apparitions (Revenan[t]s) of Hungary, or Vampires...are men who have been dead for some considerable time, it may be for a long period or it may be for a shorter period, and these issue forth from their graves and come to disturb the living, whose blood they suck and drain. These vampires appear visibly to men, they knock loudly at their doors and cause the sound to re-echo throughout the whole house, and once they have gained a foothold death generally follows. To this sort of Apparition is given the name Vampire or Oupire, which in the Slavonic tongues means a bloodsucker. The only way to obtain deliverance from their molestations is by disinterring the dead body, by cutting off the head, by driving a stake through the breast, by transfixing the heart, or by burning the corpse to ashes. (qtd. in Summers, *Kith* 28-29)

The most famous European case study, also related in Calmet's *Traité*, was of Arnold Paole (or Paul), a Hungarian soldier who returned home from the Turkish wars, died, rose from his grave to feed on family and friends and contaminate the cattle of the surrounding countryside. The story was printed as factual in the *London Journal* in 1732, and many times retold throughout the 18th and 19th centuries (Frayling, *Vampyres* 20-21).

Frayling remarks on the ironic necessity for "the philosophers of the Age of Reason in France, Germany, and Italy...to come to grips with well-publicized epidemics of vampirism emanating from eastern Europe" (19). In his *Dictionnaire Infernal* (1820), Collin de Plancy remarks,

The most astonishing thing about these accounts of vampirism is that they shared the honour of astounding the eighteenth century with our greatest philosophers. They terrified Prussia, Silesia, Bohemia, and the whole of northern Europe, at precisely the same time as wise men in England and France were attacking superstition and popular error with the utmost confidence. (qtd. in Frayling 19)

Voltaire remained skeptical: "True vampires are the monks who eat at the expense of both kings and people" (*Dictionnaire Philosophique* [1764], qtd. in Twitchell 13); but Jean-Jacques Rousseau wrote in his "Letter to the Archbishop of Paris," "If ever there was in the world a warranted and proven history, it is that of vampires: nothing is lacking, official reports, testimonials of persons of standing, of surgeons, of clergymen, of judges; the judicial evidence is all-embracing" (qtd. in Twitchell 6). Louis XV became interested and asked Richelieu to conduct an investigation, and Horace Walpole wrote to Lady Ossory of George II, "I know that our late King, though not apt to believe more than his neighbors, had no doubt of the existence of vampires, and their banquets on the dead" (qtd. in Frayling 20).

Scattered references among the century's well-known writers demonstrate that the knowledge of vampires was widespread: Alexander Pope made a joking reference to rumors about his health in a letter to William Oliver (1740): "If ever he [Pope] has walk'd above ground, he has been (like the Vampires in Germany) such a terror to all sober and innocent people, that many wish a stake were drove thro' him to keep him quiet in his grave" (4: 227); Henry Fielding in *Tom Jones* (1749): "To be denied Christian burial, and to have your Corpse buried in the Highway, and a Stake drove through you, as Farmer Halfpenny was served at Ox-Cross" (7: 349); and Oliver Goldsmith in *The Citizen of the World* (1760): "From a meal he advances to a surfeit, and at last sucks blood like a vampire" (II: 209).

The key preoccupations of the vampire myth are 1) fear of death and of dead bodies; 2) cannibalism and the equating of blood with life; and 3) sexual predation and the equating of sex with killing, and blood with semen. Obviously these are some of mankind's most basic obsessions and fears, and the superstitions and practices which grow up around them can be examined rewardingly through psychology, anthropology, and literature. Any of the three aspects can be dominant in a particular version of the myth, but perhaps most basic, and primitive, is the theme of death and resurrection.

We have always been haunted by the concept of the dead rising from their graves. In almost every culture there is a fear of dead bodies. It is natural and understandable that at some point in the process of separation and grieving, the mourner becomes alienated from the physical body of the deceased and fixes on the spirit, or soul, which we imagine to have departed from the body and either gone elsewhere or ceased to exist. The "uninhabited" body becomes increasingly alien, and as we observe the changes and deterioration brought on by decay, the corpse takes on an increasingly frightening aspect, and pity becomes laced with terror. Prostrated by sorrow, exhaustion, and loss, unable to sleep, we lie awake trying to picture what the newly buried loved one is actually doing as he "sleeps" under the ground. A sleeper eventually wakes. The story of the Resurrection of Christ is the joyous interpretation of this reawakening; the vampire is the nightmare version.

One shocking, unassimilable aspect of death is that the body is cold: so the vampire seeks warmth, the blood of living humans. The dead are lonely, so they seek to drag us down into darkness with them. Eastern European folk vampires all prey on members of their own families.

Customs which suggest a need to placate the dead are very nearly universal. The Tibetan and Egyptian Books of the Dead are elaborate textbooks on rituals for propitiating the souls of the dead. The common ancient practice, found even among Neanderthals and Cro-Magnons, of burying precious objects in the tomb, is a way of bribing the dead to stay in their graves and let us live. The ancient Greeks are thought to have poured blood on graves to keep the dead from rising, and to have piled the body with heavy stones to hold it down (see Danforth, *Death Rituals*). In some European countries including England, suicides and criminals were buried at unmarked crossroads in the hope that they might become confused and not find their way home. One function of the vampire-killer's wooden stake is to nail the body down, making sure it stays put.

In *Vampires, Burial and Death: Folklore and Reality*, Paul Barber argues that the vampire superstitions of Eastern Europe had a pragmatic and seemingly logical basis. When people die from mysterious, unknown causes, such as viruses or bacteria, the survivors become panicky and prone to suggestion, and one likely explanation is that death is a contagion which comes from the dead. Is it surprising then, that where there is fear and ignorance, every exhumation yields a vampire?

Philippe Ariès in *The Hour of Our Death* points out that attitudes toward death began to change in the 17th and 18th centuries. Civilization and its "sanitizing" effect began to alienate us from the facts of dying and decay, which before had been accepted as a natural part of life, as manifested by the charnel houses and public display of corpses at cemeteries such as Les Saintes-Innocents in Paris, for example (54-69). As these customs changed, it was no longer common knowledge, for instance, that *rigor mortis* is a temporary condition. That this state of ignorance existed is borne out by the numerous 18th-century German university treatises previously mentioned, many of which cite pliant limbs in a corpse as the sign of a vampire (Jones 103, 128-29). Further, it was not commonly known that a corpse's rate of decomposition is related, among other things, to the amount of moisture in the soil, nor that in certain climatic conditions the blood will not congeal for months, and that the body will acquire a ruddy color. Before the nails fall off as the flesh shrinks back, they may seem to grow, as many people still believe today.

Barber even has a natural explanation for the vampire's death cry when impaled with a wooden stake:

The peasants of Medvegia assumed that if the corpse groaned, it must still be alive. But a corpse does emit sounds, even when it is only moved, let alone if a stake were driven into it. This is because the compression of the chest cavity forces air past the glottis, causing a sound similar in quality and origin to the groan or cry of a living person.... A corpse that did not emit such sounds when a stake was driven into it would be unusual. ("The Real Vampire" 79-80)

The dead can indeed seem to rise from their graves, according to Barber, by the natural processes of decomposition. Buildup of gases can literally make the body float upward when the coffin is opened. Small wonder they seemed alive.

The second major element of the vampire superstition is cannibalism. Since one can die through loss of blood, it seems logical to conclude that one could return to life by drinking blood. People have always eaten people—however most civilizations develop a taboo against the practice, because, although man is a carnivorous animal, he considers his own body sacrosanct. It makes him uneasy to realize his own flesh is identical to the animal meat he consumes. Comedians Flanders and Swann show the illogicality with their joke in which the old cannibal tells his son, "If God hadn't meant people to eat people, He wouldn't have made us of meat."

In many warrior societies men drink the blood of their enemies, not to insult or desecrate them, but to gain their strength, courage, or other attributes. Summers catalogues dozens of examples of cultures in antiquity where blood sacrifice was practiced: the Greeks, Assyrians, Romans, Arabs, Scythians, Moabites, Philistines, Phoenicians, and pre-eminently, the Aztecs. More modern cultures include Australian Aborigines, Polynesians, Amazon and African tribes, Patagonians, and American Indian tribes of the Southwest. These customs involve the drinking of blood by priests and participants in the ritual, the offering of blood to a vampire deity, or some combination of both.

In the Old Testament Jehovah would accept blood sacrifice (e.g., Abraham and Isaac, called off at the last minute), but strictly prohibited the drinking of blood:

Genesis 17:11: But flesh with the life thereof, which is the blood thereof, shall ye not eat.

Deuteronomy 12:23: Only be sure that ye eat not the blood, for the blood is the life, and thou mayest not eat the life with the flesh.

Leviticus 17:10-11: And whatsoever man there be of the house of Israel...that eateth any manner of blood; I will even set my face against that soul that eateth blood, and will cut him off from among his people. For the life of the flesh is in the blood.

Holy Communion is possibly the stylized remnant of a cannibalistic ritual. Christ's blood promises everlasting life:

John 6:53-56: Verily, verily, I say unto you, except ye eat the flesh of the Son of man, and drink his blood, ye have no life in you. Whoso eateth my flesh and drinketh my blood, hath eternal life; and I will raise him up at the last day. For my flesh is meat indeed, and my blood is drink indeed. He that eateth my flesh, and drinketh my blood, dwelleth in me, and I in him.

The vampire's blood drinking is a satanic parody of the Eucharist, the sacrament of the blood of Christ. Communion wine is a promise of eternal life; human blood bestows eternal life on the vampire. Food and blood, eating and sex, are poetic metaphors that become literal in the vampire myth. As it had with witchcraft, Christianity played a major role in spreading the vampire superstition.

Credibility was also furthered by the actions thoughout history of psychopathic personalities who believed they were vampires. There are many infamous cases of isolated individuals, from Elizabeth Bathory, Vlad Tepes and Gilles de Rais, to Jeffrey Dahmer, who have acted on their misguided beliefs in the restorative power of blood.

Further, imperfectly understood diseases—cholera, rabies, tuberculosis, blood disorders such as pernicious anemia, and porphyria, whose symptoms resemble the marks of the vampire— also helped to spread the superstition, as did the discovery in the New World of *Desmodus rotundus*, the vampire bat, in the late 18th century.

Third, and perhaps most recent in its evolution, is the sexual element of vampirism. There are numerous theories on the psychological processes involved in sustaining the vampire myth. In *Totem and Taboo* Freud propounds his "primal horde" theory and the male instinct to kill the castrating father, which Maurice Richardson in "The Psychoanalysis of Count Dracula" links to the vampire myth. Freudian disciple Ernest Jones's *On the Nightmare* makes the connection of blood with semen: "A nightly visit from a beautiful or frightful being, who first exhausts the sleeper with passionate embraces, and then withdraws from him a vital fluid...can only point to nocturnal emissions accompanied by dreams of...[an] erotic nature" (119). In *Man and His Symbols* C.G. Jung sets out his theory of the negative *animus*. Jungian disciple Maud Bodkin applies Jung's theory to literature in *Archetypal Patterns in Poetry*, in which we may connect the vampire with the Demon-lover, a mythopoetic archetype recurring in the literature and "collective subconscious" of many cultures. Havelock Ellis wrote "There is scarcely any natural object with so profoundly emotional an effect as blood" (120-21). Sexual arousal connected with the sight, smell, or taste of blood was given the clinical name "hemothymia" by Dr. T. Clay Shaw in an article in *The Lancet* in 1909, and Christopher Frayling has coined the word "haemosexuality" to describe the blood basis of a vampiric relationship (388).

The sexual symbolism of the vampire is generally a late development, accomplished mainly by the English Romantic poets and taken further by the Victorians; therefore a full discussion of the sexual element belongs more properly to the later chapters of this study. However, while sexually attractive vampires are rare in folklore, the erotic meaning is present even in the most primitive vampire motifs. The oral sex symbolism of the vampire's bite is obvious. The Elizabethans called orgasm the "little death," and the kiss of the vampire brings both ecstasy and death. Clearly, the image of a supremely powerful, frightening, yet desirable man or woman who initiates one against one's will into unspeakable, dangerous, and forbidden acts points to incest fantasy. Jones writes, "The incest complex, which underlies the Incubus belief, shows itself equally in the Vampire one...the whole superstition is shot through with the theme of guilt" (127).

In general sexual vampire predators are male, and victims are female. There is an important female subspecies, a kind of succubus or demonic woman derived from the Greek *empusa* and the Roman *lamia*, evolving into the *fin-de-siècle femme fatale*, but this demon does not have the specific blood-sucking characteristic of the vampire. Unfortunately, the literary works that are based on this interesting archetype present a difficulty for inclusion in this study: they tend not to have been dramatized. Examples include Goethe's "Die Braut von Korinth" (1797), Coleridge's *Christabel* (1797-1800), Keats's "La Belle Dame Sans Merci" (1819) and *Lamia* (1820), E.T.A. Hoffmann's "Aurelia" (1820), Gautier's "La Morte Amoureuse" (1831), Poe's "Berenice" (1833), Baudelaire's *Les Métamorphoses du Vampire* (1857), Le Fanu's *Carmilla* (1872), Maurice Rollinet's *Névroses* (1883), and Kipling's "The Vampire" (1897). An exception is "Wake Not the Dead" (c. 1800), attributed to Ludvig von Tieck, dramatized in 1834 and examined in Chapter 6.

Certainly there is much guilt and masochism bound up in the heterosexual version of the vampire fantasy, which can easily be loaded with homoerotic and sadistic connotations as well. A vampire is a sexual nemesis figure, the danger underscored by the condition, in some versions of the story, that the vampire cannot attack unless the victim first invites him in. Varma makes the case for the erotic interpretation of the myth:

Like all true myths the vampire legend has been subjected to manifold interpretations, but surely it is logical within the realms of fantasy.... Sin must follow temptation. Evil may be terrible, but it is also irresistible. Even a loathsome embrace marks the naked cruelty of passion. The vampire's embrace may plumb the bottomless pit of damnation; nonetheless, it ravages the heights of heaven with rage and rapture. ("Vampire" 19-20)

In summary, the vampire, with many variations and exceptions, is a creature with the following characteristics:

1. The true vampire is a dead body, not a ghost, spectre, or demon.
2. Vampires can be either victims of a contagious disease similar to rabies, or they can be a separate species from man; they are not necessarily connected with Satan and the powers of hell.

3. They have superhuman strength, and are most powerful at night.
4. They feed on the blood of living persons.
5. Barring accident, they can "live" forever.
6. They have command over lower animals, and can change into wolves or bats (a recent development; when vampire bats were discovered in South America in the 1770s, as mentioned previously, they were quickly grafted onto the persona of Old World vampire).
7. Vampires live in graves and shun the light.
8. Since they are already dead, they are exceedingly difficult to destroy.

It must be emphasized that this is an evolving definition, and not every characteristic applies in each case. Lord Ruthven, for instance, the most prominent vampire figure of the 19th century, does not qualify as a true vampire because he does not literally drink blood. The Romantic poets tend to take the myth less literally, and, as it becomes a poetic metaphor, it loses its specifics almost entirely.[2]

Traditional remedies against the vampire, some of very ancient origin, include the stake, called Transfixion by the Catholic church, made of iron or a particular wood—oak, whitethorn, hawthorn, maple, or aspen; decapitation; fire; running or boiling water; garlic stuffed in the mouth; a consecrated sword or silver bullet; icons or crosses; a male virgin on a white horse crossing over the sleeping vampire's grave. The extreme aversion to sunlight does not come from folklore but from the movies. The first vampire to disintegrate in the rays of the sun was in F.W. Murnau's *Nosferatu* (1922).

Of the dozens of ways one could become a vampire, some are to be an illegitimate child of illegitimate parents; a heretic; a wizard; an excommunicate; a suicide; a homosexual; a victim of incest; a miser; a person born with a cleft palate, tail, or caul; a seventh child of the same sex; a child born with teeth or born on Christmas or between Christmas and Epiphany; an unbaptized child; an unhappy child; a child whose mother when pregnant has been deprived of salt or has been gazed on by a vampire; a blue-eyed or dark-eyed person (whichever is unusual for the region); one with a ruddy (porphyriac) or pale (anemic) complexion; one who eats the flesh of a lamb killed by a wolf; one whose grave is jumped over by a wolf, cat, bird, or boy; and of course, one who is bitten by a vampire, or (more modern) one who drinks a vampire's blood.

Montague Summers provides us with a few more loathsome details on the vampire's general appearance:

The vampire is generally described as being exceedingly gaunt and lean with a hideous countenance and eyes wherein are glinting the red fires of perdition. When, however, he has satiated his lust for warm human blood his body becomes horribly puffed and bloated, as though he were some great leech gorged and replete to bursting. Cold as ice, or it may be fevered and burning as a hot coal, the skin is deathly pale, but the lips are very full and rich, blub and red; the teeth white and gleaming, and the canine teeth wherewith he bites deep into the neck of his prey to suck thence the vital streams which re-animate his body and invigorate all his forces appear notably sharp and pointed. Often his mouth curls back in a vulpine snarl which bares these fangs...In Bulgaria, it is thought that the Vampire who returns from the tomb has only one nostril; and in certain districts of Poland he is supposed to have a sharp point at the end of his tongue like the sting of a bee. It is said that the palms of a vampire's hands are downy with hair, and the nails are always curved and crooked, often well-nigh the length of a bird's claw, the quicks dirty and foul with clots and gouts of black blood. His breath is unbearably fetid and rank with corruption, the stench of the charnel. (*Kith* 179)

Ornella Volta's description is equally repulsive:

An emaciated face, with a phosphorescent pallor...many thick hairs on his body which are often reddish in colour, and often has hair in the palms of his hands...and blue eyes...swollen, sensual lips covering sharp canine teeth...extremely long fingernails, pointed ears like bats, foetid breath, and [they] move jerkily, showing a tendency to suffer from epilepsy. Their bite has anaesthetizing powers. (145)

To see how such a creature could be transformed into an attractive lover, we must turn to the Romantics.

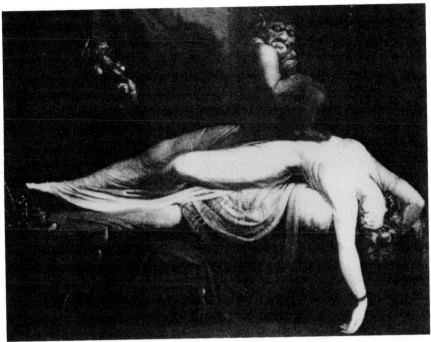

Henry Fuseli, "The Nightmare" (1781), Detroit Institute of the Arts.

Francisco Goya, "Las Resultas" (c. 1815), *Los Disastres de la Guerra.*

# Chapter 2

# Evolution

But first on earth, as Vampyre sent,
Thy corse shall from its tomb be rent;
Then ghastly haunt thy native place,
And suck the blood of all thy race;
There from thy daughter, sister, wife,
At midnight drain the stream of life;
Yet loathe the banquet, which perforce
Must feed thy livid, living corse,
Thy victims, ere they yet expire,
Shall know the demon for their sire;
As cursing thee, thou cursing them,
Thy flowers are withered on the stem.

—Lord Byron, "The Giaour"

Three very unlikely progeny of the Age of Reason were the gothic novel, Romantic poetry, and melodrama. The three genres, which emerge only very roughly in that order, are so overlapped and intertwined, develop so differently in Germany, England, and France, and play so important a role in the evolution of the vampire as a literary motif, that it seems almost impossible to find an orderly way to discuss them—by nation, genre, or chronology. But with some skipping about, it may be possible to avoid going over the same ground three times. This chapter will carry the discussion of gothic novels, *Sturm und Drang*, and Romantic poetry to 1819, culminating in an analysis of John Polidori's *The Vampyre*, the important work which generated a dozen or more vampire melodramas in Paris and London in 1820.

Although the gothic novel is usually said to be a precursor of Romanticism, it continued through the Romantic period, through the 19th century, and in fact exists today as a viable genre. Strangely, vampires are not specifically mentioned in any piece of gothic literature until Polidori's *The Vampire* in 1819.[1] However, besides its

**26**

contribution of atmospheric focus on the uncanny and fantastic, the gothic novel develops a character archetype, the sinister priest (to be discussed later in this chapter) which would be grafted onto the vampire of folklore and further transmuted by the Romantics into the vampire of the 19th-century stage.

In the mid-18th century, when an interest in the past came into vogue, particularly the Middle Ages with its picturesque ruins (architecture erroneously attributed to the Goths), the word "gothic" was revived, carrying with it a hint of revolt against the orderliness and symmetry of classicism. For writers, "gothic" conjured up the barbarism, vigorous energy, and superstition of an exotic, if nebulous, past. As Margaret Carter in *Specter or Delusion: The Supernatural in Gothic Fiction* points out, the word has two meanings: 18th-century writers use it interchangeably with "medieval"; modern critics use it to designate 18th-century fiction which was modeled on the medieval romance, and later works that grew out of that tradition. She also points out that the gothic novelists were, in some ways, "imitating a construct of their own minds" (6).

Gothic fiction is haunted by "the numinous," a weightier, more solemn word for "supernatural" coined by the theologian Rudolf Otto in *The Idea of the Holy*, which seems to mean a combination of religious ecstasy and terror, *mysterium tremendum et fascinans* (5). Despite the many weaknesses of the genre—heavy plotting, stereotyped characters, stilted dialogue, prolixity—the gothic novel has a strong appeal to the imagination, to some extent explained by Freud's definition of the *unheimlich* ("the uncanny") as "something which is secretly familiar, which has undergone repression and then returned from it" (*Works* 7: 245). It is the Freudian "touch of strange" which gives gothic fiction its haunting, mysterious-yet-familiar quality. The genre is typified by ambiguity between natural and supernatural, good and evil; madness, alienation, sexual deviation, apparitions from the other world, the fantastic, the macabre, and the doppelgänger, or hidden self.

The first gothic novel is agreed to be Horace Walpole's *The Castle of Otranto* (1764), but the first distinguished writer in the genre was Ann Radcliffe, who in *The Italian* (1797) introduces a character-type which would become a staple of gothic fiction: the mad priest Schedoni, the sinister monk and proto-vampire:

Among his associates no one loved him, many disliked him, and more feared him. His figure was striking, but not so from grace; it was tall, and,

though extremely thin, his limbs were large and uncouth.... There was
something terrible in its air; something almost superhuman. His cowl too,
as it threw a shade over the livid paleness of his face, increased its severe
character, and gave an effect to his large melancholy eye, which
approached to horror.... An habitual gloom and severity prevailed over
the deep lines of his countenance; and his eyes were so piercing that they
seemed to penetrate, at a single glance, into the hearts of men, and to
read their most secret thoughts; few persons could support their scrutiny;
or even endure to meet them twice. (34-35)

There is some dispute among scholars about the publication
dates of Radcliffe's *The Italian* (Railo, 1794; Praz, 1797) and
Matthew Gregory "Monk" Lewis's *The Monk* (Summers, 1795; Praz,
1796), so it is a matter of conjecture as to which monk, Radcliffe's
Schedoni or Lewis's Ambrosio, influenced the other. Mario Praz
notes that both first appear in the "odor of sanctity," both commit
horrible crimes, and both end as victims of the Inquisition (62). *The
Monk* contains scenes of torture, sadism, cross-dressing, demons,
devil worship, cabalistic rites, a temptress/succubus disguised as
monk, and three ghosts including a bleeding nun. Despite its
unevenness, infantile excesses, and occasional lapses of taste, *The
Monk* is the paradigmatic gothic novel. Lewis also wrote at least
fifteen plays, including the very successful *The Castle Spectre* (1798),
one of the first English melodramas.

The demonic monk, almost but never quite a vampire, reached
an apogee of sorts in Lewis's novel, which was drawn on by many
19th-century writers. Charles Robert Maturin's *Melmouth the
Wanderer* (1820) follows a hero who is, according to Praz, "a kind
of Wandering Jew crossed with Byronic vampire" (78) (also a Faust
figure since he has sold his soul to Satan and at his end is 150
years old), equipped with mesmeric eyes, who disrupts a wedding
feast and, simply by staring, causes the bride to die and the
bridegroom to go mad. Mary Shelley's *Valperga* (1823) contains a
satanic hero, Castrucchio, "a majestic figure and a countenance
beautiful but sad, and tarnished by the expression of pride which
animated it" (qtd. in Praz 116). Eugène Sue generally avoids the
supernatural but develops the satanic villain/hero, typically in
*Latréaumont* (1838). Paul Féval's Rio-Santo in *Les Mystéres de
Londres* (1844) is another portrait of Byron:

He was a man of some thirty years at least in appearance, of a good height,
elegant and of an aristocratic bearing. As for his face, it offered a remarkable

type of beauty; his high, broad forehead was unwrinkled, but crossed from top to bottom by a scar which was nearly imperceptible when his features were at rest, and enveloped by a magnificent mane of black hair. One could not see his eyes, but beneath their lower lids their power could be sensed. The face of the dreamer was pale and smooth as a baby's.... Young women had reveries about his dreaming eye, ravaged face, aquiline nose, and his smile that was infernal yet divine. His naturally curling locks, in careless disarray, fell in graceful waves.... "I know that you are powerful, my lord," replied the countess..."powerful in evil as a fallen angel."[2]

The Marquis de Sade must also be mentioned, although it is difficult to assess how widely known his writing was in its own time. *Justine* and *Juliette* (final versions 1797) depict vampires of a sort, such as the Muscovite giant Minski, who eats human flesh and makes furniture out of the victim's bones; the Comte de Grenade and the monster Rodin, whose orgies are crowned with the pleasures of flowing blood. Byron and de Sade, "the Satanic lord" and "the divine Marquis," as Praz calls them, both contributed elements of depravity to the personality of the vampire, both through their work and through the public perception of their lives. Agreeing with Freud's often-stated opinion that the infantile conception of sex is always sadistic in nature, Linda Bayer-Berenbaum in *The Gothic Imagination* notes that sexual perversion is as important an element in gothicism as the supernatural:

Gothicism is no more inclined to accept sexual restriction than psychological or aesthetic confinement. Sexual excess functions physically as madness does psychologically; one drive, one intention, becomes overpowering, all-consuming. Sexual perversions are important in gothic literature for their intensity born of repression and for the expansion they provide in the range of sexual practice. Homosexuality, sodomy, incest, rape, or group copulations are inserted into ordinary experience in order to destroy the boundary line between the normal and the perverse. (39-40)

After the advent of Lord Ruthven in Polidori's *The Vampyre* in 1819 (which will be discussed after tracing its roots in Romanticism), vampires of the Byronic type began to appear in French and English gothic fiction of the *Schauer-romantik* school: Cyprien Bérard's sequel to Polidori, *Lord Ruthven ou les vampires* (1820); Charles Nodier's *Smarra* (1821) in which a sinister incubus puts the lovers to death after a feast; Prosper Mérimée's *La Guzla* (1825-26), in which we encounter the Bey of Moina, another vampire with deadly eyes: "Who could escape the fascination of his gaze? His mouth is bloody and smiles like that of a sleeping man tortured by a frightful love [Qui pourrait éviter la fascination de son regard?...Sa bouche est sanglante et sourit comme celle d'un homme endormi et tourmenté d'un amour hideux]" (qtd. in Praz 79); James Malcolm Rymer's *Varney the Vampire* (c. 1847); Dumas père's *The Pale-Faced Lady* (1848); "The Mysterious Stranger" (anon., 1860); and Bram Stoker's *Dracula* (1897).

Perhaps the attraction of the supernatural for gothic writers is attributable to the suppressed impulses—neurotic and erotic—of educated society, or to the traces of religious feeling which remained in the scientific man of the Enlightenment, which could not be totally effaced by rationality. The attraction to the inexplicable (*unauswickelbar*) was one predilection they held in common with the Romantics.

The hallmarks of Romanticism were exaltation of the individual, of freedom and revolution, of art and artists, of nature, idealization of the distant past, and revolt against the literary *ancien regime*. In his writings Jean-Jacques Rousseau praised emotion over reason, subjectivity over objectivity, and eulogized the "noble savage," natural man, denigrating civilization and its evils. Other more troubled and muddy wellsprings may have been the guilt which accompanies the decline of religious feeling, and the swing of the pendulum away from the Enlightenment's love of reason. The concept of dualism—that there is more to the mind than its rational surface, that it contains a darker, hidden self—is one of the basic characteristics of Romanticism. The dark twin—Cain, Caliban, Mephistopheles, Karl Moor, Mr. Hyde, the vampire—is the poetic metaphor by which Romanticism externalized the unconscious. R.E. Foust in "Monstrous Image: Theory of Fantasy Antagonists," writes:

This fantasy antagonist is a "psycho-pomp," a visual metaphor for our divided condition, a way of speaking the unspeakable. The monster mediates between the daylight society of the self-created Ego and the boggy night country of the inchoate and imperfectly repressed Id. Thus the antagonist is not something external to ourselves, merely a threat occasioning the intervention of the Hero (although this also occurs). It is our chthonic *doppelgänger*, our *semblable*, our "secret sharer." It seems to stare at us with mingled loathing and longing from some dark geography lying in a past we attempt repeatedly to forget. The adversary's fate—its eternal malevolence, its more-than-human pitifulness, its universal doom—constitutes a chapter in the spiritual autobiography of the human race. (452-53)

The five major English Romantic poets—Wordsworth, Coleridge, Byron, Shelley, and Keats—all wrote significant works on vampires (the only questionable example being Wordsworth's "The Leech Gatherer" (1800), where vampirism is only implied). Continuing the themes of death, transcendence, and morbid preoccupations of the Graveyard poets of the 1740s and 1750s, the Romantics adapted the vampire from German sources, an early example being Heinrich August Ossenfelder's "Der Vampyr" (1748), roughly contemporaneous with Calmet's *Traité* and the vampire dissertations of German universities. It is here quoted in its entirety:

> My dearest little girl believes
> Constant, firm, and steady,
> In the old teachings
> Of her devout mother,
> As people of the Theyse [River]
> Have always deeply believed
> In deadly vampires.
> Now wait, little Christina,
> You don't want to love me;
> I will have revenge on you,
> And drinking the Tokay wine [of your blood],
> I will become a vampire.
> And when you are softly sleeping,
> Then I will suck up
> The fresh crimson of your cheeks.
> And if you are afraid
> When I kiss you,
> And kiss you as a vampire,
> And if you are trembling
> And faint in my arms,
> Feebly sinking into death,
> Then I will ask you,
> Is my teaching better
> Than your good mother's?[3]

More influential in England was Gottfried August Bürger's "Lenore" (1773), concerning Wilhelm, a Crusader killed in King

Frederick's wars who returns from the grave to claim his fiancée, and containing the refrain, "Denn die Todten reiten schnell [For the dead travel fast]," quoted to such chilling effect in Stoker's *Dracula*. Translated into English in the 1790s in at least eight different versions including those by William Taylor and Sir Walter Scott, it became quite famous. Shelley made a copy in his own hand and liked to read it aloud. Among the many derivative English works spawned by "Lenore" were Monk Lewis's ballad, "Alonzo the Brave and the Fair Imogene," and John Stagg's "The Vampyre" (1810), whose hero and heroine, Lord Herman and Gertrude, are terrorized by Sigismund, a particularly grisly vampire-beast.

In William Blake's "Jerusalem" (1804-17) the vampire appears symbolically as a bat, signifying the destructive powers inherent in man's nature. Shelley's vampire was Count Cenci in the verse drama, *The Cenci* (1819), concerning a depraved and unnatural father who one by one "devours" his own children.[4]

The powerful sub-genre of the female vampire begins with Goethe's "Die Braut von Korinth" (1797), taken from the Roman story by Phlegon of Tralles (see Chapter 1), in which a young Athenian is awakened at midnight by his dead lover, who tells him:

> From the silent graveyard I am driven,
> Still to seek the joys I missed,—though dust—,
> Still to love him, who from me was riven,
> Suck his life-blood from his heart with gust.
> Once he is destroyed,
> Others are decoyed,
> And the young fall victim to my lust.[5]

Germaine de Staël commented in *De l'Allemagne* on Goethe's "mixture of love and terror, funereal voluptuousness, a perfect union of death and life" in which "love is allied with the grave, and beauty itself seems nothing but a frightful apparition [mélange d'amour et d'effroi, volupté funebre, une union redoutable de la mort et de la vie...l'amour fait alliance avec la tombe, la beauté même ne semble qu'une apparition effrayante]" (II: xiii, 207). Goethe's Bride mothered a line of female vampires: Coleridge's "Christabel" (Part One: 1797; Part Two: 1800) with its suggestive and fragmentary evocation of Lady Geraldine, whose undescribed but terrifying breasts once made Shelley bolt from the room where it was being recited, conjuring in his imagination a woman's breasts with eyes instead of nipples, according to John Polidori, who was present.[6]

Robert Southey's *Thalaba the Destroyer* (1797-1800) devotes Book VIII to a vampire bride, and is wonderfully exotic and macabre, with the first vampire-staking in English poetry, performed by her own father:

> And o'er the chamber of the tomb
>     There spread a lurid gleam,
> Like the reflection of a sulphur fire;
>         And in that hideous light
>     Oneiza stood before them. It was she...
>     Her very lineaments...and such as death
> Had changed them, livid cheeks and lips of blue;
>         But in her eye there dwelt
>         Brightness more terrible
>     Than all the loathsomeness of death.
>     "Still art thou living, wretch?"
> In hollow tones she cried to Thalaba;
>         "And must I nightly leave my grave
>         To tell thee, still in vain,
>         God hath abandoned thee?"
>
> "This is not she!" the Old Man exclaim'd;
>         "A Fiend; a manifest Fiend!"
> And to the youth he held his lance;
>         "Strike and deliver thyself!"
>     "Strike HER!" cried Thalaba,
>     And palsied of all power,
> Gazed fearfully upon the dreadful form.
> . . . . . . . . . . . . . . . . . . . . . . . . . . . . . . . . .
>     When Moath, firm of heart,
> Perform'd the bidding: through the vampire corpse
>         Thrust his lance; it fell,
>         And howling with the wound,
>         Its fiendish tenant fled.
>     A sapphire light fell on them,
> And garmented with glory, in their sight
>         Oneiza's spirit stood. (VIII: 9, 10)

Then followed Keats's demonic women, "La Belle Dame Sans Merci" (1819) and *Lamia* (1820), taken from the *Life of Apollonius of Tyana* (see Chapter 1), which tells of a serpent with the form of a woman who seems to truly love Lycius, while the sage, behaving like a jealous rival, exposes her.

George Gordon, Lord Byron, came to embody the vampire in the public mind, and James Twitchell writes that the Byronic image is the main impetus in transforming the monster-vampire of folklore into a Romantic hero:

To a considerable extent the myth's currency is a tribute to this one man, for not only was Byron one of the first to think seriously about telling a vampire story, he also constructed the skeleton that would support the vampire in its many reincarnations. By the early nineteenth century the Byronic Hero already had many of the mythic qualities of the vampire: here was the melancholy libertine in the open shirt, the nocturnal lover and destroyer, the maudlin, self-pitying, and moody titan, only a few years away from Nietzsche's Superman. (*Living Dead* 75)

The view, shared by Twitchell and Praz, that the Byronic Fatal Man was the genesis of 19th-century vampire literature is challenged by Peter Thorslev in *The Byronic Hero*:

Praz maintains that for the fashion of vampirism too, "Byron was largely responsible," and sure enough, a few pages later, the Byronic Hero has an added attribute, and we read of "the vampire loves of the Byronic Fatal Man." This attribute Praz bases on a passing reference in one poem and on the fragment of a ghost story written as a joke.... For the most part the Byronic Hero was a typical Romantic lover, and nowhere in all of the poems is he referred to either literally or figuratively as a vampire-lover. (9)

But as Twitchell points out, Thorslev is overlooking Manfred, the Corsair, Conrad, Lara, and the Giaour, all to some extent self-portraits, and all of whom share "a love of darkness, hypnotic eyes, an obsession with the destructive side of love, sneering smiles, and quivering lips" (*Living Dead* 24).

In "The Giaour" (1813), quoted at the beginning of this chapter, a Mohammedan curse is laid upon the hero, that he will become a vampire, drink the blood of his wife and daughters, and be cursed by them. Manfred, the quintessential Romantic hero, is an outcast wanderer whose crime, which he elliptically confesses to the Chamois Hunter, was that he had feasted, either literally or metaphorically, on the hymeneal blood of his own sister, which we may or may not take as autobiographical. (Byron boasted to his wife that he had committed incest with his half-sister, Augusta Leigh.)

Not with my hand, but heart—which broke her heart;
It gazed on mine, and withered. I have shed
Blood, but not hers—and yet her blood was shed;
I saw—and could not stanch it.. (II, ii, 118-22)

Byron's image of the vampire has a tragic, remorseful quality which transformed it for many later writers.

Combining the tradition of the gothic novel with the vampire themes of German and English Romantic poetry, John Polidori's novella, *The Vampyre* (1819) was the first treatment of the vampire in English prose. This seminal work created an immediate sensation and is the source for nearly every vampire play through the century in England and France until the advent of *Dracula* in 1897.

In the convoluted manner which events have a way of taking in real life, *The Vampyre* is both a theft from Byron and a portrait of him. Byron, who remarked that he "awoke one morning to find myself famous," made himself infamous: the scandal of his divorce from Arabella Milbanke and various incidents and affairs surrounding it (including homosexual experiments) forced him to abandon English society. According to Twitchell, "He was exiled from drawing rooms, spat upon in the streets, and cast in the role of social pariah, almost a vampire among men" (*Living Dead* 104).

Byron hired John Polidori to be his physician and traveling companion on his self-imposed exile to the Continent. "Polly-Dolly," as Byron called him, was half-Scottish and half-Italian, fluent in English, Italian, and French, a connoisseur of gothic novels, future uncle to Christina and Dante Gabriel Rossetti, and the youngest man ever to take a medical degree from the University of Edinburgh, writing his dissertation on mesmerism and somnambulism. As a Grand Tour companion, however, he proved to be a poor choice—he was moody, cantankerous, sullen, vain, and given to tantrums and jealousies. In one incident he petulantly asked his employer, "Pray, what is there excepting writing poetry that I cannot do better than you?" Byron replied, "Three things. First, I can hit with a pistol the keyhole of that door. Secondly, I can swim across the river to yonder point. And thirdly, I can give you a damned good thrashing" (qtd. in Marchand, *Byron* 2: 219). The mystery is why Byron tolerated him as long as he did. He wrote to his publisher John Murray (who incidentally had secretly hired Polidori to keep a diary of the journey for publication), "I was never much more disgusted with any human production than with the eternal nonsense, and tracasseries, and emptiness, and ill humor, and vanity of that young person" (qtd. in Bleiler xxxv). Perhaps he was amused by Polidori's sulks, and enjoyed goading him.

They reached Geneva in the summer of 1816, where they met with the Shelleys—Percy Bysshe Shelley, his not-quite wife Mary Godwin Shelley, and her half-sister Claire Clairmont, who had previously been Byron's mistress, was pregnant by him, and would bear him a daughter, Allegra.[7] Byron leased the Villa Diodati on the shore of Lake Geneva, and the Shelleys took Maison Chappius, a few minutes' walk distant.

The irascible Polidori took a jealous and violent dislike to Shelley and tried to challenge him to a duel over a boat race. All dosed themselves with ether, opium, and laudanum; Shelley suffered from hallucinations. There were séances, and discussions of the new science of galvanism, which was thought to be a technique of bringing dead limbs to life, reviving the dead with electricity (which would figure prominently in Mary Shelley's *Frankenstein*). Ghost stories were told, "Christabel" was read aloud, as was a book of German horror stories in French translation, *Fantasmagoriana*.[8] Then Byron proposed a sort of horror decameron, as Mary Shelley relates:

"We will each write a ghost story," said Lord Byron; and his proposition was acceded to. There were four of us. The noble author began a tale, a fragment which he printed at the end of his poem of Mazeppa. Shelley, more apt to embody ideas and sentiments in the radiance of brilliant imagery and in the music of the most melodious verse that adorns our language, than to invent the machinery of a story, commenced one founded on the experiences of his early life. Poor Polidori had some terrible idea about a skull-headed lady, who was so punished for peeping through a keyhole—what to see I forget—something very shocking and wrong, of course…. The illustrious poets, also, annoyed by the platitude of prose, speedily relinquished their uncongenial task.[9]

Polidori, however, made an outline or rough draft of Byron's abandoned fragment, and when he returned to England in 1817, having been dismissed by Byron and in need of money, he spun out his own version of the story from the fragment and sold it to Colburn's *New Monthly Magazine* for thirty pounds as part of "A Letter from Geneva, with Anecdotes of Lord Byron." The story is prefaced by an account of the circle at Lake Geneva in the summer of 1816, Polidori referring to himself throughout in the third person (assuming he, not the magazine's editor, is the author of the preface)[10] and very craftily implying the story is Byron's:

It was afterwards proposed, in the course of conversation, that each of the company present should write a tale depending upon some supernatural agency, which was undertaken by Lord B., the physician, and one of the ladies before mentioned. I obtained the outline of each of these stories as a great favor, and herewith forward them to you, as I was assured you would feel as much curiosity as myself, to peruse the *ébauches* of so great a genius, and those immediately under his influence. (*Three Gothic Novels* 260)

The farrago over the story's authorship has been exhaustively analyzed by D.L. MacDonald in *Poor Polidori: A Critical Biography of the Author of "The Vampyre"*, who concludes that the intent to deceive was probably the publisher's, not Polidori's (178-87).

Following the "Preface" is an "Introduction" which traces the origin of the vampire superstition from the Near East through modern Greece and to the West, cites a few 18th-century European cases from Calmet's *Traité*, and quotes the vampire curse in "The Giaour," and Southey's *Thalaba*.

Polidori's vampire is named Lord Ruthven (pronounced "rivven"), taken from *Glenarvon* (1816, also published by Colburn) a *roman à clef* by Lady Caroline Lamb, whose notorious affair with Byron had done much to drive him out of polite society and eventually out of England altogether. Her novel depicts the poet as the heartless libertine Ruthven Glenarvon, a Scottish nobleman who, after a vile career of preying on numerous women, is carried off by supernatural forces à la Don Giovanni. Byron remarked contemptuously, "As for the likeness, the picture can't be good—I did not sit long enough" (qtd. in Frayling, *Vampyres* 8). Lamb herself is caricatured in *The Vampyre* as a brazen, importunate (if unsuccessful) sexual adventuress, who "threw herself in his way, and did all but put on the dress of a mountebank, to attract his notice...[but] even her unappalled impudence was baffled, and she left the field" (265).

Polidori's description of Ruthven is as follows:

...a cold grey eye, which, fixing upon the object's face, did not seem to penetrate, and at one glance to pierce through to the inward workings of the heart, but fell upon the cheek with a leaden ray that weighed upon the skin it could not pass.... In spite of the deadly hue, which never gained a warmer tint, either from the blush of modesty, or from the strong emotion of passion, though its form and outline were beautiful, many of the female hunters after notoriety attempted to win his attentions. (265)

A synopsis of the story, with excerpts and commentary, is included in Appendix B.

Despite a mixed reception in England,[11] the story had an astounding success. It was issued as a book by Sherwood, Nelly and Jones, went to five printings in 1819 alone, and was translated into three French versions and two German ones. Goethe pronounced it the finest thing Byron had ever written, and E.T.A. Hoffmann commented on Byron's "remarkable knack for the weird and the horrible" in his *Serapion Brethren* (Bleiler xxxviii). There was suddenly a vampire craze in Paris and Amédée Pichot in 1824 declared that the story did more to popularize Byron in France than all his other works put together (Summers, *Kith* 290). The influence of the piece on French writers was so great that it was denounced by Academicians:

Be horrified by that literature of cannibals that feasts on scraps of human flesh and drinks the blood of women and children; it would betray your heart without giving a better image to your mind. Take horror, above all, at that misanthropic poetry, or rather infernal, that seems to have received its mission from Satan himself.[12]

Byron, in the meanwhile, vociferously but futilely denied his authorship of *The Vampyre*—to his publisher, John Murray: "Damn 'The Vampire,'—what do I know of Vampires? it must be some bookselling imposture—contradict it in a solemn paragraph" (*Letters* 41); and to the French public: "I have...a personal dislike to 'vampires,' and the little acquaintance I have with them would by no means induce me to divulge their secrets" (*Works* 4: 288). But Byron's denials and Polidori's subsequent claims of authorship were of little consequence where money was to be made: Byron's name was infinitely more profitable. When publishers insisted on including it in editions of his collected works, he was forced to publish his own fragment, consisting of nine pages and differing in many respects from Polidori.

In Byron's "Fragment of a Novel" the vampire is named Augustus Darvell. It is narrated in the first person by the (unnamed) Aubrey character; contains only the death and burial scenes;

involves business about a ring to be thrown in the Bay of Eleusis; breaks off suddenly before the vampire's resurrection; and includes some naturalistic conversation (Polidori's version has only a few lines of dialogue). Byron's vampire does not seem particularly evil and debauches no one in the course of the story. Some aspects are superior to Polidori's version: the use of singular, evocative, exotic words like glowing jewels—"Ephesus," "Sardis," "serrugee," "janizary," "caravanserai," "Sulieman," "ataghan"; the very effective setting of the death scene in an ancient Turkish cemetery; and the symbolic appearance of a stork with a snake in its beak at the moment of Darvell's death. The many differences should have acquitted Polidori of the charge of plagiarism, but public opinion, particularly in France, could not accept the idea that the first story was not Byron's. Polidori died two years later in 1821, destitute and alone, possibly of a drug overdose, at the age of 25.

MacDonald points out that Polidori made four innovations in the character of the vampire which would remain part of his persona for the next century (193-99):

1. He is a resurrected dead body. (This is not new, but more strongly emphasized than before.)
2. He is an aristocrat. The vampire of folklore had been a peasant, preying on his family and neighbors. Ruthven's predations are in the manner of a Don Giovanni or Count Almaviva exercising *droit du seigneur*.
3. He is a traveller, a "mysterious stranger," mobile, restless, and in search of new victims.
4. He is a seducer. Polidori added malevolent charm to the personality, linking it with Byron.

To these modifications, we should add another pointed out by Carol Senf in *The Vampire in Nineteenth-Century Literature*: he has a supernatural relationship with the moon (34). The connection between vampires and moonlight seems to have occurred first in Byron's "Fragment," embellished by Polidori. This lunar power will prove extremely important in the many stage plays involving Ruthven.

The importance of *The Vampyre* is summed up by Twitchell:

Polidori's most important innovation…is the introduction of an active villain, a villain as eager to suck the life from his fictional compatriots as is the author to scare the life out of his audience. Not only was Polidori the first to use the figure of the vampire in prose, but he also seems, like

Coleridge and Keats, one of the first to understand its psychological possibilities. For Polidori seems to use the myth in part as an analogy to explain how people interact. To Ianthe and Miss Aubrey, Lord Ruthven is an actual vampire, a horrid demon, but to Aubrey, Ruthven is a parasite of a different sort, a psychological sponge. Ruthven never "attacks" Aubrey, never sucks his blood; but there does seem to be some energy exchange between the two men. (112)

It is the psychic relationship between vampire and victim that appealed most to the Romantic poets: vampirism as a metaphor for the predatory nature of human relationships—man and woman, parent and child, philosopher and madman, artist and subject—all devour one another's souls. Construed to its broadest possibility, there is an element of vampirism in every human relationship, because, according to the Romantics, in every human relationship one person is enlarged and the other is diminished.

The transformed Romantic vampire, a demon-lover who dies and yet loves, has a strong religious component as well. Linking gothic sensibility with the Romantic preoccupation with love and death, the vampire, as Bayer-Berenbaum notes,

...is an interesting example of the gothic distortion of a religious notion and the attempt to express overtly what Christianity had implied.... The living dead is a more immanent expression of the religious notion of life *after* death.... Further, the vampire is neither human nor divine but a combination of the two; he is a spirit incarnate in life, not all-powerful yet not a mortal. Like the saint or savior, he is all-suffering, a perverted Christ figure who offers the damnation of eternal life in this world rather than the salvation of eternal life in the next. (35)

It was through Polidori's novella that the vampire, powerful and complex creature of the Romantic imagination, made his transition from page to stage.

**Chapter 3**

# Paris, 1820

The vampire will terrorize, with his horrible love, the dreams of all women; and soon, no doubt, this monster, still exhumed, will lend his immobile mask, his sepulchral voice, his "dead grey eye," he will offer, I say, all that melodramatic apparatus to the Melpomene of the boulevards; and then what success is not in store for him![1]
— Charles Nodier, *Les Démons de la nuit*

Within a year of the publication of Polidori's *The Vampyre*, a dramatization of the story was presented in Paris at the Théâtre de la Porte-Saint-Martin. It was the work of three writers: Pierre François Adolphe Carmouche (1797-1868); Achille, Marquis de Jouffrey d'Abbans (1785-1859); and Charles Nodier (1780-1844). My discussion of this seminal play will include commentary on the play's role in developing the genres of melodrama and Romantic drama; analysis of the plot and the influence of secondary sources (*Ossian, Glenarvon, Don Giovanni*); investigation of the staging and the artists involved in creating the production, and the critical reception the play received. Further, the enormous success of *Le Vampire* spawned a series of imitations and parodies, making vampires the rage of Paris for the next several years; these derivative works will also be analyzed. In conclusion, possible reasons will be considered for the phenomenal popular response to this play.

A chronological listing of the plays, with première dates, theatres, and publication information is to be found in Appendix A; plot summaries and illustrative passages in Appendix B; biographical material on playwrights, actors, designers, and others in Appendix C; and cast lists in Appendix D.

The distinctions between French Romantic drama and melodrama must be drawn before analyzing the importance of *Le Vampire* in the development of both genres. Melodrama predates Romanticism and outlives it, and, like the gothic novel, is a form which survives in somewhat altered state up to the present day. Although there are some earlier examples, in general melodrama

**41**

came into being as a way of circumventing Napoleon's 1807 Moscow Decree outlawing irregular genres: it purported not to be drama at all but pantomime accompanied by music. Jean-Jacques Rousseau had previously used the word "mélodrame" in this way (and perhaps coined it) to describe his *Pygmalion* and *Le Devin du Village* in 1770, though they had no immediate successors. Other strands of influence can be traced to Diderot's theories of sentimental drama, and to the writings of Beaumarchais: "It is time to interest a people and make flow its tears for an event which may be supposed real and taking place before their eyes, among the citizens; it would never fail to produce emotion."[2] That is, it was to be theatre of pure emotion, of and for the common people.

"I write for those who cannot read" is a statement imputed to Guilbert de Pixérécourt (1773-1844) who, followed by Victor Ducange and Louis Caigniez, fixed the features of the form for the next hundred years with *Victor, ou l'Enfant de la forêt* (1798), *Coelina, l'Enfant de mystère* (1800), and more than 120 other plays. Among his plot sources were gothic novels and German sword-and-cape drama. Nodier's *Le Vampire*, while barely qualifying for the legal definition of melodrama by containing only one song, conforms to the characteristics of the genre as developed by Pixérécourt and as they existed in early 19th-century France in the following ways:

1. A simplified and idealized portrait of human existence, a world of black and white.
2. A powerful and fascinating villain who is the moving force of the plot.
3. A virtuous heroine persecuted by the villain.
4. An episodic plot; thrilling stage action.
5. Acts ending in strong climaxes.
6. Emphasis on ocular rather than literary theatre.
7. Emphasis on physical action.
8. Coincidence and surprise, rather than inexorable fate.
9. A mixture of comedy, pathos, thrills—no purity of genre. (*Le Vampire* contains no real comedy, however.)
10. Musical underscoring of dialogue.
11. Singing and dancing.
12. A happy ending.

Christopher Prendergast, in *Balzac, Fiction and Melodrama* (7-8), puts forth six further characteristics of the genre in terms of thematic content:

1. Antithesis: a Manichean view of the world divided into good and evil, with no grey areas.
2. Hyperbole: good and evil existing only in extreme form.
3. Stereotype: recognizable characters, generic hero and heroine, comic-helper, black (diabolical, *e.g.*, Simon Legree) or white (wormish, hypocritical, *e.g.*, Uriah Heep) villain.
4. Mystery: sudden revelation, concealed parenthood, who-done-it.
5. Coincidence: miraculous escapes from inescapable situations, long-lost twins, chance triumphing over fate.
6. Poetic justice: reward and punishment meted out in this world, not the next.

Melodrama's powerful hold on French popular taste can be accounted for in two ways: first, when a style such as neoclassicism becomes the official "high art" of a culture, it becomes hide-bound by rules and authority imposed from above, and tends to become derivative, pretentious, repetitive, and self-devouring. Melodrama, with its flaunting of the rules, vitality, and responsivity to the public pulse, was an innovative and quickly evolving form. Like jazz with its lower-class origins and crude energy, it had a "trickle-up" effect, eventually infecting the higher art forms. Focused on the box office, melodrama looks not to eternity but to tomorrow night.

Second, there is a dark side to melodrama, very much exemplified by *Le Vampire*, which is its emphasis on sex, cruelty, and the macabre. The Boulevard du Temple was often called "le Boulevard du Crime," not only because of the usual subject matter of the melodrama houses, but also because of the nature of the audiences which frequented those theatres. The heavy sexual content of plays such as *Le Vampire*, and its violence, probably intensified the sense of danger. The atmosphere of the Boulevard du Crime is beautifully evoked in Marcel Carne's film, *Les Enfants du Paradis* (1943).

In addition to its place as an example of gothic melodrama, *Le Vampire* is also in some ways a proto-Romantic drama. A. Owen Aldridge in "The Vampire Theme: Dumas père and the English Stage" writes, "Without question, Nodier's play should be interpreted as a manifestation of French Romanticism, a precursor of *Hernani*" (314).

Melodrama paved the way for Romantic drama by popularizing the departure from neoclassic rules and creating a large potential audience. The Romantic period in France was brief (from 1830 with Victor Hugo's *Hernani* to 1842 with the failure of Hugo's *Les Burgraves*), but its influence was far-reaching. Distinguished from melodrama (which typically has three acts) by the five-act structure, the use of verse, and the unhappy ending, Romantic drama shares so many characteristics with melodrama that the genres overlap in more ways than they differ.

One characteristic distinguishing Romantic drama from melodrama was the divided hero—drawn from Schiller's Franz Moor in *Die Räuber* (1782), Goethe's Faust (1808) and ultimately from Hamlet or even Orestes—a protagonist in conflict with himself and with the moral order. In several ways this description fits Nodier's Rutwen in *Le Vampire*. The end of the play, in which he is destroyed, can be seen as tragic. Romanticism's moral reading of the universe is considerably more complex than melodrama's.

Since melodrama is a form of theatre which depends as much, if not more, on the physical production and the acting for its effects as it does on the written script, it is important to consider these elements to obtain a truer picture of what the experience of the play was really like in its historical context. Therefore, as stated in the Introduction of this work, I will consider these plays from the point of view of theatre history as well as that of literary criticism.

Napoleon's defeat and exile in 1815 had removed many of the restrictions imposed on the theatres of Paris limiting their number and repertory.[3] The Théâtre de la Porte-Saint-Martin had been one of the minor houses, whose license to produce melodrama granted in 1806 had been rescinded by the 1807 Moscow Decree. After petitioning for two years, it was granted permission to stage "acrobatics, historic tableaux, military displays and prologues" (qtd. in Carlson, *French Stage* 55). Interpreting these restrictions more and more broadly, it was again punished and closed in 1811. It re-opened under the Restoration, first under the direction of Saint-Romain, then under Jean-Toussaint Merle with a strong leaning toward the literature of England and Germany, specializing particularly in gothic melodrama and horror. Typical offerings, besides *Le Vampire* (1820), were *Les Chefs écossais* (1819), *Le Doge de Venice* (1821), *Chateau de Kenilworth* (1822), Pixérécourt's *Château de Loch-Leven ou l'Evasion de Marie Stuart* (probably the only Mary Stuart play which does not end with her execution), and *Le Monstre et le magicien* (1826; Nodier, Merle, and Béraud's version of Mary Shelley's *Frankenstein*; the monster, a mime role, was played by the English actor T.P. Cooke, the first to play Ruthven in London. See Chapter 4 and Appendix C). Additionally, according to Maurice Albert in *Les Théâtres des Boulevards*, it produced *La Fiancée de Lammermoor, Hamlet, Le*

*Marchand de Venice*, and *Les Sorcières d'Écosse* (*Macbeth*). In these lists we see ample testimony of the French taste for things English (especially Scottish history). Merle, the theatre's director, carried his anglophilia so far as to import British actors to Paris, disastrously with the Penley troupe's *Othello* and *School for Scandal* in 1822, but preparing the way for the triumphant visit of Charles Kemble's company in 1827 and William Macready's in 1828.[4]

The Porte-Saint-Martin was a large and well-equipped theatre on the Boulevard du Temple, specially equipped for the staging of melodramatic spectacle by its machinist, Poulet, and its resident designer, Pierre-Luc-Charles Ciceri (1782-1868). Its machinery could create floods, storms, sinking ships, fires, thunder and lightning—for the apotheosis of *Faust* the stage divided in half, showing both heaven and hell (Carlson 51) Maurice Albert writes:

The Porte-Saint-Martin was in those times a fortunate theatre. But it well merited the flattering preference, already old and established, shown by the patronage of all classes of society, even the royal family. It owed that favor to the intelligence of its directors, to the talent of its actors, who were called Frédérick Lemaître, Bocage, and Mme. Dorval, to its love of novelty, to its audacious inventions, to the great expenditures of money happily borne, and finally to its many efforts to bring together under its roof all sorts of attractions scattered on other stages.[5]

Of the three co-authors of *Le Vampire*, Achille Jouffrey, a historian, seems never to have written another play;[6] Pierre Carmouche wrote at least 150 between 1815 and 1830. He was a practiced and prolific writer of comedy-vaudeville and boulevard farce, who frequently collaborated with some of the other playwrights to be mentioned in this chapter.[7]

However, the most important of the three was Charles Nodier. Although he wrote only four or possibly five plays,[8] he is considered one of the fathers of French Romanticism and an important literary influence on the age. He was an early champion of Shakespeare and the German pre-Romantic writers. Defending melodrama in his newspaper columns and in his introduction to the printed works of his friend Pixérécourt, Nodier praised the literature of England and Germany, two nations which were not very popular in France at that period, no doubt stemming from the Battle of Waterloo (1815) and the striving of the Germans and English to unseat France as the dominant culture and political power in Europe, a position it had held for 150 years.

Nodier was a Royalist who courted the favor of the restored Louis XVIII (although he had served Napoleon during the Empire), but he was a revolutionary in his ideas about art. In a commentary on Germaine de Staël's *De l'Allemagne* (1814), he wrote:

Today, the *mélodrame* is indispensable. I cannot conceive of anything that could be put in its place, and whatever efforts are made to destroy it, or to render it ridiculous...will never succeed.... *Mélodrame*, leaving aside for the moment considerations of technique, is German romantic tragedy. If among people of wit who make a habit of poking fun at it, there had been found a genius who had the courage to face adverse criticism, to desire to earn the first palm in a new career, to evoke that masculine and terrifying muse of Schiller and Goethe whose secrets Madame de Staël reveals so eloquently, do you know where the second Théâtre Française would be? Most likely on the Boulevards. (*Débats*, 8 November 1818; qtd. in Oliver, *Charles Nodier* 89)

He was shortly to answer his own summons. In his 1819 review of the Faber translation of Polidori's *The Vampyre*, he wrote of Romanticism:

Positive truths do not flatter the imagination, which so loves untruth that it prefers frightening illusions to the depiction of an agreeable, but natural, emotion. This latest shift in human idiosyncrasy, tired of ordinary emotions, is what is called the romantic genre.... We know where we are in politics; in poetry we have reached the age of the nightmare and of the vampires. (*Débats*, 1 July 1819; qtd. in Oliver 89-90)

Nodier was already familiar with vampires, having come across the legends in the course of his travels in "Illyria" and discussed them in an article in *le Télégrafe officiel*, 11 April 1813. In an article in *le Drapeau blanc*, 1 July 1819, he treats the subject quite seriously:

The myth of the vampire is perhaps the most universal of our superstitions. Everywhere it has the authority of tradition; nor does it lack the support of theology or of medicine. Even philosophy has spoken of it. [La fable du vampire est peut-être la plus universelle de nos superstitions...Elle a partout l'autorité de la tradition: elle ne manque ni de celle de la théologie ni de celle de la médicine. La philosophie même en a parlé.]

Later he would tell the young and impressionable Alexandre Dumas père that he had seen an Illyrian vampire with his own eyes, which Dumas recounts at length in *Mes Mémoires* (1863; see Chapter 7).

The first vampire novel, *Lord Ruthven ou les vampires* by Cyprien Bérard, underwent a curious fandango of denied and claimed authorship that is reminiscent of the Polidori-Byron case, except that the roles are reversed. In his biography of Nodier, Alfred Richard Oliver concludes, "He was at least a silent partner to the publishing artifice and had very likely written the novel in the first place" (90). Bérard, his close friend and manager of the Théâtre de Vaudevilles, had only one other published work, a prosaic report on theatre management.

*Lord Ruthven ou les vampires*, a sequel to Polidori, concerns the vampire's further adventures, this time in Italy, where he has made an unwilling vampire of Bettina, and is pursued by her fiancé Leontî. Ruthven, under the assumed name Lord Seymour, becomes engaged to the Duke of Modena's daughter, whom he victimizes on their wedding night. Leontî accuses Ruthven of being a vampire, challenges and kills him, then commits suicide. When Ruthven revives from death in his usual fashion, the truth is revealed, and he is killed in a ritualistic manner: he is staked and his eyes are gouged out.

If Nodier is the author of the piece, he was simultaneously working with Carmouche and Jouffrey on the stage adaptation of the original story. *Le Vampire, mélodrame en trois actes et prologue*, outstanding example of the first sub-genre of melodrama, the gothic, premiered 13 June 1820 at the Porte-Saint-Martin. The leading roles were performed by the great Romantic actors Monsieur Philippe (Emmanuel de la Villenie, d. 1824) and Marie Dorval (Marie Delauney, 1789-1849). Biographical material on these actors appears in Appendix C.

Nodier shifts the scene from the London and Greece of Polidori's story to the Inner Hebrides of Scotland. The first possible explanation for the change of locale is that Ruthven was a Scottish nobleman in both Polidori's *The Vampyre* and Lamb's *Glenarvon*. Second, for the French, Ruthven *was* Lord Byron, whose family seat and heritage, through his mother Catherine Gordon, were Scottish. Third, the French, perhaps with a fond nostalgia for the "Auld Alliance" with Scotland of the 16th century, seem to have found Scotland an exotic locale and developed a romantic attachment to it which mystified and bemused the English. For example in 1804, Lesueur's *Les Bardes* was a spectacular production at l'Opéra, glorifying "gothic" Scotland and showing, in the fourth act, Ossian sleeping in his cave surrounded by the spirits of heroes and warriors in the mists of Celtic twilight (Carlson 37-38). Ossian was the invention of one James Macpherson, who pretended to have collected the poems of a medieval Scot and published them in 1760-63. The hoax was finally "exploded" by Dr. Johnson, who challenged Macpherson to a duel, but France "went on swooning over the imaginary bard" (Kendrick, *Thrill of Fear* 51). Nodier, whose fondness for all things Scottish is well noted, took names from the "Ossian" poems such as Ituriel, angel of the moon; Oscar, ancient bard and semi-mystic "génie des Mariages;" and Malvina,[9] heroine of the piece; and set his prologue in the Grotto of Staffa. Having also shifted the time period from Polidori's unspecified but not distant past to "gothic" Scotland, Nodier's employment of a pistol for the killing of Rutwen is incongruous, but an inconsistency typical of Romantic drama.

"Ruthven" (which the English pronounce "rivven") in the play is spelled "Rutwen" and pronounced "root-wain"; the French may have adored the Scots but they were clueless as to pronunciation as were the Germans, who pronounced it "rott-ven" (see Chapter 6). The character is more redolent of Lord Byron than of Calmet, particularly the Byron portrayed in Caroline Lamb's *Glenarvon*. She describes the protagonist, Clarence de Ruthven, Lord of Glenarvon, as follows:

It was one of those faces which, having once beheld, we never afterwards forget. It seemed as if the soul of passion had been stamped and printed upon every feature. The eye beamed into life as it threw up its dark ardent gaze, with a look nearly of inspiration, while the proud curl of the upper lip expressed haughtiness and bitter contempt; yet, even mixed with these fierce characteristic feelings, an air of melancholy and dejection shaded over and softened every harsher expression. (II: 29)

Rutwen is not a typical melodrama villain; he has many characteristics of the Romantic anti-hero: he has feelings of despair, and his passion for Malvina seems genuine. Nodier has altered the character from the cold, serpent-like fiend with the dead grey eyes of Polidori's tale—Rutwen is a fallen angel, lonely and desperate for human love.

Exactly what Rutwen is planning to do to Malvina on their wedding night is not made clear, but there are references to "virgin blood." He attempts to rape Lovette, the peasant bride, and his need for blood means he will mutilate if not kill her. The Prologue makes clear that many women have been murdered by him through the centuries; he has ravaged and ravished his way through 20 countries. His is "the love that brings death," yet he is presented as an attractive, ardent, seductive young man with hypnotic eyes, and an "inconceivable charm." He speaks passionately of love, and is "powerfully moved at the sight of his beloved" (McFarland 32).

O my friend, how my whole being is revived at seeing her. You know me, blighted with unhappiness, alone on earth; you saw me always ready to leave without regret the emptiness which envelops me to search for another emptiness still unknown. This angel, this angel alone can hold me to life; it is from her that I await a new life: it almost seems to me that I drink it in through her eyes. O Malvina, let your lips confirm so sweet a hope! (I, vii, 25)[10]

In Malvina's "dream" he calls to her piteously, he seems to be asking for help. The combination of pity and fear has always been a powerful one; add to it erotic attraction and the mixture is potent. Rutwen embodies an extremely powerful archetype, the "dark stranger." A love-affair with a vampire, possibly at the price of death, is the horror version of one of the basic human encounters, which for women is always a gamble with fate.

Richard Switzer in "Lord Ruthven and the Vampires" notes that the subplot involving the second couple, Lovette and Edgar, seems to be drawn from Da Ponte's libretto for Mozart's opera *Don Giovanni* (1787), especially the "Là ci darem la mano" scene between the Don and Zerlina, who is saved by her fiancé Masetto (111). The source is an excellent one, and the borrowed personality of Don Giovanni works well in fleshing out the Polidori vampire. His sudden unslakeable desire for the peasant bride is in the long-standing tradition of rakes, although it has the effect of undermining our sympathy. Perhaps we are to understand that he is driven by hunger and desperation: a storm prevents his return to the neighboring island to consummate his own wedding night.

As Ronald McFarland points out, Nodier has shifted the focus of attention from Aubray to Malvina, another characteristic of French melodrama (which always found Ophelia more interesting than Hamlet). McFarland also notes that the French dramatists have somewhat improved Aubray's motivations from Polidori's original

ones, by making him owe Rutwen his life, and thus made him a
more plausible, if flatter, character (26, 28).

Other changes made by Nodier include the elimination of
Ianthe from the plot, and the addition of stock characters and
*confidants* to aid the exposition: Brigitte, a rather colorless
companion for Malvina, and "Scottish" types, Scop and Petterson.

One other device Nodier has added is the necessity for the
vampire to marry his victims. Polidori's Ruthven married Miss
Aubrey, but his other victims were taken without benefit of clergy.
However the death of a bride on her wedding night is a feature of
gothic romances dating back to Bürger's "Lenore" (1748, qtd. in
Chapter 2).

Ginette Picat-Guinoiseau, editor of a new critical edition of
Nodier's dramatic works and author of a critical biography, *Nodier
et le théâtre*, argues that Nodier's changes elevate the Polidori
material to a level approaching tragedy:

Polidori's short story has furnished *Le Vampire* with some givens: the
personalities of the protagonists, the recollection of the customs of
vampires, the hallucinatory events of a premonitory nature, the past
"death" of the vampire, the exigence of the oath, and finally the intrusion
of madness. From this little bit of material the authors have created a
powerful work with clever doses of the tragic, the dramatic, and the
melodramatic.[11]

The Prologue of *Le Vampire* provided the great Romantic
designer, Ciceri, with the opportunity to create the Cave of Staffa, a
flying moon spirit, tombs rising from the earth and releasing their
spirits. The description in the script reads:

At the rise of the curtain, the sky is dark and everything confused. It grows
lighter little by little. The stage is transformed to a basaltic grotto whose tall
prisms terminate in unequal angles near the sky. The hanging drops are
revealed. The circumference of the grotto is strewn with tombs of diverse
shapes, with columns, pyramids, and cubes of a crude workmanship. On a
tomb downstage a young girl is lying, plunged in the most profound sleep.
Her head is resting on one arm, and is covered by her veil and her hair.
The light has grown progressively brighter. The angel of the moon, in a
floating white gown, addresses Oscar. (Prologue 1)[12]

Then follows a room in the Château de Staffa, an outdoor peasant
wedding scene, then "a vast gothic vestibule, the door of the chapel

at the rear" [un grand vestibule gothique, la porte de la chapelle ...au fond] (III, i, 44). The final scene featured demons rising out of the earth, an exterminating angel, and a rain of fire. We may be sure that Ciceri created a denouement to make one's hair stand on end.

RUTWEN: Annihilation! Annihilation!
(He drops his dagger and tries to flee. Phantoms rise from the earth and drag him down with them; the exterminating angel appears in a cloud; lightning flashes and the phantoms disappear with Rutwen. Rain of fire.) GENERAL TABLEAU (III, S. dernière, 56)[13]

The new scholarly edition of the text by Picat-Guinoiseau compares the printed text published by J.N. Barba (1820) with two earlier manuscripts ("fonds de la censure des Archives Nationales, F[18]601"). They contain some word variations, additional scenes, music cues, stage directions, and a slightly different ending:

His arm, which was raised, falls. Lightning rumbles. The back of the stage opens and one sees the ghosts of the vampire's victims. They are young women covered with veils who pursue him showing their torn bosoms from which blood still flows. At that moment the angel of love crosses the stage in a luminous chariot.
    ALL (seized with fright): O heaven! (Thunder groans more loudly and falls on the vampire, who is engulfed.) CURTAIN (III, vii, 125-26)[14]

We may presume that the inventions of Ciceri dictated the more spectacular finale of the published version. This fiery finish (again à la *Don Giovanni*) reverses Polidori's denouement and fulfills one of Pixérécourt's rules for melodrama: a happy ending.[15]
    The play contains a peasant ballet, the bard's song, and the supernatural prologue, which could be described as a masque. The music, written especially for the production, was by Alexandre Piccini. As Picat-Guinoiseau comments:

Piccini, the great specialist of the genre, knew how to compose... punctuations for the action which were evocative and pathetic; songs for the soloists and the chorus;...and finally, dance, in the form of a ballet which illustrates the harmony of the world while the adverse events have already been put into motion.... The music could be descriptive, could "paint" or "express" a tempest or storm; it could underscore the words; it could be the background of an entire scene. The scenic indications evoke a kind of film score. The music poetizes the action.[16]

This is an important point. Musical evocation of the subtext, creating an aural poetry underscoring the action, a convention now taken for granted in film, is one of the signature innovations of melodrama.

The dialogue is in prose, and studded with colorful English locutions such as "Mylord," "Sir," "Miss," and "Par St. Georges!" Montague Summers comments:

The dialogue of this melodrama is spirited, the situations striking and well managed, and even in reading the play, one can clearly visualize that upon the stage it must have been extraordinarily effective, especially when set off with all the attractions of the scene painter's glowing perspectives, the magic craft of the subtle machinist, and the richest adornment of romantic costume. Even before he had introduced the Vampire to the boards Nodier had prophesied that this macabre monster would win a veritable triumph, and his prediction was amply fulfilled. (*Kith* 293)

Picat-Guinoiseau remarks:

The theatre of Nodier is situated at that ill-defined margin between melodrama and literature. (Melo)drama was for him a game, the rules of which he applied himself to follow correctly, but while he plays, he expresses himself. One could question certain tics of language; this theatre nevertheless constitutes an original and fetching work whose power of seduction surpasses simple pathos to touch the depths that literature explores and magnifies.[17]

The success of *Le Vampire* was extraordinary. Even the playscript sold out, and went through several printings:

All Paris flocked to see *Le Vampire*, and nightly the Porte-Saint-Martin was packed to the doors. Philippe and Madame Dorval were applauded to the echo by enthusiastic audiences who recalled them again and again after the final tableau. Even the book of the play had an immense circulation and every morning Barba's counter was freshly stocked with huge piles of the duodecimo, which rapidly diminished during the day. (Summers, *Kith* 293)

The critical reception of *Le Vampire* was quite hostile, perhaps because of its enormous success. Critics focused on the play's supposed immorality:

The melodrama of the *Vampire* in which one sees a monster who sucks the blood of little girls and which offers scenes which an honest woman could not view without blushing [Le mélodrame du *Vampire* dans lequel on voit paraître un monstre qui suce le sang des petites filles et qui offre des Tableaux qu'une honnête femme ne peut voir sans rougir]. (*Les Lettres Normandes* [1820] XI: 93)

To balance the success of *The Vampire*, disgusting melodrama, so monstrous that the authors, Messieurs Ch. Nodier and Carmouche have not dared to make themselves known, the Porte-Saint-Martin is getting ready to present the literal translation, in prose, of Schiller's *Maria Stuart* [Pour balancer le succès du *Vampire*, mélodrame dégoutant et si monstreux que les auteurs MM. Ch. Nodier et Carmouche n'ont pas osé se faire connaître, le théâtre de la Porte-Saint-Martin se prépare à représenter la traduction littérale, en prose, de *Marie Stuart* de Schiller]. (*Conservateur littéraire* [1820] II: 245)

In the wings of the theatre, the vampire Ruthven tries to violate or suck [the blood of] the young bride who flees before him. Is this a moral situation? The whole play indirectly represents God as a weak or odious being who abandons the world to the demons of hell [Le vampire Ruthven veut violer ou sucer dans les coulisses une jeune fiancée qui fuit devant lui sur le théâtre: cette situation est-elle morale?...Toute la pièce représente indirectment Dieu comme un être faible ou odieux qui abandonne le monde aux génies de l'enfer]. (*Histoire des Vampires et des spectres Malfaisons*, Paris, 1820)

Melodrama itself had many detractors, whose two main arguments consisted of the familiar complaint against mixed or "impure" genre, and the threat to public morals. Michel Hennin, in "De l'anarchie théâtrale" called for a total ban on melodrama, which showed "dethroned kings, cast-off princes, rebellious subjects, homicides, guilty wives, seduced daughters [les rois détronés, des princes dépouillés, des sujets rebelles, des homicides, des femmes coupables, des filles séduites]" (qtd. in Summers, *Kith* 294). Using Saint Augustine's argument, Hennin condemns melodrama for "les larmes inutiles" which it caused to flow. Further, it debased public taste and destroyed reason. The anonymous "Essai sur l'Etat actuel des théâtres de Paris" fulminated:

Was not melodrama becoming the school of disobedience?... What misshapen language melodrama spoke! With what liberties it denatured history! With what errors it nourished the public in "mixing up epochs and deeds!" What false ideas it expounded! How, in the midst of all this uproar, could amiable and discreet works be heard again? What became, with melodrama, of the cult of great writers? They were rushing into an abyss. That cartoon from the beginning of the century that showed Melpomene and Thalia in flight before melodrama, who brandished a dagger and was followed by a band of brigands, was it not too prophetic?[18]

However, melodrama could not be suppressed. It was "unquestionably the dominant dramatic genre of the century" (Carlson, *French Stage* 3).

As Eric Bentley writes in *The Life of the Drama*, melodrama focuses on the actor. Bentley's argument is that Richard III, for example, paradoxically is a greater *acting* role than Lear, though *King Lear* is a much greater play. Illustrating his argument with the examples of Edmund Kean and Henry Irving, he says that great actors "hypnotize" audiences by force of personality, enabling the spectators to reach visceral and emotional heights possible only in the theatre and far transcending the written word.

Once we see the hypnotic character of melodramatic theatre we see in a new light the fact that this theatre often actually presents cases of hypnotic and kindred states of mind.... There is a primitive Pirandellianism in the fact that the relationship with the audience becomes part of the play itself by an analogy with the action presented onstage.... Edmund Kean could make Lord Byron faint and women give birth prematurely without much aid from the plot...In rejecting bad melodramatic acting, the twentieth century has fallen into the error of condemning melodramatic acting as such, and today the task of the actors is to rediscover and recreate a lost grandeur. (176-78)

Of course, neoclassic tragedy dealt with emotion and focused on the art of acting, but because of the rules of decorum, the characters are reduced to talking about their feelings; in melodrama, characters "act out" violently. Emotion divorced from action is not as interesting to *watch*. The "sense of danger," which Kenneth Tynan has referred to as an essential element of great acting, is especially served by the violence of melodrama.

The cult of the personality of the actor (and Philippe's often-mentioned magnetic good looks), combined with the implied sexual threat of the vampire's lust for blood, and the touch of the uncanny, the foreign, the "alien," are all components of Rutwen's power as a theatrical image.

One natural reaction when something frightening powerfully seizes the public imagination, is to make fun of it. In *Le Mélodrame* Paul Ginisty remarks:

The most famous melodramas were the most parodied.... One of the proofs of its vitality was the parody, which exercised its fantasy upon melodrama, and parody is one form of consecration [Les mélodrames les plus fameux furent très parodiés.... Une des preuves de sa vitalité c'était la parodie qui exercait sur lui sa fantaisie, et la parodie est une manière de consécration]. (184)

Also, as John Cawelti in *Adventure, Mystery and Romance: Formula Stories as Art and Popular Culture* points out, horror is always very close to comedy. "To objectify a terror by giving it a specific form is closely related to the basic rhythm of comedy in which a situation presented as dangerous or disturbing turns out suddenly to be far less so than we thought (49)." For these reasons (along with the profit-motive of piggy-backing on a phenomenal commercial success) Paris was presented with at least six more vampire plays within the space of a few weeks. As Montague Summers writes:

Immediately upon the furore created by Nodier's *Le Vampire* at the Porte-Saint-Martin in 1819 [sic] vampire plays of every kind from the most luridly sensational to the most farcically ridiculous pressed on to the boards. A contemporary critic cries: "There is not a theatre in Paris without its Vampire! At the Porte-Saint-Martin we have *le Vampire*; at the Vaudeville *le Vampire* again; at the Variétés *les trois Vampires ou la clair de la lune*." (*Kith* 303)

The parodies omit the original's blood and violence, hinging instead on the tired device of mistaken identity, although some are more interesting in that they put comic focus on the vampire's ability to die repeatedly and pop back up again, which seems to have tickled the French funny-bone.

Eugène Scribe (1791-1861) and Mélesville (pseudonym of Anne Honoré Joseph Duveyrier), with whom he wrote more than forty plays, put their comedy-vaudeville, *Le Vampire*, also called *Le Vampire Amoureux*, on the boards of the Théâtre du Vaudeville on 15 June 1820, two days after the opening of Nodier's play. This swiftness suggests the possibility of industrial spying, not surprising considering that Carmouche and Merle frequently collaborated with

Mélesville and Scribe in various combinations. Neil Cole Arvin, a Scribe biographer, writes that at this early period in his career, Scribe was transforming the nature of vaudeville from its earlier bucolic tradition with conventional shepherds and country patois, and turning to the manners and mores of Restoration society which he found close to hand. In 1820 he was already the most popular provider of French "gaiety" (13).

Scribe's *Le Vampire* is an elegant farce in one act and 17 scenes. There are about 20 songs; in the custom of the time they consisted of new words set to popular tunes, not newly composed for the play. The setting is Hungary (suggesting that the playwrights had read Calmet's *Traité*), in a gothic chateau. The play concerns Adolphe de Valberg, a young soldier who pretends to have died several times in the course of the action, and his romantic involvement with the sisters Mansfred (cf. Byron's *Manfred*).

While Scribe's piece played at the Vaudeville, Nicholas Brazier (1783-1838), Gabriel Lurieu, and Armand d'Artois opened their *Les Trois Vampires ou le clair de la lune* at the Variétés a week later on 22 June 1820. This was a one-act folie-vaudeville with about 15 songs. The plot concerns old M. Gobetout, a Byron devotee, defending his daughters against three supposed vampires, actually their sweethearts. It contains amusing references to the Porte-Saint-Martin *Vampire*. Brazier cranked out more than 210 similar trifles between 1815 and 1830.

*Encore un Vampire*, another farce involving mistaken identity, was published under the name Emile B.L., the pseudonym of Michel Nicholas Balesson de Rougemont, and a fourth, *Les Etrennes d'un vampire*, a burlesque by Auguste Rousseau, was advertised as being copied from a manuscript "trouvé au cimetière de Père-Lachaise" (Summers, *Kith* 305).

Marc Antoine Madeleine Désaugiers (1772-1827) contributed *Cadet Buteux, vampire, avec relation véridique du prologue et des trois actes de cet épouvantable mélodrame écrit sous la dictée de ce passeux du Gros Caillou, par son secrétaire Désaugiers*. The published libretto bore the words, "Vivent les morts!" The Cadet Buteux plays were a series of one-man versions of popular plays, all sung (no dialogue) to popular tunes. The pieces are send-ups of the originals in the style of the present-day "Forbidden Broadway."[19]

Another 1820 vaudeville-burlesque was called *Le Vampire, mélodrame en trois actes, paroles de Pierre de la Fosse de la rue des Morts*. It also contains a satiric reference to the Nodier play:

Reading for a political penny,
Place Royale, on a bench,
I fall, the trick is diabolical,
On the right spot, on the "White Flag" [a newspaper].

I get a ticket, not for the parterre,
Those seats are reserved for friends.
Without the help of Father St. Peter,
With thirteen cents I mount to Paradise [the highest seats].

In the last row, quiet, let everyone shut up!
Lower your voices, they cry from the front.
The curtain rises, and much to my discomfort,
Believe it, I see Père Lachaise [a Parisian cemetery]
From the back row.[20]

The popular success of Nodier's melodrama, inspiring no less than six parodies within a few weeks, was so great that the company revived the play with the same cast in 1823. It was a performance of this revival that Alexandre Dumas père saw when he first arrived in Paris and describes in such vivid detail, along with his encounter with Nodier, in *Mes Mémoires* (Ch. 23-27). Also in that year the Porte-Saint-Martin mounted the *Polichinel Vampire* (ballet-pantomime-divertissement en un acte et à spectacle) by François Alexis Blache, the resident ballet master.[21] Montague Summers states that this ballet played the Circus Maurice in 1822 (*Kith* 305), but this is contradicted by the title page of the printed text (Paris: Pollet, 1823), which places the première at the Porte-Saint-Martin on 27 May 1823. The music was by M. Alexandre; Polichinel was danced by Mazurier, Merlin by Vissot, Léontina by Mme. Florentine.

The author's preface gives a defense of the piece against his detractors, but says nothing about vampires. The text is a scenario without dialogue in eight scenes.[22] The setting is the seashore of the Isle of Mutes, containing a great oak tree, a green meadow, the palace of Prince Huberto, and the house of "Bergamilia." A voyage in a hot-air balloon is featured in the plot; these were a fairly new invention and all the rage in Paris. Like the parodies previously discussed, this charming piece contains no real vampire character, but testifies to the continuing vampire craze in Paris through 1823. Merely adding the word "vampire" to the title apparently could draw in a guaranteed audience.[23]

The Nodier/Carmouche/Jouffrey *Vampire* inspired 1) a huge popular success; 2) a hostile critical response and a debate on public morals; 3) half a dozen parodies; and 4) adaptations and sequels for the next 80 years. How can one cut through the detritus and overlaying dross of so many imitations and see the play freshly, as if for the first time; how can one account for its power? First, there must have been a deep psychic response in Parisian society to the material. Taking the approach of new historicism, Jonathan Gray, in "A Historical Examination of Vampires in 1820s Paris Boulevard Theatre," a paper given at the 1992 conference of the Popular Culture Association, theorized that Rutwen represented the *ancien regime*, the old order destroyed by the forces of the Revolution. Nodier does display a complex love-hate attitude both toward his protagonist and toward the monarchy, neither of which would "stay dead." I think, however, that Rutwen seems much more likely to be a stand-in for Napoleon, if we take Nodier at his word for a reborn Royalist. Napoleon, driven from power in 1815, lurked menacingly offshore on his island of exile and was always a threat to "resurrect" himself, like the vampire, until his death in 1821.

The influence of mesmerism, or animal magnetism, is also to be considered, a pseudo-science verging on occultism which claimed as disciples many of the leading figures of Romanticism. Robert Darnton in *Mesmerism and the End of the Enlightenment in France* writes,

Because the Enlightenment had dealt some damaging blows to religious orthodoxy,...many latter-day philosophies therefore attempted to develop a nonorthodox system that would account for irrationality and for the existence of evil.... Religious mysticism provided these philosophers with the richest source of the irrational...from convulsionaries like the mesmerists...[to] Swedenborgianism, martinsism, Rosicrucianism, alchemy, physiognomy, and many other currents of spiritualism. (127)

This was a period of turbulence and upheaval, a generation that had lived through the Terror, and, quite reasonably, had lost their faith in reason. Christopher Frayling in *Vampires: Lord Ruthven to Count Dracula*, writes:

As a member of a mesmerist lodge in Paris put it, "The reign of Voltaire and of the *Encyclopédistes* is collapsing. One finally gets tired of cold reasoning. We must have livelier, more delicious delights. Some of the sublime, the incomprehensible, the supernatural." Not only did an interest in vampirology—as part of a wider concern with the exotic and the occult—become fashionable but certain Parisian newspapers exploited this interest by featuring reports of vampire-like monsters which had been "sighted" in South America. (35)

The vampire craze hit Paris at the same time as the *fantasmagorie*, the magic lantern shows with their projected images of demons, bats and ghosts. Its impact was probably also enhanced by France's ingrained and notorious xenophobia: the source of *Le Vampire* was English, but in it the Englishman is portrayed as a demonic serial killer and a walking corpse. But Rutwen is not merely a negative figure, and the response to him is ambiguous. He represents sublimated sexuality, the thrill of fear, and the erotic threat of the unknown. In his preface to Nodier's *Lord Ruthven ou les vampires*, Max Milner comments:

The epidemic of vampires that falls upon France at the moment when the *Poetic Meditations* gives a totally different image of Romanticism, was the domain of Nodier. But he himself felt that the attraction of vampirism was not unconnected with what happens in the psyche of the sleeper, that is to say, with that which we call the unconscious. "Inductions do not fail," he wrote, "to prove for certain that the most terrifying aberrations of man— sorcery, lycanthropy, vampirism—are the diseases of the sleeper, like somnambulism and nightmare." The fantasy of a sexual aggression, at once delicious and deadly, constitutes the absolute weapon of this "Lovelace of the tombs," as he is called by a critic of the epoch.[24]

Perhaps Rutwen embodied the spectre of Napoleon, or the monstrous violence of the Reign of Terror (still within living memory); whatever vampires really meant to the French public in 1820, they were a subject which received treatment on every level from the serious to the facetious, and were a social and cultural as well as a literary phenomenon. The number of concurrent productions playing on the Boulevard du Crime, as well as in other minor houses, attests to the public appetite.

Lastly, I return to Eric Bentley's remarks on the power of the actor. The vampire, rising out of folklore as a monster, and passing through metamorphosis into a demon lover in Romantic poetry, comes into his own only when embodied by an actor on the stage. The living actor in relationship to a living audience, like a tiger in the drawing room, brings terror and pity to life.

# LE VAMPIRE,

### MÉLODRAME EN TROIS ACTES,

## AVEC UN PROLOGUE,

### Par MM. ***;

Musique de M. Alexandre PICCINI;

Décors de M. CICERI;

Représenté, pour la première fois, à Paris, sur le Théâtre
de la Porte-Saint-Martin, le 13 Juin 1820.

Prix : 1 fr. 25 c.

## PARIS,

AU MAGASIN GÉNÉRAL DE PIÈCES DE THÉATRE,

CHEZ J.-N. BARBA, LIBRAIRE,
Editeur des Œuvres de Pigault-Lebrun,
PALAIS-ROYAL, DERRIÈRE LE THÉATRE FRANÇAIS, N°. 51.

1820.

Title page, Nodier.

# LE VAMPIRE,

## COMÉDIE-VAUDEVILLE EN UN ACTE;

### Par MM. E. SCRIBE et MÉLESVILLE.

Représentée pour la première fois, sur le Théâtre
du Vaudeville, le 15 juin 1820.

Prix : 1 fr. 5o cent.

A PARIS,

Chez GUIBERT , libraire, Quai des Augustins, n°. 25.

DE L'IMPRIMERIE D'Anthe. BOUCHER,
SUCCESSEUR DE L.-G. MICHAUD,
RUE DES BONS-ENFANTS, N°. 54.

M. DCCC. XX.

Title page, Scribe.

# POLICHINEL

## VAMPIRE,

Ballet-pantomime et Divertissemens burlesques en un
Acte et à Spectacle,

### PAR M. BLACHE FILS,

Musique de M. ALEXANDRE,

REPRÉSENTÉ POUR LA PREMIÈRE FOIS, A PARIS, SUR LE
THEATRE DE LA PORTE SAINT-MARTIN, LE 27 MAI 1823.

PRIX : 50 Cent.

PARIS.

POLLET, LIBRAIRE-EDITEUR DE PIÈCES DE THÉATRE
RUE DU TEMPLE, N°. 36, VIS-A-VIS CELLE CHAPON.

1825.

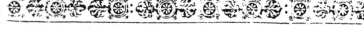

Title page, Blache.

Ciceri's scene designs for Acts One and Two of Nodier's *Vampire* (1820).

M. Philippe as Ruthwen.

Marie Dorval as Malvina.

# Chapter 4

# London, 1820

Mr. Samuel James Arnold...had placed in my hands, for adaptation, a French melodrama, entitled "Le Vampire," the scene of which was laid, with the usual recklessness of French dramatists, in Scotland, where the superstition never existed. I vainly endeavored to induce Mr. Arnold to let me change it to some place in the east of Europe. He had set his heart on Scotch music and dresses—the latter, by the way, were in stock—laughed at my scruples, assured me that the public would neither know nor care—and in those days they certainly did not—and therefore left for me nothing but to do my best with it. The result was most satisfactory to the management. The situations were novel and effective; the music lively and popular; the cast strong, comprising T.P. Cooke, who made a great hit in the principal character, Harley, Bartley, Pearman, Mrs. Chatterley, and Miss Love. The trap now so well known as "the Vampire trap" was invented for this piece; the final disappearance of the Vampire caused quite a sensation. The melodrama had a long run, was often revived, and is to this day a stock piece in the country. I had an opportunity years afterwards, however, to treat the same subject in a manner much more satisfactory to myself, and, as it happened, in the same theatre, under the same management; but of that anon.

—James Robinson Planché, *Recollections and Reflections*

Planché's adaptation, *The Vampire, or the Bride of the Isles*, opened at the English Opera House in London on 9 August 1820, two months after Nodier's *Le Vampire* opened in Paris. It too was followed by a string of imitations—vampire plays by W.T. Moncrieff, Charles Edward Walker, Edward Fitzball, St. John Dorset, and two more works by Planché, a burletta and an opera. In the analysis of these works, the interest lies not in their similarities, which are numerous, since all are more or less variations on the basic plot of the French original, but in how they differ, both from Nodier and from each other. The examination of these plays—Planché in this chapter and the others in the next—is a study in adaptations.

One proof of the popularity of Planché's melodrama is that, in addition to stage revivals, it was reprinted many times, demonstrating its continued popularity late in the century. The authoritative modern edition of the text was edited by Donald Roy for Cambridge University Press in 1986.[1] Before turning to a discussion of the play itself, I would first like to examine the London cultural milieu and the nature of the audience for English melodrama, and to what extent differences between it and the French audience produced differences between Planché's play and Nodier's.

Though not with the intensity of Paris, London too experienced a vampire craze in the 1820s. Vampires had seized the imagination of the English Romantic poets, as has been noted in Chapter 2, and there was some flirtation with the belief among the intelligentsia. Attesting to the lively public interest, two articles appeared in the *New Monthly Magazine*, a kind of unofficial vampire gazette, having published Polidori's short story in 1819 and given a rave review to the Planché play in 1820 (quoted later in this chapter). It was a literary magazine, but had broad circulation and carried articles of general interest. The anonymous author gives a sense that vampires were very topical, while demonstrating great ambivalence himself and taking a little of every position on the subject. He feels that anything so interesting to the French deserves investigation:

Since the appearance of the story of the *Vampire*, the conversation of private parties has frequently turned on the subject; and the discussion has been prolonged and invigorated by the pieces brought out at the theatres, as well of Paris as of London. Vampirism, at one period, had almost superseded politics, at Paris, in the journals of that lively and inquisitive city, during an interval of national expectation.[?] The French literati, whom nothing escapes, desirous of displaying their learning, have brushed off the dust of repose and oblivion from more than one story applicable to the enquiry; of which the intent of the present paper is to set a specimen before our readers. ("On Vampires and Vampirism," *New Monthly Magazine and Universal Register* 14 [1820], 548)

The article then relates a number of supposed case histories— Poland, 1810; Germany, 1805; Greece, 1701; and a detailed version of the Arnold Paul case (Austria, 1732) drawn from Calmet's *Traité*. (See Chapter 1.) Paul supposedly passed on the contagion of vampirism by sucking the blood of cows which were later eaten by persons who in turn became vampires. This proves to be too much for the credulity of the author, who ends on a skeptical and playful note:

But—here we stop:—for should it once become a popular opinion among us, that cattle which have been sucked may become the vehicles of infection, who can foresee the consequences on John Bull's roast-beef stomach?...The most powerful protector against supernatural visitations is a good conscience. Excellent is the advice of the sagacious Sir Hugh Evans to the crest-fallen knight of the round belly, in the last scene of the Merry Wives of Windsor:—"Sir John Falstaff, serve Got, and leave your sinful desires, and fairies (vampires) will not pinse you." ("On Vampires and Vampirism," New Monthly Magazine and Universal Register 14 [1820], 551-52)

The public appetite was judged to be unsated, and a second article appeared in 1823. The author, "D," also begins by twitting the French for their susceptibility and faddishness:

[Vampires are] introduced into popular novels, represented as figuring at the drawing room, shining in fashionable assemblies, favourites with the ladies, and this not alone in barbarous London, but forming the delight and admiration of elegant audiences in the superlatively polished capital of...[France]. Indeed, their success among our refined and delicately nerved neighbors has infinitely surpassed what they have met with among ourselves. We are not aware that many of our dramatists have hitherto attempted to draw tears for the pathetic amours of these interesting bloodsuckers.... But at Paris he [Ruthven] has been received with rapturous applause at almost all the spectacles, from the Odeon to the Porte-St.-Martin; all the presses of the Palais Royal have for the last two years been employed in celebrating, and describing, and speculating on him and his adventures, and in putting forth perpetual nouveautés on all the cognate topics—"Infernal Dictionaries"—"Demoniana"—"Ombres Sanglantes"...Where are the descendants of the Encyclopaediasts and the worshippers of the goddess Reason, when Parisian readers and audiences are running mad after "loups-garoux" and "apparitions nocturnes"?" ("On Vampirism," New Monthly Magazine and Literary Journal 7 [1823], 140)

Calling the myth of vampires a "monkish imposition," "D" denounces the superstition as unhealthy and unworthy of a civilized nation, "one of the most extraordinary and most revolting superstitions which ever disturbed the brains of any semi-barbarous people, most frightfully embodying the principle of evil, the most terrific incarnation of the bad demon, which ignorance and fanaticism ever suggested to the weak and the deluded" (140-41). But then, perversely, he reverses his position and goes on unskeptically to reexamine all the cases described in the previous article, supplemented by a number of others culled from Calmet, and advances the supposition that the origin of the belief can be traced through the Greek Orthodox Church to classical Greek mythology—the lamiae, Strygis, Stryx, and so forth. The article breaks off suddenly with no conclusion either way.

The preface to the second Cumberland edition (1830) of Planché's *Vampire*, signed "D.G.," tries to set forth the arguments logically, but bases its analysis on incomplete medical facts:

Some are of the opinion that they are really miraculous—others look upon them as the mere effects of whim and prejudice. Others, again, think there is nothing in them but what is very plain and natural, the persons not being dead, but acting upon other bodies in a more natural way. There are others who attribute the whole to the operation of the devil.... Others will have it, that it is not the dead themselves which eat their own bodies and clothes, but that it is done by serpents, mice, moles...and *Striges*, which are a species of birds that eat the flesh and suck the blood of animals. Some have maintained, that these instances are chiefly remarked in women, and at times when the plague reigns. But there are examples of these spectres in both sexes;—nay rather more frequently in men; though it must be confessed that those who die of the plague, or by poison, frenzy, drunkenness...are more apt to come again; probably because their blood does not congeal so easily. (3-6)

The author quotes the Gravedigger in *Hamlet* as an authority on dead bodies and rotting, cites the usual classical references, the standard case histories from Calmet.

From these and other articles, we can deduce that the reading English public had a more than nodding acquaintance with vampires in the 1820s.

The question of what audience went to the theatre is a complex one, with variations depending on the period and the country. London was subject to large shifts of population in this period. An important historical source is Henry Mayhew's pioneering sociological study, *London Labour and the London Poor* (1851), which gives a picture as vivid as Charles Dickens's fictional accounts of the subculture of poverty and the underclasses which comprised much of the new audience for theatre in the 19th century. Mayhew writes that in 1815 there were 1,319,851 paupers in England, or 5 percent of the population, which he lists at 20,892,670 as of 1821 (IV:316-18).[2] Most of the poor were to be found in the populous cities, drawn there by the first stage of the Industrial Revolution. Mayhew estimates an illiteracy rate of 20 percent, based on the fact that one person in five signed his or her marriage license with an X. We may assume the rate to be substantially higher, since many illiterate persons learn how to sign their names, and since, among the poorest classes, marriage was a luxury. A series of tables at the conclusion of *London Labour and the London Poor* on crime rates and illegitimacy estimates the population in London in 1840 at about one and a half million, with 80,000 prostitutes (IV: 206). This would be approximately one woman out of every nine. He estimates 30,000 "professional" beggars.

Theatre audiences reflected the changing nature of the society as a whole. Clive Barker, in his essay "A Theatre for Poor People," writes that the first evidence of new audiences attempting to break the cultural hegemony was Palmer's failed effort to open the Royalty in 1787, to which I would add the Old Price Riots of 1809, lasting sixty days at John Philip Kemble's Covent Garden, ending in the theatre's capitulation and the lower classes' taking possession of the pit as well as the gallery. Population shifts—the poor coming in and the middle classes departing—were particularly acute in the areas surrounding the patent theatres:

I want to advance one further argument for the decline of the Patent Houses. They were obnoxiously sited. [Friedrich] Engels in his list of urban horrors singles out the area. "In the immediate neighborhood of Drury Lane Theatre, are some of the worst streets in the whole metropolis, Charles, King and Park Streets in which houses are inhabited from cellar to garret exclusively by poor families." [*The Condition of the Working Class in England—1844*] Standing immediately to the west of the Patent Theatres were the two worst "rookeries" in London—St. Giles, teeming with starving Irish, and Seven Dials, characterised by Dickens as the worst area of London.... The concentration of beggars, prostitutes and criminals in the area obviously made theatre-going...a hazardous and most unpleasant activity. (17-18)

But the working poor did attend the theatre, according to Mayhew:

The other amusements [in addition to dog fights and rat killing] of this class of the community are the theatre and the penny concert, and their visits are almost entirely confined to...the theatres of the Surrey-side—the Surrey, the Victoria [Coburg]...and Astley's.... Three times a week is the average attendance at theatres and dances.... "Love and murder, suits us best sir (says an informant) but within these few years I think there's a great deal more liking for deep tragedies among us. They set man a thinking; but then we all consider they go on too long." (I: 15)

In keeping with the economic hardship of the times, the theatres were beset by bankruptcies, the actors by the prospect of starvation and prostitution. Many serious writers were driven out of theatre altogether, since the profession of playwright was both disreputable and unprofitable.[3]

The explanation for the sharp rift between poetry and drama was in part created by a peculiar legal situation which had many similarities with that of French theatres. The Licensing Act of 1737 that gave the monopoly in legitimate drama to the patent houses forced the minor houses[4] to fall back on other genres: melodrama and the legally amorphous term, burletta (which came to mean any sort of piece so long as it contained at least five songs). These circumstances produced the beginnings of a popular entertainment industry. As Walter Kendrick in *The Thrill of Fear: 250 Years of Scary Entertainment* writes:

The period from the late eighteenth century to about the middle of the nineteenth seems...to have been a rare interval in the history of Western theater when the playhouse was neither middle-class nor aristocratic but genuinely popular. And though their value judgments differ, all authorities agree that by the middle of the nineteenth century...the performing arts were well launched on a process of sorting into the categories of highbrow and lowbrow, elite and popular, polite and vulgar, that we now take for granted. (108-09)

How could the theatres deal with the problem of their houses, now too enlarged to effectively present legitimate drama, and meet the demands of the new, rowdier and less literate audience? The answer came in the form of Monk Lewis's *The Castle Spectre*, containing elements from Schiller's *Die Räuber*, Walpole's *Castle of Otranto*, and various plays by Kotzebue, produced at Drury Lane in 1797 under the management of Richard Brinsley Sheridan, who, according to Lewis, was very much opposed to the introduction of the ghost:

Never was any poor soul so ill-used as Evelina's, previou
herself before the audience. The friends to whom I read
managers to whom I presented it, and the actors who wei
all combined to persecute my spectre, and requested me
ghost to the green-room. Aware that, without her, my catastrophe would
closely resemble that of *The Grecian Daughter*, I resolved upon retaining
her. The event justified my obstinacy. The spectre was as well treated
before the curtain as she had been ill-used behind it; and as she continues
to make her appearance nightly, with increased applause, I think myself
under great obligations to her and her representative. (qtd. in Railo 100)

This play (though there are precedents) introduced gothic
melodrama to English audiences. Lewis proceeded to write 15
more similar works, and soon had many imitators. It was
discovered that the new audience had a taste for blood, dungeons,
and the supernatural, and that the problems of the buildings could
be dealt with by offering the sensational visuals of melodrama with
plots borrowed from the French. In 1802 Drury Lane offered
Thomas Holcroft's *A Tale of Mystery*, the first English play to use
the word "melodrama" on the playbill and a line-for-line translation
of Pixérécourt's *Coelina, Enfant de Mystère*. With *The Castle
Spectre* as a prototype, gothic melodrama became the dominant
form for the first quarter of the century.

The attempt to conceptualize the audience for melodrama, and
the vampire plays in particular, involves difficulty because of the
lack of solid data on past audiences. Based on the evidence of
diaries, journals, contemporaneous newspaper accounts, and
similar documents, one can conclude that in general melodrama
developed at the beginning of the 19th century in England as a
genre which appealed to a largely sub-literate audience, while the
educated class patronized the opera, and the middle class deserted
theatre entirely. A typical piece of evidence is the journal of
Hermann Pückler-Muskau, a visitor to London in 1826, who was
much struck by the crude behavior of the audience:

The most striking thing to a foreigner in English theatres is the unheard-of
coarseness and brutality of the audiences. The consequence of this is that
the higher and more civilized classes go only to the Italian Opera, and very
rarely visit their national theatre.... English freedom here degenerates into
the rudest license, and it is not uncommon...to hear some coarse
expression shouted from the galleries in stentor voice. This is
followed...either by loud laughter or approbation.... Another cause for the

absence of respectable families is the resort of hundreds of those unhappy women with whom London swarms. They are to be seen of every degree.... Between the acts they fill the large and handsome "foyers" and exhibit their boundless effrontery in the most revolting manner. It is most strange that in no country on earth is this afflicting and humiliating spectacle so openly exhibited as in the religious and decorous England. (*Tour in England, Ireland and France in the Years 1826, 1827, 1828 and 1829* [Philadelphia: 1833] qtd. in *A Source Book in Theatrical History* 476)

A playwright confronting such an audience would need to know a few tricks. As to the kind of play that would hold the attention of such customers, W.T. Moncrieff, prolific playwright and author of one of the vampire plays, remarked in 1820, "The frequenters of the minor theatres would listen to nothing like a lengthened dialogue on the stage. They required incessant action and shifting of the scene. Pieces that appealed to the eye and to the ear...were the only things likely to succeed; for the gods held sway not in the gallery only (their ancient privileged region) but in the boxes and pit" (qtd. in Booth, *English Melodrama* 61). In Planché's *The Drama at Home* (1844), a character says, "The public want startling effects, madam, not fine language or natural acting.... Get your effects, madam, no matter how, but get them, and the faster the better" (qtd. in Booth 61). A costermonger whom Mayhew interviewed told him, "Of *Hamlet* we can make neither head nor side; and nine out of ten of us...would like it to be confined to the ghost scenes, and the funeral, and the killing off at the last. *Macbeth* would be better liked, if it was only the witches and the fighting" (Mayhew I: 15). Since fights, villains, and the supernatural were sure-fire draws, *The Vampire* was a natural choice for this audience.

The Lyceum (in the Strand, next to Drury Lane), which produced *The Vampire*, was opened as a place of public entertainment in 1769 by a Dr. Arnold, who built a theatre on the property in 1795, with a license to present "exhibits, entertainments, phantasmagoria and waxworks" (qtd. in Booth lv).[5] His son, Samuel James Arnold, then became the manager, and gained permission to stage opera and musical drama in the summers, refurbished his theatre between 1816-17 at a cost of 80,000 pounds, equipped it with gas lighting (the first London theatre to use gas for *stage* lighting), and renamed it the English Opera House. In 1820 he presented Planché's *The Vampire*, a great popular success. It returned with the same cast in June of 1821 and was revived again in 1829 with two of the same actors in minor roles. In that year the English Opera House also presented Heinrich Marschner's opera *Der Vampyr*, with English libretto by Planché. (See Chapter 6.)

The theatre burned down in 1830, was redesigned by Samuel Beazley (who changed the entrance to Wellington Street), resumed the name Lyceum, and became a showcase for extravaganzas under the management team of Mme. Vestris, Charles Mathews, and Planché (1847-55). It came into its final glory when Henry Irving assumed the management in 1878 (and where *Dracula* received its first staged reading in 1897; see Chapter 9). Although it offered lighter fare as well, we could conclude that the English Opera House at this period was a genre house similar to the Porte-Saint-Martin, specializing in gothic melodrama, though it had many rivals and imitators, particularly in the rougher district south of the Thames.

From this brief survey of its history, the Lyceum/ English Opera House seems a thoroughly respectable establishment, but studies dealing purely in theatre history often seem to brush over the real character of these institutions. Even Drury Lane and Covent Garden were not places where the middle classes felt as ease, as the Pückler-Muskau journal informs us, and the reputations of the minor theatres in the 1820s were decidedly *louche*. In fact, as Mayhew states in *London Labour and the London Poor*, the main attraction of the Lyceum may not have been its theatrical offerings:

There is a coffee-house in Wellington Street, on the Covent Garden side of the Lyceum Theatre, in fact adjoining the playhouse, where women may take their men; but the police cannot interfere with it, because it is a coffee-house, and not a house of ill-fame, properly so called. The proprietor is not supposed to know who his customers are. A man comes with a woman and asks for a bed-room.... A subterranean passage, I am told, running under the Lyceum connects this with some supper-rooms on the other side of the theatre, which belongs to the same man who is proprietor of the coffee and chop house. (I: 238)

Attending a performance of Planché's *The Vampire* at the English Opera House, Pückler-Muskau wrote:

There was no opera, however. Instead we had terrible melodramas. First *Frankenstein*...and then *the Vampire*, after a well-known tale falsely attributed to Lord Byron. The principal part in both was acted by Mr. T.P. Cooke, who is distinguished for a very handsome person, skillful acting and a remarkable dignified, noble deportment. The acting was, indeed, admirable throughout, but the pieces so stupid and monstrous that it was impossible to sit out the performance. (qtd. in Frayling, *Vampyres* 38)

This strikes me as harsh criticism indeed. *The Vampire*, like all of Planché's oeuvre, is marked by its delicacy, wit, fantasy, skilled dialogue, and sound construction. A formidable presence as playwright, designer, and director in the English theatre for half a century, Planché wrote between 180 and 200 theatre pieces, including burlettas, farces, pantomimes, interludes, extravaganzas, revues, masques, outdoor spectacles, operas, and operettas, and was one of the most popular playwrights of his era. *The Vampire*, coming early in his career, is in many ways atypical of his work—he wrote very few melodramas, and little else in the gothic genre. But in other ways, Nodier's *Vampire* was an obvious choice of source material for him: it was French, it dealt with the supernatural, and it was exotic. As for vampires, though he employed the theme in three of his works, for Planché they were obviously a bit of whimsy on a par with fairies and leprechauns, but his audiences— uneducated, rustic (or at least newly citified), and superstitious— may have felt otherwise.

Although Planché traveled to Paris several times to gather plays, he specifically states in his *Recollections* that he was given Nodier's script by Samuel Arnold, manager of the English Opera House. Apparently he did not see the production (or Ciceri's set designs) at the Porte-Saint-Martin.

Unusually, the stage bill for the ninth performance, 19 August 1820, credits the French original:

A new Romantick Melodrama (partially taken from a celebrated Piece which has for some weeks past attracted all Paris).... The effect produced on crowded audiences by *The Vampire* is perfectly electrical. The applause at the conclusion of each performance has lasted for several minutes, and its success is nightly attested by shouts of approbation.—The publick demand will be answered by a repetition every evening.

Marvin Carlson's essay, "Theatre Audiences and the Reading of Performance" in *Interpreting the Theatrical Past*, notes the importance of analyzing advertisements, playbills, programs, reviews, and the like in assessing the way in which a "theatre

event" was perceived by its audience, or "interpretive community"
(90). From the "big bill" for *The Vampire*, we can extrapolate that it
was considered an asset that the source play was French; so was
the fact that it was brand new. Also, the production is advertised as
"a shocker" and a visual *tour de force*. The bill goes on to state:

THIS PIECE IS FOUNDED ON the various Traditions concerning THE VAMPIRES,
which assert that they are *Spirits*, deprived of all *Hope* of *Futurity*, by the
Crimes committed in their Mortal State—but, that they are permitted to
roum [sic] the Earth, in whatever Forms they please, with *Supernatural
Powers of Fascination*—and, that they cannot be destroyed, so long as
they sustain their dreadful Existence, by imbibing the BLOOD OF FEMALE
VICTIMS, whom they are first compelled to marry.

From this I surmise that the myth was not yet in general currency
with the play's intended audience. A handbill with a sketch of the
vision scene of the prologue, where Margaret dreams of Ruthven,
suggests that this was considered one of the play's highlights.
Mention of Lord Byron is conspicuously absent from any of the
play's publicity—the poet was far less popular in his own country
than in France.

In his article "The Vampire Theme: Dumas père and the English
Stage" A. Owen Aldridge notes, "Oddly enough, Planché in the
printed version apologized 'to the Public for the liberty which has
been taken with a Levantine superstition, by transplanting it to the
Scottish Isles.' This suggests that he was personally responsible for
the Scottish setting, whereas of course it already existed in Nodier's
version" (315). However in the *Recollections*, printed many years
later, Planché clears up this confusion, partly as a way of
denigrating his original work in comparison with his libretto for
Heinrich Marschner's opera, *Der Vampyr* (1829), for which he
succeeded in shifting the scene to Hungary. He states that Arnold
insisted on retaining the Scottish setting since he already had the
costumes in stock. (See the beginning of this chapter for the
relevant passage.)

Planché did as much as he could otherwise to dismantle the
Scottish gothicisms of the piece, however. He discards the Ossianic
names in the prologue, Oscar and Ituriel, and replaces them with
Rosicrucian and Shakespearean names: Unda, Spirit of the Flood,
and Ariel, Spirit of the Air. The opening sequence, in blank verse,
is now between two female characters, and very reminiscent of the
masque in *The Tempest* (IV, i) with Iris, Ceres, and Juno. Ronald

McFarland in "*The Vampire*: A Study in Adaptations" makes the interesting point that, in the prologue, by associating Ruthven with "Cromal the Bloody" (probably a misprint for "Cormal" from Macpherson's *Ossian*), Planché anticipates Bram Stoker, who in *Dracula* (1897) theorized a human antecedent (Vlad Tepes) for his vampire.

Assessing the qualities and talents of the company at the English Opera House (expounded in Appendix C), I think it is probable that Planché tailored the *Vampire* roles to these actors, who, despite some comings and goings, were more or less the resident company in the summer of 1820. Planché eliminates Oscar, the Celtic bard, and substitutes McSwill, a low-comedy dialect part. Malvina becomes Margaret; her brother Aubray becomes her father, Lord Ronald, Baron of the Isles. Edgar, Nodier's peasant hero, becomes Robert, an Englishman, now promoted to Lord Ruthven's steward. McFarland comments that "Planché's final alteration of the script is to have Robert save Lord Ronald from Ruthven's dagger, thus investing the slight hero's role in the person of the working class attendant rather than the aristocrat, a change that no doubt was calculated to appeal to the proletarian audience" (32).

Although the ballet is omitted, there are ten songs—the spirit quartetto, drinking songs, rowing songs, Scottish love ballads, and more.[6] Most of the singing is done by Effie and Robert (Lovette and Edgar in the French version), probably because the actors possessed sweet voices and could carry the music. Margaret and Ruthven do not sing.

Planché seems to have read Polidori's short story as well as Nodier's play, because he gives McSwill a narrative of the murder of Ianthe (which took place in Greece) as a local legend of a long-ago murder in the Cave of Staffa. Also, in the death scene Ruthven instructs Lord Ronald to throw his ring into the sea, a detail the playwright has culled not from Nodier or Polidori, but from Byron's "Fragment," the ur-source.

The major change, however, is one of tone. The hen-pecked, heavy-brogued drunkard McSwill, is partnered by the termagant Bridget, a straight *confidante* in Nodier. This larger component of low ethnic humor—McSwill gets pinched by the ear, hides under the table from Bridget, and has a number of drunk scenes and boozing songs—contrasts with the tragic characters in the time-honored tradition of Shakespeare. Perhaps, as this was to be perforce a Scottish play, Planché was thinking of the drunken

Porter in *Macbeth*. At any rate it demonstrates that, even on the most popular level, the French and English differ in their taste for purity of genre.

Margaret seems much more conventional and uninteresting than Malvina; her speech is all stock phrases. Rather than merely staggering at the first sight of Ruthven, she faints dead away.

An original stroke of Planché's is to give Ruthven a soliloquy revealing that the vampire is torn by remorse and self-loathing:

Demon as I am, that walk the earth to slaughter and devour! The little that remains of heart within this wizard frame, sustained alone by human blood, shrinks from the appalling act of planting misery in the bosom of this veteran chieftain. Still must the fearful sacrifice be made, and suddenly, for the approaching night will find my wretched frame exhausted—and darkness—worse than death—annihilation is my lot! Margaret! unhappy maid! thou art my destined prey! thy blood must feed a Vampire's life, and prove the food of his disgusting banquet. (I, ii, 26-27)

Nothing like this occurs in Nodier, making the English vampire a much more anguished and divided character, although I note he is more sorry for the father than for the intended victim. Ruthven seems less in the throes of sexual passion than Rutwen, more transported by a "loftier sentiment," and thus less Byronesque than the French vampire. Planché provides a noble motive for Ruthven's sudden interest in Effie: "Should I surprise her heart, as by my gifted spell I may, the tribute that prolongs existence may be paid, and Margaret may (at least awhile) be spared" [I, iii, 30]. This change shows the weakness of Planché's concept of the vampire's nature, and detracts from the character's persona in two ways: first, his reasoning is, if someone must be raped and murdered, better a lower-class girl than a high-born lady. Second, it attributes his power of seduction to magic; this diminishes the vampire and vitiates the sexual content.

Although Planché has compressed the play from three acts to two, the running time is probably longer—about one and a half hours—because there are more scenes and nine added songs. The severe stormy weather of the French play is held off by Planché until the very end of the play; rather than continual thunder and lightning we get a big thunderclap and howling wind just at the end. As a substitute we have more spectacle: a night scene in the Cave of Staffa, the comings and goings of the boats, a fight on the rocks, and the spectacular death of Ruthven who is struck by lightning and vanishes into the earth. It was for this effect that Planché devised the "vampire trap," two doors on springs which allowed the actor to instantly vanish into the floor, an invention still in use today in plays dealing with the supernatural.

Planché shrewdly tightened the suspense by giving the vampire only until the setting of the moon to accomplish his design, and the moon figures very prominently in the language and as a visual element of the play. In a paper presented at the 1992 City University of New York Conference on Victorian Theatre and Theatricality, "Escaping the Vampire Trap," Nina Auerbach pointed out the importance that Ruthven's relationship with the moon assumes in Planché's (and later Boucicault's) version of the story:

The two most famous stage vampires, Planché's Byronic Ruthven and Dion Boucicault's Alan Raby, claim heavenly bodies, not earthly ones, for while they drink women's blood to survive, they are enthralled by the moon that bred them.... In the final diabolical wedding, we watch not the monster and the maiden, but the sinking moon which plunges Ruthven into the abyss when it sets before the ceremony.... The moon's dominance in the nineteenth-century theatre makes the stage vampire a cosmic virtuoso, ascending and descending perpetually, both above and beneath his audience's time and space. It removes him from the sphere of blood and the body, aligning him instead with Shakespearean enchantment, with fairies, with the magic of a semi-phantasmal Nature on the verge of refining matter into spirit. Ricocheting between moon and abyss, their ascending and descending vampires are cosmically supreme, at times surmounting physicality altogether.... Planché brought the moon to Victorian vampire theatre; it plays no role in his French source, *Le Vampire*. (7-11)

Auerbach's images are wonderful, but Planché's *Vampire* is 17 years short of being a Victorian play,[7] and she exaggerates to say the moon makes no appearance in Nodier's play. It functions, as it does in Polidori, as the restorer of life after Rutwen's death in Act II, though it does not figure in his destruction at the end of the play. (In Polidori's story, of course, the vampire triumphs.) Also, it is odd that Auerbach visualizes the vampire trap as a mechanism for sudden ascents as well as descents: "Depending on its placement, the vampire trap allowed the actor to be alternately body and spirit; the trap in the floor catapulted him back and forth between hell and heaven, while the trap in the flats endowed him with the semblance of immateriality as he moved in and out of walls" (6-7). As defined by Michael Booth and others, the trap would seem to have been used in the final scene for Ruthven's disappearance, not throughout the play. Montague Summers provides the following description (which he quotes but gives no citation):

A vampire trap consists of two or more flaps, usually india-rubber, through which the sprite can disappear almost instantly, where he falls into a blanket fixed to the under surface of the stage. As with the star trap, this trap is secured against accidents by placing another piece or *slide*, fitting close beneath when not required, and removed when the prompter's bell gives the signal to make ready. (*Kith* 306)[8]

Although it is possible the vampire trap could have been used in the prologue when the vampire rises from the tomb of Cromal, in my opinion Planché was too theatrically astute to ruin the *coup de théâtre* of the finale, where Ruthven instantly disappears in a flash of lightning. The actor-manager John Coleman in *Fifty Years of an Actor's Life* wrote of the amazement and terror this effect produced in him when, as a boy, he saw a touring-company performance in Derby: "When I recall that gruesome Scottish horror feeding upon the blood of young maidens and throwing himself headlong through the solid stage, and vanishing into the regions below amidst flames of red fire, I protest I shudder at it now" (I: 30, qtd. in Roy 4). The stage bill advertised the effect with the puff, "The effect produced upon crowded audiences by *The Vampire* is perfectly electrical."

Despite some felicitous individual lines and a much greater suspense and temporal urgency, I think the English *Vampire* is a lesser work than the French one. The addition of low dialect comedy, however it may heighten the sense of Scottish ethnicity for English audiences, diminishes the power of the central characters— they lose both focus and stage time. Donald Roy praises the comic relief and additional characters:

The fearful, superstitious servant Scop of the French version becomes the bibulous ne'er-do-well McSwill, thus infusing a contrapuntal strain of comedy and providing an ideal role for Harley; the heroine's brother is altered to a father who...welcomes her vampirical fiancé with the extra emotional warmth due to a son-surrogate; and the Ossian-like bard is omitted altogether as too improbable for English (and certainly Scottish) audiences. (Roy 4)

But McFarland thinks the additions are incongruous:

The mixture of elements, though heralded by the anonymous writer of an introduction to the printed text of the play as an "agreeable *melange* of the tragic and the comic," never really works. The comic scenes and the romantic songs seem always to be superimposed upon the serious framework that Planché borrowed from the French dramatists. (30)

McFarland further points out that while Planché supplied McSwill with two Scottish drinking songs, he failed to endow him with any plot function.

The main weakness, in my opinion, is that Planché misunderstands the nature of the erotic relationship between vampire and victim. To give Ruthven a sense of self-disgust and a guilty conscience adds dimension to the character, but loses the important point in that his desire for her is both sexual and murderous, "haemosexual," in Christopher Frayling's coinage. He is a jaded rake in the tradition of *Clarissa*'s Lovelace, and to attribute Margaret's attraction to him to "magic" undermines Nodier's insight into human nature—our attraction to the danger of the "dark stranger" (which Ibsen plumbs so deeply in *The Lady from the Sea*)—and completely misses the power of the central myth of vampires.

In terms of staging, the outstanding features were the effects of moon and water, and the vampire trap. Acting as his own designer, Planché presumably wrote to his own strengths. Martin Meisel in *Realizations: Narrative, Pictorial, and Theatrical Arts in Nineteenth-Century England* calls Planché one of the first English designers to move toward what he terms "pictorial realization":

The enveloping medium of melodrama, here romantic and picturesque, and Planché's emphasis on the contemplation of the picture so that it may make its full effect, are characteristic of the new age. Planché is interested in realizing, not merely the speaking configuration, but the persons in their authentic habit and as much of the scene itself as possible.... Planché was an antiquarian by temperament, and as a considerable pioneer of scenic development in his own right, very much attuned to the visual. (112, 114)

He writes that Planché scripts emphasized situations that could be illustrated by tableaux, which were such important elements in melodrama that they were often described in the stage bills. In envisioning the effects Planché created, one should remember that the English Opera House was the first London theatre to use gas lighting for its stage effects.

The printed version of the play lists the original costumes. Some of the more interesting:

The Vampire (Ruthven)—Silver breast-plate, studded with steel buttons—plaid kelt—cloak,—flesh arms and leggings—sandals—grey cloak, to form the attitude as he ascends from the tomb.

Lady Margaret—White satin dress, trimmed with plaid and silver—plaid silk sash—Scotch hat and feather.

Ronald—Crimson shirt, with large clasps down the front—plaid cloak—flesh arms and leggings—sandals—sword and belt—Scotch hat and feathers.

McSwill—Red plaid jacket, waistcoat, and kelt—philibeg—flesh leggings—plaid stockings—black shoes and buckles—Scotch cap.

Effie—Black velvet body and tabs—plaid petticoat, trimmed with black—blue ribbon in the hair—plaid sash.

From these costumes, it is apparent that Planché too set the play in the vague past of gothicism, as is also evidenced by his occasional use of archaisms in the dialogue. As Montague Summers cryptically remarks, "This is in the true transpontine tradition of Ossianic attire" (*Kith* 307). Summers seems to be using "transpontine" to mean "across the sea," referring to the French origin of the play and the hyper-romanticized French concept of Scottish dress. But the literal meaning of "transpontine" is "across the bridge," and several theatre historians explain that it became a derogatory term referring to the extremely violent and crude melodrama produced by the rougher theatres on the south bank of the Thames. The English Opera House was not "Surrey-side," so Summers's comment as it stands makes no sense.

T.P. Cooke, who became the most prominent actor of melodrama of the age, created the role of Ruthven. For a survey of his career (and other actors in the cast), see Appendix C. William Hazlitt called Cooke's performance "spirited and imposing,"[9] and *The British Stage* called it "one of the most vigorous and effective specimens of melodramatic acting we ever remember to have witnessed; his expressive countenance and commanding figure are displayed to great advantage, and his whole appearance is extremely picturesque" (4 [1820], qtd. in Nichols 75).

Two aspects of Cooke's career are unusual: first, he was among the first English actors to perform in France, where he appeared as Frankenstein's Monster in a play co-authored by Nodier (see Appendix C). While his appearances in Paris predate the visit of William Charles Macready in 1827 (usually credited as the first English actor to perform successfully in Paris), he arrived after the (unsuccessful) visit of the Penley troupe in 1822, brought, as was Cooke, by J.T. Merle to the Porte-Saint-Martin. Of his success in Paris, Ginette Picat-Guinoiseau comments:

Here we find the most illustrious names of Romanticism. Casting aside the contemporary fame of Vampire Philippe, as famous in France as Vampire Cooke was in England, Cooke who interpreted the monster so gloriously on both sides of the Channel, we also find Frédérick Lemaître as Mephisto, and, as nearly all the heroines from Malvina to Marguerite, the great Marie Dorval.[10]

The other unusual aspect of Cooke's career is that he was also a director, before that profession was recognized or the word in common usage. The big bill for the London *Vampire* states, "The Action of the Melodrama under the direction of Mr. T.P. Cooke," a very unusual credit, and one of the earliest such usages. He was also credited with the "melodramatic business" of the Adelphi's *Flying Dutchman* in 1827. Stephen Wischhusen in *The Hour of One: Six Gothic Melodramas* speculates, "Perhaps it was because he was so successful in melodramatic roles that his name appearing as director as well as among the players would be an assurance of a high standard" (25).

Nina Auerbach ascribes the ascension of the stage director to the egotism and desire for control of the men who played the vampire (Cooke and Dion Boucicault): "*The Vampire* and *The Phantom* are, in a sense, about the megalomania of their male stars: T.P. Cooke not only played Lord Ruthven but directed *The Vampire*, seizing prematurely, in 1820, the comprehensive control of the actor-managers who colonized the late Victorian stage; Boucicault both wrote *The Phantom* and played its title role" ("Escaping" 10-11). However, Boucicault's biographers state that the role of Alan Raby was written for Charles Kean and taken over by the playwright only after Kean's refusal of it (see Chapter 7); as for T.P. Cooke's megalomania, it seems logical that the increasingly complex mechanics of staging melodramatic spectacle required someone to be in charge. The theatre manager had the authority to hire and fire and controlled the money; the prompter usually had the responsibility to rehearse the actors; the machinist and the designer (sometimes several) controlled the technical aspects (and a playwright-designer like Planché probably had a lot of power); but someone has to oversee the production and set the priorities— vacuums of authority tend to be filled by strong personalities. *The Vampire* came early in Cooke's career; he was in no sense a powerful actor-manager in 1820. Perhaps Arnold and Planché simply needed help coordinating the acting with the scenic and musical elements of the production. As a former seaman, Cooke may have learned a sense of order and the value of keeping everything shipshape. William Oxberry, theatrical memoirist and fellow actor who apparently observed the proto-director at work, commented:

As a stage manager, our hero has judgement, unwearied industry, and exemplary patience. His directions are given with mildness, but enforced with firmness. He never exerts his authority over the wretch beneath him, or tamely submits to the blown-up fool above him. As a man, we have ever heard Mr. Cooke's name mentioned with respect and delight. His manners are unassuming—his habits domestic. (*Oxberry's Dramatic Biography and Green Room Spy* I: 260)

Samuel Arnold seems to have been an *éminence grise* also. Planché states that Arnold placed the French play in his hands, and insisted on the Scottish locale because he had the costumes on hand, the singers in residence, the Scottish tunes already in mind.

The critical reaction to Planché's *Vampire* displayed none of the jealousy or moral outrage that the French press had shown to Nodier's work. Many were struck by the beautiful scenic elements contrived by Planché, though several scolded him for transposing the scene to Scotland, which must have vexed him greatly. Nor was there any hint of condescension—that this was merely a minor-house production, and low genre fare for the vulgar masses. As we see by the peregrinations of the actors between the patent and minor houses (see Appendix C), there was no separate and higher standard for actors at the major theatres. The most important writers on theatre were lavish in their praise. The following review by William Hazlitt (which hardly suggests a subliterate audience) is reprinted in George Rowell's *Victorian Dramatic Criticism* (204):

The new Dramatic Romance (or whatever it is called) of *the Vampire* is, upon the whole, the most splendid spectacle we have ever seen…. On the stage it is a little shocking to the feelings, and incongruous to the sense, to see a spirit in human shape,—in the shape of a real *Earl*, and what is more, of a *Scotch* Earl—going about seeking whom it may marry and then devour, to lengthen out its own abhorred and anomalous being.... The scenery of this piece is its greatest charm, and it is inimitable. We have seen sparkling and overpowering effects of this kind before; but to the splendor of a transparency were here added all the harmony and mellowness of the finest painting.... In the scene where the moonlight fell on the dying form of Ruthven (the Vampire) it was like a fairy glory, forming a palace of emerald light: the body seemed to drink its balmy essence, and to revive in it without a miracle. The line, "See how the moon sleeps with Endymion," came into the mind for the beauty and gorgeousness of the picture, notwithstanding the repugnance of every circumstance and feeling.... This melodrama succeeds very well: and it succeeds in spite of Mr. Kean's last nights. ("The Drama," IX, *The London Magazine*, September 1820)

The critic of *The Times* wrote:

A new dramatic romance, called *The Vampire; or the Bride of the Isles* was brought out last night at this theatre. It is one of those productions which, uniting dialogue, and music with scenery of more than ordinary splendor, aided likewise by some admixture of pantomime, pass in the theatrical nomenclature under the title of *melodrames*.... It has but little pretension and calls not for a rigorous judgement. The decorations are suitable, if not magnificent; and the incidental music consists of a selection of favourite Scottish airs. One of the duets was executed with infinite sweetness and taste by Miss Carew and Pearman. The performers engaged exerted themselves with considerable effect, and the whole drama met with a most encouraging reception. It was to have been produced on Monday last, but the death of the Duchess of York led to a suspension, for two days, of all theatrical entertainments. ("English Opera House," *The Times*, 10 August 1820)

The *New Monthly Magazine*, the "vampire gazette," gave the most glowing reviews:

The celebrated story of the Vampire, which has been successfully dramatized at Paris, has supplied materials for one of the best melodrames, we have ever seen at this or any other theatre. The superstition on which it is found[ed]...has so much of the disgusting, that there appeared considerable hazard in its representation on the stage. This danger has, however, been admirably avoided in the new drama—where the literal design of the fiend is so little obtruded on us, that we feel throughout only a pleasing horror.... The interest of this piece fascinates like a spell.... All the acting, indeed, is admirably calculated to aid the illusion. Bartley excellently represents the stout-hearted baron, both in his frank dealing while he suspects no evil, and in the contest between his paternal agony and his honour, when he knows the frightful truth which he may not reveal. Mr. T.P. Cooke, whom we have long regarded as an actor of unappreciated talent, has secured a high place in the public esteem, by his performance of the Vampire. In his fearful action—his triumphant smiles—his very assumed softness of tone and demeanor—he gives us the idea of a being not of this world. Harley, as a drunken servant, is amusing as usual, and sings an excellent song. Mrs. Chatterley's appearance and manner, as Lady Margaret, have a picturesque elegance which even now rarely graces the stage, and her action, where she sees in Lord Ruthven the phantom of her dream, and where she is spell-bound by his fascinations, is exceedingly beautiful and impressive. The scenery is the most complete we have ever seen. The vast cave of Staffa, with its heavy, metallic grandeur—the basaltic columns narrowing into jagged recesses, with the sea flowing in large waves among them, and rippling gently to the shore—the sweet moonlight falling on the gigantic bulk of Ruthven as he lies expiring on the bank—and the chapel when the painted window is thrown open, the moon is seen dipping into the sea, the bridegroom disappears through the stage as if by magic, and a broad red glare is cast over the exquisite group of amazed spectators—form a series of the most striking and harmonious pictures which the stage has ever presented. ("English Opera House," *New Monthly Magazine* 14, 80, 1 September 1820, 321-22)

The preface to the Cumberland edition (1830) of the play contains some remarks on the production:

The author of this melodrama has transplanted a Levantic superstition to the Scottish Isles.... The subject is ingeniously treated, and exhibits an agreeable *melange* of the terrific and the comic. T.P. Cooke in the *Vampire*, and Harley in *McSwill*, were extremely well contrasted. Some old Scotch airs were introduced with beautiful effect. The Vampire was highly successful, but not *more* so than it deserved to be. (10)

The success of the play was such that within three months it reached New York, opening at Stephen Price's Anthony Street Theatre on October 22, 1820; Price's company was in residence there because the Park Theatre had burned down. Joseph Ireland's *Records of the New York Stage* erroneously states that the play was "founded on Scott's beautiful poem...It was received with great favor" (II: 366). The English production toured the provinces, reaching Hull by December 1820; Bath in January 1821; Durham in April; and returning to London in June to re-open the summer season of the English Opera House, which revived it in 1829 with Mr. J. Vining as the vampire and Miss Grey as Margaret, and again in 1839 with Charles Diddear and Miss Rainforth. Productions were also mounted by the Sadler's Wells in 1838 with Mr. Cathcart and Mrs. Robert Honner, and by the Victoria (Royal Coburg) in 1841 with Mr. Hicks and Emmeline Montague (*Victorian Plays* 393).

The Planché *Vampire* will be compared with its successors in the next chapter, in a general discussion of the English vampire plays of the 1820s and their social implications.

## Theatre Royal, English Opera House, Strand.

This Evening, SATURDAY, August 19th, 1820;

Will be presented (FIFTEENTH TIME) an entirely new OPERATICK DRAMA, in Three Acts, called

# Woman's Will—A Riddle !

WITH ENTIRELY NEW MUSICK, SCENERY, DRESSES AND DECORATIONS.
The OVERTURE and MUSICK composed by Mr DAVY, with the exception of Two Songs by Mr. PINDAR, of Bath.
The SCENERY designed and executed by Mr. CAPON, Mr. A THISELTON, Mr. GILL, and Assistants.
The DRESSES by Mr. HEAD, Mrs. BROOKES, &c. &c.

Duke of Milan, Mr. ROWBOTHAM,     Count Vitaldi, Mr. BARTLEY,
Cæsario, Mr. PEARMAN,     Corvino, Mr. HARLEY,
1st Lord, Mr. WEBSTER,—  2nd Lord, Mr. LOGUE,   Officer, Mr. MINTON,
Principal Priest, Mr Moss,     Attendant Priests, Mr. FISHER, Mr. KENNETH,
Children of the Chapel, Master COOTE, Miss E. LANCASTER,
Nobles of the Court, Messrs Bowman, Collingbourn, Elsmore, Jenkins, Laws, Nichols, H. Phillips, R. Phillips,
Proud, Shaw, Spentley, &c. &c.

Duchess of Mantua, Mrs. W. S. CHATTERLEY,
Princess Clementine, Miss KELLY,     Isabel, Miss CAREW,
Ladies of the Court, Mesdames & Misses Hobbs, Jerrolds, Lancaster, Lodge, Manuell, Mews, Miller, Newton, Shaw, Tokely, Webster.

The EPILOGUE, in Character, by Miss KELLY.

In the course of the Opera, the following new Scenes will be exhibited.
An ANTI-CHAMBER of the DUCAL PALACE.   (Gill)    SALOON and BANQUET HALL.   (A Thiselton.)
An ANTIENT STREET of POINTED ARCHITECTURE, selected entirely from remains of the middle ages.  (Capon.)
ANTI-CHAMBER adjoining the PALACE-CHAPEL.  (A. Thiselton)

To which will be added (NINTH TIME) a NEW ROMANTICK MELODRAMA, (partly taken from a celebrated Piece which
has for some Weeks past attracted all Paris) in THREE PARTS, founded on THE CELEBRATED TALE, called

## "THE VAMPIRE"

The OVERTURE from OSCAR & MALVINA, composed by the late Mr. REEVE.
The INCANTATION and CHARM in the INTRODUCTORY VISION, by Mr. M. MOSS.
The VOCAL MUSICK selected from the SCOTTISH MELODIES——The Melodramatick Musick composed by Mr. HART.
The SCENERY, including correct Views of the BASALTICK COLUMNS of The ISLAND of STAFFA, with The
GROTTO and CAVE of FINGAL, entirely new, by Mr. A THISELTON, Mr. SMITH, and Assistants.
The ACTION of the MELODRAMA under the direction of Mr. T. P. COOKE.

### Characters in the Introductory Vision.

The Vampire, Mr. T. P. COOKE,
Lady Margaret,    Mrs. W. S. CHATTERLEY,
Unda, (Spirit of the Flood) Miss LOVE,     Ariel, (Spirit of the Air) Miss WORGMAN.

### Characters in the Drama.

Ruthven, (Earl of Marsden) Mr. T. P. COOKE,   Ronald, (Baron of the Isles) Mr. BARTLEY,
Robert, (a Retainer of the Baron) Mr. PEARMAN,  Mc.Swill, (Henchman to the Baron) Mr. HARLEY,
Andrew, (Steward to the Earl of Marsden) Mr. MINTON,     Father Francis, Mr. SHAW,
Lady Margaret, (Daughter to Lord Ronald) Mrs. W. S. CHATTERLEY,
Bridget, (Housekeeper to Lord Ronald) Mrs. GROVE,
Effie, (Daughter to Andrew, and betrothed to Robert) Miss CAREW.

THIS PIECE IS FOUNDED ON
the various Traditions concerning THE VAMPIRES, which assert that they are Spirits, deprived of all Hope of
Futurity, by the Crimes committed in their Mortal State—but, that they are permitted to roam the Earth, in
whatever Forms they please, with Supernatural Powers of Fascination—and, that they cannot be destroyed, so
long as they sustain their dreadful Existence, by imbibing the BLOOD of FEMALE VICTIMS,
whom they are first compelled to marry.

The effect produced on crowded audiences by THE VAMPIRE is perfectly electrical. The
applause at the conclusion of each performance has lasted for several minutes, and its success is nightly
testified by shouts of approbation.—The publick demand will be answered by a repetition, every evening.

The highly successful Opera of WOMANS WILL—A RIDDLE, will be repeated this evening,
and twice next week.

### THE SPACIOUS SALOON

Has been again tastefully fitted up, with a NEW DESIGN, representing

## AN ILLUMINATED ORIENTAL GARDEN

and will be opened as usual at EIGHT o'Clock, for the admittance of the SECOND PRICE, which commences at NINE.
Stage Manager, Mr. BARLEY.     Leader of the Band, Mr. MOUNTAIN.

Boxes 4s. Second Price 3s.   Pit 3s. Second Price 1s 6d.  Lower Gallery 2s. Second Price 1s.  Upper Gallery 1s. Second Price 6d.
PRIVATE BOXES may be had nightly of Mr. SAYERSON, of whom Places are to be taken, at the Box Office, Strand Entrance,
from Ten till Four; also at PEARMAN's Library, 170, New Bond Street.
Doors open at half-past Six, the Performance to begin at Seven—No Money returned—[Lowndes, Printer, MarquisCourt, DruryLane

On Monday will be produced (First Time) a new ex-tempore, temporary, Sketch, to be called
### "PATENT SEASONS."
The Characters by     Mr. WRENCH,   Mr. HARLEY,   Mr. WILKINSON,   Mr. PEARMAN,
Miss CAREW,  -  Miss KELLY.
After which (10th time) The VAMPIRE; to which will be added (First Time) an entirely NEW FARCE, in Two Acts, which has been
some time in preparation, to be called

## WHANG FONG:
or
## HOW REMARKABLE!

The Musick composed by Mr. PINDAR, of Bath.
Principal Characters by Mr. PEARMAN,   Mr. HARLEY,   Mr. T.P. COOKE,   Mr. WILKINSON,   Mr. LANCASTER,
Mrs. GROVE,    Miss LOVE.
Mrs. PINDAR, (from the Theatre Scarborough, being her first appearance on a London stage.)

Playbill, J.R. Planché's *The Vampire*, English Opera House, 1820.

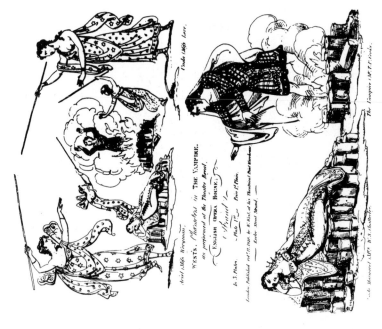

Planché's *Vampire*, engraving by J. Findlay (Enthoven Collection).

Illustration, Richardson edition of Planché's *Vampire*.

Mʳ T. P. COOKE.
AS
RODERICK DHU.

Mʳˢ CHATTERLEY.
AS
LADY TEAZLE.

# THE VAMPIRE;

OR, THE BRIDE OF THE ISLES:

A ROMANTIC MELO-DRAMA,

In Two Acts,

## BY J. R. PLANCHÉ,

*Author of Charles the XII. The Merchants' Wedding, A Woman Never Vext, The Mason of Buda, The Brigand, A Daughter to Marry, &c.*

PRINTED FROM THE ACTING COPY, WITH REMARKS, BIOGRAPHICAL AND CRITICAL, BY D—G.

To which are added,

A DESCRIPTION OF THE COSTUME,—CAST OF THE CHARACTERS, ENTRANCES AND EXITS,—RELATIVE POSITIONS OF THE PERFORMERS ON THE STAGE,—AND THE WHOLE OF THE STAGE BUSINESS.

As performed at the

THEATRES ROYAL, LONDON.

EMBELLISHED WITH A FINE ENGRAVING,

By Mr. Bonner, from a Drawing taken in the Theatre, by Mr. R. Cruikshank.

LONDON:

JOHN CUMBERLAND, 6, BRECKNOCK PLACE, CAMDEN NEW TOWN.

R. Cruikshank, Del.                        G. W. Bonner, Sc.

The Vampire.

Lady Margaret. Hold! hold! I am thine;—the moon has set.

Act II. Scene 4.

Title page, Planché.

# Chapter 5

# London, 1820-23

Davie: Horrible to relate, they found the body of the young bride pale and bleeding; the marks of human teeth upon her throat—proved her to have been the victim of a Vampire!

Sandy: That's a sort of drinking not at all in my way—I like whiskey.

—W.T. Moncrieff, *The Vampire*

Early-19th-century English theatres were characterized by the increasing unruliness and coarseness of the new audience; a gradual loss of the apron forestage and increasing importance of the proscenium, the "picture frame" which signals the supremacy of the visual image over language; and the greatly expanded size of the houses, resulting in an acting and staging style which William Axton in *Circle of Fire* describes as typified by "sweeping gestures, flamboyant costume, mass blocking, spectacular effect, machinery, business, miming—and by music, song, and dance.... Little wonder that the 19th century produced so little great drama and so much delightful theatre" (26). Walter Kendrick writes of the period:

It was the rowdy theater of the nineteenth century into which Lewis moved after shocking the polite world with *The Monk*. Not a highly genteel place, it would soon get less so, thanks in part to Lewis's efforts. The...theater, however, was the true heir of the horrid novel, quickly latching on to its favorite effects, intensifying them to a degree that the printed word was incapable of, and maintaining its delight in horrors long after written fiction had grown tired of them.... Captious though ...theatrical audiences could be, freehanded with rotten fruit on occasion, they seem to have suspended disbelief enthusiastically.... They eagerly took part in the make-believe, gleefully riding the waves of emotion that playwrights, actors, and stage technicians set surging. Virtually any emotion would do, so long as it came sharp and clear, trimmed of tedious nuances. Across that spectrum, artificial fear traced a fiery blue stripe. (109-14)

Foremost in the pack of "horrors," as they were called, were vampire plays. The huge success of Planché's *Vampire* could not go unnoticed by other London theatres and playwrights, and a very close imitation was produced in the same year by W. T. Moncrieff (1794-1857) at the Royal Coburg Theatre. Moncrieff turned out four plays in 1820, a particularly busy year for him: a serious domestic drama, *The Lear of Private Life*; a gothic melodrama, *The Ravens of Orleans*; one of the first nautical melodramas, *The Wreck of the Medusa*;[1] and *The Vampire*. Many of Moncrieff's plays seem to have been attempts to cash in on his rivals' successes; for instance, his *The Cataract of the Ganges* (1823), an Eastern spectacular melodrama, was presented in competition with Edward Fitzball's *Thalaba the Destroyer* (discussed later in this chapter), and advertised many of the same effects. This was certainly the case with *The Vampire*, for which not even the name was changed.

In the "Remarks" (dated November 7, 1829) prefacing the printed edition of Moncrieff's play, the author rehashes the foundations for the vampire myth, quotes the relevant passages from Byron's "The Giaour" and Southey's *Thalaba the Destroyer*, then makes an original argument supporting the play's change of venue to Scotland:

Sir Walter Scott's translation of the Eyrbyggia Saga...is a tale of dreadful Vampyrism...which refutes the attempt to confine the superstition to the more *Southern* parts of the world; this will also be some apology for the author of this drama, in placing its scene in Scotland, which, on its first production, was loudly exclaimed against.... But surely...it will not require any great stretch of the imagination to...place it in a country where the belief in witchcraft, and its attendant devilries,—wraiths, goblins, and ghosts of every description, was universal. Indeed there can be but little doubt of its ancient ascendance in our own island, for it strikes us in the highest degree probable, that our custom of driving a stake though the body of a *felo-de-se* [suicide]...has its origin in the popular horror of the self-murderer—in the apprehension of his becoming a Vampire. (vi)[2]

The author argues that similar beliefs and customs in such widely separated parts of the world as Britain and Hungary are some proof of the truth behind the superstitions. He concludes with comments on the production, disingenuously failing to acknowledge Planché:

Those who witnessed its first representation...will no doubt remember it as being possessed of that soul-thrilling and intense interest, which was new to them: it was the precursor and origin of all the tales of terror which have been dramatized for the stage, and...the wonderful success, with which it was attended, obtained for it many imitators; and as was recently the case with *Der Freischütz*, the Vampire made his appearance on every stage, both in town and country. The scenic effect, the appalling incidents, and the terrific *denouement*, were never before equalled, and attended by the novelty of the situations, and the powerful interest attached to the tale itself, which the report of its being from the pen of the noblest poet of the day [Byron], was calculated to produce, we know of no dramatic production that ever met with such great, and (we may add) deserved success. (vii)

Before discussing Moncrieff's *Vampire*, I will turn to an examination of the Royal Coburg Theatre and its audience, for which the play was created. Built in 1818 and named in honor of Princess Charlotte's husband, the Coburg quickly became one of the most disreputable theatres in London. Located on Waterloo Road in the dangerous neighborhood of New Cut south of the Thames, it was believed to be "largely graced by the presence of embryo and mature convicts (*Letters from a Theatrical Scene Painter* qtd. in Booth, *English Melodrama* 54). Ernest Bradlee Watson in *Sheridan to Robertson: A Study of the Nineteenth Century Stage* calls the Coburg the most debased of the minor houses, and sums up its reputation:

The *Inquisitor* flays it for its "miserable mummery," and Hazlitt...found it "nothing but an exhibition of the most petulant cockneyism and vulgar slang." It had become a "Bridewell or a brothel" patronized by "... pickpockets, prostitutes, and mountebanks." The audience came "not to admire...but to vilify and degrade everything"; they "laughed, hooted, nick-named, and pelted [the actors] with oranges and witticisms, to show their unruly contempt for them and their art" [*London Magazine*, 3 March 1820]. Although Junius Brutus Booth, and even Edmund Kean, at times resorted to this stage, Davidge, the proprietor, was content to supply his noisy patrons with entertainment to their taste. (429)

Few of the gentry dared to venture into this unsavory area, in spite of stage bills which advertised that the Coburg provided armed guards against the robbers who lurked on Waterloo Bridge. T.P. Cooke, who had managed and acted at the Coburg, "pointed out that its audience, like others in outlying districts, was essentially a local one. It was possible that gallerygoers at the Coburg might also frequent the major theatres, he allowed, but the Coburg audience as a whole was 'almost restricted to that theatre' and essentially different from that of the Surrey, despite its short distance away" (*Revels* VI: 158). The Coburg had to rely on the rough local audience which liked its entertainment bloody and lurid, a style characterized by the derisive term, "transpontine melodrama," meaning "across the bridge," or south of the Thames.

Although still quite new, the Coburg was refurbished in 1820, and among the improvements was an unusual curtain made of 63 pieces of mirror-glass which reflected the entire audience. Perhaps the semiotic meaning was "Your own lives are reflected on this stage."[3] The improvements had no effect on the clientele, however. The audience seems to have been a young one, full of rambunctious adolescent boys. Here are excerpts from Henry Mayhew's wonderful description in *London Labour and the London Poor* of a typical night at the Coburg:

On a good attractive night, the rush of costers to the threepenny gallery of the Coburg...is peculiar and almost awful.... On the occasion of a piece with a good murder in it, the crowd will frequently collect as early as three o'clock in the afternoon.... To anyone unaccustomed to be pressed flat it would be impossible to enter with the mob.... There are few grown-up men that go to the "Vic" gallery. The generality of visitors are lads from about twelve to three-and-twenty...the gallery audience consists mainly of costermongers.... The gallery...is one of the largest in London. It will hold from 1500 up to 2000 people, and runs back to so great a distance, that the end of it is lost in shadow.... When the gallery is well packed, it is usual to see piles of boys on each other's shoulders at the back, while on the partition boards, dividing off the slips, lads will pitch themselves, despite the spikes.... When the orchestra begins playing, before "the gods" have settled into their seats, it is impossible to hear a note of music.... By-and-by a youngster, who has come in late, jumps up over the shoulders at the door, and doubling himself into a ball, rolls down over the heads in front, leaving a trail of commotion for each one as he passes aims a blow at the fellow. Presently a fight is sure to begin, and then every one rises from his seat whistling and shouting;...the audience waving their hands till the moving mass seems like microscopic eels in paste.... The "Vic" gallery is not to be moved by touching sentiment. They prefer vigorous exercise to any emotional speech.... Altogether the gallery audience do not seem to be of a gentle nature. One poor lad shouted out in a crying tone, "that he couldn't see," and instantly a dozen voices demanded "that he should be thrown over."...No delay between the pieces will be allowed, and should the interval appear too long, some one

will shout out—referring to the curtain—"Pull up that there winder blind!"
or they will call to the orchestra, saying, "Now then you catgut scrapers!
Let's have a ha'purth of liveliness." Neither will they suffer a play to
proceed until they have a good view of the stage, and "Higher the blue" is
constantly shouted, when the sky is too low, or "Light up the moon,"
when the transparency is rather dim. (I: 18-19)

Later the Coburg became a music hall, was renamed the Royal
Victoria in 1833, closed in the 1880s, and reopened as a temperance
hall. In this century it flourished as the Old Vic under Lillian Bayliss,
and in 1963 became the temporary home of the National Theatre. It
is currently in use, and houses the Young Vic company.

The Coburg in 1820 seems to have possessed the perfect
ambience for Moncrieff's *Vampire*. The piece is a much cruder and
more blatant theft of Planché than Planché is of Nodier. Moncrieff
was also aware of Nodier's play, since he takes some elements from
it that Planché omits. He changes Margaret back to Malvina, but
retains the name Margaret for the maid (named Bridget in Planché
and Nodier). Sir Ronald becomes Sir Malcolm and is changed back
to Malvina's brother, and (in a startling burst of originality) Ruthven
becomes Ruthwold. The low-comedy drunk, McSwill, becomes
Sandy Mull, and is made the love interest of Effie, now called
Jeannie Mucklegear. There are only three songs and no ballet.

Moncrieff's biggest innovation is the addition of a conventional
hero. Unlike Nodier's peasant Edgar, Moncrieff's Edgar is the Chief
of Lorn, and a suitor to Malvina supplanted by Ruthwold. In this
new configuration we may discern traces of Walter Scott's *The
Bride of the Lammermoors*, which also features a broken
engagement, a rejected fiancé named Edgar, and a brother whose
meddling in his sister's love life brings on catastrophe. Another new
character is Mac Dirk, a stock Scottish warrior in the line of
Shakespeare's Black Douglas in *Henry IV, Part One*.

The play opens with a chorus of singing vampires in the Cave
of Fingal. Planché's Rosicrucian names were judged too arcane for
the South Bank audience, so Moncrieff substitutes Terra, Genius of
the Earth, a male role, and Lunaria, a Moon Spirit. He thereby
presents himself with a difficulty: in this version the moon is
contradictorily both the ally and enemy of the vampire. Although
Ruthwold is revived by the moon's rays, Lunaria explains she does
this very unwillingly. Moncrieff sets a 24-hour time limit on the
vampire's life, and establishes the phrase, "At the hour of one," as
a refrain to be repeated throughout the play.[4]

Upon recognizing Ruthwold as the figure in her dream, this Malvina neither shudders not faints, but screams. Ruthwold's soliloquy is of far less interest than Ruthven's: it is merely a reiteration, in standard villain-ese, of what has just transpired (for the benefit of inattentive audience members):

Your sister once made mine, I bid defiance to the world;—hasten, hasten, I entreat you! (Exit Sir Malcolm.) Fool! to let the meteor light of friendship blind his dull eyes to the sure ruin of his sister!—so young, so lovely;— even I could pity her, should she refuse;—should the Hour of One arrive, and my victim have escaped me!—horrid thought! (I, i, 21)

Despite the borrowings from the superior French original, Moncrieff's play is much the poorest of the three. The crudeness of the writing shows in the many asides for all the characters (explaining the obvious), and the amateurish superfluity of exclamation points and dashes. This weakness of technique is surprising, considered in contrast to the inventiveness of this playwright's *Tom and Jerry* and *Eugene Aram*. The vampire's enigmatic and romantic character is completely eclipsed by villainish mustache-twirling. The addition of the Edgar character demonstrates Moncrieff's lack of comprehension that the key to the story is that the vampire *is* the romantic lead. It seems Moncrieff felt his audience would have been stymied by an attractive or divided villain, relying as they did on visual cues to tell them what was happening onstage. The playwright resorts to the stock formula in order to meet audience expectations, resulting in a loss of nuance, depth, and literary quality.

Some of the tinkering might be explained by the necessity of tailoring the piece to the company—perhaps no character men were available for the father or McSwill, but there was a leading man in the company, a Mr. Blanchard, who could sing, play the harp, and handle a sword; so possibly the role of Edgar was patched together for him. (The character disguises himself as an old bard like Nodier's Oscar and sings the ballad of warning accompanying himself on the harp.)

Ruthwold is listed as being played by a Mr. Kemble. The most likely candidate from this large acting family is Henry Stephen Kemble (1789-1836), son of the Stephen Kemble who was a famous Falstaff. One of the least well known of the family, he was a ranting, bombastic performer, known for his loud voice and foot-stamping, who led a dissolute life offstage. (See Appendix C.)

A character named Ruthven also appeared in Charles Edward Walker's *Warlock of the Glen* (Covent Garden, 2 December 1820). This was another Scottish gothic melodrama, an early effort by the author of the better-known *Wallace* (1821), a five-act tragedy. In this play, Ruthven is not a vampire or even a warlock, and receives only seventh billing. The play contains no vampires, but shares its Scottish locale, gothic ambience, and interest in the supernatural with the vampire plays. It seems the English, dreary and overfamiliar as they may have found Scotland themselves, sheepishly followed the French vogue which found it romantic, exotic, and a natural setting for wizards and sorceresses (and vampires).

In 1821 a neoclassic tragedy, *The Vampire*, by St. John Dorset (1802-27, pseudonym of Hugo John Belfour), was published with a dedication to William Charles Macready and probably conceived as a vehicle for him. It was not produced, but went through at least two printings, and so reached a reading public at least. The *London Magazine* review compared it favorably with "the revolting egotism which pervades every page of Lord Byron's works.... That such compositions as Lord Byron's could retain their popularity was impossible; they are the children of a diseased imagination and came into the world bearing within them the seeds of early dissolution" (qtd. in Frayling 10).[5]

In his "Advertizement" which prefaces the play, Dorset wrote, "In submitting this Tragedy to the perusal of a generous public, it may be deemed superfluous to premise, that the chief personage of the drama is no blood-sucker. A *goût* so barbarous and *bizarre*, however it may assimilate with the usual horrors of the melodrama, must be very derogatory to the chaste dignity of the tragic muse" (Dorset n.p.). Intrigued by the theme of Planché's melodrama at the same time he was disgusted by it, he quotes a review of the play as his inspiration:

The *Examiner* newspaper, in noticing the melodrama of the Vampire, as performed last season at the English Opera House, makes use of the following language: "There are Vampires who waste the heart and happiness of those they are connected with, Vampires of avarice, Vampires of spleen, Vampires of debauchery, Vampires in all the shapes of selfishness and domestic tyranny. What is the seducer and abandoner of a trusting young girl, but a Vampire not sufficiently alive to the harm of his own cruelty? What is a husband who marries for money, and then tramples upon his wife, but a Vampire? What is the "poisonous bosom-snake" of Milton but a female Vampire, wearing a man's heart out by holding him without loving him?" The above observations, in conjunction with other circumstances, afforded the original idea of the present production. (n.p.)

Dorset remarks that he took advantage of a lacuna in the historical records of tenth-century Egypt to create an amoral Persian prince, Abdalla, whose vampire-like personality almost succeeds in seizing the throne of Egypt through his talent for lying, betrayal, seduction, and murder. Ironically, given the high-minded sentiments in his "Advertizement," Dorset's *Vampire* is by far the bloodiest of them all: many characters—and all the females—die violently onstage. The play is over-written and marred by a great deal of motiveless hugger-mugger, but Dorset's neoclassic *Vampire* is a serious and ambitious effort by a 19-year-old writer. He published another tragedy, *Montezuma*, in 1822, was ordained a priest in 1826, and died the following year at 25.

Neither Dorset's *Vampire* nor Walker's *Warlock* are really vampire plays, but both demonstrate, on different levels, the widespread interest in the vampire theme.

In the same year, Planché wrote a delightful and improbable vampire burletta, *Giovanni the Vampire!!! or How Shall We Get Rid of Him?*, presented at the fashionable Adelphi Theatre on 15 January 1821. This incredibly prolific playwright had an extraordinarily productive year even for him: the burletta was the first of ten pieces he wrote for the Adelphi winter season, and according to Donald Roy, he was at the same time supplying plays to the Sadler's Wells, Haymarket, and English Opera House (36). *Giovanni the Vampire* was one of a series of satirical pieces by various authors on the Don Juan theme.[6] A. Owen Aldridge in "The Vampire Theme: Dumas père and the English Stage" states that Planché was the first to have the ingenious notion of combining Don Juan with the vampire (312-24), but Richard Switzer points out that the Nodier *Vampire* borrowed the Zerlina subplot from Da Ponte's libretto for Mozart's *Don Giovanni* (111).

The thrust of Planché's satire was that, although all the Giovanni plays ended with the Don going down in flames, he always reappeared in a sequel the following season. It struck Planché that he had as many lives, and much the same predilections, as the vampire, and he facetiously proposed to kill them both off:

The Public...will readily acknowledge the wonderful resemblance which exists between the notorious Don Giovanni, and the supernatural being aforesaid; not only, in their insatiable thirst for blood, and *penchant* for the fair sex, but in the innumerable resuscitations that both have, and still continue to experience. To put this libertine entirely *"hors de combat"*— to clap, as it were, an extinguisher upon his burning passions—to prevent, by "total annihilation" his ever again becoming the bugbear of "Children who are young, or children who are old["]; as the great Cervantes killed Don Quixotte [sic], to preclude the probability of his adventures being extended by other pens—is the design of the present production, and will doubtless meet the hearty concurrence of the Suppressors of Vice, whether officially or privately situated, to whom it is most respectfully dedicated by the Author. (1)

Planché's burlettas differ from the usual potpourri of offerings under the name "burletta," by adhering more strictly to the classic definition, e.g., a good-natured spoofing of a legend or classical myth following the form of *opera seria*, that is, recitative and aria. Planché's burlettas—many of which, such as *Olympic Revels* and *Olympic Devils*, were written as vehicles for Mme. Vestris—gave the form its typically British flavor: elegance, whimsy, and droll seriousness. They pointed the way to the style of Gilbert and Sullivan, especially the device of semi-operatic music accompanying nonsensical lyrics full of puns and doggerel, so that the music was both the agent and the object of the satire (Dircks 78).

Apparently only portions of the text survive; the 1821 John Lowndes edition printed only the cast list, the Introductory Vision, and the lyrics. There were three parts to the piece: the prologue-vision scene; the burletta itself; and the procession and ballet. As far as can be judged from the surviving fragments, this was an amusing and witty piece of theatre, differing from the French send-ups of Nodier in that the vampire was a breeches role, played by Mrs. Waylett. (See Appendix C.) Robertson Davies in *The Mirror of Nature* comments on this very British phenomenon:

The study of nineteenth-century burlesque is of the greatest psychological interest, for much of its attraction lay in its transvestite element. The leading comedian played a female role, and the hero was represented by a pretty girl with a striking stage personality and excellent legs.... If a drama made a hit in the nineteenth century, it was not long before a burlesque version of it appeared in a popular theatre. There must have been a large group of playgoers who were so well acquainted with what was on the serious stage that they were able to appreciate genial and often subtle burlesque versions on the lighter stage…. This was an instance of *enantiodromia*: the heavily weighted moral drama ran into a farcical anti-masque, a burlesque of itself. (56)

Planché's satire is directed at the London theatre scene, and its habit of retelling the same old story, milking a proven cow to death. He takes double aim, both at the Giovanni plays and at his own *Vampire*. While this is a genuine parody of the original, rather than a tangentially related play like Scribe's or Brazier's (to Nodier's), any real sting is removed by the fact that the author is parodying himself. One wonders if, in the lost text, there were any mention of Moncrieff, who wrote two Giovanni plays and stole Planché's *Vampire* for the South Bank.

As Aldridge remarks, Planché failed to exterminate either Don Giovanni or Ruthven, and many more sequels of each were to follow. But it was with the classic burletta in this fanciful style, further developed in his many collaborations with Vestris and Mathews at the Olympic, that he influenced the course of English light opera, culminating in the works of Gilbert and Sullivan. Considering the delightful qualities of Planché's vampire burletta, one is taken aback to read in Mayhew's *London Labour and the London Poor* that a prospective play-goer might have been taking his life into his hands to attend the Adelphi:

Many novelists, philanthropists, and newspaper writers have dwelt much upon the horrible character of a series of subterranean chambers or vaults in the vicinity of the Strand, called the Adelphi Arches…. where parties were decoyed by thieves, blacklegs, and prostitutes, and swindled, then drugged, and subsequently thrown from this door into the darkness of what must have seemed to them another world, and were left, when they came to themselves, to find their way out as best they could. (IV: 239)

Nonetheless, the Adelphi had a much more fashionable ambience and better reputation than the Coburg. First called the Sans Pareil, it opened in 1806 under Charles Didbin with a license for music and dancing, and was renamed the Adelphi in 1819. Watson writes that "what the Olympic did to civilize burlesque was done in part for melodrama at the Adelphi," and that they were the two most important minor houses in London (74-75). The Adelphi staged many Walter Scott adaptations and gothic melodramas affectionately known as "the horrors." Watson mentions *Cruchley's Picture of London* (1835), a guidebook referring to it as "by far the most fashionably attended of the minor theatres" (75). It became the melodrama house *par excellence*, famous for the "Adelphi guests," a group of extras in fancy-dress who appeared in every play in the same costumes and groupings. It was rebuilt in 1858 and 1901 and renamed the Century (Nicoll 218).

Next in the series, on 18 April 1823 the Coburg presented another play which featured a vampire among the characters, *Thalaba the Destroyer*, based on Robert Southey's poem. The play bill lists the author as E. Ball, who, theatre historian Frank Rahill informs us, was actually the very prolific Edward Fitzball (1792-1873), whose penchant for gothic stage effects earned him the nickname, "Blue-fire Fitzball" (159). He wrote many successful gothic, nautical, and crime melodramas, as well as oriental spectacle extravaganzas, of which *Thalaba* is an outstanding specimen. It played in competition with Moncrieff's *The Cataract of the Ganges*, an Eastern spectacle melodrama complete with Grand Brahmins, Rajahs, Pavilions of Pleasure, temples, palaces, and battle scenes. It was far out-lavished by *Thalaba*, whose stage bill advertised a winged serpent, a colossal statue that comes to life, a giant war elephant, a flight of locusts, an enchanted cavern, a grand storm chorus, the "precipitation of Thalaba and Oneiza down the cataract of Bodelmandel," a ruined cemetery, "desperate conflict and storming of the fortress," all ending with "the Destruction of the Tyrant and Restoration of Thalaba to his Crown and Kingdom."

In Southey's epic poem, Thalaba is a warrior who discovers that his true love, Oneiza, who dies on their wedding day, is a vampire. In Book VIII, Thalaba, with Oneiza's father, Moath, descends into her tomb, where the vampire bride is dispatched in customary fashion with a stake through the heart. (The passage is quoted in Chapter 2.) But in melodrama, the heroine, though she may have little to do or say, is indispensable since it is necessary to rescue her from various dreadful fates; therefore Fitzball substitutes Thalaba's mother, Zeinah, for the vampire episode. After her shade is purified, Zeinah becomes a protective deity for the rest of the action. One amazing effect, according to Michael Booth, was a message written in smoke, "Obey thy mother's ghost." The Coburg also made great use of its blue flame effect, and they had a splendid grotto setting:

An enchanted cavern beneath the waters of Bodelmandel, with the waves gently agitated above—an opening in the background, transparently showing the water's depth and the bed of the ocean, an immense pillar of rock, overhung with coral shells and submarine plants. KAWLA discovered seated on a throne of amber and attended by water demons—HAG, OKBA, and demons over a cauldron. (qtd. in Booth, *English Melodrama* 90)

One wonders if the management of the Coburg might have thriftily recycled *The Vampire*'s Cave of Fingal set for this scene, adding a scrim for the underwater effect.

On the bill with *Thalaba* was *Frankenstein, the Demon of Switzerland* by H.M. Milner, a very early example of a horror double bill. Citing the example of *Frankenstein* coupled with *The Vampire* at the English Opera House in 1828, Frayling comments, "If by chance the theatre-going public began to find his adventures *too* predictable, he could always join forces with his fellow monster from 1816 to keep the box office busy" (*Vampyres* 37).

Considered together, the English vampire plays of the 1820s, while variations on a theme, each have a unique flavor. A surprising number gothic melodramas are set in Scotland, a country distinctly less exotic to the English than to the French, and the touches of authentic local color that the English playwrights added tend to demystify as they particularize. Scottish drinking songs, lairds and chieftains, kilts and kelpies, highland flings and heavy brogues—is this a milieu for a vampire? As we will see in Bram Stoker's *Dracula*, one essential ingredient of the vampire myth is his "otherness," his foreignness, which is weakened (for the English, at least) by the Scottish identity. However, Planché's attempt to identify Ruthven as the reincarnated "Cromal" (Cormal), may be a subtle appeal to racist attitudes. Celts, after all, are not Anglo-Saxons.

Also, we can detect in these plays a rising (but as yet not very pronounced) hostility toward the upper classes. In Planché, the highborn Margaret is susceptible to the decadent male aristocrat, but Effie stoutly resists his attempted enforcement of *droit de seigneur*. These elements are present in Nodier's drama, but become more pronounced in Planché because of the increased importance of Robert, a prototypic working-class hero, who saves both Lord Ronald and Margaret in the final moment. This becomes muddled in Moncrieff's version, where Robert again becomes Edgar, but is of the aristocratic class. Edgar drives the plot and actually supplants the vampire by marrying Malvina. The reason for this could have been because of the qualities of the available actors, but also because Moncrieff fell back on the stock characters of formula melodrama. His Ruthwold is a pure "black" villain, without romantic appeal (as in Nodier), twinges of conscience (Planché), or satanically derived powers (later vampires). In all the plays, the traditional family guardian, the father/brother, Aubray/Ronald/ Malcolm, is shown to be ineffectual and blind.

Dorset's tragedy attempts to broaden the definition of vampirism to a kind of pervasive and predatory amoralism in human relationships, especially in the manipulation of women, considered vulnerable and compliant by nature and nurture. This theme would be taken up by many poets and novelists throughout the 19th century.

Planché's burletta, in making the vampire a transvestite role, however light and innocent the context, points the way to the increasing sexual ambiguity of the vampire which we will discover in its evolution, ending with the *fin-de-siècle* bisexuality of Dracula. Mrs. Waylett, the Adelphi vampire, was reputed to be very beautiful and to have a captivating voice. She was known as "Queen of the Ballad Singers."

The first quarter of the 19th century was an age of gothic sensibility, with a dark taste for violence and morbidity in stark contrast with the 18th-century atmosphere of light and learning, (and taste for high comedy of manners and sentimental drama). Two of the greatest of the gothics, Mary Shelley's *Frankenstein* (1818) and Charles Maturin's *Melmoth the Wanderer* (1821) were published at this time, and so popular was the genre that Jane Austen wrote a satire of the literary craze for gothicism, *Northanger Abbey*, in 1817. We may also note Thomas De Quincey's essays, "On Murder Considered as One of the Fine Arts," the first part published in 1827, and his "On the Knocking at the Gate in *Macbeth*" in 1823, both suggesting that murder was a fit subject for aesthetic appreciation. Accounts of grisly murders, such as the Ratcliffe Highway murders of 1811, were popular items in pulp journals, taken up and recited by street "patterers," and quickly dramatized and put on the stage in penny gaff theatres (i.e., disreputable music halls where the admission was a penny and one could stay as long as one liked, as the performance was continuous and included a bit of everything). "Artificial fear" was also the main attraction of gothic melodrama: blood, sexual violence, and supernatural demons surrounded by blue fire.

This was a period of cultural stress, caused by the social changes and population shifts produced by the Industrial Revolution as referred to in the previous chapter. Also, the fact that England had been ruled for ten years by an extravagant and dissolute regent for an almost invisible king who was known to be insane, may have produced an uneasiness in the public unconscious which led to these morbid preoccupations. Recently, historians have speculated that the cause of George III's insanity was porphyria, a hereditary metabolic disorder which causes dementia, a red discoloration of the skin, and extreme aversion to light. These of course are the classic signs of the vampire, and sufferers from the disease were often mistaken for vampires in Slavic countries. During the Regency (1812-20), the mad old king was hidden away in locked and secret chambers of Windsor Castle, while the Prince of Wales pursued his dissipated career. The old king's condition was unmentionable in polite society—there was a voluntary moratorium on productions of *King Lear* in this era. When George III died at 82 in 1820, there was a sudden spate of *Lears*, including Moncrieff's *The Lear of Private Life*. Also, vampire plays suddenly proliferated at the same time. Perhaps these were also portraits of the mad king from another angle of vision, or perhaps combined the most lurid aspects of father and son in one personality.

Beyond the possible hidden association with the two Georges, these plays are relatively innocent excursions on the surface of the subconscious. On the whole, they seem sexually naive; they are too simple to mix love and death. These vampires are definitely "bad guys," and there is plenty of enthusiastic talk of gory deeds, but no women (as yet) are killed; we see no glorification of blood-lust. The English playwrights make little effort to enter into the vampire's psychology. Kendrick comments:

Gothic villains may be self-blind, but their minds are all of a piece. No part leads a separate, hidden life, as the fiendish dark sides of innumerable post-Freudian psychopaths do.... On the early nineteenth-century stage, where villains obligingly informed the audience of their nefarious schemes, villainous shallowness became almost ludicrous—though, of course, stage villains were no more shallow than were the good guys they menace. (156)

Of course, all these stage vampires end in the fiery pit, satisfying the demands of poetic justice, but they experience a lot of pleasure on the way, and the adventure of the plays is to experience vicariously the working out of the vampire's designs on his victims (as in *Richard III*, for example). We are allied, not with the luscious victim, but the predator. Feminist critics argue that every spectator perforce identifies with the male subject, through whose eyes we gaze at the female characters as objects of possession.[7] The gaze appropriates—the action of any play or film is that we either "get" the woman or she gets away. Vampires merely put the action on a more primitive level.

These tendencies toward violence against females in art, while milder than what was served up by Shakespeare and the Jacobeans, for example, and very tame compared to the pervasive misogyny of the *fin-de-siècle*, were entering a new cycle in the 1820s.

The female victim is passive: she does not as yet "deserve her fate," and, indeed, is saved at the last moment in every example but Dorset's. These are good girls, whose virtue consists of obedience (so there is no need to punish them, as in *Dracula*). If any Malvina or Margaret were *defying* her brother or father for the forbidden love of a vampire, we would have another, and perhaps better, story. The basic action, as it stands, is that an innocent girl is placed in temporary jeopardy by her careless guardian, but escapes unharmed due to the fortunate arrival of her sweetheart, confirming one of melodrama's most cherished tenets: that providence will come to the rescue. Any more ambiguous handling of the moral issues would have been unsatisfactory to the patrons of these theatres, who demanded simple, easy-to-follow schematic characterization, a plot structure that followed a familiar formula, and a denouement that satisfied the demands of poetic justice, with violated social norms restored, virtue rescued, and evil banished to the infernal regions beneath the stage.

Who were the audience for these plays? Were these minor theatres filled with audiences of adolescent hoodlums ambitious to be serial killers? One thinks especially of the Coburg, den of cutthroats and whores as it was reputed to be. I was especially struck by Mayhew's observation that the audience for Moncrieff's *Vampire* at the Coburg consisted mainly of teen-age boys, much like the audience for today's slasher films. Here we come to the even-yet-unanswered question of the relationship of pornography to behavior. But nobody in England was raising this question at this time, as they were in France in the critical reaction to Nodier's *Vampire* (and indeed had been doing so since d'Aubignac in the

17th century, with his vision of the theatre as a school of morality for the lower classes).

James Twitchell in *The Living Dead* remarks that the study of vampires in literature is in some ways a depressing exercise because, examined chronologically, the vampire "is a mythic figure who rather than developing new sophistication and sharpness, becomes instead tedious and dull" (5). In the plays examined in this chapter we see this process of deterioration already taking place. As much as Planché seems to weaken and dilute the rich thematic substance and ambiguity of Nodier's play, so much further does Moncrieff vulgarize and oversimplify the material as he found it in Planché. The complex figure of the vampire created by the Romantic poets is reduced, in three quick steps and within a year, to stock villain.

As happened in France, the vampire was almost instantly subjected to satiric treatment (in Planché's burletta), is relegated to a supporting role in *Thalaba*, and actually is reduced to a supernumerary in *The Warlock of the Glen*.

The division of English and French theatres into major and minor houses was one of the contributing factors that created a division between elite and popular culture. In *The Thrill of Fear: 250 Years of Scary Entertainment*, Walter Kendrick comments:

"Popular culture," indeed, had not yet been clearly defined as such, nor had it been parceled out into the categories we recognize today. Affective entertainment—which aims to stir your feelings and can be labeled according to the feeling it goes after [e.g., "horror film"]—gradually slid down the scale of respectability until it hit rock bottom in the popular ghetto. (155)

In the 1820s this division into hierarchies was in process but not yet in place. While no vampires appeared at the Comédie Française, Covent Garden, or Drury Lane, they did invade the most elite art form, opera. In 1828, two vampire operas were being written in Germany, and one would find its way, through Planché, to England.

Mʳ. H. KEMBLE.

Engraved by J.Rogers from a Picture

Mᴿˢ WAYLETT.

# Royal Coburg Theatre.

ACTING-MANAGER MR HUNTLEY.

### First Night of an entirely New & most Impressive Melo-Drama!
SECOND WEEK OF THE SPLENDID ROMANCE OF THALABA THE DESTROYER.

☞The Rapturous Applause from Overflowing and Elegant Audiences, which Nightly hails the New Dramatic Romance, founded on the celebrated Poem of THALABA THE DESTROYER, by R. Southey, Esq. Poet Laureat, has surpassed the Proprietor's most sanguine Expectation.—The Characteristic Splendor of the Costume and Scenery, and the extent and ingenuity of the Machinery, are universally allowed to do ample justice to the magnificent Creation of the Poet's Imagination.

MONDAY, Aug. 18th, 1823,—And During the Week,—At Half-past Six precisely,
Will be Presented an entirely New Melo-Dramatic Romance, founded on Southey's celebrated Poem of Thalaba, written by E. Ball, Esq. with New Music, Scenery, Machinery, Dresses and Decorations, Called,

# THALABA
## THE DESTROYER!

The Music & New Overture composed by Mr. T. Hughes.—The Scenery by Messrs. Wilkins, Jones, Stanfield, Jun. and Assistants.—The Machinery by Mr. Burroughs.—The Properties by Mr. Blamire.—The Dresses by Mr. Smythers, Messds. Cross and Follet. The New Ballet & Processions arranged by Monsieur Le CLERCQ, and the Piece Produced under the immediate Direction of Mr. HUNTLEY.

Thalaba, the Destroyer,......Brought up as an Arabian Peasant,......Mr. STANLEY.
Moath, an Old Arabian, Mr. HARWOOD. Samba, a Black Slave, Mr. SLOMAN. Hassed, Usurping Sultan of the Isles, Mr. BENGOUGH. Hafna, Zelem, and Ali, Officers of the Sultan, Mr. HILL, Mr. HAINES, and Mr. HOWELL. Okman, Zoar, Haaric, Morab, Abuer, Persian Chiefs, Messrs. HONOR, COOPER, ANBURY, HOBBS, BOULANGER, FISHER. Abdalda, a Demon, assuming various Characters, Mr. BRADLEY. Okba, a Fiend, Mr. JONES. Moussain Hag, Mr. MORRIS. Oneiza, - - - - Daughter of Moath, beloved by Thalaba, - - - - Miss EDMISTON. Zeinab, Spirit of Thalaba's Mother, Mrs. BRADLEY. Kawla, Enchantress of the Isles, Mrs. STANLY. Marmina, Peri of Faith, Miss BURNETT. Fairy Fiends, Upas, Mrs. TENNANT. Semi, Miss GASKILL. Monfa, Mrs. YOUNG. Cindombere, Mrs. WESTON.

In Act II.—A NEW GRAND ASIATIC PAS DE DEUX, by Monsieur and Madame Le CLERCQ.

| Act 1. | Act 3. |
|---|---|
| The Sepulchre of Zeinab by Moonlight, WILKINS. | A RUINED CEMETERY, JONES. |
| **AWFUL INCANTATION.** | ENTRANCE TO THE SILVER CAVERN, |
| ROMANTIC PASS, WILKINS. | Guarded by a Stupendous Winged Serpent, JONES. |
| Cottage of Moath in the Valley of Date Trees, WILKINS. | Interior of the Silver Cavern, |
| Thalaba's Chamber in the Cottage of Moath, WILKINS. | **COLOSSAL STATUE AND ALTAR,** |
| Act 2. | Bearing the 7 Enchanted Lights & Burning Sword, JONES. |
| COTTAGE OF MOATH BY SUN-RISE. | VALLEY OF THE MOUNTAINS, JONES. |
| Impressive Appearance and Flight of the Locusts. | *Procession of Thalaba's Army,* |
| Apartment in the Sultan's Palace, STANFIELD, Jun. | WITH HIS APPEARANCE ON A |
| MOUNTAINOUS PASS & MAGIC WELL, WILKINS. | **WAR ELEPHANT** |
| Splendid Pavilion in the Sultan's Palace, | Towers and Fortifications of Badelmandel, |
| IN WHICH WILL BE INTRODUCED | Wilkins & Jones. |
| **A Grand Procession and Ballet.** | **Desperate Conflict,** |
| PRINCIPAL DANCERS, | **STORMING OF THE FORTRESS,** |
| Mons. & Mad. Le CLERCQ, Masters HUMMERSTON and WIFLAND. | With the Destruction of the Tyrant, |
| A VIEW NEAR THE ROCK OF BADELMANDEL. | **AND RESTORATION OF THALABA** |
| **Enchanted Cavern** | *To his CROWN and KINGDOM.* |
| Beneath the WATERS of Badelmandel, WILKINS. | |
| **GRAND STORM CHORUS,** | |
| And Precipitation of Thalaba & Oneiza down the Cataract of Badelmandel, With their Miraculous Escape. | |

After which will be Revived, (Second Time these Two Years,) the very favorite Petite Comedy, Called,

# THE SECRET.

The Characters by Messrs. HILL, HAINES, HARWOOD.    Mrs. POPE and Mrs. De BOOR.

☞The Proprietor ever anxious to produce Novelty, has engaged that eminent Artist, Mr. STANFIELD, (by Permission of R. W. ELLISTON, Esq.) to paint a New Elegant Picturesque Drop Scene, to be exhibited at the End of this Piece.

*⁎* In the Construction of the New Melo-Drame, founded upon the Terrific Romance of "FRANKENSTEIN," every care has been taken to avoid any points that might be deemed objectionable in Principle and Morality; and, the Manager trusts, that instead of being offensive to the Feelings of the most Fastidious, this Drama will be found to convey an instructive Lesson, through the Medium of the most Novel and Impressive Effects.

The whole to conclude with an entirely New Dramatic Romance, of a peculiar Interest, founded on the Popular and Singular Romance of the same Name, with New Music, Scenery, Dresses and Decorations, to be Called,

# FRANKENSTEIN!
## Or, THE DEMON OF SWITZERLAND.

Music by Mr. T. Hughes.—Scenery by Messrs. Wilkins, Jones, and Assistants.—Dresses by Mr. Smythers, Messds. Cross and Follet.—Properties by Mr. Blamire.—Machinery by Mr. Burroughs—And the Piece written by Mr. H. M. Milner.

Frankenstein, a Student of Geneva, Mr. STANLEY. Clairville, his Friend, Mr. HILL. Mr. Theodorus, Cornelius, Maximan Lightbody, Mr. SLOMAN. Ludolf, Mr. JACOBSON. Ruric, Mr. COOPER. Villager, Mr. REEVES.

Clara, Sister of Clairville, Mrs. POPE. Maud, his Mother, Mrs. WESTON. Eliza, Sister to Clairville, Mrs. TENNANT. Swiss Villagers, Messrs. Morris, Prond, Waring, Boulanger, Gouge, Dowing. Messda. Brock, Fairbrother, Davis, De Boor, Gough, Grisdale.

Boxes 4s 3s.    Pit 2s.    Gal. 1s.    Doors open at Half-past 5, begin at Half-past 6    Second Price at Half-past 8.
☞Places to be taken of Mr. A. R. Bowes, at the New Box Office, in the Grand Marine Saloon of the Theatre, and of whom may be had Private Boxes Nightly, also First Admissions for the Season, and for the Accommodation of the Nobility and Gentry at the West End of the Town, at the Western Exchange, Old Bond-street, and at No. 182, Piccadilly, opposite Burlington-House.    [T. Romney, Printer, Lambeth.]

*Thalaba* playbill.

**The Vampire.**

*Ruth.*   Ha! some one coming!—I must seize my prize!

Act 2. Scene 2

Frontispiece, Richardson edition of Moncrieff's *Vampire.*

# Chapter 6

# German Influence, 1829-34

Your spell has recalled me from the grave
With magical desire;
You quickened me with passion's flame—
And now you can't quench the fire.

Oh, press your lips against my lips!
For the breath of life I've waited!
I drink your soul down to the dregs:
The dead can never be sated.[1]

—Heinrich Heine, *Dr. Faust*

The English treatments of the vampire theme were all derived from the French; that is, from Nodier via Planché, in turn based on an English source, Polidori, who had drawn his material from the German Romantics via Byron. In this convoluted process, the horror content had become very much diluted: the vampire was treated rather sympathetically (especially in Nodier and Planché). His terrible ending could evoke pity, and his designs on the heroine, in terms of drinking her blood, were de-emphasized in many plays.

For the French, the interest was in the tragic love story. Nodier's Malvina at the end has no alternative lover, and is left alone. The theme of the abandoned bride is Romanticism at its most pale and sentimental. Since all the plays, English and French, were derived from the one seminal short story, its power had become attenuated.

But the roots of Romanticism were in Germany, and German writers continued to treat the vampire theme with freshness and vigor, and with much more emphasis on the carnivorous and violent aspects of the vampire's *modus vivendi*, and with particular interest in the sub-genre of the female vampire. Vampires had been a subject of continuous interest in Germany from the time of the dozens of university treatises and scientific studies in the 18th century (see Chapter 1). In addition to the poems of Bürger, Goethe, and Ossenfelder, there were such works of the *schauer-romantik* school as "Aurelia" in *Die Erzühlungen der Serapion-*

**110**

*brüder* (1819-20) in which Count Hippolitus discovers that his
bride is a vampire, by E.T.A. Hoffmann (1776-1822), "the
archpriest of ultra-German Romanticism" (Varma, *Gothic Flame*
154), and "Wake Not the Dead" (c. 1800), a short story about a
vampire wife attributed to Ludwig Tieck.[2]

In 1829 and 1834 two examples of the German treatment of
the vampire theme were seen on the London stage: Heinrich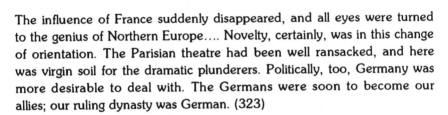
Marschner's opera *Der Vampyr* and George Blink's *The Vampire
Bride*, an adaptation of Tieck's short story. They were part of a
resurgence of German influence on English literary taste. Allardyce
Nicoll conjectures on the reasons why England turned from France
to Germany as a cultural influence:

The influence of France suddenly disappeared, and all eyes were turned
to the genius of Northern Europe.... Novelty, certainly, was in this change
of orientation. The Parisian theatre had been well ransacked, and here
was virgin soil for the dramatic plunderers. Politically, too, Germany was
more desirable to deal with. The Germans were soon to become our
allies; our ruling dynasty was German. (323)

Carl Maria von Weber's *Der Freischütz* (1821), a romantic
opera dealing with the supernatural—especially its Wolf Glen scene
with its invocation of evil spirits—was an enormous popular success
everywhere. It "spread like wildfire all over Germany...set German
Romantic opera on its road and dealt the death blow to the
century-long Italian reign in German theatre" (Grout 366). Its
popularity in England was due to the fact that it was a refreshing
change from the French and Italian emphasis on lovelorn heroines,
to the originality of Weber's music, and to the novelty of his
treatment of the macabre—devils appearing onstage evoked the
Faust plays of both cultures by Goethe and Marlowe. The opera
was very influential, and inspired many English imitations. Michael
Booth remarks:

The supernatural horrors of Weber's *Der Freischütz* were immensely
popular on the English stage, with four melodramas and two burlesques of
it in 1824 alone. The scene in which Caspar casts the magic bullets crams
as many weird effects into a few minutes as any play: ghouls, serpents,
wheels of fire, skeleton stag, horse and hounds in the air, storm, thunder,
lightning, uprooted trees, split rocks, a river of blood, and the climactic
appearance in flames of Zamiel, the dreaded Black Huntsman. (*English
Melodrama* 85)

English opera embraced German horror with enthusiasm. Christopher Frayling comments that "Operatic horror shows were so popular by autumn 1826 that the journal...*Opera Glass* ran a ten-stanza poem entitled 'The Devil Amoung the Players,' which described how even the best singers seemed to have become diabolically possessed by *The Vampyre, Frankenstein,* and *Faustus*" (*Vampyres* 38).

Greatly under the influence of *Der Freischütz*, Weber's disciple Heinrich August Marschner (1795-1861), composed *Der Vampyr* in 1827 to a libretto by Wilhelm August Wohlbrück, his brother-in-law, a popular actor.[3] Wohlbrück's source was an 1821 German adaptation of Nodier's *Le Vampire* by Heinrich Ludwig Ritter, *Der Vampyr, oder die todten Braut*, "Romantiches Schauspiel in drei Acten" first performed in Karlsruhe on 1 March 1821 (Palmer 84).

The opera premiered in Leipzig on 28 March 1828 with Marianne Wohlbrück, the composer's wife and librettist's sister, in the leading soprano role of Malwine. The role of Ruthwen (pronounced rott-ven) was written for the famous basso, Eduard Genast. *Der Vampyr* was very successful and eventually joined the repertory of most of the leading German opera houses.

The libretto for *Der Vampyr* is based on the Nodier melodrama via Ritter, but the plot is given a Faustian framework: in the opening scene, highly evocative of the *Freischütz* Wolf-Glen scene, Ruthwen cavorts with witches and ghosts and a Satan-like Vampyrmeister, whom Ruthwen begs for more time on earth. He is given three years on the condition that he obtain for his master three virgin brides. This bargain with the devil is typically Germanic, resonant not only of Faust's bargain, but of numerous German fairy tales. Nowhere in the previous French or English plays have we been shown a specific connection between the vampire and satanic powers.

Janthe (Ianthe in Polidori's story, appearing for the first time in a dramatized version), an innocent young girl, is the first victim, whom Ruthwen easily seduces. In the opera's most famous aria (the only piece to be performed as an excerpt today, and that rarely), he sings of the joy of killing:

> Ah, what pleasure from beautiful eyes,
> From flowering breasts, new life
> In a wondrous drink,
> To suck all this in with one kiss!
> Ah, what pleasure in loving caresses,

With lustful daring
To coaxingly nip
The sweetest blood
Like nectar of roses
From crimson lips!
And when the burning thirst is quenched,
And when the blood has flowed from the heart,
And when they groan, filled with terror,
Ha ha, what delight!
What pleasure, with new lust,
Their death agony is fresh life!
Poor darling, white as snow,
No doubt you feel pain in your heart.
Ah, once I felt these pangs
Of fear in my warm heart
Which heaven created for feeling.
Don't remind me in these fresh tones
Of the curse of the heavens!
I understand your cry!
Ah, what pleasure![4] (I, no. 2)

These bloodthirsty sentiments are set to a surprisingly jaunty dance tune, which shockingly invites the hearer to participate in a sense of pleasure and release, almost as his accomplices. This vampire, a kind of Gilles de Rais, expresses no sorrow or doubt, just brutal enjoyment and sexual excitement at the act of killing, in contrast with the soliloquy of Planché's Ruthven, expressing remorse and self-contempt.

Janthe's murdered body is found in a cave by her father, Lord Berkley, who stabs Ruthven. He is brought back from the dead by Edgar Aubry, tenor and romantic lead. (The "romantic" ranking of the characters is established by the vocal range assigned by the composer: almost universally in opera, basses and baritones are "heavies" and tenors are heroes.)

The fact that Janthe and later Emmy appear onstage, are seduced and brutally killed undermines Ruthwen's claim of love for Malwine—she is just one of a series.[5]

In Wohlbrück's alteration, Lord Humprey Davenaut instructs his daughter, Malwine, to break off her engagement to Aubry in favor of Ruthwen, now calling himself the Earl von Marsden, but she resists and remains faithful to Aubry. Thus Wohlbrück (as Moncrieff had done previously) introduces an alternative, previously displaced lover for Malwine, so that the ending can display poetic justice, and further removing Ruthwen from any pretension to the position of romantic lead. He is clearly an interloper (as in Moncrieff's play), but Wohlbrück's scheme introduces more psychological complexity: Aubry is guilty because of his previous (and hidden) relationship with Ruthwen. As in the Polidori source, there is a subtle hint of homosexuality in the relationship, also of psychic vampirism. As D.L. MacDonald in *Poor Polidori: A Critical Biography of the Author of "The Vampyre"* points out, the Wohlbrück libretto greatly strengthens Aubry's motivation: "Aubry has to keep his oath because of a new superstition deftly improvised by Wohlbrück and explained by the vampire in a scene closely based on *The Giaour*: if he breaks it, he will become a vampire himself" (191). Aubry knows Ruthwen's secret, and is complicit in it; his involvement with the vampire threatens the life of the woman he loves.

The second act brings in the subplot of the peasant couple (derived from Da Ponte/Mozart through Nodier and the English playwrights: Zerlina/Masetto, Lovette/Edgar, Effie/Robert, Jeannie/Sandy), now called Emmy and Georg Diddin. Emmy's *Romanze*, "Den bleichen Mann," was so admired by Richard Wagner that he used it as the model, both in form and text, for Senta's ballad in *Der fliegende Holländer* (1841) (*New Oxford Dictionary of Music* 513). Wagner's admiration for *Der Vampyr* is well documented: in 1833 he composed an extensive new *allegro* for Aubry's aria, "Wie ein schöner Frühlingsmorgen" (II, no. 15). Indeed, Wagner's Dutchman, like Ruthwen a bass role, shares many characteristics with Marschner's vampire: his immortal life, his damnation, and his search for a victim who will sacrifice herself for him. Wagner's opera has more in common with Marschner's than the Flying Dutchman melodramas from which Wagner drew his plot: the relationship between Ruthwen and Emmy is paralleled in Senta's attraction to the dark, silent stranger who captains a ghost ship with a crew of dead men, a strange and powerful love for which she is willing to sacrifice her life. MacDonald gives a slightly different version of Wagner's involvement:

Wagner, who conducted the opera in 1833, was interested enough in it to suggest some revisions, which Marschner was wise enough to accept, and *The Flying Dutchman*...is built around Senta's ballad about the Dutchman, as Marschner's is around Emmy's ballad about the vampire, and both ballads describe the central figures in precisely the same terms, as *der bleiche Mann*, the pale man. Both these pale men seek their salvation, in different ways, from women—the main practical difference being that Emmy is drained and Senta is drowned. (199)

Wohlbrück introduces folk elements and scenes of comedy, but unlike Planché and Moncrieff who use them as relief, he uses them theatrically to heighten the sense of horror. Gerald Abraham in *The Oxford Dictionary of Music* provides a good analysis of the effect:

The apparently irrelevant scene in Act II, in which four yokels...drink themselves into a stupor and are hauled over the coals by Blunt's indignant wife, gives rise to a brilliant *coup de théâtre*. It follows Ruthwen's wooing of the peasant bride Emmy, and is terminated abruptly by shots as her bridegroom, finding her ravished body, fires at the escaping murderer; the chill realization of what has been going on offstage is immensely effective. (199)

In its review of the English Opera House production on 26 August 1829, *The Times* remarked, "One of the most original compositions in the opera is the drinking quartette with which the third act opens. It was sung in the true spirit of mirth and conviviality, and was warmly encored" (qtd. in Palmer 288). In thus mixing tragedy with comedy and folk elements, Marschner was following the suggestions of his friend E.T.A. Hoffmann, who commented, "Only in the truly Romantic could comedy mix so fittingly with tragedy that both are fused in a total effect, and the mind of the listener is seized in a special and marvelous way" (qtd. in Köhler, *New Grove Dictionary*, 1980 ed., 702).

Contextualizing the place of *Der Vampyr* in the history of opera, the modern scholar and music historian Volkmar Köhler assigns it an important place as a bridge between Weber and Wagner in German Romantic opera:

He created a protagonist psychologically divided within himself in *Der Vampyr*.... The technique of combining in one personality what (until Weber) had generally been presented in two separate characters had its roots in Mozart's *Don Giovanni* and was developed in the dramas of the "Sturm und Drang" period; this was supplemented by the Romantic penchant for the supernatural. These ideas were stimulated in Marschner by Tieck and his circle.... His operas have much less local flavour than those of Weber, as is evident even in *Der Vampyr*, with its many changes of scene and its melodramatic treatment of the arch-vampire....

Marschner's predilection for character drama led to a great extension of psychological meaning within the opera: his music, although immediately concerned with its particular moment, can only be fully understood within the context of the entire plot. The music shrewdly portrays the inner developments of mind and spirit, and Marschner used every means to capture this accurately and with dynamic fluency.... His readiness to sacrifice music for dramatic ends is demonstrated by his preference for melodrama, of which he was the greatest exponent. (*New Grove*, 1980 ed., 701-02)[6]

Psychologically divided characters are typical of Romantic drama, but atypical of melodrama, where characters are for the most part schematically good or evil. Marschner was one of the first to delineate psychological complexity through music, one of the few—besides Mozart—to attempt it. The link between Ruthwen and Don Giovanni is also to be noted—both characters seem unaware of their own contradictions; both are self-destructive; both believe they love women while actually despising them; both end by descending into the fiery pit.

Abraham makes a much more negative modern assessment of Marschner's achievement, calling *Der Vampyr* "a mixture of diabolism and sexual pathology:"

Marschner...became intoxicated by the license to horrify, without commanding Weber's invention or musical control.... The central character...is a psychopath who murders and drinks the blood of his virgin-victims, apparently during intercourse. These exploits are a condition of his pact with the devil.... The authors...treat his performances with relish, wasting little time or sympathy on the victims or their bereaved relatives.... Ruthwen, like Don Giovanni, at least has the courage of his convictions (if they can be so termed) and commits two murderous rapes in the course of the opera.... [Marschner] could draw peasants, perhaps because he was himself a peasant at heart.... He lacks the lightness of touch—he deals in goblins and demons, never the fairies of *Oberon*. (*New Oxford* 507-10)

Presumably Abraham would give the above as reasons why *Der Vampyr* is not included in the modern operatic canon. Nevertheless, while disliking the subject matter and questioning the morality of the treatment, he yet finds some qualities to admire in terms of theatricality and stage-worthiness:

Marschner's strength lay in his gift for theatre: *Der Vampyr*, for all its gaucheries of plot, comes off remarkably well even today.... One of his most successful gambits is his use of *mélodrame* in scenes of darkness, terror, and extreme emotion.... His peasants are boorish, though not without rough humour; his nature pieces evoke the nocturnal and sinister.... His orchestration...has undeniable power. (509-10)[7]

Marschner retains the Scottish locale and attempts to give a "Shakespearean" flavor to his *Vampyr*, judging from the character names he chooses: besides those from Nodier (Ruthwen, Malwine, Edgar Aubry), he tries for local color with Berkley, Humprey Davenaut, John Perth, Toms Blunt, James Gadshill, Richard Scrop, Robert Green, and Georg Didden. Scotland was an exotic place to a 19th-century Leipzig musician. These efforts at Anglicization were undone when J.R. Planché was selected to write the English libretto:

In the summer of 1829 I had the opportunity of treating the subject of "The Vampire" in accordance with my own ideas of propriety. The French melodrama had been converted into an opera for the German stage, and the music composed by Marschner.

Mr. Hawes, who had obtained a score of it, having induced Mr. Arnold to produce it at the Lyceum [formerly English Opera House], I was engaged to write the libretto, and consequently laid the scene of action in Hungary, where the superstition exists to this day, substituted for a Scotch chieftain a Wallachian boyard, and in many other respects improved upon my earlier version. The opera was extremely well sung, and the costumes novel as well as correct...respecting the national dresses of the Magyars and Wallachians.

I am surprised that Marschner's most dramatic and melodious works, *Der Vampyr*, *Die Judin*, &c., have not been introduced to our more advanced musical audiences at one or other of our great operatic establishments. (*Recollections* I: 151-52)

Planché's reference to "my own ideas of propriety" we may presume refers to his residual irritation at being coaxed by the English Opera House management to retain the Scottish locale in his 1820 adaptation of the Nodier original (and the twitting he took for it from the press), despite his conviction that the play would be more appropriately set in Eastern Europe. His statement that the origin of the superstition is Hungarian is almost correct. But there is no indication that he tried to soften the coarseness and violence of the German opera to make it more resemble his own or Nodier's more genteel versions. The German Ruthwen kills two women in the course of the action—there was no way around this while maintaining the integrity of the piece. Planché's main focus at this period in his career was authenticity of costume and scenery, a life-long vocation to which he contributed much innovation and reform.

Planché was the obvious choice for the English librettist, having written the English adaptation of Nodier's play and therefore thoroughly familiar with the material; also, he had worked in 1826 with Weber on *Oberon*, for which he was the original librettist, not a translator. This highly successful production opened at the Lyceum on 25 March 1829[8] and ran for 60 nights, in the same season and at the same theatre as the revival of Planché's own melodrama, *The Vampire, or the Bride of the Isles*, which opened on 28 September. The Lyceum in 1829 surely deserved to be called the "theatre of vampires," or "the House of Ruthven," having staged two separate works featuring this character in the same season.

Considered aesthetically, Marschner's *Vampyr*, even in its English/Hungarian incarnation, is more viscerally disturbing than the English and French works which preceded it, because 1) the music itself acts as an intensifier; 2) the opera includes many of the harsher elements of the Polidori source which are omitted in the plays; and 3) Wohlbrück's conception of Ruthwen's character is that of a brutal and depraved serial killer. The dosage of horror is higher in *Der Vampyr* than in the diluted French version by Nodier, further softened by the English imitations.

Marschner's opera also had a close imitator: Peter Josef von Lindpainter (1791-1856) composed an opera also named *Der Vampyr* which opened in Stuttgart on 21 September 1828, seven months after Marschner's work opened in Leipzig.[9] The libretto of Lindpainter's *Vampyr*, by Cäsar Max Heigel, is much less extreme than Wohlbrück's, and despite the switched-around names and character functions, reprises the Nodier plot. Briefly stated, the action is shifted to France, and the vampire is Graf (Count) Aubri. Port D'Amour is the father who breaks his daughter Isolde's engagement to Count Hippolyte in favor of the vampire suitor. Invoking the aid of demonic powers to help him seduce Lorette (Lovette *et al.*, the same basic peasant girl in all the versions) on her wedding night, Aubri is killed by Hippolyte. He makes Hippolyte swear not to reveal his death until midnight, still hoping to make Isolde his prey, but she throws herself on God's protection, and the vampire's time runs out with the usual fiery results.[10]

For a time Lindpainter's opera competed successfully with Marschner's in Germany, but eventually was overshadowed. Lindpainter's other works, now mainly of academic interest, are highly derivative of Weber, Schumann, and Mendelssohn.

Marschner's opera has been revived in this century in Passau (1973), London (1976), and the Boston Conservatory (1980). Writing of the Passau production, which featured a bat motif in the designs, A. Dean Palmer comments:

Ruthven, unlike Dracula, never had any connection with bats. These and other pieces of evidence support the contention that the Ruthven-Dracula tradition is a historically continuous one despite minor dissimilarities between the characters, and that Marschner's opera, even if rarely staged today, was an important contribution to that tradition. (96)

In 1992 the BBC made a film version of the opera directed by Nigel Finch with the BBC Philharmonia and the Britten Singers under the musical direction of David Parry (on video release in this country by CBS/Fox). With a new English libretto by Charles Hart and chicly designed by Jim Grant, this postmodern treatment, obviously conceived as a film, sets some of the action in a rooftop swimming pool and a number of other architecturally interesting spaces. Updated to modern London among the rich and jaded jet set, this reconceived version paints all the characters as cynical and tarnished, following, with gory detail, the trail of a handsome serial killer among the rich and gullible. The body of one victim is discovered by parking-garage attendants in the trunk of the vampire's Mercedes. The incongruity between the stylish, jaundiced, slang-filled lyrics and the full-blown German Romantic score is almost too much at times; nevertheless it is meticulously sung and performed with gusto (and a great deal of nudity) by the young British cast, including Omar Ebraham as Riply the Vampire (Ruthwen), Fiona O'Neill as Miranda Davenaut the Heiress (Malwine), Philip Salmon as Alex (Aubry), Willemijn van Gent as Ginny the Fashion Model (Ianthe), and Sally-Ann Sheperdson as Emma the Executive (Emma), and narrated by Robert Stephens.

Ludwig Tieck's short story, "Wake Not the Dead" (c. 1800) with its female vampire, Brunhilda, is of the line of Goethe's "Die Bräut von Korinth" (1797), in turn derived from the Roman story of

Phlegon of Tralles (see Chapters 1 and 2). Though vampires were plentiful in German literature, Brunhilda was the first of the female vampires to reach the English stage, in *The Vampire Bride, or the Tenant of the Tomb*, the melodrama by George Blink based on Tieck's short story, in 1834.

Of the surveys of 19th-century theatre history consulted for this study, only Michael Booth's *English Melodrama* mentions this work, comparing it to the Planché and Boucicault vampire plays: "An early equivalent of the modern horror film is what might be called monster melodrama, a branch of the Gothic. Here the main attraction is commonly a non-human fiend of terrible powers who makes the lives of hero and heroine even more trying than usual. Vampires were a popular subject" (84). He goes on to give a brief plot summary, but, atypically for him, does not mention the date or theatre of the premiere, which are also omitted from both editions of the play.[11]

"Wake Not the Dead," one of the most outstanding works in the gothic horror genre, is a sexual allegory which cautions against the excesses of love. The story concerns a Burgundian lord, Walter, who cannot accept the death of his beloved wife, Brunhilda, in spite of the fact that his new wife, Swanhilda, has borne him two children. He persuades a sorcerer to bring Brunhilda back to life, not realizing that, having passed through death, she must return as a vampire, "an artificial life.... All that Brunhilda now possessed was a chilled existence, colder than that of the snake" (*Vampyres* 176). She preys on the vassals' children at first, and finally devours Walter's own sons. When Swanhilda discovers the truth, she curses Walter and commits suicide. He wakes one night to find Brunhilda sucking at his chest, her lips covered with blood. "Monster...is it thus that you love me?" She replies, "Aye, even as the dead love.... I was obliged to pamper myself with warm youthful blood in order that I might satisfy thy furious desires.... Thou hadst the courage to love the dead—to take into thy bed one who had been sleeping in the grave, the bedfellow of the worm" (188-89).

Finally, Walter realizes what he has done, and, with the sorcerer's aid, he kills Brunhilda with a consecrated dagger. Wandering in anguish and still obsessed with the memory of his vampire wife, he meets a strange woman, "a female figure clad in black [with] a raven on her hand.... Wonderfully did she resemble Swanhilda, except that her locks were brown and her eye dark and full of fire." She comes home with him, and restores peace and joy to the castle for a short while, but, at the height of Walter's happiness, she transforms into a serpent and "entwining him in its horrid folds crushed him to death," as the castle sinks into the earth and a voice cries, "Wake Not the Dead."

This superb story is certainly on a plane with, if not surpassing, Polidori's "Vampyre." It can be read on many levels, psychological and allegorical. The blonde Swanhilda and dark Brunhilda are surely doubles, like *Swan Lake*'s Odette and Odile, two aspects of one personality. Especially intriguing and frightening is the fact that Swanhilda, as the stranger, avenges the murder of Brunhilda, suggesting that the "good" wife and the "bad" wife are somehow the same; that all women are one woman: the Other, Goethe's Eternal Feminine. The stranger's metamorphosis into a snake makes her cousin to Keats's Lamia, to Coleridge's Lady Geraldine in *Christabel*, to the 15th-century French legends of the fairy Mélusine, to the Hindu goddess Kali and the Naginis, and to the Minoan snake goddesses. A woman who turns into a snake is certainly a phallic woman, an image of loathing carried to hysterical extremes in Bram Stoker's *Lair of the White Worm* (1911). Compared to the Polidori short story, "Wake Not the Dead" is more profound, both because of its closer linkage with primitive myth— the earliest vampires preyed on their own families—and because of Tieck's insight involving *coincidentia oppositorium*: finding antithesis within the symbol—mother and vampire, wife and succubus—and the terror inherent in the beloved and familiar.

*The Vampire Bride, or the Tenant of the Tomb*, "a romantic drama in two acts," by George Blink, author of *More Schemes, The Speculator, Blind Man's Bluff*, and *The Tiger at Large*, had two published editions: J. Duncombe's in 1834 and T.H. Lacy's in 1854. The Duncombe edition states, "as now performed at the London theatres" on the title page, and "Time of Representation, an hour and a quarter." The costume plot is also listed, and is of interest because it establishes a gothic period, and because of the predominance of white in all the costumes.

Blink's drama, in blank verse and prose, is set in a gothic castle in Thurwalden, the first vampire melodrama to use a non-Scottish setting. The plot follows Tieck, with the very great exception of the insertion of three comic servants, Annetta, Jansen, and a cobbler and carpenter appropriately named Kibitz. Their matrimonial wrangling takes up as much, if not more, stage time than the main characters. This uneasy marriage of genres is in my opinion a detriment to the artistic unity of the play. More like *Abbott and Costello Meet the Wolf Man* than *Macbeth*, where the drunken porter scene heightens the sense of terror, this large subplot serves to diminish it, swamping the play and almost dividing it into two incompatible halves, so jarringly out of key that they seem to be of different worlds. Rather than deepening the tragedy by contrast, the theoretical function of comic relief, it tends to make the serious characters appear ludicrous.

The raising of Brunhilda is the most spectacular scene in the play and the subject of the illustration used as the frontispiece in both editions of the play. The blue-fire effect is specified in the stage directions.

With the minor exception of the small role of Zeinah in Fitzball's *Thalaba* (1823), Brunhilda is the first female vampire on the English stage, and a remarkably vicious one. Unlike the English Ruthvens, her blood-drinking is not glossed over or sanctified by matrimony, but graphically described. She leaves a wide swath of death—men, women, and children alike. The vampire woman's hunger for children is a complete reversal of the universal image of the nurturing mother: rather than nursing infants with her breast milk, she sucks their blood. Instead of giving birth, she brings death. In the confrontation scene between husband and vampire, heavily laced with symbolic imagery of sexual starvation, the author plays ironically with the sexual double-entendres of cold and heat:

> BRUNHILDA: You brought me back to life, but thought not of
> The means whereby on earth I was to live:
> All that
> I now possess, is an existence, chill'd
> And colder than the snake. Give me thy hand. (takes his hand)
> Am I not cold?
>
> LORD WALTER:                    Colder than death! (shuddering)
>
> BRUNHILDA: A living statue. And 'twas requisite,
> That a magic draught should animate the dull
> Slow current in my veins. —
> Human blood! warm—fresh from the arteries.
> This is the hellish drink for which I've thirsted
> And even when beside thee I have laid, [sic]
> I have long'd to taste of thine.
>
> . . . . . . . . . . . . . . . . . . . . . . . . . . . . . . . . . .
> LORD WALTER:                    Begone!
>
> BRUNHILDA: Begone? Know you not I cannot leave you? (I, v, 15)

The substitution of Brunhilda for Swanhilda as the avenging stranger (and necessary omission of the serpent transformation; instead, the uxorious Walter is dragged into the earth in a shower of fire) simplifies Tieck's symbolism considerably and loses some of its resonance, but makes for a very theatrical finale. The tidier ending diminishes the menacing theme of the sisterhood of women, and substitutes a simpler parable of obsessive love and its power to destroy lives.

This story of a love that transcends the grave is a nightmare version of the classical myths of Orpheus and Eurydice, of Admetus and Alcestis. Ernest Jones, writing of vampires in *On the Nightmare*, speculates that, along with sexual desire and the longing for reunion with the dead, there is "equally pronounced dread of such a contingency" (105). Fear of the dead, Jones writes, is derived equally from love and hate, and he quotes Freud's dictum that morbid fear always signifies repressed sexual desire. *The Vampire Bride* could almost have been written to illustrate this theory. Walter's love of Brunhilda, to the exclusion of his living wife and children, is true necrophilia:

The dead being allows everything, can offer no resistance, and the relationship has none of the inconvenient consequences that sexuality may bring in its train in life. The phantasy of loving such a being can therefore make a strong appeal to the sadistic side of the sexual instinct.... Necrophilia ranks as perhaps the most extreme imaginable perversion of the love instinct.... In superstition necrophilia is more correctly represented by the idea of the...ghoul, but this is in many ways connected with that of the Vampire itself. (Jones 111-12)

Since the London theatre where *The Vampire Bride* played is unknown, we cannot speculate on its intended audience. However the play's aspiration to tragedy and its resemblance to the earliest versions of the vampire myth, in which the vampire preys on members of its own family of both sexes, connect it with the primitive archetypal motif, the "archaic remnants," as Jung puts it, of primordial images cast up by the collective unconscious—the vampire and the snake mother (67).

*The Vampire Bride* has a psychological profundity deeper than any of the Ruthven plays. Ruthven, the handsome stranger who is not what he seems, is far less frightening than the mother who is "not in the giving vein." Some mothers kill. Reflected in no other English play of its period, this theme of the demonic woman was more often pursued in French literature, and would reach its apotheosis in *fin-de-siècle* Symbolist drama and poetry. *The Vampire Bride* seems more of that period than its own, where it stands entirely alone, without imitators, and seems to have been almost entirely forgotten. A modern revival of the play would be a worthy project, but the dramaturge would be well advised to cut back on the comic scenes to make the piece viable, thus respecting Tieck's integrity, if not Blink's.

This remarkable play had no immediate successors; however, an American adaptation was produced in 1863. The manuscript prompt book of the play is in the Billy Rose Collection of the Lincoln Center Library for the Performing Arts, its title page reading, "*Brunhilda, or Wake Not the Dead*, altered and adapted from *The Vampire Bride* by E.F. Taylor for Barnum's Museum, New York, September, 1863."

The first Barnum Museum, located at Ann Street and Broadway in New York, was an unusual American institution which made a unique contribution to the character of American theatre. P.T. Barnum (1810-91) envisioned the Lecture Room of his museum as a place of "family entertainment" where "men and women, adults and children, could intermingle safe in the knowledge that no indelicacies would assault their senses, onstage or off," according to A.H. Saxon in his biography, *P.T. Barnum: The Legend and the Man* (105).

Typical American audiences of this period apparently surpassed the rowdiness of their English and French counterparts, and drunkenness was a particular problem:

Spectators, particularly those in the upper galleries, were given to demonstrating their disapproval of actors and playwrights in no uncertain terms, often to the detriment of those seated below; drunkenness was rife in the front of the house and, to a somewhat lesser extent, on the other side of the footlights as well; prostitutes openly solicited in corridors and boxes.... trading on the theatre's reputation as a haunt for dissipation and vice.... A respectable person thought twice about going to the theatre. He thought even harder before exposing his wife or sweetheart to these conditions. Children were almost never taken there. But all this was gradually to change...thanks largely to the determined efforts of Barnum and a handful of other managers. (Saxon 104-05)

The Lecture Room of Barnum's Museum was actually a lavishly appointed theatre seating 3000 spectators on the second floor of the building, where Barnum's eclectic collection of the world's oddities (including living human beings) was displayed. From 1841 until the museum burned in 1865, it offered such morally uplifting temperance and abolitionist works as *The Drunkard, or Ten Nights in a Barroom* and *Uncle Tom's Cabin,* and domestic and romantic dramas such as *The Curate's Daughter, The Trials of a Village Girl, The Man, the Spirit, and the Mortal, The Octoroon,* and a very popular and sensational version of Byron's poem, *Mazeppa.* By the 1860s the offerings were veering away from the morally uplifting and toward spectacle, display of female flesh, and gothic melodrama. A 40-member *corps de ballet* was permanently employed, and fairy extravaganzas in the French style were offered, as well as *Macbeth* and other Shakespeare plays performed by the child prodigies Kate and Ellen Bateman. Performances were free with museum admission, although upgrades in seating could be purchased. Saxon states that the museum sold 34 million tickets under Barnum's management, more tickets in proportion to the 1860 American population than Disney theme parks' tickets to today's population (108). Taylor's *Brunhilda* was offered in 1863, two years before the Museum burned to the ground and Barnum rebuilt it further uptown.

The first part of the manuscript of *Brunhilda* uses the printed text of Blink's *Vampire Bride* with extensive handmade cuts and revisions. After II, iii, however, it is completely rewritten. Briefly, the added scenes, larded with bits of chewed-up Shakespeare, include a second rising of Brunhilda, at which Walter stabs and shoots her (for good measure), and a witches' sabbath with spirits and devils. It ends almost identically with the English original, with only a few word changes in Brunhilda's final speech. The Sorcerer is called Herman the Astrologer in this version; Annetta becomes Annella; and the children are given names—Albert and Christine. The prompt book gives the helpful annotation "Playing time—47 minutes. No waiting between acts."

In this American version, we see a more heroic, action-oriented Walter—many of his self-pitying speeches are cut, and he is given a mad scene and an attempted suicide. Brunhilda is an aggressive and sexually attractive vampire, backed up in this version by a whole coven of demons and witches. The fact that she is shot, after stabbing proves ineffective, suggests that the Barnum production may have ignored the gothic setting as well as increasing the violence quotient. Cutting half an hour of playing time—almost a third of the play—and the inclusion of a ballet and the repeated killing of Brunhilda, illustrate the usual American taste for action and spectacle over dialogue.

The subject matter of *Brunhilda* seems unusually lurid for a palace of temperance and Christian morality. Barnum, in a letter to *The Nation*, remarked that he was "often grieved that the taste of the million was not more elevated," and maintained that his theatre offered theatrical entertainment in a purified form: "No vulgar word or gesture, and not a profane expression, was *ever* allowed on my stage! Even in Shakespeare's plays, I unflinchingly and unvaryingly cut out vulgarity and profanity. I am sensitive on these points because I was always extremely *squeamish* in my determination to allow nothing objectionable on my stage" (qtd. in Saxon 107). The presentation at the Barnum Museum of *Brunhilda*, a violent and (for its time) sexually graphic vampire melodrama, very much undercuts the veracity of these remarks.

Considering the *Der Vampyr* and *The Vampire Bride* together, one could conclude that the audiences in the late 1820s and early 1830s were receptive to increasing violence in their entertainment. It should also be noted that neither work is a cheap thriller intended for a transpontine audience of the lowest common denominator. One is in the "elitist" form of an opera; the other is a Romantic tragedy.

It is worth noting that in these works and those examined in the preceding chapters, the vampire always has a tinge of the foreign and exotic in his persona. For the French, he was the English/Scottish personification of Lord Byron, with emphasis on his prowess as a lover. For Planché, he was a Celtic Scot, but more of a gentleman, and colored by Shakespearean touches, reflecting Planché's taste for Shakespearean enchantment, and as Nina Auerbach points out, the poetic imagery of the moon. Dorset's nihilistic vampire is a Persian interloper in Egyptian society. Marschner's vampire is an Elizabethan-era Scottish lord, thus exoticized for German audiences; but for English consumption Planché converted him into a Wallachian (Hungarian) boyar. Blink sets his story in medieval Germany; "Thurwalden" indeed has an ominous "foreign" sound.

It is the opinion of Richard Switzer that the more often the Ruthven story was adapted, the more insipid it became:

In this evolution Lord Ruthven can be viewed only as a harmful influence. Wherever this one vampire continues as the central figure, the resultant works are uniformly mediocre.... Lord Ruthven then is the supreme example of lack of discriminatory taste on the part both of public and of authors, and a witness to the reactionary force exerted by the public in the evolution of literary genres. (112)

This seems to me to a valid assessment. As we have examined each adaptation, in turn, of the Polidori "Vampyre," the story has evolved by increments, gradually adding details which seem minor in themselves, until the late plays bear very little resemblance to the original. Marschner's opera proves the exception: a fresh jolt of German brutality was needed to remind English audiences of what vampires really were—not wicked moon fairies but vicious killers.

The great vogue for gothic novels was temporarily dead in England, to be revived in mid-century with the penny-dreadfuls, notably *Varney the Vampire*; onstage, nothing followed until Boucicault's *Vampire* in 1852, another version of Polidori. But the fresh infusion of primitive vampirism from the East, seen in Marschner's *Vampyr* and Blink's *Vampire Bride*, anticipates the trend in France reflected in a series of lectures given by the Polish playwright Adam Mickiewicz in the 1840s, which, together with the bizarre and notorious case of Sergeant Bertrand in 1849, rekindled the French interest in vampires, and attracted the attention of Alexandre Dumas *père*. Lord Ruthven still had not worn out his welcome.

Heinrich Ramsburg, illustration of Marschner's *Vampyr*, repr. *Galerie zu den Opern* (Kiel: Wissenschaftliche für Literatur und Kunst, 1935).

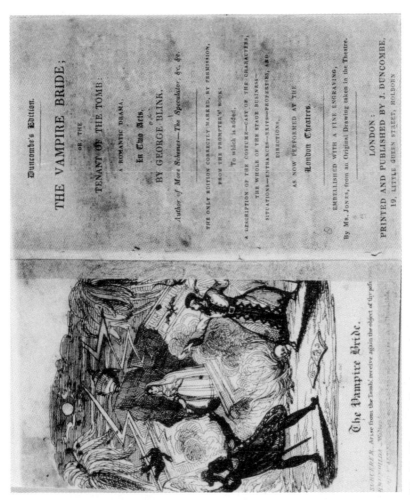

Blink's *Vampire Bride.*

Illustration from the first English edition of Tieck's "Wake Not the Dead."

# Chapter 7

# Paris, London, and America, 1851-62

How then are we to account for the taste which maintained for so long the works of terror and blood? Most easily. It is the privilege of the ignorant and the weak to love superstition. The only strong mental sensation they are capable of is *fear*.... There are millions of minds that have no resource between vapid sentimentality, and the ridiculous spectra of the nursery.
—James Malcolm Rymer, *Popular Writing* (1842)

In Paris, after the initial flood of the 1820s, the fascination with vampires subsided but remained a small but steady current. Works of fiction, such as Mérimée's *La Guzla* (1827), Théophile Gautier's *La Morte Amoureuese* (1836), and Paul Féval's *Les Mystères de Londres* (1844) continued to be produced, while on the stage there was only a minor entry, another comedy-vaudeville called *Le Vampire* by Eugène Deligny (1816-81) at the Théâtre de Variétés, 11 July 1844.

Readers of French newspapers could not have escaped the subject of vampires in 1849, when the famous case of Sergeant Bertrand, known throughout France as "the Vampire," was given sensational play for many weeks. Bertrand was actually the exact opposite of a vampire, a necrophiliac, who for a number of months had been desecrating graves in Parisian cemeteries and mutilating corpses. The police laid a trap for him, and, wounding him in an ambush, traced him to a military hospital and discovered him to be a sergeant in the French army. At his trial his doctors offered an insanity defense, but he was judged sane and sentenced to a year's imprisonment.[1] Sergeant Bertrand the Vampire became a staple of French pulp fiction and music-hall songs. The case is cited in this study not as evidence that vampires were running amok in Paris, but that public interest was still running high 30 years after Nodier's *Le Vampire*, and that a play on the subject stood a good chance of commercial success.

Interest in vampires was alive and healthy in intellectual circles, and was given a boost when the subject was discussed in the lectures of the Polish playwright Adam Mickiewicz (1798-1855) at the Collège de France in 1843. Now considered Poland's most important Romantic poet and playwright, Mickiewicz spent most of his life in exile in Russia, Germany, Italy, and France. In the 16th lecture of the series, on the subject of Slavic drama, Mickiewicz advanced the 20th-century view that theatre should be a tool for awakening the masses to social awareness, and called for the theatre to reach beyond its conventions and bourgeois concerns to a more all-inclusive audience. But Mickiewicz was also a mystic and a student of cultural ethnology who believed in the power of theatre as sacred ritual, not only through the communal religious experience of the participants, but also as a form of communion with the dead. In remarks prefacing his translation of Mickiewicz's lecture on Slavic drama, Daniel Gerould writes: "The poet stresses that the theatrical communion is not merely with the living, but most importantly with the dead. The invoking of the spirits of departed ancestors in a pagan ceremony becomes for Mickiewicz the model for the theatre as a sacred rite" (92). In the lecture, Mickiewicz states that the Slavic people are, like the Celtic race, gifted with poetic imagination and sensitivity to the supernatural, and have a particular ability to communicate with spirits:

The Slavic people have, above all, believed in the existence of what are called *vampires*, and they have even developed a philosophical theory of vampirism.... This belief is nothing other than faith in the individuality of the human spirit, in the individuality of spirits in general, and nowhere is this belief as strong as it is among the Slavic people. That is why no pantheistic theory will ever manage to take root there; the national instinct rebuffs it. We know from history and mythology that the cult of spirits was an important part of Slavic religion: to this very day there is the custom of invoking the dead in Lithuania and elsewhere; and of all the Slavic sacred rites the most important and solemn is the ceremony of calling forth the spirits of the dead. (94)

Mickiewicz saw the ancient Lithuanian rites of ancestor worship as a basis for a national Polish drama not only rooted in myth and ritual, but also employing all modern technological means, and combining many forms of art, thus anticipating Wagner's *Gesamtkunstwerks*. His attempt to create such a drama was the cycle trilogy, *Forefathers' Eve* (first version, 1823; final and entirely different version, 1832), not produced until 1901 by Slanislau

Wyspiański (1869-1907), the painter, poet, and playwright who was the founder of modern Polish drama.

*Forefathers' Eve* is a drama centered on the conflict between good and evil in the spirit of Konrad, the protagonist, who evolves into the personification of the Polish people. Part Three concerns the twice-yearly feast held in cemeteries in which the dead are invited to partake, a custom also observed in Greece and in many Catholic countries on All Souls Day. The play makes extensive use of folklore elements in the last scene. The song of the vampire is sung by Konrad:

> Song lay cold with the grave:
>   Blood it sniffed from underground.
> Up it rose as vampires crave
>   Blood of any victims found.
>       Vengeance, vengeance on the foe,
>       God upon our side or no!
> . . . . . . . . . . . . . . . . . . . . . . . . . . . . .
> Then spoke Song: "I'll walk by night.
>   First I'll gnaw each brother worm;
> Whomsoever my fangs bite
>   Shall, like me, take vampire's form."
>       Vengeance, vengeance on the foe,
>       God upon our side or no!
>
> Then we'll seek the foe at last,
>   Suck his blood, and body hew
> Into bits and nail it fast
>   Lest he rise a vampire too.
> Then we'll take his soul to hell,
>   Stamp on it with all our might,
> Squeeze its last immortal yell;
>   As it groans, we'll scratch and bite.
>       Vengeance, vengeance on the foe,
>       God upon our side or no! (98-99)

There are echoes, but probably no connection, with the treatment of the vampire theme in William Blake's *Jerusalem* (1816), in which the Spectre, embodied in Blake's drawings in the form of a bat, symbolizes the destructive forces—despair, envy, pride, hostility, anxiety, and melancholy—in the mind of Los, who stands for mankind.

Although *Forefathers' Eve* was not produced in Paris, the lectures of Mickiewicz, as the first holder of the chair in Slavic literature at the Collége de France, must have been known among intellectuals and writers.

When Alexandre Dumas père (1802-70) first came to Paris as a young man in 1823, the first play he saw was the weird and famous melodrama *Le Vampire,* and the story of his adventure at the Porte-Saint-Martin fills five chapters of his memoirs (73-78). The difficulty he encountered getting into the theatre attests to the play's continued popularity. He sat next to a well-dressed elderly gentleman reading an antique cookbook, Elzévir's *Le Patissier François* (1655). Unknown to Dumas, this was the play's author, the erudite, elegant, and eccentric Charles Nodier. The two engaged in a wide-ranging conversation—cuisine, travel, Roman history, claques—and of course came around to the subject of vampires. Nodier assured Dumas that in "Illyria" (Spalatro) he had seen a vampire with his own eyes, an old man whose corpse came back to the house of his sons, asking for food and drink. The grave was opened, with the usual results:

"But, when one came to the tomb of Kisilova—that was the name of the old man—he was found with open eyes and crimson mouth, powerfully breathing and yet immobile, like one dead. A stake was thrust through his heart; he gave a great cry, and blood flowed from his mouth. Then he was put on the pyre and burnt, and they threw his ashes to the wind.... Some time later, I left the country, so that I never learned whether his son had become a vampire like him."

"Why would he have become a vampire like him?" I asked.

"Ah! Because it's customary; persons who die by vampirism become vampires."

"Truly, you say that as if it were a proven fact."

"But it is indeed a fact, proven, known and recorded!" (136-93)[2]

As further proof of the existence of vampires, Nodier offered the example of rotifers, microscopic animals, dead in their dry state, which repeatedly come back to life when a drop of water is placed on the specimen slide.

The performance began, and Dumas was enthralled. He thought Philippe "marvelous," Madame Dorval "wonderful," and referred to Jenny Vertpré (Lovette) as "cette gracieuse miniature de Mlle. Mars" (qtd. in Gorman 254). But Nodier groaned, fidgeted, made caustic remarks, and was angrily hissed by his neighbors. At intermission he announced he could no longer bear the terrible play and pretended to leave, but turned up in one of the boxes, whistling (the French equivalent of booing) at a climactic moment. Finally he was ejected from the theatre.

As a result of this chance meeting, Dumas became a protegé of Nodier's, and was accepted into the circle of Romantics around him. Richard S. Stowe comments, "Important for the budding author, in 1828 Nodier opened to him the doors of his salon at the Arsenal Library. There at the regular Sunday evening receptions he met the leaders of the Romantic movement—Vigny, Lamartine, Hugo, and, later, Balzac, Musset, Mérimée, Delacroix—and himself became a part of the group" (23). Nodier also encouraged him as a playwright, and presented Dumas's first attempt at historical tragedy, *Christine*, to the reading committee of the Comédie Française with his enthusiastic endorsement.

In addition to his career as a novelist, Dumas wrote a number of historical dramas in a style somewhere between melodrama and Romantic drama, *Henry III et sa cour* (1829) and *La Tour de Nesle* (1832) being outstanding examples. They ignore the unities; many have tragic endings but are written in prose, and are in the swashbuckling style of Victor Hugo, in turn derived from a synthesis of Schiller and Shakespeare, with a smattering of Pixérécourt in the use of spectacle. He wrote more than 100 plays, usually preferring to work with a co-author.

The most prolific period of Dumas's career coincides with a period of political upheaval in France—the revolution of 1848 and formation of the Second Republic. One casualty of the changing regimes was Dumas's major producer, the Théâtre Historique, and in 1851 Dumas and his collaborator Albert Maquet shifted their theatrical home base of operations to the Ambigu-Comique, one of Napoleon I's original four minor genre theatres. In the Moscow Decree of 1807 it was designated as the theatre for melodrama and pantomime. Pixérécourt had some of his greatest successes there, and it was one of the earliest of the small theatres to compete with the major houses in lavish display:

The Ambigu displays all its machines in a manner which attracts the crowd that eagerly attends this theatre: picturesque and well-made sets, novel costumes perfectly adapted to the dramatic situations, prettily designed ballets performed by dancers nearly as good as the Opera's, military maneuvers, stage fights, nothing is neglected to satisfy the spectators. (*Lettres sur les différents théâtres de Paris, 1800*, qtd. in Ginisty 213)[3]

By the 1840s the Ambigu, along with the Gaité and the Porte-Saint-Martin, were the traditional homes of melodrama, with the difference that its emphasis was on spectacle, and, in common with the Gaité, the fairy play. Marvin Carlson states, however, that the Ambigu's major offering in 1851, the year of *Le Vampire*, was Bourgeois and Dennery's *Marthe et Marie* (*French Stage* 167).

Dumas's *Le Vampire*, "drame fantastique en cinq actes, en dix tableaux," opened at the Ambigu-Comique on 20 December 1851,[4] and featured the noted boulevard actors Monsieur Arnault (François Alphonse Arnault), Jane Essler, and Joseph Laurent (see Appendix C). In his commentary on *Le Vampire*, Richard Switzer remarks, "At least one of the authors, no doubt Maquet, appears to have studied all the material available on the subject, since the play is a synthesis of all the previous incarnations of Ruthven" (111).[5]

Among the added supernatural characters is the fairy Mélusine,[6] derived from Jean d'Arras (15th century), a being who turns into a snake every Saturday and kills the husband who spies on her, but here the benevolent protector of the family of Gilbert, the hero. In the masque scene of Act Two a tapestry comes to life, and Mélusine and her troupe of sylphs, hunters, shepherds, ondines, and salamanders, along with the portraits of Gilbert's ancestors, the barons of Tiffauges, step down from the walls and sing this warning:

> Mélusine: Know who this man of somber face is,
>    What plot he weaves;
> This man, like us, is a child of darkness,
>    But an accursed child.
>
> His night is too profound even for our eyes.
>    For what dreadful purpose
> Does God permit him to live in this world,
>    This immortal assassin?
>
> No one knows; God puts his whitest doves
>    In his fatal hand,
> And one can follow his tracks
>    By the graves that open along his path.
>                              (Gilbert stirs in anguish.)
>
> No virgin escapes the murders he amasses;
>    The hideous oppressor

Braves the elements and governs space...
Gilbert: O my sister, O my sister!

Mélusine: Hardly has Juana, his victim, died,
   When the spectral ravisher,
Flying up from his tomb, returns to the carnage.
Gilbert: O my sister, O my sister!

Mélusine: Yesterday he tried to kill our son on the plain,
   Because this blood-bathed bridegroom
Wished to deprive Hélène of her protector...
Gilbert: O my sister, O my sister!

Mélusine: Let us pray that all-powerful God
   Inspires Gilbert with great will.
Ruthven is a demon, Ruthven is a vampire;
   His love, it is death! (III, ii, 476-77)[7]

Another new character is La Goule, supernatural antagonist to Ruthwen, and lover of the romantic hero Gilbert, for whom she sacrifices her immortal life. It is mentioned that she eats nothing but a few grains of rice a day, a detail taken, as A. Owen Aldridge points out, from the "Histoire de Sidi Nouman" in *Les Mille et une nuits...traduit par Galland* (1839), which identifies the strange woman as a ghoul, or female vampire. Sidi Nouman was "a beautiful bride who eats nothing but rice, which she nibbles grain by grain, and eventually is perceived in the cemetery devouring a corpse which had been buried the same day" (319). Also of interest is the comedy part of Lazare, of the line of Figaro and Leporello, half Spanish *gracioso*, half comic helper out of English melodrama. Montague Summers comments, "Lazare is a capital character, but the intrusion from Oriental legend of the ghoul cannot be considered happy. On the other hand, the appearance of Mélusine...is certainly effective" (*Kith* 299).

This is a much more elaborate work than those which preceded it, with its five acts, ten tableaux, episodes set in Spain, Brittany, and Circassia, and its three heroines, two of whom become victims of the vampire. The plot would be adapted a number of times in the next thirty years in England: twice by Boucicault, and once by Augustus Harris. Elements of it—the tapestry scene in particular—surfaced in Gilbert and Sullivan's *Ruddygore*.

Dumas reveals a remarkable instinct for vivid visual images. In the revival by moonlight, which takes place on a jagged cliff,

Ruthwen unfurls enormous wings and flies off into the night sky. Later he emerges from the depths of the sea. In the last scene, stunningly set in a snow-covered cemetery lit by a full red moon, he is sealed forever in a marble tomb.

The Dumas *Vampire* adds a new element to the vampire's nature: the revenge motif. Ruthwen's prey is the three women, but he seems to be using them as a way to get at Gilbert, whom he pursues for three years, and is only defeated in his third assault. This element of psychic vampirism is present in the Polidori short story, but obscured in the melodramas which were derived from it. Because of the necessity imposed by poetic justice, the previous stage Ruthvens never carry out their murders. Dumas's vision is much darker—this vampire succeeds and keeps coming back. He wants all of Gilbert's women, predating the image of Dracula as the "primal hoarder," Freud's hypothesis of the father who must be killed to release the tribe's women to the younger men.

Maquet sued Dumas, claiming co-authorship of this play and others. Dumas, desperate for money to pay his debts, claimed sole credit for the piece. Most critics ever since have argued the opposite and attributed the play to Maquet. *Le Vampire* has largely been forgotten, never translated into English (except as plagiarized by Augustus Harris), and never given a separate printing beyond Michel Lévy's edition of the complete works (1863). Frank Rahill praises its theatricality: "In *Le Vampire*, reworked from Nodier's play in the fifties, a veritable supernatural carnival is introduced. Dumas managed to bring it all off; he was, in that hackneyed but indispensable phrase, a born dramatist. Nearly everything he wrote for the stage is alive with dynamic action and nervous with expertly contrived suspense" (76). Summers compares it unfavorably with Nodier:

This drama of Dumas is infinitely more elaborate than the play of Nodier, but I am not altogether certain whether it is in some respects so good a work. The first two acts attain a high level; the scene in the tapestry chamber would be most picturesque upon the stage; there are several other telling situations and effective speeches, but as a whole it is too prolix, and we feel that the episode of Antonia in particular is an anticlimax. Nor...can one consider the figure of the ghoul entirely in keeping with the rest. Had the level of the opening scenes been maintained we should possess an excellent piece of work. But without concentration and compression that was hardly possible, and here we have the secret of Nodier's success.... It will be remarked that in his treatment of the vampire tradition Dumas has adapted the legend that the vampire must year by year rejuvenate his waning forces by absorbing the life of another and sucking from another's veins fresh blood, a detail which although it may recommend itself to, and legitimately be used by, the dramatist and the writer of romances, is actually inexact and but rarely to be met with, and only then in folk-lore not of the first value. (*Kith* 302, 299)

*Le Vampire* was Dumas's last play before leaving Paris in 1852, when the Dictatorship was terminated and Louis-Napoleon was crowned Napoleon III, commencing the era of the Second Empire. Gorman writes, "Gathering what cash he could for immediate expenses and taking with him a tiny negro lad [Alexis] that 'the little Dorval' had once brought to him for a page, he boarded the train for Brussels. Behind him was wreckage" (356). According to Marvin Carlson this was an artistic exile as well as a political one:

The evolving political situation doubtless had its effect on the last days of romanticism. Hugo and Dumas had received a certain support from the old regime. Deprived of that, and frightened by Louis-Napoleon's dictatorial ambitions, both felt obliged to leave France.... The new President dissolved the Assembly and ordered the arrest of prominent political opponents..... The defeat of the later experiments by Hugo and Dumas, and the success of such minor rivals as Ponsard showed clearly that the impetus of the romantic movement had died well before the Revolution of 1848 gave the politics, and the culture, of the nation a new direction. (*French Stage* 115)

Although critics usually define the period of French Romanticism as bounded by the success of Hugo's *Hernani* (1830) and the failure of his *Les Burgraves* (1843), one could also argue that the French "Romantic melodrama" came in with Nodier's *Vampire* (1820), and went out with Dumas's *Vampire* (1851). "Romantic melodrama" is a mongrel phrase, but Dumas and Nodier certainly qualify as Romantic writers, and both wrote melodrama.

The only vampire play to follow Dumas on the Paris stage in the next few years was also presented at the Ambigu-Comique, a minor offering by Albert Masquelier,[8] *Le Vampire de la Rue Charlot*, a one-act vaudeville, on 18 March 1855. In London the story was very different. Six months after the Paris production, an adaptation of the Dumas *Vampire* by Dion Boucicault was produced at the Princess Theatre in June 1852.

In England the vampire had metamorphosed into a figure of popular mythology. In the 1840s the penny-dreadful serial, *Varney the Vampire, or the Feast of Blood,*[9] by James Malcolm Rymer (or possibly Thomas Preskett Prest, author of *Sweeney Todd, the Demon Barber of Fleet Street*[10]), was one of the first mass-market serial shockers. *Varney* is an epic of 868 pages crammed with carnage, sex, violence, and "godalmighty muckamuck." Jan Perkowski, in *The Darkling: A Treatise on Slavic Vampirism*, comments on the appeal of the vampire theme to its new and broader audience:

Rife with gothic melodrama, the romantic vampire theme appealed not only to the educated few, but achieved instant popularity among the broad masses. As in France, imitations were soon to follow, and before long there was another genre crossover to the penny dreadful, a popular prose genre in novel format composed of serial chapters packed with action and melodrama, which would be published weekly. This genre is doubtless a result of England's industrial revolution, which provided fast and inexpensive printing techniques coupled with a ready market of large urban concentrations of semi-literate workers. Thus the penny-dreadful— a penny was the cost of a weekly installment and dreadful because of the subject matter—became England's proletarian fiction genre. (128-29)

A Scottish civil engineer, Rymer was a skilled producer of pulp literature. Some titles give a flavor of his typical subject matter: *Ada, the Betrayed; Owlet, the Robber Prince, or, the Unknown Highwayman; A Smuggler Cutter, or, the Cavern in the Cliff;* and *The Raft and the Spray. Varney the Vampyre* was first issued in 1847 by Edwin Lloyd's of Shoreditch, and reissued in penny parts in 1853.[11]

Although almost all modern writers on vampire lore dismiss *Varney* as ludicrously bad, they regard it with a sneaking affection. David Skal writes, "A transfusion of energy...which even today retains an odd, campy fascination. A far cry from literature...almost the definition of hack writing" (*Hollywood Gothic* 16), and Leonard Wolf comments, "*Varney* is Grand Guignol writing at its childlike best" (*Dream* 169).

Writers who are paid by the page for their work do not regard a coherent plot as a prime necessity, but require instead galloping pace, thrills, suspense, plenty of gore and great gobs of female flesh, and prurient, if not quite pornographic, bedroom scenes. The preface includes a brief disclaimer—are there vampires? Yes and no:

A belief in the existence of vampires first took its rise in Norway and Sweden, from whence it rapidly spread to more southern regions, taking a firm hold of the imaginations of the more credulous portion of mankind. The following romance is collected from seemingly the most authentic sources, and the Author must leave the question of credibility entirely to his readers. (qtd. in Senf 42)[12]

Depending on what chapter one is reading, Varney has survived from the days of Henry IV, or the Interregnum, and become a vampire either by suicide or by killing his wife and son, for which he was hanged during the Restoration, the first of his many deaths. The story transpires in rural England, but occasionally moves to London, Bath, and Europe. Sometimes Varney is tall, handsome, and sexually compelling, but in the opening chapter, he is a monster:

It [the face] is perfectly white—perfectly bloodless. The eyes look like polished tin; the lips are drawn back, and the principal feature next to those dreadful eyes is the teeth—the fearful looking teeth—projecting like those of some wild animal, hideously, glaringly white, and fang-like. It approaches the bed with a strange gliding movement. It clashes together the long nails that literally appear to hang from the finger ends.... But her eyes are fascinated. The glance of a serpent could not have produced a greater effect upon her than did the fixed gaze of those awful metallic-looking eyes that were bent on her face.... She drew her breath short and thick. Her bosom heaves, and her limbs tremble, yet she cannot withdraw her eyes from the marble-looking face. He holds her with his glittering eye [cf. Coleridge, *The Rime of the Ancient Mariner*].... With a sudden rush that could not be foreseen—with a strange howling cry that was enough to awaken terror in every breast, the figure seized the long tresses of her hair, and twining them round his bony hands he held her to the bed.... The glassy, horrible eyes of the figure ran over that angelic form with hideous satisfaction—horrible profanation. He drags her head to the bed's edge. He forces it back by the long hair still entwined in his grasp. With a plunge he seizes her neck in his fang-like teeth—a gush of blood, and a hideous sucking noise follows. *The girl has swooned, and the vampyre is at his hideous repast!* (42-44)

The woman in the opening chapter is Flora Bannerworth, who survives and becomes sexually attracted to Varney, and, like Stoker's Lucy, becomes a sleepwalker. Like Varney, Stoker's Dracula becomes younger and more attractive in the course of the novel.

Perkowski feels that *Varney* is not really a novel at all, but a string of picaresque adventures loosely connected through the figure of Varney, whose characteristics are themselves unstable. Varney is several centuries old, and lives on the blood of virgins and near relatives. He does not eat or drink, can starve for lack of blood, but the sea and earth will not receive him. He sleeps in his grave, but not always. He is humanly vulnerable, and, like Ruthven, revives by moonlight. (Rymer gives a minor character who appears in Venice the name Count Polidori.) Also borrowed from Ruthven are the cold grey eye, white face, supernatural strength, and power of seduction. Varney is the first vampire to wear a black cape. All but one of his female victims survive, and she (Clara) becomes a vampire. After her resurrection she is discovered, staked by an angry mob, and buried at a crossroad. Perkowski states:

The dominant theme is erotic. Varney's attacks are like rape. After an attack his victim is sullied, develops a horror of men, and cannot then marry…. Unlike Ruthven (the ruthless) Varney gains the sympathy of the reader, in that he is presented as an earthbound Dantéesque figure condemned to the torment of committing repulsive acts for crimes committed before his first "death." Apparently redemption is possible, but he does not achieve it. (130)

In a more careful reading of *Varney* than most other critics', Carol Senf in *The Vampire in Nineteenth Century Literature* points out that the source of much of the evil in the novel is money. The greed and selfishness of some of the human characters are actually shocking to Varney. Senf adds that the author makes numerous connections between vampirism and economic parasitism:

Moreover, by stressing the cruelty of human beings, the author makes Varney appear even less cruel. For example, after the mob's destruction of Clara, Varney alone mourns: "I thought that I had steeled my heart against all gentle impulses: that I had crushed—aye, completely crushed dove-eyed pity in my heart, but it is not so, and still sufficient of my once human feelings clings to me to make me grieve for thee, Clara Crofton, thou victim" (Ch. CCVII). Although Varney eventually becomes disgusted with his bloodthirsty deeds, the human characters seemingly never tire of their cruelty, either to Varney or each other. The following passage…[is] a profound recognition that the vampire is a projection of humanity's cruelty: "…and as often was the miserable man [Varney] hunted from his place of refuge only to seek another, from which he was in like manner hunted by those who thirsted for his blood" (Ch. LXXXVII). The writer does not go on to develop this connection to any extent, but the metaphoric connection between the vampire's behavior and reprehensible human behavior will be made frequently by realistic novelists and social writers later in the century. (46-47)

Filled with self-loathing and disgust, Varney wishes to die, which in his case is not easily accomplished. After surviving literally dozens of deaths in 220 chapters, he finally succeeds in incinerating himself:

You will make what haste you can, from the mountain, inasmuch as it is covered with sulphurous vapours, inimical to human life, and when you reach the city...you will say that you accompanied Varney the Vampyre to the crater of Mount Vesuvius, and that, tired and disgusted with a life of horror, he flung himself in to prevent the possibility of a reanimation of his remains. (CCXX)[13]

Senf writes that the public discussion of vampires in mid-19th-century England centered on rational, scientific explanations of phenomena associated with vampires—diseases which could account for the symptoms (both of vampires and victims), and aberrant mental diseases (23). In 1847 *Blackwoods* magazine printed an article attributing the belief in vampires to premature burial, and in 1855 an article in *Household Words* agreed with that argument. One sure sign that vampires had seized the public imagination was that men of science felt obliged to explain them away.

With his skill in predicting the tides of popular taste, Dion Boucicault (1820-90), in his capacity as literary advisor to Charles Kean, decided that a vampire play would be a splendid vehicle for that actor, and having seen the Dumas *Vampire* in Paris in 1851, set about tailoring the piece to suit.

Charles Kean (1811-68) was instrumental in bringing the fashionable audience back into the theatre, and, as lessee of the Princess Theatre, had the particular patronage of Queen Victoria, who in 1848 appointed Kean to the newly revived office of Master of the Revels. Kean was the son of Edmund Kean; was married to his leading lady, Ellen Tree; and had toured America a number of times in a repertory of Shakespeare. He also had a beautiful young Scottish ward, Agnes Robertson, with whom Boucicault fell in love (and possibly married) during the production of *The Vampire*. (See Appendix C.)

The Princess was a fairly new theatre, the last to open before the passage of the Theatre Regulation Act of 1843. It was noteworthy as a showcase for American actors: Edwin Forrest, Charlotte Cushman, Anna Cora Mowatt, and E.L. Davenport all performed there. As manager of the Princess, Kean set about perfecting the school of pictorial realism in scene design begun by Planché. This was a theatre of massive spectacle. David Krause, in *The Dolmen Boucicault*, lists some of the technical aspects of Kean's theatrical style:

The diorama, in anticipation of the revolving stage, an apparatus that propelled a series of panoramic scenes across the stage; sliding traps in the floor for mobile ghosts, and overhead wires for hovering or flying figures; limelight illuminations, projected by heating lime in an oxyhydrogen flame; overhead lights with coloured glass; water scenes constructed in huge tanks with moving ships and waterfalls; sheets of gauze for simulated water scenes, and gauze curtains for supernatural scenes; off-stage treadmills for wind and storm effects, and sheets of zinc for thunder; lavishly constructed historical sets in period street scenes, and interior scenes with accurately reproduced furniture and trappings. These devices, especially for historical plays, became such a passion with Charles Kean that he printed extra "fly-leaves" as part of his play-bills in which he explained, with antiquarian detail, all the sources and authorities for his "authentic" constructions. (23)

The plays which Boucicault wrote for Kean at the Princess, calculated to take full advantage of all these technical resources, included *The Vampire* (1851), *Pauline* (1851), *The Corsican Brothers* (1852), *Genevieve; or, The Reign of Terror* (1853, *Chevalier de la Maison-Rouge*), all adaptations of Dumas; and *Faust and Margaret* (1854, adaptation of Michel Carré's version), and *Louis VI, King of France* (1855, Casimir de la Vigne).[14]

As mentioned previously, *The Vampire* was written as a vehicle for Kean and intended as an afterpiece for his benefit night. Since Kean was already performing in *Trial of Love* on the same bill, he refused the role (perhaps also thinking it beneath him), so Boucicault took the part himself, appearing under his own name for the first time in London. Biographer Richard Fawkes analyzes the motivations:

As Kean had anticipated, the announcement that Boucicault was to appear in his own play provoked widespread interest. Boucicault was a well known figure, a colourful character who featured in the gossip columns.... The public, with encouragement from the press, couldn't wait to see him onstage. For Boucicault, the venture was more than a calculated move to increase the box-office take for the Keans' benefit night.... He had had to accept a flat fee [for writing the play], and a three-act after-piece would not add much to his account; as an actor, however, he would be able to more than double his earnings. (74)

It is possible that this play was never published. The only text of the Boucicault *Vampire* that I could locate was a manuscript prompt book in the Billy Rose Collection of the Lincoln Center Library for the Performing Arts. The title page states, "Copied for James Wallack, Esq., New York, by T.H. Edmonds, prompter, Royal Princess Theatre, London, 1852." The 87-page handwritten manuscript contains blocking, set diagrams, sound and music cues, flat cues, and lists of properties. It lists the average running time as one hour and 45 minutes.

*The Vampire, A Phantasm in Three Dramas*, is a loose adaptation of Dumas, transported to Wales. Boucicault incorporates only the first two acts of the French play, enclosing them in a time-travel frame in which each of the three acts takes place 100 years apart, and a new group of characters, descendants of the previous group, do battle with the immortal vampire, Sir Alan Raby (a.k.a. Gervase Rookwood). The device possibly is drawn from Maturin's *Melmoth the Wanderer* (1820) which also traces the career of an accursed Byronic hero whose bargain with Satan gives him eternal life. Other more remote models might be the Flying Dutchman, Faust, and the Wandering Jew. The Third Drama (Act Three), which takes place on 15 August 1860, would have been eight years in the future when the play was first produced. The play incorporates many elements of *Varney* as well, particularly the vampire's interest in real estate, and his flowing cape.

In place of the tapestry scene in Dumas (and in my opinion an improvement on it), in a dream sequence the portraits of the heroine's ancestors (previous victims of the vampire) come to life and step down out of their frames to warn her of her danger:

ALICE: What have I done, there is some dread emotion twined around my heart and chokes its throb. Can this be love, no—no—it is a frenzied fascination. What did I vow, not my love—no—my gratitude, yet is it gratitude that makes me tremble thus? (turning to portraits) Oh, you ancestors of my race, why do your eyes seek me with that mournful gaze—why have you no tongues to tell me—what is this spell that overpowers me thus—and leaves me—senseless—thus—ah...

(Music. Lucy glides out of her frame.)

LUCY: The weary time has fled, and year succeeding year
A hundred have been told, the appointed hour is near.
Too well the curse of Raby marks this fatal day,
The Phantom has returned to seek another prey.
A virgin of his race, who if she yield her heart
Will with her ebbing life, another life impart.
Another hundred years he will achieve, and doom
Our lives that live in him, unto a living tomb.
Obstructed, uncovert, in earth we must remain,
While mortal lives like ours the Phantom's life sustain.
(Glides back to the portrait)
Speed, moments, speed, oh, haste the tardy midnight's chime,
That we may sleep in peace until the end of time. (II, i, 50)

Apparently Boucicault played the Welsh vampire with a broad Irish accent. Several writers comment on this: "Oddly enough Boucicault's brogue, which always came out strong except in dialect parts, did not seem anachronistic. Vampires, forsooth, may be classed as cosmopolites, not being indigenous to any particular clime. The play, an altogether weird and dreadful thing, was announced on the bills as 'a spectral drama in three dreams'" (Walsh 45-46).

*The Vampire* was one of Boucicault's few critical failures, although he received good notices for his acting: "He looked the vampire to perfection, and spoke and acted it exceedingly well. His deathly hue and rigid cast of countenance, his high and bald forehead and spare figure, his measured accents and grave demeanor, were all in keeping, and his 'make-up' in each act quite a study" (*Era*, qtd. in Fawkes 74). Even Queen Victoria was amused: "Mr. Boucicault, who is very handsome and has a fine voice, acted very impressively. I can never forget his livid face and fixed look, in the first two Dramas. It quite haunts me." She commissioned a watercolor of him in the role, and returned a week later to see another performance, at which she recanted her first opinion. "It does not bear seeing a second time, and is, in fact, very trashy" (qtd. in Fawkes 74). Mr. Kean's secretary is reported to have called it "a mistake about which the less said the better." Henry Morley's review was very negative, with snippets of Shakespeare to lend it a magisterial tone:

If there be truth in the old adage, that "when things are at the worst they must mend," the bettering of Spectral Melodrama is not distant; for it has reached the extreme point of inanity in the new piece which was produced on Monday at the Princess's Theatre.... Its plot is chiefly copied from a piece which some years ago turned the Lyceum into a Chamber of Horrors; but it has been spun out into three parts...the little period of a century has been interposed between each part, and, in order that the outrage on the possible shall be complete, the third part is projected forward into the year that will be 1860! By this ingenious arrangement, the resuscitation of the original *Vampire* has been enabled to supply the lovers of the revolting...with three acts of murder...but, as the delicate process of vampirical killing is exactly after the same pattern in each case, the horror is quite worn out before the career of the creature terminates. Nothing but tedious trash remains.

To an "honest ghost" one has no objection; but an animated corpse which goes about in Christian attire, and although never known to eat, or drink, or shake hands, is allowed to sit at good men's feasts; which renews its odious life every hundred years by sucking a young lady's blood, after fascinating her by motions which resemble mesmerism burlesqued...such a ghost as this passes all bounds of toleration.

The monster of absurdity was personated by its reviver, Mr. Boucicault, with due paleness of visage, stealthiness of pace, and solemnity of tone; the scenery, especially a moonlit ridge amidst the heights of Snowdon, was beautiful, and the costumes were prettily diversified; but the dreary repetition of fantastical horror almost exhausted even the patience which a benefit enjoins. Unfortunately, the mischief of such a piece, produced at a respectable theatre, does not end with the weariness of the spectators, who come to shudder and remain to yawn; for it is not only "beside the purpose of playing," but directly contravenes it; and though it may be too dull to pervert the tastes of those who witness its vapid extravagances, it has power to bring discredit on the most genial of arts.[15]

The 19-year-old Agnes Robertson also received bad reviews as Alice Peveryl: "Not exactly suited to her character...convulsive and spasmodic, and unintelligible in her efforts to be forceful" (*Era*, qtd. in Fawkes 75). Boucicault was able to make this up to her by writing a specially tailored vehicle, *The Prima-Donna*, which opened in September 1852 at the Princess, and was very successful.

A disagreement arose between Kean and Boucicault. "Kayne— I mayne Kean—was about to throw me over," as he wrote to John Coleman (qtd. in Fawkes 35), and in 1853 Boucicault and Robertson sailed for New York, where they remained until 1860. There he began a campaign, as mentor and manager, to promote her career, writing such vehicles for her as *The Fairy Star, The Young Actress, Agnes Robertson at Home, The Cat Changed into a Woman, Rachel is Coming, The Octoroon,* and *The Phantom.* They acted for the two top New York managements, Lester Wallack and Laura Keene, and toured Boston, Montreal, Chicago, St. Louis, and New Orleans.

Robertson, known in America as "the fairy star," was exceptionally beautiful, could sing and dance, excelled at breeches roles, and was at her best in light comedy. *The Phantom,* calling for a heavier style, was probably in the repertory for ballast and was published under the heading "Boucicault's Dramatic Works, forming the Repertoire of Agnes Robertson" (New York: Samuel French, 1857).

Summers, Aldridge, Hogan, and all other critics whose works were consulted for this study, mention Boucicault's *Vampire* only in passing, stating that *The Phantom* is a shortened version of it, and proceed to analyze the latter play. But in fact Boucicault made considerable alterations, and retained less than ten percent of the dialogue from the earlier play. The fact that *The Vampire* exists only in manuscript form has perpetuated these erroneous conclusions.

In his first American period (there was a second hegira from 1870 until his death in 1890), Boucicault began to move away from costume drama and toward realism. The major changes from *The Vampire* to *The Phantom* were, first, simplification—jettisoning the technically demanding portrait scene and the cemetery with its rising tombs, and eliminating many of the small roles; second, an increase in the proportion of comedy, particularly ethnic humor; and third, an entirely new set of characters in the last act and a different ending. Unhappy losses in the shortened version include the evolving line of Welshmen, Rhys, Rys, and Rees; the elaborate time scheme; and the entire second act. (*The Phantom*'s time references are very muddled in the 1857 Samuel French edition, with conflicting lines setting the second act in 1704, 1755, and 1857.)

Robertson is also given a dual role in this version, playing Lucy and Ada (her original role of Alice is cut), while Boucicault continued to play the Phantom and Alan Raby (actually one role).

*The Phantom,* first presented in Philadelphia in 1856, opened in New York at Wallack's Lyceum in 1857, and played at Niblo's Garden in 1858. Wallack's had opened in 1852 on the ruins of Brougham's Lyceum, and was advertised by the management as

"One of the Most Beautiful and Commodious Theatres in the World." In *Annals of the New York Stage*, George Odell wrote:

Decidedly one of the most important events in the history of the New York stage was the establishment of Wallack's Theatre.... There was nothing haphazard about the productions of this house throughout its best years; care for minutest details distinguished the management, a finish of acting glorified every play, and the best the English dramatists had done was presented on that stage, night after night, for years. Nothing like Wallack's Theatre, I am convinced, had existed in New York previously to 1852; nothing quite like it existed after 1880. (6: 213)

The fact that Boucicault showcased *The Phantom* at this prestigious theatre suggests that he thought it was one of his outstanding productions.

As the play toured America, Boucicault experimented with a number of versions of the play, at one point reverting to the Scottish identity of previous Ruthvens: Alan Raby became Sir Alan Ruthven, Lord of Lochiel, and the play was set in the Scottish highlands, at the ruins of Ravensleigh, and "the Wolf's Craig [sic]," with a spectacular storm and burial scene on the peak of Ben Nevis. In this version there is a 200-year interval between the acts. Boucicault brought the Scottish version to London on 28 August 1861 at the Theatre Royal, New Adelphi, where Planché's *Giovanni the Vampire* had played in 1823. It played the following year at Drury Lane on a double bill with *The Octoroon*. A critic wrote: "A new version of the old drama of the Vampire, called the Phantom, in which the author enacted an Irish ghost, who could only be brought back to corporeal existence by being laid in 'the moonbames,' afterward supplemented the Octoroon, but with only doubtful success" (qtd. in Baker 433).

Another American production of Boucicault's Welsh version of *The Phantom*, probably pirated since he is not credited on the play bill, was given in 1862 at Liberty Hall,[16] under the name, "The Grand Legendary Drama, *Vampire! or, The Spectre of Mount Snowden!* [sic]," starring Harry Langdon as the Vampire and Alan Raby, and Annie Senter as Lucy and Ada, under the management of J.C. Myers. The bill, for the opening night of 29 May 1862, carried the following legend:

This strange monster is well authenticated—chiefly known in Germany. It is said that if a dead person be exposed to the first rays of the rising moon which touch the earth, a false life is installed [instilled] into the corpse, which possesses movement and all signs of ordinary existence, except that there is no pulsation in the heart. This creature, living against the will of Heaven, eats not, drinks not, nor does he require the refreshment of sleep. This Phantom recruits his life by drawing the life blood from the veins of the living, but more especially it chooses victims from amongst maidens pure and spotless. As the body of this monster is bloodless, so his face is said to be as pale as death. The Vampire can be destroyed by fire or by bullet, which must pierce his heart.[17]

That this background information was provided in the production's advertising suggests that vampire lore was strange and new to Americans, or it may simply have been part of the promotional hype.

The question arises, how familiar were Americans of this period with the legend of the vampire? Normally we tend to associate the Puritans of New England with witch-killing, but a recent article in *The New York Times* (31 October 1993) makes the surprising claim that they also unearthed corpses and performed vampire-killing rituals. Quoting Dr. Paul S. Sledzik, curator of the anatomical collection of the National Museum of Health and Medicine in Washington, D.C., the article states:

Bodies from 18th and 19th-century New England graves appear to have been dug up within a few months or years of death and then mutilated.... Dr. Sledzik said his research shows such beliefs were common...as late as 1892, particularly among families that were often struck with tuberculosis.... "When someone died of consumption, it was believed they could come back from the dead and drain the life of their living relatives.... In order to stop this, family members would go into the grave and somehow attempt to kill the person again.... In the American tradition, just causing some disruption to the body was the way to kill a vampire." The stake-through-the-heart approach, he said, was a European tradition not practiced by Americans. (A: 36)

This is particularly interesting because Agnes Robertson's role of Ada is a consumptive only in the American version.

Modern critical commentary on *The Phantom* is very sparse (and for *The Vampire* appears to be nonexistent). Robert Goode Hogan calls the play "a delightful bit of spooky *Kitsch*...which counterpoints a good deal of effective theatrical humor in the low characters against the pasteboard horrors of the main plot" (69). Summers comments:

*The Phantom* is, of course, somewhat old-fashioned and a little stilted, as was the mode, in its diction. No doubt some of the situations could be revised and far more neatly turned, yet on the whole I conceive that it should prove of its kind excellent fare in the theatre, and some scenes, at least, in capable hands were not without emotional appeal, I had almost said a certain impressiveness.... I notice that Boucicault has in certain scenes borrowed his situations pretty freely from *Le Vampire* of Dumas, and occasionally he has even conveyed actual dialogue from the French play. (*Kith* 318, 315)

Boucicault's own assessment is more scathing: "I can spin out these rough-and-tumble dramas as a hen lays eggs. It's a degrading occupation, but more money has been made out of guano than out of poetry" (qtd. in *The Oxford Companion to American Theatre* 97).

Another version of Dumas's *Vampire* was given in London in 1859 at the Grecian Theatre, an adaptation by Augustus Glossop Harris entitled *Ruthven*, "a drama in four acts." Harris was the father of the Augustus Harris (1851-95) who in the 1880s became an impresario of burlesque-extravaganzas at Drury Lane.

The Grecian Theatre, in Shepherdess Walk, Hoxton, previously the Royal Eagle Saloon, was opened by Thomas "Brayvo" Rouse in 1832 as a variety theatre. Several important mid-century actors and singers got their start at the Grecian. In 1851 it came under the management of Benjamin Conquest, and became known for ballets and Christmas shows. Presumably the younger Augustus Harris learned his trade here. Conquest rebuilt the Grecian in 1876, and in 1879 sold it to the Salvation Army (*Revels* VI: liv).

Harris's *Ruthven* is really a line-for-line translation of Dumas, changing a few locations and employing a few minor cuts and simplifications, and a slightly different ending. Like Moncrieff, he adds soliloquies to clarify the action and telegraph a character's intentions for the simpler audience members. Harris's Gilbert kills Ruthven with a pistol instead of a sword; Mélusine is omitted, so Gilbert deduces who Ruthven is from hints dropped by the "Ghoule;" the last act is moved from the Black Sea to the Bay of Naples. One original bit of business, which, ironically, would be retained in vampire plays and films ever after, is that Gilbert gives Helene a wedding present of "an amulet in the form of a cross." Ziska retrieves it from her dead body; it is then given to Antonia as protection, and serves to repel the vampire.

A. Owen Aldridge is quite censorious of Harris's very blatant plagiarism in an age of plagiarism:

Even though greater tolerance has traditionally been extended to dramatists than to poets and novelists in the matter of borrowing from other writers, Harris's drama is so close to the original that it cannot possibly be explained euphemistically as an adaptation. In a sense, Harris was paying a great compliment to Dumas by appropriating the work wholesale, but at the same time he was perpetrating a fraud on his audiences by his arrant plagiarism. (324)

However, Harris's primary skill and interest was not in creative writing but in producing plays and making money. His originality lay in the way he staged the piece and how he advertised it. Some excerpts from the play bill give an idea of his skills as an entrepreneur:

A new Powerful Legendary Drama, from the Pen of A. Harris, Esq., produced on a Scale of Unparalleled Splendour...RUTHVEN!!.... Part 3rd.—Bridal Chamber of Helene. Love—the Faithful Servant—revelations—TOO LATE—the DEATH KISS—Arrival of Gilbert—the FALL from the TURRET. THE TURRET MOAT—Discovery of the Body.... The Chapel!! ABDUCTION OF ANTONIA—the VAMPIRE'S REVENGE—Midnight—the CHARMED AMULET. DEATH OF RUTHVEN. THE ASCENSION OF THE GHOULE! THE LIME LIGHT BY MR. MORGAN.

The four plays examined in this chapter—by Dumas, the two by Boucicault, and by Harris—are all variations on the same story. The best version is Boucicault's *Vampire*. Taking the best parts of Dumas's *drame-fantastique*, omitting the fairies and ghouls but adding fantastic elements of his own, such as the three-layered parallel structure, and the 300-year battle against an ageless enemy, Boucicault's is unlike any vampire play before or after it. By this device, Boucicault is able to make something truly theatrical out of the vampire's immortality. His identical entrances in Acts One and Two, 100 years apart, must have been quite an eerie *coup de théâtre*. The three-century structure also allows the excellent device of the unfolding evolution of the primitive peasant Watkyn Rhys, through Watly Rys, into Walter Rees, an educated and formidable opponent for the vampire.

Although other playwrights make mention of Ruthven's hypnotic effect on women, Boucicault is the first writer with sufficient skill in dialogue to create a believable scene for a woman attempting to struggle out of a state of trance. Lucy, Alice, and Ada are certainly prototypes for Stoker's Lucy and Mina, and for George du Maurier's *Trilby*.

The ideas involved in the staging were impressive: the use of scrim in the dream sequence to show the room as it looked 100 years before in its ruined state, with the picture frames coming down and the portraits coming to life, reveals the sure hand of a master. Another fine touch is the clock tower, a presence throughout the drama embodying the theme of the passing of time, and becoming pivotal when Rees sets the hands back an hour, as time, an ally of the vampire, is turned against him at the play's climax.

Boucicault's *Vampire* and *Phantom* are quite different, and *The Phantom* is in many ways inferior, and certainly less ambitious. The increased proportion of comedy was probably to please the taste of American audiences, but unlike George Blink (*The Vampire Bride*, 1834), for example, Boucicault could write genuinely funny lines without disrupting the atmosphere of the main plot. George Rowell does not mention either play specifically, but compares Boucicault favorably with the authors of two earlier vampire plays:

In short, the sensation scenes of Boucicault's plays are not merely more ingenious than those of a Moncrieff or Fitzball. They are expertly woven into the fabric of the play, so that they emerge as the pivot of the story, not its *raison d'être*; nor is the novelty of the sensation scene made the excuse for a total lack of character, plausibility, or intelligence. Boucicault was above all things thorough. (57)

Because *The Phantom* is in most respects a different play from *The Vampire*, it may be said to be the first American vampire play, since it premiered in Philadelphia in 1856 and toured extensively in America before coming to London.[18] However, productions of Planché's *Vampire* were presented in America in the 1820s (see Chapter 3). David Skal's statement in *Hollywood Gothic*, "The Phantom had the distinction of being the first vampire play exported from England to America" (16), is erroneous in every respect.

In terms of the development of the vampire figure, the plays of the 1850s add an elaborate plot structure which displays the repetitive and compulsive nature of the vampire's killings. In Dumas's Gilbert, we have an echo of the psychic vampirism between Ruthven and Aubrey in Polidori. Thanks to Varney,

Ruthven/Raby becomes more suave. Varney—in some chapters—has a social conscience and a sense of remorse like Planché's Ruthven, but this aspect is not developed. In structure and atmosphere, *Varney* contributes much more to *Dracula*.

These vampires reflect the changed social and sexual attitudes of the 1850s: they are much more formidable, frightening opponents, figures of nemesis with great powers: Dumas's Ruthwen is equipped with wings and the ability to fly and to survive under water, pursuing Gilbert across Spain and France to Asia Minor. Boucicault's Raby haunts a family through many generations, a threat from out of the past which hounds the Peveryls like inexorable fate. He wants their land as well as their souls and bodies, thus fusing the vampire with the dreaded bloodsucking villain of many American melodramas, the landlord.

They are no longer seeking marriage: the attacks are sudden and violent (but still offstage), and some of the women are killed. They are not acquiescent victims; Juana, Hélène, Lucy, and Alice fight for their lives. An interesting detail in *The Phantom* is that the vampire prefers a nubile female, but in an emergency is willing to make do with a male.

The vampires are beginning to acquire the paraphernalia and habits with which they are associated today in pop culture—the cape (Rymer), the aversion to the cross (Harris), the nocturnal existence—most vampire appearances in these plays occur at night. Thus, these are theatrical, not folkloric, characteristics.

Boucicault was the first and only person to write, direct, and perform his own version of the vampire—and he liked the role so well he did it twice. In the Dumas model Gilbert, structurally at least, is the protagonist and romantic hero, but Boucicault cuts back the Gilbert character to a secondary role appearing only in the first act, and places himself as the vampire firmly center stage, providing himself with three leading ladies. The fact that he was in love with Agnes Robertson when he wrote the scenes between Alan Raby and Alice Peveryl, lends the character intensity and seductive charm. The part is wonderfully theatrical, certainly an actor's role.

Boucicault also adds an interesting note of religious mania to the character. As he did with miscegenation in *The Octoroon*, he seems to be making a somewhat veiled attack on organized religion, and the mesmeric power of religious fanatics to control vulnerable minds. It is not clearly indicated whether the vampire is practicing hypnosis on his victims, but he definitely controls their minds, and the influence is shown to be evil. The theatre has shown us evil churchmen—

Tartuffe, Rasputin, Reverend Davidson—but only Boucicault has had the inspiration to make a vampire of a holy priest.

Hogan, while preferring Boucicault's Irish plays and Regency comedies to the sensation plays, praises his craftsmanship and theatricality:

Some of this entertainment was extremely successful in its day, and if *The Phantom* or *Belle Lamar* were revived today they might still have a twitch or two of stage life about them…. These plays may take up an honorable position in the enduring minor drama, along with the plays of Etheridge, Cibber, Aphra Behn, and Colman the Elder. And that is really no ignoble position at all. (111)

Title page, Rymer.

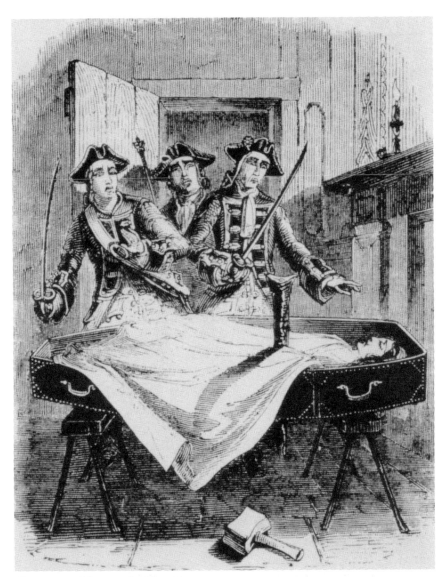

Illustration, *Varney the Vampire*.

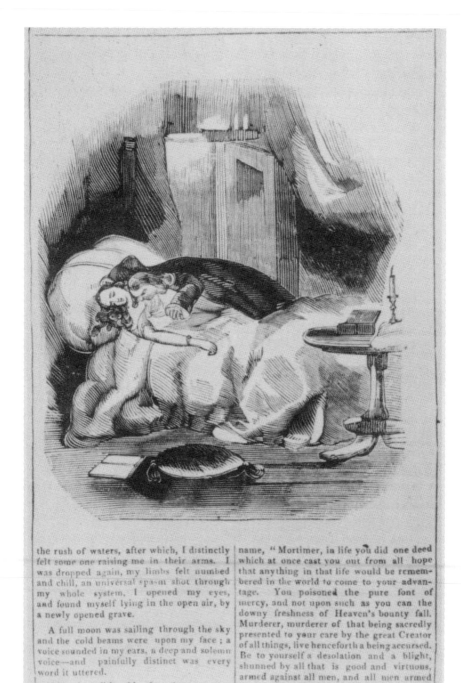

the rush of waters, after which, I distinctly felt some one raising me in their arms. I was dropped again, my limbs felt numbed and chill, an universal spasm shot through my whole system. I opened my eyes, and found myself lying in the open air, by a newly opened grave.

A full moon was sailing through the sky and the cold beams were upon my face; a voice sounded in my ears, a deep and solemn voice—and painfully distinct was every word it uttered.

"Mortimer," it said, for that was my name, "Mortimer, in life you did one deed which at once cast you out from all hope that anything in that life would be remembered in the world to come to your advantage. You poisoned the pure font of mercy, and not upon such as you can the downy freshness of Heaven's bounty fall. Murderer, murderer of that being sacredly presented to your care by the great Creator of all things, live henceforth a being accursed. Be to yourself a desolation and a blight, shunned by all that is good and virtuous, armed against all men, and all men armed against thee, Varney the Vampyre."

Illustration, *Varney the Vampire.*

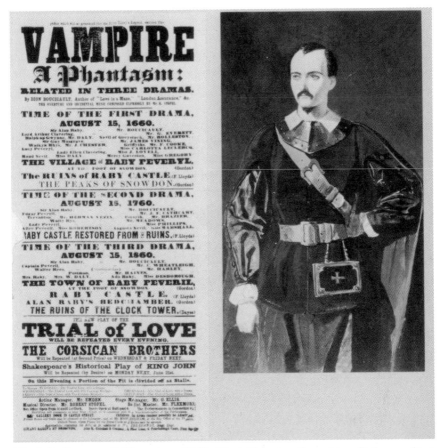

Playbill, Boucicault *Vampire*, 1851. Dion Boucicault as Alan Raby; earliest known portrait (1851), commissioned by Queen Victoria (Victoria and Albert Museum).

Frontispiece, *The Phantom* (Boucicault).

### Boucicault's Dramatic Works,

#### FORMING THE REPERTOIRE OF

## MISS AGNES ROBERTSON.
### No. III.

———————— •••• ————————

# THE PHANTOM:

A DRAMA, IN TWO ACTS.

BY

*Dion Boucicault.*

*Author of " London Assurance," " Old Heads and Young Hearts,"*
*" The Willow Copse," " Used Up," " Love in a Maze," " The*
*Irish Heiress," " Andy Blake," " The Young Actress,"*
*" The Corsican Brothers," " The Phan-*
*tom," &c. &c.*

### NEW-YORK:
#### 1856.

Title page, Boucicault.

# Liberty Hall.

MANAGER, - - - - - - - - J. C. MYERS.
STAGE MANAGER, - - - - - ASA CUSHMAN, Jr.

## SPLENDID ATTRACTION.
### Another Great Drama.

This Evening will be presented the grand Legendary Drama of the

# VAMPIRE!

This strange monster is well authenticated—chiefly known in Germany.  It is said that if a dead person be exposed to the first rays of the rising moon which touch the earth, a false life is installed into the corpse, which possesses movement and all signs of ordinary existence, except that there is no pulsation in the heart.  This creature, living against the will of Heaven, eats not, drinks not, nor does he require the refreshment of sleep.  This Phantom recruits his life by drawing the life blood from the veins of the living, but more especially it chooses victims from amongst maidens pure and spotless.  As the body of this monster is bloodless, so his face is said to be as pale as death.  The Vampire can be bestroyed by fire or by bullet, which must pierce his heart.

| LUCY PEVERYL, ADA RABY, } | MISS ANNIE SENTER. |
|---|---|
| THE VAMPIRE, ALAN RABY, } | MR. HARRY LANGDON, |

## Thursday Evening, May 29th, 1862,

Will be presented for the first time in this city the Legendy Drama in 2 acts entitled the

# VAMPIRE!

### Or, The Spectre of Mount Snowden!

| The Vampire, | - - - - | Mr. Harry Langdon |
|---|---|---|
| LORD ALBERT CLAVERING, | - - - | MR. C. E BIDWELL |
| SIR HUGH NEVILLE, | - - - | MR. W. C RAYMOND |
| SIR GUY MUSGROVE, | - - - | MR. A. CUSHMAN |
| RALPH SWINE, | - - | MR. M. HURLEY |
| DAVY ROEBECK, | - - - | MR. H. F. STONE |
| Lucy Peveryl, | - - - - | Miss Annie Senter |
| MAUDE OF GREYSTOCK, | - - - | MISS MINNIE JACKSON |
| JANET, | - - - | MRS. H. F STONE |

100 years are supposed to have elapsed between the 1st and 2d. acts.

| Alan Raby, | - - - | Mr. Harry Langdon |
|---|---|---|
| COLONEL RABY, | - - - | MR. W. C. RAYMOND |
| EDGAR, (his son,) | - - - | MR. C. E. BIDWELL |
| DR. REESE, | - - - | MR. J. MURRAY |
| CORPORAL STUMP, | - - - | MR. H. F. STONE |
| CURATE, | - - | MR. M. HURLEY |
| Ada Raby, | - - - - | Miss Annie Senter |
| JENNY, | - - - - | MISS ANNIE HYATT |

| Favorite Songs, | Mrs. H. F. Stone. |
|---|---|
| Grand Pas Seul, | Miss Minnie Jackson. |

To conclude with the drama in one act, entitled

# ROBERT MACAIRE!

### Or, The Two Murderers!

| ROBERT MACAIRE, | - - - | MR. HARRY LANGDON. |
|---|---|---|
| Jaques Strop, | - - - Mr. H. F. Stone | Charles, - - - - Mr. M. Hurley |
| Mons. Dumont, | - - - Mr. J. Murray | Francois, - - - - Mr. Merewether |
| Germeuil, | - - Mr. W. C. Raymond | Marie, - - - Miss Annie Hyatt |
| Pierre, | - - - Mr. C. E. Bidwell | Clementina, - - - Mrs. H. F. Stone |

☞Friday Evening, May 30, Benefit of J. C. MYERS, and last night of the season.

## Admission 15 and 25 Cents. : : : Reserved Seats 35 Cents.
### DOORS OPEN AT 7—TO COMMENCE AT 7 3-4 O'CLOCK.

☞ Seats can be procured at the Box Office from 10 to 12 o'clock, and from 2 to 4 ☜

Playbill, Liberty Hall.

Will be Performed a New Powerful Legendary Drama, in Four Parts, from the Pen of A. Harris, Esq., produced on a Scale of Unparalleled Splendour, and entitled

# R U T H V E N ! !

## Part 1st.—COURTYARD of a SPANISH POSADA.

The Wedding—the Unlucky Servant—the Lonely Traveller—Ten Louis for a Guide—More Travellers—a Pic-nic Party—Storming the Posada - the Unknown—the Fearful History of Tormenar—the Expedition—Supper, Supper.

## INTERIOR OF THE CASTLE OF TORMENAR.

The Ghoule's Victim—the Arrival of the Pic-nic at their Destinations—the Preparations for Supper—Fires Lighted—Room well Lit—Ghost Stories over Supper—Sudden and Unexpected Appearance of Ruthven—the Alarm—Supper Finished—a Resting Place for the Night—the Discovery of the Dead Body—Death of Juanna and Ruthven—Ruthven's Last Request.

### THE HEIGHTS OF TORMENAR.

THE MOONBEAMS.    .    .    .    "Thanks, Gilbert, thou hast kept thy Oath."

## Part 2nd.—Gardens of the Chateau de Tiffanges.

A Sister's Love—the Return of Gilbert - the Betrothed—the Recognition and supposed Madness of Gilbert—the Marriage—Interview between the Unknown and Ruthven—the Warning.

RUSTIC FETE    -    .    .    by Mrs.

## Part 3rd.—Bridal Chamber of Helene.

Love—the Faithful Servant—Revelations—Too Late—the Vampire's Bride—the Death Kiss—Arrival of Gilbert—the Fall from the Turret.

## THE TURRET MOAT—Discovery of the Body.

## Part 4th.—An Apartment overlooking the Bay of Naples.

The Unknown and her Rival—Gilbert and his Bride—the Interview and Threat of the Unknown—the Storm—Lazaro out Fishing—the Sacrifice of the Unknown.

## THE CHAPEL !!

Abduction of Antonia - the Vampire's Revenge—Midnight—the Charmed Amulet.

### DEATH OF RUTHVEN.

# THE ASCENSION OF THE GHOULE!

THE LIME LIGHT BY MR. MORGAN.

Advertisement, Augustus Harris's *Ruthven*.

# Chapter 8

# Satire and Misogyny, 1872-88

ALAN: All's over! (falls down flat)
ALL:            Oh!
ALAN:                    Don't feel the slightest pain!
Oh! put me in the limelight! quick I'm dyin',
A poet's life and essence is moonshine!
                    —Robert Reece, *The Vampire*

Boucicault's *Vampire* gives us a portrait gallery of murder victims who come to life to warn their descendant of the danger of a lurking vampire; Gilbert and Sullivan's *Ruddygore* gives us a gallery of vampires who descend from their frames to castigate their reluctant descendant, Ruthven Murgatroyd, to get on with the evil-deed business or face unpleasant consequences. And Robert Reece's *The Vampire* gives us an Irish writer vampire, Alan Raby, who sucks other people's plots rather than their blood. The vampire melodrama was the subject of some excellent satire in the 1870s and 1880s, but why did they wait so long? Boucicault's play was more than 20 years old in 1872 when Reece's play was produced; *Ruddygore* came in 1887, and Richard Henry's *The Vampire's Victim* in 1888. Boucicault himself had left England for America in 1870. Perhaps these playwrights retained vivid childhood memories of being taken by their parents to the 1851 *Vampire* at the Princess or the 1862 *Phantom* at the Adelphi and Drury Lane.

The subject of vampires was still *au courant* in the popular press. An article by Charles Dickens, Jr., appeared in 1871 in *All the Year Round*, one of the most popular Victorian magazines. The piece recaps the evolution of the superstition in some detail, from William of "Newberry" [Newbury] through Tournefort and Calmet to the Sergeant Bertrand case of 1849. The vampire plays of the 1820s are mentioned: "Fifty years ago, vampyre literature had a temporary run of public favour. The Vampyre, or the Bride of the Isles, a drama, and The Vampyre, a melodrama in two acts, were presented at the theatres; the hero being enacted by some performer who had the art of making himself gaunt and ghastly on occasions" (*Dracula Scrapbook* 20). The piece ends on a skeptical note.

The temper of the times in the last quarter of the century in both England and France was becoming more misogynistic, and a diffused version of the vampire theme was being employed to delineate the psychology of the female sexual predator, on the stage by the Symbolists and in art by the pre-Raphaelites. Examples in fiction are D.H. Friston's "The Dark Blue" (1871-72), Sheridan Le Fanu's "Carmilla" (1872), Rudyard Kipling's "The Vampire" (1897), Hulme Nisbet's "The Vampire Maid," and Rachilde's "The Blood Drinker" (both 1900).[1] Some of these are not actual vampires but soul-sappers, demonic women. As in Baudelaire's poem "Le Vampire," vampirism is often not treated literally but equated with sexual degradation, enslavement to the body's appetites, and female voraciousness. Mrs. Patrick Campbell has been called the first "vamp," and Philip Burne-Jones's painting "The Vampire" was rumored to be a portrait of her.

On the London stage, however, more money and fun was to be had in making sport of the male vampires of "transpontine" melodrama, now on its last legs. While realistic drama was being written successfully by T.W. Robertson, who would be followed by Arthur Wing Pinero and Henry Arthur Jones, the most popular form of entertainment in England at this period was the burlesque extravaganza. A staple for writers of this kind of theatre was the cannibalizing and sending-up of old plays. Naturally Boucicault provided a large and tempting target.

Robert Reece's *The Vampire*, "an Original Burlesque," was produced at the Royal Strand Theatre, under the management of Mrs. Swanborough, on 15 August 1872. Reece was the author of many other satiric pieces with facetious titles such as *The Very Last Days of Pompeii, Prometheus, or the Man on the Rock, Lady of the Lake Plaid in a New Tartan, Agamemnon and Cassandra, or the Prophet and Loss of Troy,* and *Faust in a Fog.*

The direct butt of Reece's humor in this case was Boucicault's 1851 *The Vampire,* which had been billed as "a Phantasm in Three Dramas." Reece's satire was subtitled "a Bit of Moonshine in Three Rays." The playbill states that the play is based on "a German legend, Lord Byron's story, and a Boucicaultian drama." It was directed by Mrs. Swansborough, Mr. J. Wallace, and Mr. Reece, with new music by John Fitzgerald, scenery by H.P. Hall, and costumes by Mrs. Richardson.

Reece's *Vampire* is written in rhymed couplets crammed with excruciating puns, which was characteristic of the genre. The male juvenile leads were played by women. The story concerns an Irish writer of gothic penny-dreadfuls who attempts to steal plots from lady novelists. The concept of female writers was apparently funny on its own. One of them, Lady Moonstone, throws herself successively at all the male characters—none accepts her. There is a mean streak of female-intellectual bashing in the play, as well as Irish baiting. Boucicault's Irish accent (and multi-national persona) is the object of ridicule:

> My name's Alan Raby, I come from *Llangollen*,
>   A place which the English can never pronounce!
> I love a fair maid dressed in airiest *muthlin*,
>   (A rhyme I've achieved with a good deal of bounce!)
> . . . . . . . . . . . . . . . . . . . . . . . . . . . . . .
> I can't make up my mind
>   In this my trade of rogue,
> Which pays the best to speak
>   The Welsh or Irish brogue?
> . . . . . . . . . . . . . . . . . . . . . . .
> To find a Paddy idiotic
>   Singing Welsh airs patriotic,
> Of two lands a strange exotic—
> . . . . . . . . . . . . . . . . . . . . . . .
> Shuffling, and changing, not knowing his mind,
>   To either or neither, or both disinclined,
> But just at this moment these mountains suggest
>   That Welsh for my purpose perhaps might be best.

(Ray 3rd, 21)

The role of the Hibernian plagiarist who lives on other's brains was a great success for Edward Terry. *Era*'s review, 18 August 1872, said, "Mr. Terry's make-up as the Vampire was something extraordinary, and he worked with unflagging energy to add 'go' to the novelty." *The Illustrated London News*, 24 August 1872, added that he played "with the broadest of brogues and the most ghastly of faces...seeking to filch the notebooks of tourists from which he may gather materials for a three-volume novel which he has been engaged by a publisher to compose." The *News* critic thought the subject matter was inappropriate for travesty, while the *Era* critic thought it a great success: "The author was cordially greeted upon his appearance before the curtain, and the latest Strand burlesque may be noted as an undoubted success."

The mood was similar in Paris, where the vampire theme was treated in a light-hearted way in Eugène de Richemont and Léon Frank's one-act operetta, *Vampire et loup garou, ou le violon de voyage* (1870), music by Blangy; and in Emile Durafour's one-act folie-vaudeville, *Le Vampire de Montlignon*, presented at the Pépinière on December 27, 1879.[2]

The taste for satire was emblematic of the age, as was the fondness for the froth and pretty tunes of light opera: the partnership of Gilbert and Sullivan produced the most successful pieces of this kind ever written. The stylistic predecessor of English comic opera was the French *opéra bouffe*, presided over by Jacques Offenbach (1819-80), whose witty and infectiously melodious light operas were the signature theatre pieces of the Second Empire. Offenbach's works differ from Gilbert and Sullivan's in that they tend to be comedy or farce rather than genre satires, and they are often based on classical subjects, similar to Planché's burlettas. Also, they exude a playful sexuality and interest in females entirely absent from the English team. A part of the humor in Gilbert and Sullivan is the perfunctory and mechanical way in which Gilbert handles the couplings of the juvenile and ingenue, typically characterized as a genial nincompoop and a mercenary minx; and the pure horror of the fate of the androgynous patterer (the true leading role) when he is mated with the male-devouring contralto. As Robertson Davies observes in *The Mirror of Nature*:

Part of the [sexual] disillusion [of the era] expresses itself in the disagreeable portraits of middle-aged women and especially unmarried women that are a part of these plays. The sexual desire that is denied to the pure young girl is often exhibited in a gross form in the characters of old maids...and W.S. Gilbert is a notable offender in this respect—man-hungry harpies, ravening for husbands. There is an ugly juvenility about this sort of comedy. But what do you expect from a society that equates ignorance with virtue and conspires to treat half the human race as untrustworthy cretins? (98)

Sullivan's music has a kind of pompous, bombastic dignity that, coupled with lyrics of a peculiar blend of cleverness, flippancy, and nonsense, and delivered by singers in a deadpan operatic style, embodies what the rest of the world has come to regard as the essence of British humor, that is, incongruity of style and content.

It is ironic that most of the world is still familiar with the Gilbert and Sullivan parodies, but not with the works on which these parodies were based, the popular genres of Victorian melodrama.[3] *Trial by Jury* (1875) burlesques the conventions of traditional courtroom drama; *The Sorcerer* (1877), while aspiring to satirize grand opera, really takes aim at lighter works such as Donizetti's *L'elisir d'amore*; *H.M.S. Pinafore* (1878) is of course a send-up of nautical melodrama, the most prominent among dozens being Jerrold's *Black Ey'd Susan* (1829); *The Pirates of Penzance* (1879) is a typical adventure/kidnapping melodrama. *Patience* (1881) parodies not a previous play but the entire aesthetic movement, and caricatures Oscar Wilde. *Iolanthe* (1882) and *The Mikado* (1885) are political satires, and *Princess Ida* (1884) takes aim at feminism using the framework of Tennyson's "The Princess."

Gilbert and Sullivan were brought into partnership by Richard D'Oyly Carte (1844-1901), composer of light operas, lecture and concert manager of such luminaries as Oscar Wilde and Matthew Arnold, and manager of the Royalty Theatre. D'Oyly Carte functioned as producer, shared with Gilbert the directing responsibilities, managed the touring companies all over the world, and in 1881 built the Savoy Theatre, the first to be lighted entirely by electricity, especially to house their works.[4]

*Ruddygore; or, the Witch's Curse!*, as it was first named, "an Entirely Original Supernatural Opera in Two Acts," opened on 22 January 1887 at the Savoy, immediately following *The Mikado*, the most successful of the collaborations, which had to be closed after a two-year run to make room for the new piece.[5]

Gilbert and Sullivan scholars whose field is primarily music have only a vague idea of the object of Gilbert's satire in *Ruddygore*. The reason for this is doubtless that Boucicault's *Vampire* was unpublished, and theatre historians almost all state that it is a version of *The Phantom*, which lacks the portrait scene. For instance, Thomas F. Dunhill in *Sullivan's Comic Operas: A Critical Appreciation*, writes, "Gilbert's libretto was intended to satirize the 'transpontine' type of melodrama which...was, by the time *Ruddigore* [as it later came to be spelled; see p. 170] appeared, almost confined to the provinces and the London theatres south of the Thames. As a skit, therefore, it was a trifle belated, but the story was founded upon a genuinely humorous idea" (143). Neither Planché's nor Boucicault's *Vampire* was transpontine, the Lyceum (English Opera House) and the Princess Theatre both being eminently respectable theatres north of the

Thames. (William Moncrieff's *Vampire*, at the Coburg, was indeed transpontine.) S.J. Adair Fitz-gerald, in *The Story of the Savoy Opera*, is also vague on antecedents: "*Ruddigore* was a deliberate burlesque...of the old Surrey and Victoria [Coburg] dramas, that were already in themselves somewhat stale and old-fashioned...[and] of the ghostly not to say ghastly Monk Lewis, and the simple imbecilities of old-time domestic drama" (129). None of the critics mention Boucicault's *Vampire*, obviously the model because of the portrait scene and several other details to be discussed. No blood-sucking actually occurs in *Ruddygore*, but "ruddy" was a British euphemism for "bloody," a fact which became a problem for the Savoy. One can also discern traces of Verdi's *Il Trovatore*, echoed in the drum rolls and opening chords of the overture, in the theme of a family curse hurled by a witch as she is burned at the stake, and the two warring brothers, rivals for the love of one woman.

From vampire melodrama is taken the dual identity motif: the wicked Sir Ruthven tries to mask his identity and live as a simple farmer, Robin Oakapple, embodiment of all that is stout and true in British manhood, and perhaps based on Shakespeare's Orlando, since Oakapple is also followed by a faithful servant, old Adam Goodheart. The heroine, Rose Maybud, knows nothing of Ruthven's past, a device from Act Two of Boucicault's *Vampire* (Alice and Raby), and also from Planché (Margaret and Ruthven), the comic twist being that the shy farmer, Oakapple, is his true personality, and the wicked lord Ruthven his unwillingly assumed one.

*Martyn Green's Treasury of Gilbert and Sullivan*, written by the leading comic performer of the D'Oyly Carte Company from 1934 to 1951, and detailing traditional performance practices, explains how the transformation of Oakapple into Ruthven was accomplished, even though there are no stage directions to that effect in any published version:

As Robin comes to the end of his solo, which he has sung in the best "mellerdramatic" manner, Zorah steps forward and asks him to dance. He refuses the offer, because the transformation from good to evil has already begun to take place. With a violent scowl on his face he storms offstage and within the space of two minutes he changes his wig to that of the second act, applies make-up—heavy eyebrows, dark rings under his eyes, etc.... He flings a cape around his shoulders, seizes a hunting crop with a lash, and re-enters, cracking the whip.... All but Old Adam run off, terrified and screaming. Old Adam pleads with Robin—now Sir Ruthven—but Robin cracks his whip again and the venerable Adam jumps like a jack-in-the-box and scuttles off the stage, followed by the bad Baronet who is still cracking his whip. (523)

This stage business was handed down from the first Ruthven, George Grossmith (under Gilbert's direction), through Henry Lytton, who temporarily took over the role in the second week when Grossmith fell ill, to Martyn Green.

In the second act, set in the picture gallery of Ruddygore Castle, the parody of Boucicault begins to come to the fore. The portraits come to life, and the ghosts begin to berate Ruthven for falling short in the crime-a-day department. While the device of ancestor portraits coming to life had been used elsewhere (Offenbach's *The Tales of Hoffmann*, for example), the following exchange can only refer to Boucicault's *Phantom*, which played London in 1862 in a version with a Scottish setting (see Chapter 7), in which the living vampire's signature is discovered on a 200-year-old will, and he is accused of forgery:

> ROBIN (melodramatically): On Wednesday, I forged a will.
> SIR RODERIC: Whose will?
> ROBIN: My own.
> RODERIC: My good sir, you can't forge your own will!
> ROBIN: Can't I though! I like that! I *did*! Besides, if a man can't forge his own will, whose will can he forge?
> 1ST GHOST: There's something in that.
> 2ND GHOST: Yes, it seems reasonable.
> 3RD GHOST: At first sight it does.
> 4TH GHOST: Fallacy somewhere, I fancy! (II, 296)

Accustomed to roaring success with their efforts, Gilbert and Sullivan and D'Oyly Carte were surprised to receive a mixed reception on the opening night, and even a few boos. The opera was judged to be too ghastly, too long, and too serious. The title was a major problem. "Ruddy" had become rather too close to "bloody," and, amazingly, this was enough to prevent many "nice" people from attending. After 11 days, the spelling was changed to *Ruddigore*, but it was too little and too late, and the complaints continued. Gilbert later declared that he had been tempted to call the piece "*Kensington* Gore; or, Not So Good as the Mikado," or "Robin and Richard Were Two Pretty Men." Of the several versions of the following anecdote, Deems Taylor's is succinct:

A friend of Gilbert's, meeting him on the street, said, "How's *Bloodygore* going?"

"You mean, *Ruddygore*," said Gilbert.

"Same thing," remarked the friend.

"Indeed?" observed Gilbert icily. "Then if I say that I admire your ruddy countenance—which I do—it means that I like your bloody cheek—which I don't." (Taylor 298)

On 24 January 1887 the critic of the *London Times* wrote:

The production of Gilbert and Sullivan's new operetta, *Ruddygore*...(a most unfortunate name, by-the-by), was...accompanied by a phenomenon never before experienced at the Savoy Theatre.... A small but very determined minority mingled its hisses.... We have no hesitation in attributing them to the feebleness of the second act and the downright stupidity of its dénouement. (qtd. in Allen 270)

*The New York Times* on January 23 was similar: "When the curtain fell there was hissing—the first ever heard in the Savoy Theatre. The audience even voiced sentiments in words and there were shouts and cries such as these: 'Take off this rot' 'Give us *The Mikado!*'" The second act, which contains most of the references to *The Vampire*, was the problem, according to the *St. James Gazette*: "Gradually the enthusiasm faded away and was hardly to be revived...Shortly after the beginning of the second act the interest of the story had begun to flag, until at last the plot had seemed within an ace of collapsing altogether" (qtd. in Allen 273).

Accordingly, cuts and changes were in order: "It was, for the Savoy, a very stormy first night," recalled Rutland Barrington, who played Despard, and it was "responsible for what had been hitherto an unheard-of occurrence with us, a rehearsal the morning after the production, for cuts" (qtd. in Allen 276). Some of the changes included: eliminating much of the ghost scene music (felt by some modern critics to be the best section of the score); cutting half of the duet of Robin and Adam opening Act Two; omitting the name change from Adam Goodheart to Gideon Crawle; substituting a new patter song for Robin; deleting the snide references to Sunday School, Superior Court, and the French Navy (which had brought a protest from *Le Figaro*, the offending lines being, "Why, we're such sturdy British salts/While she's only a Parley-voo"). Sir Roderic's entrance through the vampire trap was cut, and he alone is revived at the end, instead of the whole chorus of ancestors, and a new finale is substituted which repeats the Act One bridesmaids' chorus. These "drastic" revisions, along with the change of title spelling to *Ruddigore*, were inserted on 2 February 1887, 11 days after the opening, and the opera went on to an excellent run of 288 performances; fewer, however, than *Pirates of Penzance* (363), *Patience* (578), *Iolanthe* (398), or *The Mikado* (672). "I could do with a few more such failures," Gilbert is said to have remarked (Allen 305).

*Ruddigore* was not revived until 1920 on a provincial tour of the D'Oyly Carte Company, and then brought to London with many more cuts and revisions, including a new overture and finale by Geoffrey Toye. This is the version in which *Ruddigore* is performed today.[6] Never as popular or as often performed as the others, perhaps because of the difficulties of staging the portrait scene and the lack of easily detachable "hit tunes," *Ruddigore* is a favorite among true Savoyards. Sullivan called the score of *Ruddygore* his favorite (Fitz-gerald 150), and Dunhill calls the music attractive and the libretto brilliant, summing up his fondness for the piece as follows:

*Ruddigore* may not be the most consistent or the most continuously effective of the Savoy operas, and it is never likely to be amongst the most popular. Nevertheless it can boast of qualities of imagination to which none of the others, save perhaps *Iolanthe*, can lay equal claim. G.K. Chesterton has declared that the satire of Gilbert is, by itself, "too intelligent to be intelligible." This paradoxical statement seems especially applicable to the text of *Ruddigore*. Sullivan had a severe task before him when he undertook to set this libretto, with its crude contrasts, its unbelievable motives, and its somewhat harsh character-drawing. He succeeded, as he always did, by the persuasion of his melodies and by the gentle elusive humor which softened everything it touched. When Gilbert was merely crafty Sullivan was sincere. When Gilbert had his tongue in his cheek Sullivan wore his heart on his sleeve. It was the only possible way. (153)

Such was the superciliousness of the times that even a parody could not go unparodied. On 19 March 1887, Toole's Theatre presented *Ruddy George, or Robin Redbreast*, "a Musical Parody in one act," by H.G.F. Taylor, with music by Percy Reeve. It also featured a picture gallery scene, but with portraits of Gilbert, Sullivan, and D'Oyly Carte as the depraved ancestors. Since the manager John L. Toole was a friend, Gilbert attended a performance and sat in a box, afterwards going backstage to show his good sportsmanship and chat with the actors. Fitz-gerald comments that the piece was not nearly so witty as it should have been (134-35).

*Frankenstein, or, The Vampire's Victim*, a Christmas burlesque extravaganza which opened at the Gaiety Theatre on 24 December 1887, is a minor piece compared with *Ruddygore*, but was also a great commercial success. It was written by Richard Henry, a pseudonym for Richard Butler and Henry Chance Newton, editor and theatre critic, respectively, of *The Referee*. An extensive list of credits in the program demonstrates that the production was quite elaborate: the director was Charles Harris; the designers were W. Beverley, Hawes Crawen, E.A. Banks, and W. Perkins; the music was by Meyer Lutz; costumes by Percy Anderson; choreography by John D'Auban; electrical effects by Berry and Company; and furs by the Alaska and Hudson's Bay Fur Store. There was an orchestra of fifty players and a chorus of one hundred voices.

The Gaiety, next door to the Lyceum on Wellington Street and the Strand, was opened by John Hollingshead in 1868 with a triple bill that included Gilbert's "Original Operatic Extravaganza," *Robert the Devil*, and where the first Gilbert and Sullivan collaboration, *Thespis*, played in 1872.

The Victorian equivalent of such "B" movies as *Dracula Meets the Wolf Man, The Vampire's Victim* brings together the two most popular figures of spectral melodrama: Dr. Frankenstein, here a breeches role, and the vampire, in this case the Viscount Visconti. There is also a vampire girlfriend, Mary Ann, and a vampire club. Steven Earl Forrey, in *Hideous Progenies: Dramatizations of Frankenstein from Mary Shelley to the Present*, remarks:

"Extravagance" would be the word to describe *Vampire's Victim*. Not content with one Creature, it also includes a terra cotta model and two vampires. Thus, it is the first dramatization to place on stage the creations of Mary Shelley and John Polidori. Like its flashy costumes, *Vampire's Victim* emphasized staging over the plot, prompting critics to lament the earlier, purer style of burlesque-extravaganza as practiced by Planché and Vestris. (67)

According to Forrey, Fred Leslie's performance as the Monster caricatured Oscar Wilde, and for his first entrance he was costumed *en travestie* as Galatea.

The extremely tenuous and whimsical plot concerns the difficulty vampires encounter drawing sustenance from the Monster, who is made of pottery ("clay" being taken to mean terra cotta). There is a scene in a Vampire Club, and a finale aboard a ship which sails to the North Pole. A critic for the *Pall Mall Budget*, 29 December 1887, praised the concluding spectacle:

[It is] as pretty a picture as has ever been put on the stage, representing a Christmassy scene in the Arctic regions, with the monster ship, shining with icicles, half embedded in snow, and surrounded by ice floes.... The lights go down, and then the picture changes to a lovely transformation scene, representing the land of the Sun, peopled by gods and their satellites in brilliant attire. There is a glowing procession of Northern Lights and Planets, and the Stars and their satellites dance. (qtd. in Forrey 76)

It is not a strong piece of dramaturgy, as the critic of *The Saturday Review*, 31 December 1887, observed:

If the author had read some of those delightful extravanganzas which Planché and Vestris produced many years ago at the Lyceum, he would at once have perceived that, however light and amusing were those exquisite productions, however clever the allusions which they contained to political and other passing events, nothing was introduced which did not in some way bear directly upon the plot. This certainly was not the case in Mr. "Richard Henry's" last work, in which there is scarcely a song, duet, or chorus which contains a line concerning the dramatic situation in which it is sung. The actors sing about Trafalgar Square...Mr. Gladstone, the Jubilee, and the Irish question, but say little or nothing about poor Frankenstein and the uncanny work of art which he has, to his sorrow, endowed with life. (qtd. in Forrey 77)

*The Vampire's Victim* was considered too long for a burlesque in the 1880s, employing a three-act structure more typical of the early burlesques of the 1870s, such as Hollingshead's *The Forty Thieves* (1878), a form which anticipated musical comedy. Forrey remarks:

[*The Vampire's Victim*] appeared during the last gasps of burlesque-extravaganza and represents one of the weakest versions of the myth, albeit one of the slickest pieces of Frankensteinian entertainment.... [It] represents its final demise under the assault of opera bouffe and opera comique.... As the manager of the Gaiety Theatre, John Hollingshead, later remarked: "The return of Fred Leslie and Miss Ellen Farren from their American and Australian trip, necessitated the production of a strong bill for Christmas, 1887-8." [Hollingshead, *Good Old Gaiety* (London: Gaiety Theatre, 1903), 54.] The play enjoyed 106 performances, the longest run of any British dramatization of the novel. (54-55)

Although audiences have always liked parodies of what horrified, these three British satires demonstrate a powerful urge in this period to debunk and belittle what had chilled and thrilled the fathers and mothers of their audiences. Lord Ruthven had at last exhausted himself, and was now a figure of fun. None of these vampires succeeds in inflicting harm on anyone, and indeed none threatens to do so, unless one considers pilfering a notebook (Reece) or irritating an old woman (Gilbert and Sullivan) to be serious trespasses. Robin Oakapple finds the Ruthven persona a wearisome burden; Henry's Viscount Visconti is harmless and lovelorn; and Reece's Alan Raby, the gothic novelist, is actually a clown role.

Amid all the rollicking fun of these trifling pieces, we should not fail to notice the strain of misogyny that runs through all of them. It is not really the vampire that is the object of satire here but, with surprising regularity, women writers (e.g., "That singular anomaly, the lady novelist, I don't think she'd be missed" from *The Mikado* and Oscar Wilde's Miss Prism in *The Importance of Being Earnest*). Elaine Showalter in *Sexual Anarchy: Gender and Culture at the Fin de Siècle*, points out that in the 1870s and 80s women had written 40 percent of the novels in England and 75 percent in America, dominating the periodical press as well (76-77). Now the male establishment was intent on driving them out, and ridicule was a potent weapon.

The 1880s was a peculiar period of quiet before the intellectual storm—the great disorienting revelations of Darwin and Marx on human nature were known but not yet commonly accepted, and the third explosion of man's self-image, Freud's theory of the unconscious, was still to come, as well as the revolt of the New Woman. In the 1890s this disorientation would manifest itself in the theatre in the revolutionary works of the Naturalists and the Symbolists. Meanwhile, audiences were content with light-weight satire of what had gone before, in the cases of *The Vampire, Ruddygore*, and *The Vampire's Victim* proving that, unlike their foolish forebears, they were too sophisticated to be frightened of vampires. Dracula was waiting in the wings.

# THE VAMPIRE.

## An Original Burlesque,

WRITTEN BY

## R. REECE,

(*Member of the Dramatic Authors' Society.*)

AUTHOR OF

The Very Last Days of Pompeii; Perfect Love, or Oberon's Triumph; Little Robin Hood, or Quite a New Beau; Whittington Junior, and his Sensation Cat; Undine; Brown and the Brahmin, or Captain Pop and the Princess Pretty Eyes; The Stranger, Stranger than Ever: Chilperic; Prometheus, or the Man on the Rock; Lady of the Lake Plaid in a New Tartan; Ulf the Minstrel, or the Player, the Princess, and the Prophecy; Castle Grim; Love's Limit; Game of Dominoes; Farewell of the Fairies; A Wild Cherry; Knights of the Cross; Wicklow Rose; Agamemnon and Cassandra, or the Prophet and Loss of Troy; Last of the Paladins; Our Quiet Chateau (German Reed's); A Public Dinner (John Parry's); Honeydove's Troubles; The Ambassadress; A Fancy Fair; Aladdin, or the Tale of a Moderator; On the Road; A Pleasant Evening; Guy Mannering Disguised; Ingomar, or the Noble Savage; Latest Edition of the Lady of the Lake (Liverpool Edition); In Possession (G. Reed's); Keep Your Places; Three Graces, or the Days of the Fays; Faust in a Fog; Four Shadows; Paquita, or Love in a Frame, &c., &c.

LONDON:

E. RASCOL, PRINTER, 4, BRYDGES STREET, COVENT GARDEN.

*First Produced at the Strand Theatre, under the Management of Mrs SWANBOROUGH, on August 15th, 1872.*

## Characters.

| | |
|---|---|
| Colonel Cadwallader Raby (a retired Veteran) | Mr HARRY COX |
| Edgar (a Soldier and Poet) | Miss TOPSY VENN |
| Lord Alfred Clavering (The Colonel's guest, in love with Ada) | Miss BELLA GOODALL |
| Doctor Horace Cope (The Family Physician, a reader of Necromancy) | Mr H. J. TURNER |
| Corporal ap Shenkin (The Colonel's servant) | Mr E. CHAMBERLAINE |
| Alan Raby (The Vampire) | Mr EDWARD TERRY |
| Picturesque Peasants — Cader Idris | Miss HETHERIDGE |
| Tal y Llyn | Miss EYRE |
| Bedd Gellert | Miss RAY |
| Aberystwith | Miss BELTON |
| Llangollen | Miss ROSS |
| Ada Raby (The Colonel's Daughter) | Miss EMILY PTI |
| Lady Audley Moonstone (His guest, a fashionable novelist) | Mrs RAYMOND |
| Jenny Jones (a Servant) | Miss ROSS CULLEN |

RAY I. - - RUINS OF RABY CASTLE.

RAY II. - RABY HALL.

RAY III. - THE PEAK OF SNOWDON.

Title page, Reece.

Caricatures of first cast, Gilbert and Sullivan's *Ruddygore*.

GAIETY THEATRE.

Sole Lessee and Manager . . . . GEORGE EDWARDES.

THIS EVENING, AT 8,

**FRANKENSTEIN;**

A Melodramatic Burlesque in 3 Acts, by RICHARD HENRY.

MUSIC BY MEYER LUTZ.

Produced by CHARLES HARRIS.

DRAMATIS PERSONÆ.

| | | |
|---|---|---|
| Frankenstein | A German Medical Student | Miss NELLIE FARREN |
| Tartina | His Swiss Sweetheart | Miss MARION HOOD |
| Viva | | Miss FLORENCE DYSART |
| Il Capitano Maraschino | Of the Italian Guards | Miss JENNY ROGERS |
| Mary Ann | A Maid of Mystery | Miss MARIA JONES |
| Risotto | A Wicked-Eyeberian Ditto | Miss JENNY M'NULTY |
| Tamburina | The Bandit Virandère | Miss SYLVIA GREY |
| Goddess of the Sun | | |
| Caramella | A Shepherdess | Miss EMMA GWYNNE |
| Vanilla | Another | Miss SYBIL GREY |
| Susanna | | Miss LIZZIE WILSON |
| The Monster | Frankenstein's Invention | Mr. FRED LESLIE |
| Visconti | A Vampire Viscount | Mr. E J. LONNEN |
| The Model | A Brown Study | Mr. GEORGE STONE |
| Domenincho | | Mr. JOHN D'AUBAN |
| Mondelico | A Publican—Tartina's Parent | Mr. CYRIL MAUDE |
| Schwank | Frankenstein's Page | Mr. FRANK THORNTON |
| Dotto | A Dancing Drum-Major | Mr. CHARLIE ROSS |

BANDITS, GUARDS, SOLDIERS, SAILORS, VAMPIRES, VILLAGERS.
The PERMANENT GAIETY ORCHESTRA of 50 PERFORMERS, under the direction of HERR MEYER LUTZ.

ACTING MANAGER . . . . . . . . Mr. E. J. POTTER.

MORNING PERFORMANCE of MISS ESMERALDA, EVERY SATURDAY.

ACT I.

Scene I.—THE ITALIAN ALPS . . . . W. BEVERLEY.

Scene II.—FRANKENSTEIN'S LABORATORY . . . W. BEVERLEY

ACT II.

Scene.—SOMEWHERE IN SPAIN . . . . . HAWES CRAVEN

ACT III.

Scene I.—CLUBLAND. THE JUNIOR VAMPIRES' . E. G. BANKS

Scene II.—THE ARCTIC REGIONS . . . . W. PERKINS

Scene III.—CAVERN OF THE NORTH POLE. } . . W. PERKINS
REVIEW OF THE PLANETS }

Some of the Incidental Songs by Mr. ROBERT MARTIN and F. BOWYER. The Dresses have been Specially Designed by Mr. PERCY ANDERSON, and executed by Madame AUGUSTE and Miss FISHER. The Music of the Moonlight Ballet specially composed by Wm. FULLERTON. Furs by THE ALASKA AND HUDSON'S BAY FUR STORE. Harness by URCH & Co. Furniture by ATKINSON & Co. The Jewellery and Armour by KLEIN, of Berlin, JUDIC, of Paris, and Messrs. PHILLIPS, of London. The Electrical Effects by BERRY & Co. The Ballets by JOHN D'AUBAN. The Military Band under the direction of LOUIS BECK. Chorus of One Hundred and Twenty Voices. Chorus Mistress, Mrs. JOHNSON. Assistant Stage Manager, Mr. FRANK PARKER.

PRECEDED, AT 7.15,

BY

**"LOT 49,"**

A FARCE IN ONE ACT

(From the German of G. Von Moser),

BY W. J. FISHER.

| | | |
|---|---|---|
| Horace Newlove | | Mr. CYRIL MAUDE |
| Nubbles | (A Retired Coal Dealer) | Mr. E. HASLAM |
| Joseph | (Nubble's Son) | Mr. GEORGE STONE |
| Peter | (Servant Boy to Newlove) | Mr. FRANK THORNTON |
| Blobbs | (An "Odd Man") | Mr. CHARLES ROSS |
| Mrs. Lucy Newlove | | Miss EMMA GWYNNE |
| Polly | (Maid Servant to Newlove) | Miss SYBIL GREY |
| Messenger | | Mr. WARDES |

SCENE—NEWLOVE'S HOUSE.

Title page, Henry's Frankenstein, or The Vampire's Victim, 1888.

# Part Two

# Dracula

**Chapter 9**

# Stage Adaptations, 1897-1985

A woman drew her long black hair out tight
And fiddled whisper music on those strings
And bats with baby faces in the violet light
Whistled, and beat their wings
And crawled head downward down a blackened wall.
—T.S. Eliot, *The Waste Land*

Dracula is the king of vampires. No study of the vampire onstage would be complete without examining this dominant archetype and epitomical source, not only of the great preponderance of 20th-century vampire plays, but also of numerous reincarnations in the important 20th-century art form, film.

This book is a study of the vampire figure as treated on the 19th-century stage, which ostensibly would exclude *Dracula*, despite the fact that there was a staged reading of the piece at the Lyceum Theatre in 1897, technically justifying its inclusion. But the thematic argument is more persuasive: *Dracula* is the culmination of many currents throughout the century which preceded its publication in 1897; among vampires, Bram Stoker's Dracula sums up, supersedes, and overshadows everything that came before, and is the model and source for all that came after. Although chronologically beyond the limits of this study, 20th-century stage adaptations of *Dracula* will also be examined in this chapter for comparison with their 19th-century forebears..

Lord Ruthven was killed many times onstage, but only Count Dracula could keep him in the grave. Dracula is one of those creations that transcends the work in which it is presented—one of Jung's archetypal patterns of the subconscious and a powerful poetic image of Freud's "primal hoarder." Dracula possesses tremendous cunning, grace, strength, the ability to revert to animal form and fly through the air, an aristocratic manner, an ironic sense of humor, a commanding presence, a contempt for mankind, and a hypnotic power over women. He far surpasses Ruthven in his egotism and ambition—he seems to be planning world domination. He is one of the great fictional creations of Victorian literature.

Stoker presents the bite of Dracula as a sexual violation which brings death but also sexual arousal beyond the ordinary senses. The erotic imagery in the novel is unmistakable to us today. Should anyone doubt the sexual content of the novel, the following passage is offered:

The fair girl went on her knees and bent over me, fairly gloating. There was a deliberate voluptuousness which was both thrilling and repulsive, and as she arched her neck she actually licked her lips like an animal, till I could see in the moonlight the moisture shining on the scarlet lips and red tongue as it lapped the white sharp teeth. Lower and lower went her head as the lips went below the range of my mouth.... Then she paused and I could hear the churning sound of her tongue...and feel the hot breath on my neck. Then the skin of my throat began to tingle as one's flesh does when the hand that is to tickle it approaches nearer—nearer. I could feel the soft, shivering touch of the lips on the supersensitive skin of my throat, and the hard dents of two sharp teeth, just touching and pausing there. I closed my eyes in a languorous ecstasy and waited—waited with beating heart. (39-40)[1]

Although the critical reception of *Dracula* was mixed, there was surprisingly little objection to the erotic content: "It is horrid and creepy to the last degree" (*Pall Mall Gazette*); "Weird, powerful and horrible" (*Daily Mail*); "It is a pity that Mr. Bram Stoker was not content to employ such supernatural anti-vampire receipts as his wildest imagination might have invented without venturing on a domain where angels fear to tread" (*Punch*); "*Dracula* is highly sensational, but it is wanting in the constructive art as well as in the higher literary sense" (*Athenaeum*) (all qtd. in Glut 71). This is an amazingly passive response in view of the (at least superficial) prudery of late Victorian society.

Since the surge of scholarly interest in popular culture (and with it the horror genre) in the 1960s, there have been at least 50 critical studies and numerous articles on *Dracula*, which has grown in reputation far beyond its status as a cult classic. The levels of criticism range from academic to "pop"—many of the latter seem aimed specifically at adolescent boys, for whom Dracula seems to have a particular appeal. In the serious criticism, I see six main thematic approaches to unraveling the novel's symbolism. These categories overlap somewhat—the distinctions concern what the writers feel is the dominant theme of the book, sometimes more a question of emphasis than of disagreement.

1. *Freudian interpretation.* Most scholars now agree on the underlying sexual symbolism in *Dracula.* Maurice Richardson in "The Psychoanalysis of Ghost Stories" (1959) was the first to apply Freud's primal horde hypothesis, first articulated in *Totem and Taboo* (1913), and later amplified in *Group Psychology and the Analysis of the Ego* (1921), *The Future of an Illusion (1927), Civilization and Its Discontents* (1930), and *Moses and Monotheism* (1939). Freud's theory, based in part on Charles Darwin's speculations on the social organization of primitive man, and studies of ritual sacrifice in primitive cultures, posits a family unit (the horde) tyrannized by a single powerful male, who incestuously monopolizes all the tribe's females, and who is killed and eaten by his sons, who then reorganize the group's structure into a fraternal clan, and expiate the group guilt by ritual sacrifice to an animal god, a substitute (or totem) for the murdered father. While the mythological version takes place in a single family, in Freud's supposition this social transformation took place over thousands of years, and involved "all primeval men, including, therefore, all our ancestors" (*Moses* 102).

In Richardson's application of this theory, Dracula represents the evil father who hoards the tribe's women and is killed by the sons. As Richardson memorably phrases it, *Dracula* is "a kind of incestuous, necrophilious, oral-anal-sadistic all-in wrestling match" which takes place in "in a sort of homicidal lunatic's brothel in a crypt" ("Psychoanalysis" 427).

I think it is important to point out that Stoker reverses Freud's pattern, however: rather than making his children his sex partners, Dracula's bite makes his sex partners his children, by turning them into vampires.[2] What can be made of this? It reinforces the theme that Dracula's sexual practices are uncannily familiar, yet somehow strange—ourselves in a distorted mirror.

Other critics, such as Joseph Bierman in *"Dracula*, Prolonged Childhood Illness, and the Oral Triad," follow Richardson in his Freudian analysis. The oral triad—sleeping, eating, and being eaten—are important motifs in the novel. The blood transfusions symbolize group sex, as the novel specifically states: Van Helsing (jokingly) calls Lucy a polyandrist when the blood of three men is put in her veins (121-22).[3] This and other readings of Freudian sexual symbolism into the novel are, as James Twitchell notes, "almost a donnée of *Dracula* criticism" (*Dreadful Pleasures* 42).

2. *Theme of dualism.* Many writers, such as Alan P. Johnson in "'Dual Life': The Status of Women in Stoker's *Dracula*," make much of the dual personalities with which Stoker endows his female characters, revealing their repressed sexual natures by showing by their seemingly unconscious and uncontrollable attraction to the vampire—behavior shockingly at odds with their public personalities. Lucy seems to have a doppelgänger, or buried personality, which is manifested by her sleepwalking. Freud's theory of the unconscious, which would have a profoundly troubling effect on modern man's image of himself as a rational being, was as yet unarticulated. Instead, Stoker was drawing on the general notion of a double layer of personality, or dissociation, developed by Jean-Martin Charcot, the French neurologist who was Freud's teacher, and whose experiments with hypnosis stimulated Freud's theory of the unconscious. In fact, Charcot is mentioned in *Dracula* as a colleague of Van Helsing's (172).[4]

The unconscious lives of Lucy and Mina are a manifestation of their rebelliousness and discontent—it is through the unconscious, in Stoker's scheme of things, that they are vulnerable to Dracula, a literary technique which several of the stage adaptations use to great effect.

3. *Theme of Misogyny.* A number of psychosexual approaches in the 70s and 80s have emphasized the fear and hatred of women manifested in the book, and the view of sexuality as destructive and degrading.[5] Phyllis Roth's "Suddenly Sexual Women in Bram Stoker's *Dracula*," Judith Weissman's "Women as Vampires: *Dracula* as a Victorian Novel," and Carol Senf's *The Vampire in Nineteenth-Century English Literature* all refer to the vampire brides and the transformation of Lucy as symbols of female sexual voraciousness and malignity. Lucy is punished for her sexual awakening by being impaled with a wooden stake by her fiancé assisted by a group of supporting males. The hostile symbolism of this act is obvious. For Roth and others, this is killing of the devouring mother. Mina, the novel's "New Woman," is no such thing, according to these writers, but a docile and subservient helpmeet, mother-figure, and secretary, who in fact in her diary ridicules the New Woman's demand for social and sexual equality. David Skal, in *Hollywood Gothic*, writes:

*Dracula* can be read…as an almost transparent metaphor for the Victorian confusion, guilt, and anger over the "proper" role of women. The attack of the vampire—a male's act of oral, infantile rage—succeeds in sexualizing women, who, according to the double standard of the time, must then be punished and purified through more sex and violence. (31)

In *Idols of Perversity*, Bram Dijkstra calls *Dracula* the primary example of late Victorian demonization of woman:

Stoker's work demonstrates how thoroughly the war waged by nineteenth-century male culture against the dignity and self-respect of women had been fought.... [He wrote] perhaps without ever completely realizing what he had done, a narrative destined to become the looming twentieth century's basic commonplace book of the antifeminine obsession. (342)

One of the most extreme modern feminists, Andrea Dworkin, makes this even angrier assessment:

The women are transformed into predators, great foul parasites.... As humans, they begin to learn sex in dying. And the men, the human suitors and husbands...are given a new kind of sex too...watching the women die...[*Dracula*] goes beyond metaphor in its intuitive rendering of an oncoming century filled with sexual horror: the throat as a female genital; sex and death as synonyms; killing as a sex act; slow dying as sensuality;...mutilation of the female body as male heroism and adventure; callous, ruthless, predatory lust as the one-note meaning of sexual desire; intercourse itself needing blood...to count as a sex act in a world excited by sadomasochism, bored by the dull thud of the literal fuck. (119)

4. *Theme of Racism.* John Allen Stevenson in "A Vampire in the Mirror: The Sexuality of *Dracula*," makes the argument that the plot of the novel is a disguised interracial sexual competition, and a parable of warning against excessive exogamy (contrary to Ernest Jones, who connects vampires with repressed incestuous desire). Stevenson links the racism of the novel with England's huge colonial expansion in the 19th century. *Dracula* was published in 1897, the Diamond Jubilee of Victoria's reign. The novel displays the sublimated anxiety and guilt connected with British imperialism's subjugation of the dark races of the earth, with the racist perception of their vile smell (Dracula's rancid breath is several times referred to in the novel), their unspeakable religions, revolting sex practices, and strange coloration (Stoker emphasizes red, white, and black with his vampires—unnatural and un-English, an alien breed, altogether un-human). Stevenson concludes,

The threat Dracula represents is not the desire of the father to hoard his own women; it is an urgent need to take, to violate boundaries, a desire that must incorporate foreign blood for the very survival of his kind. For the vampire, the blood he needs, both for sex and for food, always belongs to somebody else. *Dracula* thus uncovers for us the kind of mind that sees excessive exogamy as a particularly terrifying threat.... Such fears must have been acute in late nineteenth-century Britain, plump with imperial gain, but given perhaps to the bad dream that *Dracula* embodies: what if "they" should try to colonize *us*? (147)

Dijkstra, Auerbach, and others detect anti-Semitism in the portrait of Dracula: "a vile, unevolved, grossly bestial satyr, whose inability to control his desires is...[like] one of those horrid inbred Jews everyone was worrying about at the time...for he was very emphatically Eastern European, and hence, like du Maurier's 'filthy black Hebrew,' Svengali" (Dijkstra 343). The important point is that Dracula is racially "Other."

5. *Christian allegory.* More traditional interpreters such as Clive Leatherdale and Leonard Wolf see the novel as a romance in the form of a crusade, with the forces of light arrayed against the forces of darkness (*Annotated* ix). For the British such knightly quests were associated with Saint George, the dragon-slayer and savior of innocent virgins. Wolf, who has written extensively on *Dracula*, does not take a simple or single-minded approach to the work, taking into account a number of theories. Calling it an example of Jung's "visionary novel," Wolf sees Dracula as a somewhat tragic figure (*Dream* 222-23). He sees the brotherhood of the vampire-slayers as paramount. The females are treacherous to the band of crusaders, but Wolf notes that only through Mina is the vampire destroyed.

Agreeing with the Christian crusade interpretation are Christopher Gist Raible in "Dracula: Christian Heretic," Thomas B. Byers in "Good Men and Monsters: The Defenses of *Dracula*," and Gwenyth Hood in "Sauron and Dracula,"[6] which compares the quest-structure of *Dracula* with J.R.R. Tolkien's *The Lord of the Rings*.

6. *Theme of Contagion.* An approach which strikes me as insightful is the equation of vampirism with syphilis, the fin-de-siècle plague and unmentionable symbol of filth and degradation which took victims from all strata of society. Stoker was the first writer to present a theory of vampirism as contagious disease: that a vampire's bite, like a rabid animal's, spreads infection that creates more vampires. Stoker's nephew, Daniel Farson, in his biographical study revealed his hypothesis, derived from studying the previously

unexamined coroner's report, that Stoker died of syphilis, which he contracted during or (less usefully to these surmises) shortly after the period in which he wrote *Dracula* (*Man Who Wrote Dracula* 233-35).

Most writers of the period—Ibsen (*Ghosts*) and Shaw (*Mrs. Warren's Profession*) being the honorable exceptions—dealt with the disease, when they did at all, as a punishment for immorality and for dealings with female prostitutes who personified evil and passed the poison to their male victims. In *Dracula* this revulsion is intensified: the source of the plague is the devil (Dracula), passed to women whom he enslaves and who attempt to enslave men, implying a threat of universal contagion through sex. In view of the hullabaloo in England and elsewhere over *Ghosts* in the 1880s, it is surprising that Stoker's contemporaries did not pick up on this implied theme.

Stoker himself would undoubtedly deny this, and all the other above-suggested subtexts.[7] But the question of how much of the psychosexual and symbolic content was Stoker's conscious intention is, in the last analysis, irrelevant. He has been called a second-rate writer who wrote a great book. In fact, the horror-fiction writer H.P. Lovecraft, among others, doubted that Stoker was the author (or the sole author) of *Dracula*, when he compared its quality with Stoker's other works. In a letter to Robert Barlow in 1932 he wrote:

Stoker was a very inept writer when not helped out by revisers, and his *Lair of the White Worm* is so bad that many have mistaken it for a burlesque. I know an old lady who almost had the job of revising *Dracula* back in the early 1890s—she saw the original ms., and says it was a fearful mess. Finally someone else (Stoker thought her price for the work was too high) whipped it into such shape as it now possesses. (qtd. in Florescu and McNally, *Essential* 25)

In my opinion the logical gaps in *Dracula* to which Lovecraft refers make it more mysterious. How, specifically, are vampires reproduced? If by biting, why are there not thousands, if not millions, of vampires multiplying exponentially? How did Vlad Tepes, the 15th-century Wallachian prince whom Stoker posits as Dracula's original human identity, become a vampire? In the course of the novel Dracula changes in appearance; he seems to be rejuvenated—had he been through a lean period prior to the novel's events? He flies, he turns into mist, he has command over the lower animals.

And somehow most disturbing of all to the imagination, in human form he crawls head downward down castle walls.

How do vampires live? We see only tantalizing glimpses of the hidden lives of the vampire women, who seem to be both his creations and his previous wives, and they seem to be shut up in the castle, kept in a state of sexual and physical starvation and subsisting solely on the kidnapped babies that Dracula brings them. When he leaves for England, what happens to them? Dracula also is presented as a mystery, seen only in glimpses. As Wolf points out, Dracula is "onstage" for only 58 of the novel's 390 pages (*Annotated* 350-51).

Stoker uses his zoophagous madman, Renfield, more as a poetic device than as a study of insanity. Dracula asserts mental control over the weaker-minded characters, Renfield and the two women, even before he comes in contact with them. As Wolf points out a number of times in *The Annotated Dracula*, Renfield's accelerating mental deterioration is carefully correlated with Dracula's approach to England on the *Demeter*. But Renfield functions more as a prophet and clairvoyant, a parodistic John the Baptist to Dracula's Antichrist, than as a serious study of psychosis. He fits best with the interpretation of *Dracula* as a Christian allegory, though, to my mind, he also suggests the "Holy Fool," one of Jung's archetypal patterns of the unconscious.

I propose three main sources for the character of Dracula: 1) Ruthven, in all his evolving fictional and dramatic incarnations since his creation in 1819; 2) Vlad Tepes; and 3) the great Shakespearean actor, Henry Irving, both in his personality and physical appearance, and in his portrayals of Mephistopheles, the Flying Dutchman, and, especially, Macbeth. Other critics have proposed the "sexually cold" Florence Stoker (Florescu and McNally); Oscar Wilde, who was once engaged to Florence (Farson, Skal); Svengali (Auerbach, Dijkstra); Stevenson's Mr. Hyde, and Azzo in "The Mysterious Stranger" (anon., 1860). Christopher Frayling argues that the strongest influence is *Varney the Vampire*, listing six structural similarities: 1) initiation of the heroine; 2) sexual attraction; 3) incongruity of a Slavic vampire in rural England; 4) respect of the hunter for the hunted; 5) scientific approach of the antagonists; and 6) a number of minor motifs (*Vampyres* 41). However, Leonard Wolf writes, "There is nothing in *Varney*, nothing at all, that is capable of sounding anything like the chords of dark understanding that reverberate in page after page of Stoker's *Dracula*" (*Dream* 170).

Vlad Tepes, the Impaler (1431-76), called Voivode ("lord," "prince") Dracula (meaning "son of" both "dragon" [*draco*] and "devil" [*drakul*]), roughly contemporary with England's Richard III, was a warrior-king and Romanian national hero who held back the Turks as they attempted to pass from Asia into Europe. Florescu and McNally have written two books, *In Search of Dracula* and *Dracula, Prince of Many Faces*, on this historical figure, whose usual method of punishing his enemies was impalement. He murdered at least 100,000 people, many, it seems, capriciously, often with what seems to have been a very grisly sense of humor. After his death there were many accounts of his life in German, Russian, and Romanian, beginning in 1485. One example, *About the Wild Bloodthirsty Berserker Dracula* (1499), by Ambrosius Huber of Nuremberg, states on the title page:

Here begins a very cruel frightening story about a wild bloodthirsty man, Dracula the voevod. How he impaled people and roasted them and with their heads boiled them in a kettle, and how he skinned people and hacked them to pieces like a head of cabbage. He also roasted the children of mothers and they had to eat their children themselves. And many other horrible things are written in this tract and also in which land he ruled. (qtd. in Glut 5)

But none of the chroniclers specifically call him a vampire. The teaching of the Eastern Orthodox Church, that the earth will not receive the body of an evil-doer, possibly contributed the linkage of this blood-drenched mass murderer with the legend of the vampire. Some biographers theorize that this connection was suggested to Stoker by Armenius Vambery, world traveler and scholar from the University of Budapest. Other sources of vampire material for Stoker include Le Fanu's *Carmilla* (1872), Emily Girard's "Transylvanian Superstitions" in *Nineteenth Century* (1855), Sabine Baring-Gould's *Book of Werewolves* (1865) and Sir Richard Burton's *The Thousand and One Nights* (1885). All biographers make much of the fact that Stoker did assiduous research in the British Museum on his subject, and very accurately reproduced a Transylvanian culture and countryside which he never saw. (Also to be noted is the influence of Wilkie Collins's *The Woman in White* [1860] for the epistolary form and multiple narrative voice.)

The original notes for *Dracula*, now at the Rosenbach Foundation in Philadelphia, have been examined and analyzed by Joseph S. Bierman in *Notes and Queries* (January-February 1977), Florescu and McNally in *The Essential Dracula* (1977), and excerpts published in Frayling's *Vampyres* (1991). One interesting aspect to emerge is that Stoker from the beginning planned the book as a play: the original scenario is laid out in four acts of seven scenes each, typical of the synopsis page of a Lyceum Theatre program, and the action is sketched out with stage directions and curtain lines (Frayling, *Vampyres* 300).

From the point of view of theatre history, the connection with Irving is of great interest. Stoker nowhere states that Dracula was written as a role for Irving or was based on his personality or physical characteristics, but the derivation is clear. Stoker was Irving's business manager for 27 years and had known him for ten years when he wrote *Dracula*. It occurs to me that their relationship, the most important of Stoker's life—on his part composed of worship, fear, and hatred; and on Irving's of exploitation, contempt, and fatherly affection—is remarkably similar to the relationship between Polidori and Byron. As Stoker wrote in his adulatory *Personal Reminiscences of Henry Irving*, he was enthralled from the moment of their first meeting. He first saw Irving in a production of *The Rivals* when he was a 19-year-old student at Trinity College in Dublin. Ten years later, as a theatre critic, his star-struck review of Irving's Hamlet earned him an invitation to meet his idol backstage and to a private recitation of Thomas Hood's "The Dream of Eugene Aram," where his emotional response to the actor's power was such that he fainted:

Here was power incarnate, incarnate passion.... Irving's genius floated in blazing triumph.... I burst into something like a violent fit of hysterics. Let me say, not in my own vindication, but to bring new tribute to Irving's splendid power, that I was no hysterical subject. I was no green youth; no weak individual, yielding to a superior emotional force. I was as men go a strong man, strong in many ways.... Soul had looked into soul. From that hour began a friendship as profound, as close, as lasting, as can be between two men. (I: 31-33)

The friendship grew, and when Irving acquired the Lyceum in 1878, he invited Stoker to become his business manager, a position he kept until Irving's death in 1906, although the relationship soured in the last years. In a somewhat hostile analysis, Irving's grandson, Laurence Irving, writes:

Stoker, inflated with literary and aesthetic pretensions, worshipped Irving with all the sentimental idolatry of which an Irishman is capable.... Well-intentioned, vain, impulsive, and inclined to blarneying flattery...[he] revel[ed] in the opportunity which this position gave him to rub shoulders with the great. This weakness and his emotional impetuosity handicapped him in dealing with Irving's business affairs in a forthright and sensible manner. (453)

Like Dracula, Irving was tall, thin, of a saturnine appearance. His voice was hypnotic—it had a metallic, sibilant quality. Many critics, including Bernard Shaw and Gordon Craig, commented on his rather curious pronunciation, a lisp, almost a foreign accent. His great roles were in spine-tingling melodramas such as *The Bells* and *The Flying Dutchman*,[8] roles which dealt with the demonic and the supernatural. One of Irving's greatest gifts was his ability to strike terror into an audience. William Archer wrote of him, "Hatred, malignity, and cunning dwell familiarly in his eye, his jaw can express at will indomitable resolve or grotesque and abject terror. Grim humor lurks in his eyebrows, and cruel contempt in the corners of his mouth. No actor had ever fuller command of the expression which has been happily called 'a lurid glance'" (qtd. in Booth, *Victorian Spectacular* 126). Commenting on his portrayal of Mephistopheles, Booth writes, "Irving's pale face could be mask-like, with thin, mocking lips and fixed, impenetrable, lidless eyes; or very mobile: a curl of the lip, a ghastly smile, a flicker of the eyes, an upward jerk of the eyebrows—all these worked out in exact relationship to posture and gesture, the hands as claws, the half-limp" (125). Irving's terrifying portrayal of Mephistopheles made a deep impression on Stoker, who had been involved in research for the *Faust* production, traveling to Nuremberg and elsewhere. The Lyceum's version placed the demon squarely in the spotlight, eliminating the nominal lead, Faust, almost entirely, and focusing on the satanic seduction of Ellen Terry's Marguerite. In this role, Irving was like evil personified.

Furthermore, Irving was selfish, spiteful, and egotistical, almost a kind of vampire in his personal relationships: breaking with his wife (who disapproved of acting), he never spoke to her but never divorced her; and Stoker, who had devoted his life to him, was not remembered in Irving's will. Ellen Terry, his greatest acting partner, who probably loved him as much as he was capable of being loved, describes him:

He was an egotist—an egotist of the great type, *never* "a mean egotist," as he was once slanderously described—and all his faults sprang from egotism, which is in one sense, after all, only another name for greatness. So much absorbed was he in his own achievements that he was unable or unwilling to appreciate the achievements of others. I never heard him speak in high terms of the great foreign actors and actresses who from time to time visited England. It would be easy to attribute this to jealousy, but the easy explanation is not the true one. He simply would not give himself up to appreciation. (qtd. in Auerbach, *Ellen Terry* 191)

Stoker and Terry had a close, affectionate relationship, and Terry's nickname for Stoker was "Ma," as he was the business manager who "took care" of her. She signed her notes to him, "Your dutiful daughter" (Farson 49). Auerbach suggests that not only was Irving the model for Dracula, but also Terry was the model for Lucy:

Always, there was something perverse about Irving, something not only crafty but cruel: Bram Stoker's devout reminiscence expunges the sinister, invasive magnetism that made his Dracula another unforgettable Irving caricature.... Blonde, super-feminine Lucy, who collects marriage proposals and clings adoringly to men...a sleepwalker like Lady Macbeth and a dear, giggling English rose, might be Bram Stoker's tribute to his adored Ellen Terry's most audacious performance. (200, 254)[9]

Irving's great Shakespearean roles, as Eric Bentley notes, were those that could be interpreted simply, melodramatically, (177) and had an element of the satanic—Shylock, Richard III, and most importantly for Bram Stoker, Macbeth. The great 1888 Lyceum production had a profound influence on Stoker, who was deeply involved in Irving's preparation of the role. They spent many hours discussing its finer interpretive points, and Stoker traveled to Slains Castle on Cruden Bay, a desolate, remote, and deeply superstitious part of Scotland, to soak up atmosphere for the production, and where he made preliminary notes for *Dracula*.

The parallels between *Dracula* and *Macbeth* are strikingly set out by Clive Leatherdale in *Dracula, the Novel and the Legend* (82-83): 1) Blood is a central motif in both works. The thirst for blood, metaphorical in Shakespeare and literal in Stoker, is addictive and self-perpetuating. 2) Dracula and Macbeth are both warriors, who begin as military heroes and become butchers, turning on their own people. 3) Duncan is lured into the castle and visited in his sleep, like Dracula's victim, Jonathan Harker. 4) The three witches in *Macbeth* parallel Dracula's three brides. 5) Both works deal with supernatural evil. Macbeth's pact with supernatural powers, like Dracula's, makes him more than human, until humans find the one secret way to destroy him. 6) There is a rhythmic similarity in the pronouncements when good triumphs: "The curse is lifted" and "The time is free."

To Leatherdale's list of comparisons, I would add the following: 1) Dracula's literary precursor, Lord Ruthven, was Scottish; 2) In both works most scenes take place at night, and darkness is a central image; 3) The sleepwalking motif is repeated in Lady Macbeth and Lucy; 4) There is a character named Seward in *Dracula* and one named Siward in *Macbeth*;[10] 5) Macbeth is beheaded after being killed by his victorious foes; Stoker's vampire must also be decapitated to be truly destroyed.

It seems very believable that Stoker, under the spell of this great play and Irving's powerful performance as the "fiend of Scotland," wove the vampire theme around the structure and atmosphere of *Macbeth*. In many ways, Castle Dracula is Inverness.

The first dramatic version of *Dracula, or the Un-dead* was read on the stage of the Lyceum, the site of Planché's *The Vampire* in 1820 and Marschner's *Der Vampyr* in 1829, on 18 May 1897,[11] actually predating the release of the novel. It had been quickly adapted by Stoker to protect the copyright. The reading took four hours and consisted of five acts and 47 scenes, a dozen or more differing from the novel. It is unlikely that any copy of this dramatization still exists. The audience consisted of invited guests, company members and staff, cleaning persons, and a few regulars (*Dracula Scrapbook* 53). Irving did not take part in the presentation, but apparently strolled through the theatre during the course of it, and was asked his opinion. "Dreadful!" he is said to have replied, which doubtless ended any hope Stoker had that he would be interested in the role.

The cast was composed of Lyceum company members. The first Dracula was a "Mr. Jones." Neither he nor any other cast member is mentioned anywhere in Stoker's *Reminiscences*. Nina Auerbach makes much of the fact that Ellen Terry's daughter, Edith Craig, read the role of Mina; from this it is reasonable to assume that Terry was in the audience ("Escaping" 2-3). Edith ("Edy") Craig was a bit player at the Lyceum; she later formed an experimental theatre company where she staged pageants for women's suffrage and became an outspoken lesbian.

Irving was experiencing a year of disaster in 1897. He had been knighted in 1895, the first actor to be so honored, but in 1897 he fell down a flight of stairs, injured his leg permanently, and had to close the theatre for several weeks. Then fire consumed a Lyceum storehouse and scenery and costumes for most of the repertory were destroyed. The subsequent forced closing and the emergence of rival companies bankrupted the Lyceum and Irving was forced to sell to a syndicate, which collapsed in its turn. But among the catastrophes of 1897 was his failure to recognize in *Dracula* a vehicle and money-maker which perhaps would have saved his theatre. Ill with pneumonia and pleurisy, he blamed his manager for his misfortunes and broke with Stoker. Perhaps Irving was embarrassed or subconsciously repulsed by the sexual content of the piece (although there is no evidence he ever read it). When one considers his repertory and most successful roles, he could hardly claim to be "above" melodrama. At any rate, he never played it—in my opinion, one of theatre history's great losses.

*Dracula* was never again staged in Stoker's lifetime. In the 20th century, of course, it became a theatrical phenomenon, with dozens of adaptations and thousands of productions. According to *Theatre Week* (5 October 1992), versions of *Dracula* were the sixth most frequently produced play in American professional theatre in 1992 (32).

The first successful stage adaptation of *Dracula* was written in 1924 by the popular provincial actor Hamilton Deane. Stoker's widow, Florence, gave Deane the rights to the novel "as a chance to reassert control over an authorized dramatization" (Skal, *Hollywood Gothic* 69). She was at the time involved in a lawsuit with Prana-Film over *Nosferatu*, F.W. Murnau's unauthorized 1922 film version.

Deane's play is set entirely in England, the parts of the story which transpire in Transylvania related as narrative. While making the play easier and less expensive to stage, Deane thereby eliminates the best and most spectacular parts of the book—the opening chapters, the return to Castle Dracula, the chase scene and death of Dracula. According to David Skal, Deane originally intended a prologue showing Dracula climbing head first down his castle wall, but eliminated it because of the nuisance and expense of staging it. The image was used on the play's advertisements, however. Deane reduced the novel to a conventional drawing-room melodrama in three acts: Acts One and Three in "The Study of Jonathan Harker's House on Hampstead Heath;" Act Two, "Mrs.

Harker's Boudoir," and an Epilogue in "The Coach House at Carfax." Lucy is eliminated, and her plot function taken over by Mina. Deane also converted Lucy's American suitor, Quincy Morris, into a female role, presumably to fit the casting requirements to his available actors. A typical line in "American" dialect: "Well—sometimes—way back home—I've caught a whiff of garlic, from some 'Dago' or 'Mex' in the Subway—but I never 'saw red' like the Count, just now—that's got me beat!" (qtd. in Skal 77).

The sexual and psychological elements of the novel are very much suppressed in Deane's version. There are no doppelgängers. The most conventional theme—the crusade against the forces of darkness—is in the forefront. The character of Mina, written for Mary Dora Patrick, Deane's sweetheart and later his wife, is stiflingly conventional—no hint of dark waters beneath the surface, as in Stoker's concept of the character.

Deane's lasting contributions were in the character and physical appearance of Dracula, sanitizing it of animalism—Stoker's Dracula had hairy palms and fetid breath—and suiting it to his own personality and appearance. It was Deane's idea that the Count should appear in full evening dress, as he has ever since. As Donald Glut writes:

[Deane] was two inches over six feet in height and had a lean face with piercing, almost sinister eyes. He also saw the King Vampire as a man of about fifty, with a conspicuously green face, deep voice, and suave continental mannerisms. Deane insisted that the portrayal be witty and melodramatic, but never over-acted so as to become ludicrous. Although Deane had aspirations to play the Count himself, he was forced to drape his black cape around actor Edmund Blake, whose gold front tooth made him even more striking in appearance. (Glut 80)

Skal believes that Deane foolishly chose the Van Helsing role because he thought it was a better (certainly a larger) part.

The first performance was at the Grand Theatre in Derby on 5 August 1924. Deane felt the piece was successful and kept it on the road for two years, tinkering with various elements, and trying it out in Wimbledon in the spring of 1925. The role of Dracula was taken over by Raymond Huntley, Florence Stoker's lawyer's wife's brother (a distant relationship indeed), at the age of 22, a very young Dracula (Glut 71-72). Huntley's make-up in the role included a wig with white streaks which swept upwards, suggesting devil's horns. Skal also mentions the vampire's cape and collar:

This production...introduced one of the most perennial features of the theatrical vampire—the big stand-up collar on the cape, a wardrobe idiosyncracy [sic] that has become almost synonymous with the character. Originally, the collar had a distinct theatrical function: to hide the actor's head when he stood with his back to the house, thus allowing him to slip out of the cape and down a trapdoor, effectively "disappearing" before the audience's eyes. Though the trick collar had no subsequent purpose in film adaptations, it has become a signature feature of vampire costuming for all time. (73)

*Dracula* opened in London on 14 February 1927 at the Little Theatre, then owned by José Levy, running for 391 performances despite tepid reviews:

One doubts if such a story can ever be as successful on stage as it is in print.... It was only a tiny step from the devilish to the ridiculous.... There were many breathtaking excitements.... Having seen Dracula thoroughly disposed of in the epilogue, one could go home with some degree of safety.... The ordinary Grand Guignol play is a nursery rhyme beside it. It is remarkably well acted, with Raymond Huntley in a terrifyingly sinister make-up as Dracula. (*Era*, 16 February 1927)

Much of the eerie horror has been lost in the adaptation...[but it is] a play full of incident, at times even powerful. "The locale" has been changed from a wild continental district to more prosaic London. This...lessen[s] the effectiveness. Mr. R. Huntley is capital as Dracula. (*Stage*, 17 February 1927)

The critic of *The Times* (15 February 1927), complaining of the production's sudden loud noises, wrote, "In that respect, at least, this piece displays a sure sense of theatre. There is very little of Bram Stoker in it. But most of us jumped in our seats at least once in every act." He went on the criticize the acting, especially the stilted delivery:

This was so obtrusive that it almost seemed to be an intentional device to assist in making the flesh creep. The most extraordinary phrases came from the Professor's ready tongue. If they were part of a foreigner's English equipment, it is a pity that Mr. Hamilton Deane forgot all about his foreign accent during the interval.

Another reviewer ridiculed the actors' speech:

Stuart Lomath [Seward] and Dora Mary Patrick [Mina]...[are] life-long victims of elocutionists. They articulated each syllable in a clear, toneless manner, giving to each one precisely the same value. Mr. Lomath pronounced the word "personally" as if it were spelt "Pahrs O Nally" and said "Sahr Vis" when he meant "service." Miss Patrick talked about a dreadful "Leth Are Gee" which affected her "Leems."[12]

Nevertheless the play drew audiences and made money. Deane prolonged its success with such P.T. Barnum-like stunts as hiring a nurse to be present at all performances, in case of fright-induced heart attacks, a publicity device borrowed from the Grand Guignol in Paris, which would be copied by motion-picture promoters of *Dracula* films. The play transferred to the Prince of Wales Theatre, apparently immune to the "stake-like pens" of the critics. The *Evening News* commented, "While glittering productions costing thousands of pounds have wilted and died after a week or so in the West End, *Dracula* has gone on drinking blood nightly" (qtd. in Skal 74).

Florence Stoker, having become dissatisfied with her share of the royalties, and perhaps aesthetically displeased with Deane's version, commissioned Charles Morrell to write a new and more accurate adaptation, which was produced by Harry Warburton at the Royal Court Theatre of Warrington in September of 1927. This "authorized" version contains large sections of *verbatim* dialogue from the novel and a number of Shakespearean references, especially to *The Tempest* (used in the shipwreck of the *Demeter* scene) and *A Midsummer Night's Dream*. The play lays on the horror elements with a heavier hand, and for this reason ran into some trouble with the Lord Chamberlain's office, which required cuts. Morrell's version includes the book's most powerful scenes: the breast-feeding scene between Dracula and Mina, and the branding of Mina with the Sacred Host. Morrell wrote these two excellent lines for Dracula: "I have lived too long in Italy to care for the smell of garlic," and "Come, drink of my blood, that you may become even as I" (qtd. in Skal 77).

Morrell's play was never brought to London and has never been revived. Deane's play continued successfully, at one point with three simultaneous touring productions. By the mid-1920s, Stoker's novel was approaching sales of more than 20,000 a year, a phenomenal figure for a "cult" classic.

The American rights to Deane's *Dracula* were bought by Horace Liveright, producer and publisher. Fatally for his financial career, he failed to include the film rights in this agreement, or the rights to the novel itself. Liveright saw the London production four times, quickly grasped its commercial possibilities, having "stumbled across a censor-proof way to present outrageous themes of oral sexuality, insanity, and borderline necrophilia" (Skal 79).

Liveright felt the script needed modernizing and hired John Balderston to collaborate with Deane. Balderston was a London-based American journalist for the *New York World* and author of the romantic time-travel and ghost play, *Berkeley Square*. Later he became a screenwriter, contributing to the screenplays of *Frankenstein, The Bride of Frankenstein, The Mummy, Mad Love, Prisoner of Zenda, Smilin' Through, Gaslight, Lives of the Bengal Lancers, Red River*, and *Gone With the Wind*. Balderston, a much better writer than Deane, made many improvements in the dialogue, replacing such clinkers as Deane's "I have sorrow if I have given you alarm—perhaps my footfall sounds not so heavy as that of your English ploughman," with "Forgive me. My footfall is not heavy, and your rugs are soft."[13]

Updating the action of the play to the Jazz Age, the two playwrights have Dracula cross Europe overnight in a plane to avoid sunlight. The plot is simplified even further, and characters are eliminated as well: the names and plot functions of Lucy and Mina are reversed, and all but a few references to the latter are omitted—she is already dead when the action begins. Quincey Morris and Lord Arthur Goldalming are eliminated and Seward becomes Lucy's father. Harker is now Lucy's fiancé (rather than Mina's husband), saving her for the life of a proper British wife by the sincerity of his love, assisted by Van Helsing's practical know-how with garlic, wafers, and stakes. Mina's function of leading the men to Dracula's hiding place is taken over by Renfield, many of whose scenes are treated as comedy. The other major alteration is the addition of two Cockney comedy roles, the maid, Wells, and the madhouse attendant, Butterworth, whose humorous comments on the action and lower-class courtship rites could be taken straight from George Blink's *The Vampire Bride* (1834). Wells and Butterworth are thoroughly in the line of comic-helper roles of traditional melodrama. Stoker's novel had not been without its humorous elements, with many touches of class snobbery and long passages in difficult-to-read Cockney dialect, but none of the book's original comic material made it into the stage adaptations.

Comparing Stoker's novel with the Deane/Balderston play, Gregory Waller in *American Horrors* writes:

Deane and Balderston necessarily alter the thematic focus of the novel—limiting the magnitude and the range of the threat posed by the vampire, omitting almost completely the role of faith, ritual, and community for the vampire hunters, and emphasizing certain simple, reassuring distinctions between man and women, young and old, sane and insane, good and evil, heroes and victims. What these two veterans of the popular stage turn Stoker's *Dracula* into is a compact, well-made play about vampires and madness that is presented in a thoroughly conventional, easy-to-follow, symmetrical form. (84)

Liveright's New York production, which opened 5 October 1927 at the Fulton Theatre (later renamed the Helen Hayes, now demolished) was much more elaborate than the London version, directed by Ira Hards with sets designed by Joseph Physioc and startling special effects including a convincing flying bat, a pivoting bookcase, and a trick coffin.

Bernard Jukes was retained from the British cast to repeat his Renfield in New York, but because Raymond Huntley held out for more money than Liveright was willing to pay, the American production starred the Hungarian actor Bela Lugosi as Dracula. He would ever afterward be associated with the role, playing it more than 1300 times onstage as well as the first film version, film sequels, and, as he fell on hard times, burlesque parodies including one with Abbott and Costello. In my opinion (which is based on his film portrayals), despite his classical stage training in Hungary, Lugosi was a stiff, graceless, unimaginative actor who was made by the role, rather than the reverse. Skal is of a different opinion, commenting on Lugosi's contribution:

The London Dracula was middle-aged and malignant; Lugosi presented quite a different picture: sexy, continental, with slicked-back patent-leather hair and a weird green cast to his makeup—a Latin lover from beyond the grave, Valentino gone slightly rancid. It was a combination that worked, and audiences—especially female audiences—relished, even wallowed in, the romantic paradoxes. (86-87)

American critics seemed to enjoy the play more than the British, but Lugosi's performance was universally condemned. Percy Hammond in the *New York Herald Tribune* (6 October 1927): "The torments of the first American performance might have been more alarming had the demon been illustrated less stiffly than he was by Bela Lugosi. It was a rigid hobgoblin...[more] resembling a wax man in a shop window than a suave ogre bent on nocturnal mischief-making." John Anderson in the *New York Post* (6 October 1927): "Though as foolish as the other theatrical creep machines, and often cumbersomely silly, *Dracula* should delight gooseflesh addicts and cause playgoing teeth to chatter for a good long run.... Mr. Lugosi performs Dracula with funereal decorum, suggesting more an operatically inclined but cheerless mortician than a bloodsucking fiend." Gilbert Gabriel, *New York Sun* (6 October 1927): "Sometimes the chaste Ibsen side of me said pish tush, tommyrot and unavailing things like that.... Still [Dracula] remains a spine-chilling, credo-splitting fiend, with victims of his villainies still clamorous and circling all around him.... The acting is fairly awful, maybe suitably so." Brooks Atkinson in *The New York Times* (26 September 1927, New Haven tryout): "One begins to protect oneself against the machinations of the 'undead' by watching the stage machinery whirl. One is not so frightened as one had ingenuously hoped to be." Alexander Woollcott's review in the *New York World* (6 October 1927) was vintage Woollcott: "Westward the curse of the vampires makes it way.... Ye who have fits prepare to throw them now.... It was probably undue captiousness to carp at the merely textual gaucherie of so telling a shocker as this...over which a fairly callow audience quaked delightedly last night at the Fulton. Your correspondent shook like an aspen."

The Deane/Balderston *Dracula* is a marked improvement over Deane's British version, and has proved to be one of modern theatre's most enduring and profitable warhorses. The great scenes are the duel of wills between the doctor and the vampire, whose line "You are a wise man, Professor—for one who has not lived even a single lifetime" (II, 49) is the play's most famous; Renfield's spider-eating mad scenes; Dracula's materialization in Lucy's bedroom, first as a bat, then arriving via trap door in a puff of smoke; Lucy's metamorphosis into a "vamp" and lunge at Harker's throat; and finally the discovery and destruction of Dracula in his coffin in a secret underground vault. It's all pure hokum, and very thrilling it must have been when first shown to the world. One of Balderston's best touches is Van Helsing's final curtain speech, directly addressed to the audience:

Just a moment, Ladies and Gentlemen! Just a word before you go. We hope the memories of Dracula and Renfield won't give you bad dreams, so just a word of reassurance. When you get home tonight and the lights have been turned out and you are afraid to look behind the curtains and you dread to see a face appear at the window—why, just pull yourself together and remember that after all *there are such things*. (CURTAIN) (III, ii, 74)

However, judged as dramatic literature, it is a thin and plodding piece of stagecraft, fatally overburdened with three dull straightmen—the old doctor, the father, and the juvenile—who expound endlessly on their own virtue and consume stage time while we wait for the vampire to appear. The structure is creakily mechanical, and the dialogue irritating in its hoked-up commercialized religiosity.[14] By eliminating the vampire brides and the major character, Lucy (but keeping her name), the playwrights seem at first glance to have cut back on the novel's misogyny: the composite Lucy/Mina really has no distinctive personality, serving merely as the disputed object for the adversaries, Dracula and the human males. Her sexually assertive seduction of Harker, the playwrights quickly assure us, is not the "real" Lucy, but the vampire acting through her. This total negation of personality or individual will reveals a misogyny as deep, if less overt, as Stoker's.

As one who acted the role of Lucy professionally when a very young actress in Tucson, Arizona, in 1965, I found it a frustrating though enjoyable experience. The old actor's adage "Play it straight if you want your laughs" is wise advice for portrayers of Lucy as well as Dracula. The rehearsals began with the commendable aim of a serious, scary production. We achieved this to an extent, but audiences are now too sophisticated and the script too dated for serious treatment.

The New York *Dracula* sold out for a year in advance and ran over 1000 performances. There were a number of touring productions as well. Dracula was played onstage by Percy Bradshaw, W.E. Holloway, Courtney White, Jack Reitzman, John Gregory, Robert Ballinger, Louis Hayward, Hurd Hatfield, and Edward Ansara among many others. In Britain, Hamilton Deane reassumed the role in 1939, and brought his production of the American version to the Lyceum Theatre, site of the first reading of *Dracula* in 1897, where Stoker had envisioned it as a vehicle for Irving.[15] It was directed by Bernard Jukes, who had played Renfield in the original London and New York productions, and at one point featured a guest appearance by Bela Lugosi.

*Dracula* made money for Horace Liveright, earning $2 million in 1930 alone, but he mismanaged his profits, and, since his contract with Florence Stoker did not include the film rights, he was forced to settle for the quitclaim sum of $45,000 from Universal Films (Skal 109).[16] He died in bankruptcy while others went on to make their fortunes from the property.

In America Dracula was becoming a household icon and pop phenomenon. As with Nodier's *Le Vampire* in Paris in 1820, others moved quickly to exploit its popularity with satiric take-offs, often musical-comedy adaptations. Martin Riccardo's *Vampires Unearthed: The Complete Multi-Media Vampire and Dracula Bibliography* lists about 30 stage adaptations between 1938 and 1982 (62-63). Orson Welles presented an hour-long radio adaptation for Mercury Theatre of the Air for CBS, in which he played Seward and Dracula, with Agnes Moorehead as Mina, on 1 July 1938, the year of the "War of the Worlds" hoax.[17]

In the last 25 years, there have been a number of serious adaptations of Stoker's *Dracula* and major revivals of the Deane/Balderston play. The first was *Dracula Sabbat* by Leon Katz in 1970 at the Judson Poets Theatre, Off-Broadway in New York. Directed by Lawrence Kornfield, the play was staged as a Black Mass in which a bare-chested, masked Dracula (Duane Tucker), accompanied by dancing assistant demons, witches, and vampires, "mounted" Lucy (Crystal Field) wearing a dildo (which rather mixes up Stoker's symbolism), who ecstatically cries, "I defy you, Jesus, I, the priestess of this rite whose body is now both altar and offering, to strike me with lightning...if your power is greater than my Lord and Master's." In *A Dream of Dracula* Leonard Wolf quotes this passage and comments, "Jesus was patient" (229). *Dracula Sabbat* featured nudity, eroticism, and violence, climaxing with an onstage decapitation of Lucy by her fiancé Arthur Holmwood. Jack Kroll in *Newsweek* (5 October 1970) apparently enjoyed it, calling it "perfect children's theater—because it is the product of a primal sincerity." Today the script strikes me as less a piece of blasphemy than of late-sixties kitsch, perhaps the last hurrah of the *Hair* generation.

In 1972 a new version of *Dracula* by Stanley Eveling, Alan Jackson, David Mowat, Robert Nye, Bill Watson, Clarisse Erikson, and John Downing earned favorable reviews in London, and in 1974 another version written and directed by Crane Johnson played the Royale Theatre in New York (Glut 97-98).

Snoo Wilson, a serious avant-garde playwright, wrote the first version of his *Vampire* in 1973, a disjointed commentary on the Dracula theme with vampires both literal and metaphorical appearing in a series of vignettes. It played at the Oval House in London, and was directed by Malcolm Griffiths. Peter Ansorge, in *Disrupting the Spectacle*, comments:

Though the play is full of the usual Wilsonian inconsistencies and confusing breaks in narrative...*Vampire* does have a kind of exciting intellectual coherence. We are presented with three views of the ways in which people are 'vampirized' by their backgrounds and traditions.... *Vampire* prove[s] to be a brutally effective stroke of Snoo Wilson's strange and ambitious theatrical imagination. (16)

In 1977 New York was host to three rival *Draculas*. The first was Bob Hall and David Richmond's *The Passion of Dracula*, starring Christopher Bernau and Guilia Pagano, at the Cherry Lane Theatre. It employed even more Christian iconography than the Deane/Balderston play, interpreting Dracula as an Antichrist figure who, among other things, rips out the throat of a female hypnotist. It played concurrently with the Broadway revival of the Deane/Balderston *Dracula* at the Martin Beck, starring Frank Langella. The Broadway production was directed by Dennis Rosa, and was brought in from the Nantucket Stage Company with evocative two-dimensional black-and-white settings by Edward Gorey. Critic William Glover wrote:

More chills and chuckles with *Dracula*. A pictorially nifty, suavely acted production of the original play about the famous fictional werewolf of Transylvania opened Thursday.... Frank Langella in the central role marvelously balances his characterization between sophisticated satire and melodramatic menace. His cohorts also sustain a mood of make-believe that keeps the creaky old piece rolling along. The original text...appears substantially unchanged.... Some of the early scenes drag, but when the complications pile up and some theatrical tricks, that won't be disclosed here, are conjured, *Dracula* reaches a triumphant tumult of escapist entertainment. Edward Gorey's Gothic-macabre sets are no small asset, full of bats and ghoulies and Rorshach [sic] frights. You would be batty not to see *Dracula*. (Associated Press Wire Service, 21 October 1977)

The Broadway production won the 1978 Tony Award for Best Play. (The Best Revival category was not yet established.) It had a three-year run, and Langella was succeeded by Raul Julia, Jean le Clerc, David Dukes; and Terence Stamp when the play opened in London.

Running simultaneously with the other two, a third Dracula play, *Count Dracula*, a mystery comedy by Ted Tiller, was a showcase (professional but non-paid) production offered by Equity Library Theatre.

In 1979 Marcel van Kherhoven's *Dracula Waltz* opened in Paris at the Theatre du Marais. In 1984 a "blood-and-jokes" *Dracula* by Christopher Bond (whose *Sweeney Todd* was the basis for Stephen Sondheim's musical) opened in London at the Half Moon Theatre, starring Daniel Day-Lewis and directed by the author. Half grand guignol, half spoof, it featured a female Van Helsing, expert in karate. Michael Billington commented in the *Guardian* (26 November 1984):

Mr. Day-Lewis combines daemonism with agility…. He clings to precipitous ledges with bat-like fervour and at one point swings over the audience's head like a black-cloaked Tarzan. Instead of the usual sleek dandy, he makes Dracula a brush-haired monster; and it is a pity that his final abduction is forestalled by a water jet produced by the crudest means.

It was revived in 1985 with a new cast, and ran simultaneously with *Dracula, or Out for the Count* by Charles McKeown at the Lyric Hammersmith, a camp version set in the thirties with Tim Flavin as a dancing Dracula, which drew universally bad reviews.

A theatrically and intellectually inventive adaptation of *Dracula* was made by the Scottish poet and playwright Liz Lochhead, author of *Mary Queen of Scots Got Her Head Chopped Off* and *Philomena*. It opened at the Royal Lyceum Theatre in Edinburgh on 14 March 1985, directed by Hugh Hodgart, designed by Gregory Smith, with John McGlynn as Dracula. Lochhead's particular achievement is to take Dracula back from film and to frame the story in vividly theatrical terms. Some of the scenes are seen through the eyes of the madman Renfield, who functions as a kind of chorus. More than an *hommage* to Stoker, it is a penetrating and poetic meditation on his "dream of Dracula." The women are drawn with great sympathy and individuality, as are the poor servants and the mad patients. Critics were full of admiration for Lochhead's achievement:

An astonishingly brave and ambitious piece of work…. It delves beneath the…surface of Stoker's story in an attempt to marry his imagery with modern ideas about women's sexuality; its language is a daring and often highly successful mixture of domestic naturalism and high melodrama, pun, alliteration and pure poetry.... It avoids the spoofs, sendups and cheap celluloid horrors we have come to associate with Dracula and handles the story with an almost disturbing emotional directness. Its mood emphasizes the pure tragedy of Dracula's exile from human happiness and Stoker's powerful intuition—expressed here through the atmosphere of Seward's horrible Victorian asylum—that the cruelty, bloodthirstiness and arrogance of the vampire underworld reflect human life. (*Guardian*, 16 March 1985)

One bold move...is her use of the character of Renfield, the fly-eating madman. Renfield is used by Bram Stoker primarily to anticipate the mood of horror. Lochhead goes further and keeps him onstage throughout most of the play. He lurks on his chain at the front of the stage, a damaged, pitiful reminder that some kinds of horror begin in the mind. (*Scotsman*, 16 March 1985)

The list of Dracula plays examined here is not exhaustive—but it shows us the outline of a pattern, one which repeats the stage's treatment of Polidori's Ruthven: both fictional sources were originally gutted of violent content for stage purposes. In Ruthven's case, a happy ending is tacked on to satisfy poetic justice, and the vampire is made much less formidable and cold-blooded, more romantic and attractive. Also, as the character became familiar to the public (in both England and France), musical adaptations, comedies, and satires followed the original melodrama. The same pattern evolved for Dracula. Stoker's 1897 novel is truly frightening and graphically violent—it proved too much so for Henry Irving, who had a sound commercial sense. In 1924 it was made into a very conventional drawing-room melodrama, stodgy and stiff, with almost every element of violence removed. No one but Dracula dies in the Deane and Deane/Balderston scripts, and the main subplot—the metamorphosis of Lucy and her impalement—is eliminated, as are all the most lurid elements of the novel: the vampire brides; the suggested homosexuality; the attack of the wolf, Berserker; the bloodletting scene where Dracula feeds Mina—all are lost. In their place, we get a seductive, "continental" gentleman, an intelligent and powerful adversary to Van Helsing, but still a typical black villain out of melodrama. For the erotic element, we have the materialization of Dracula in Lucy's bedroom, the kiss, and, in a following scene, the contaminated and "suddenly sexual" Lucy's attempt to seduce Harker—pretty tame stuff compared to the novel.[18]

Stoker's Dracula and Polidori's Ruthven have traits in common which are lacking in their stage versions: sardonic humor, defiance of society, and the apparent pleasure they take in playing with their victims. Both seem to enjoy using men's weakness and vanity to get at the women under their supposed protection—Aubrey's sister, Lucy, and Mina.

The 1920s stage Dracula comports himself more like Nodier's Ruthven of the 1820s than like Stoker's arch-fiend. But here too there are distinctions to be made: the stage Dracula's technique with women is more direct and physical, with an implied threat; Ruthven's appeal is more to the heart—romantic, emotional, asking for pity and love. Each is in keeping with the mores of his period. On the other hand, in Nodier, Planché, and Moncrieff, we see Ruthven on stage attempting to force himself physically on a peasant girl and "carry her off." In these plays the image of evil is evoked by contrasting what Ruthven appears to be, a romantic young lover, with his true nature. Dracula, in contrast, appears to be toying with his antagonists—they know what he is, yet he defies them: "You think you can destroy me, me, the king of my kind?" (III, i, 68). They are powerless to defend their women even with this knowledge. Boucicault's Ruthven/Raby/Rookwood is more of a mesmerist; his distinguishing power, also employed by Dracula, is the mental control he exerts over his victims, in some scenes under the guise of religion.

Regrettably, the Deane/Balderston play retains the worst elements of 19th-century melodrama—dull exposition, clap-trap, fourth-wall convention, stock characters, talkiness—with none of its power or excitement. Katz's *Dracula Sabbat* takes the material in the opposite direction, attempting to liberate it from a conventional frame. Perhaps Katz's play was better to see than to read on the page, where it comes off as childish and absurd. Lochhead's *Dracula*, on the other hand, through expressionistic poetic dialogue, direct address, and simultaneous staging, gives the vampire new vitality. The final moment demonstrates great theatrical and visual flair:

Jonathan grasps Dracula's cloak of darkness and spreads it out at their feet. They [Harker and Mina] sink down on it, kissing. Third and final set of shrieks and hammer blows. As it dies away with our lovers entwined on Dracula's cloak, white snow begins to fall, then blush-pink petals like apple blossom and confetti, darker pink and finally red, red petals as the curtain falls. (146)

What does one want from a production of *Dracula*, which Lochhead's play seems best able to deliver? Fear, erotic *frisson*, being taken out of oneself into another world, excitement, awe, catharsis: to leave the theatre with a sense of unease and to see the world newly—"There are such things." An enjoyable shiver.

Images do wear out—perhaps Dracula is overlaid and overladen with so much hucksterdom—shilling cereal and teaching math on *Sesame Street*—that he really cannot be seen freshly. Paradoxically, Stoker's Dracula, because of his mystery, elusiveness, and the lacunae in our grasp of him, was truly frightening. Now, he seems too familiar, and we know too much. The novel has been subjected to a series of poor stage adaptations, of which I feel only Lochhead's comes to grips with the essence of the material.

Where Dracula has been truly terrifying, on occasion, is in film, where he is shown in close-up.

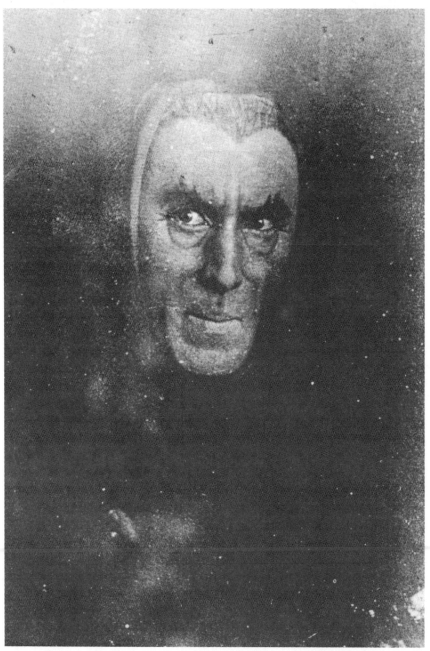

Henry Irving as Mephistopheles in *Faust* (Victoria and Albert Museum).

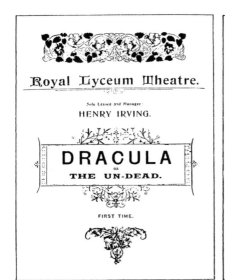

Royal Lyceum Theatre.

Sole Lessee and Manager
HENRY IRVING.

DRACULA
OR
THE UN-DEAD.

FIRST TIME.

TUESDAY, MAY 18, 1897, AT A QUARTER-PAST TEN O'CLOCK A.M.,
WILL BE PRESENTED, FOR THE FIRST TIME,

DRACULA
OR
THE UN-DEAD
IN A PROLOGUE AND FIVE ACTS
BY
BRAM STOKER.

| | |
|---|---|
| Count Dracula | Mr. JONES. |
| Jonathan Harker | Mr. PASSMORE. |
| John Seward, M.D. | Mr. RIVINGTON. |
| Professor Van Helsing | Mr. T. REYNOLDS. |
| Quincey P. Morris | Mr. WIDDICOMBE. |
| Hon. Arthur Holmwood (afterwards Lord Godalming) | Mr. INNES. |
| M. F. Renfield | Mr. HOWARD. |
| Captain Swales | Mr. GURNEY. |
| Coastguard | Mr. SIMPSON. |
| Attendant at Asylum | Mr. PORTER. |
| Mrs. Westenra | Miss GURNEY. |
| Lucy Westenra | Miss FOSTER. |
| Mina Murray (afterwards Mrs. Harker) | Miss CRAIG. |
| Servant | Miss CORNFORD. |
| Vampire Woman | Mrs. DALY. |

SYNOPSIS OF SCENERY.

Prologue: Transylvania.

SCENE 1.—Outside the Castle.
" 2.—The Count's Room.
" 3.—The same.
" 4.—The Castle.
" 5.—The Ladies' Hall.
SCENE 6.—The Count's Room.
" 7.—The same.
" 8.—The Chapel Vault.
" 9.—The Count's Room.

Act I.

SCENE 1.—The Boudoir at Hillingham.
" 2.—Dr. Seward's Study.
" 3.—The Churchyard, Whitby.
SCENE 4.—The same—Night.
" 5.—The same.

Act II.

SCENE 1.—The Boudoir—Hillingham.
" 2.—The same.
" 3.—The same.
" 4.—The same.
" 5.—Outside Hillingham.
" 6.—Lucy's Room.
" 7.—The same.
SCENE 8.—The same.
" 9.—The same.
" 10.—Mr. Harker's Meeting-Room.
" 11.—Room in the Berkeley Hotel.
" 12.—Mrs. Harker's Drawing-Room.
" 13.—The same.
" 14.—Outside the North Hospital.

Act III.

SCENE 1.—Lucy's Tomb.
" 2.—Room in the Berkeley Hotel.
SCENE 3.—Lucy's Tomb.
" 4.—Outside the Tomb.

Act IV.

SCENE 1.—Room in the Berkeley Hotel.
" 2.—Dr. Seward's Study.
" 3.—The same.
" 4.—Carfax.
" 5.—Dr. Seward's Study.
SCENE 6.—Renfield's Room.
" 7.—Mrs. Harker's Room.
" 8.—Dr. Seward's Study.
" 9.—Room in the Piccadilly House.
" 10.—Dr. Seward's Study.

Act V.

SCENE 1.—Dr. Seward's Study.
" 2.—Room in Hotel—Varna.
" 3.—Room in Hotel—Galatz.
SCENE 4.—Outside the Castle—Night.
" 5.—The same—Before Sunset.

Stage Manager ... Mr. H. J. LOVEDAY.
Musical Director ... Mr. MEREDITH BALL.
Acting Manager ... Mr. BRAM STOKER.

No fees of any kind are permitted, and the Management trust that in their endeavours to carry out this arrangement they may rely on the co-operation of the Public, who are requested, should there be any cause of complaint, to refer at once to the Acting Manager.

THE BILL OF THE PLAY IN EVERY PART OF THE HOUSE SUPPLIED WITHOUT CHARGE.

Opera Glasses can be had on Hire from the Cloak Room Attendants, One Shilling each.

This Theatre is lighted by Electricity, supplied by the Electricity Supply Corporation, Limited.

The Box Office (under the Direction of Mr. JOSEPH HURST) open from 10 to 5 and during the performance.

Private Boxes, £1 1s and £4 4s ; Stalls, 10s 6d ; Dress Circle, 7s ; Upper Circle, 4s ; Amphitheatre, 2s 6d ; Pit, 2s 6d ; Gallery, 1s

NO FEES OF ANY KIND.

NOVELLO, LONDON

Program, Lyceum, 1897.

LITTLE THEATRE

JOHN STREET, ADELPHI, STRAND

Lessee and Licensee  -  -  -  -  -  JOSÉ G. LEVY.

On MONDAY EVENING, FEBRUARY 14th, at 8.30.   Subsequent Evenings at 8.45
MATINEES:  WEDNESDAY & SATURDAY at 2.30

By arrangement with JOSÉ G. LEVY and HENRY MILLAR

HAMILTON DEANE and H. L. WARBURTON

PRESENT

THE VAMPIRE PLAY

"DRACULA"

By HAMILTON DEANE

Adapted from BRAM STOKER'S Famous Novel

| | | | |
|---|---|---|---|
| Count Dracula ... | ... | ... | RAYMOND HUNTLEY |
| Abraham van Helsing | ... | ... | HAMILTON DEANE |
| Doctor Seward . . | ... | ... | STUART LOMATH |
| Jonathan Harker | ... | ... | BERNARD GUEST |
| Quincy P. Morris | ... | ... | FRIEDA HEARN |
| Lord Godalming | ... | ... | PETER JACKSON |
| R. M. Renfield ... | ... | ... | BERNARD JUKES (By courtesy of Percy Hutchison, Esq.) |
| The Warder ... | ... | ... | JACK HOWARTH |
| The Parlourmaid | ... | ... | KILDA MACLEOD |
| The Housemaid | ... | ... | BETTY MURGATROYD |
| Mina Harker ... | ... | ... | DORA MARY PATRICK |

LITTLE THEATRE

JOHN STREET, ADELPHI, STRAND
Lessee: JOSÉ G. LEVY

Licensed by the Lord Chamberlain to JOSÉ G. LEVY

MONDAY, FEBRUARY 14th, at 8.30

By arrangement with JOSÉ G. LEVY and HENRY MILLAR

HAMILTON DEANE and H. L. WARBURTON

PRESENT

THE VAMPIRE PLAY

"DRACULA"

By

HAMILTON DEANE

Adapted from BRAM STOKER'S Famous Novel

PROGRAMME

Program, Deane's *Dracula*, London.

# FULTON THEATRE

## NEW YORK

From OCTOBER 5th 1927

# DRACULA

### A PLAY IN 3 ACTS

Adapted by HAMILTON DEANE & JOHN BALDERSTON

From the novel of the same name by BRAM STOKER

Produced by HORACE LIVERIGHT

### Cast

| | |
|---|---|
| Count Dracula | BELA LUGOSI |
| Wells | NEDDA HARRIGAN |
| Jonathan Harker | TERRENCE NEILL |
| Doctor Seward | HERBERT BUNSTON |
| Abraham Van Helsing | EDWARD VAN SLOAN |
| R. M. Renfield | BERNARD JUKES |
| Butterworth | ALFRED FRITH |
| Lucy Harker | DOROTHY PETERSON |

Program, Deane and Balderston's *Dracula*, New York.

# DRACULA
## THE INTERNATIONAL VAMPIRE PLAY

Horace Liveright, who produced The Firebrand, Hamlet in Modern Dress, Black Boy and An American Tragedy, presents a thrilling feast of the uncanny, mysterious and supernatural, *The Vampire Play*, DRACULA.

This play is founded on Bram Stoker's World Famous novel of the same name, a novel which has thrilled two generations of readers with the horror of its story, the mystery of its unfolding and the suspense of its climax.

It is safe to say that DRACULA is the most weird and spine-creeping play yet presented to an audience. It differs from all other thrillers in that it deals with the supernatural and consequently there is no awkward denouement,—no dream explanation at its conclusion.

Ira Hards, famous for his direction of "The Cat and the Canary," has directed DRACULA for Mr. Liveright. The scenic background is by Joseph Physioc.

*"The reception given 'Dracula' was most enthusiastic."*
—The Derby Daily Express.

*"If one enjoys a quick-fire procession of superquality thrills, surprises, shudders and sensations, he or she should make a point of seeing a presentation of the play. Never previously has a play so unique in theme, so remarkable in thrills and so completely overwhelming in every respect been staged in the town."* —The London Standard.

*"A really excellent thriller."*

*"You will have the time of your life."*
—The London Sketch.

*"Especially recommended for bald-headed men—it is a real hair-raiser."*
—Reynolds Illustrated News.

*"An ample feast of the uncanny and supernatural."*—The Argus, London.

*"Come away with the experience of having had more thrills than ever before in their lives."*
—The London Evening Express.

*"The jolliest blood-curdler imaginable."*—London Sunday Times.

*"I found my hour or two of horror very entertaining. So did an enthusiastic audience."*
—London Sunday News.

Scenes from the Vampire Play
DRACULA

Flyer, New York Dracula, 1927.

Program, 1973 *Dracula*. By permission of PLAYBILL ®, a registered
Trademark of PLAYBILL Incorporated, New York, NY.

Program, 1973 *Dracula*. By permission of PLAYBILL ®, a registered
Trademark of PLAYBILL Incorporated, New York, NY.

Program, 1973 *Dracula*. By permission of PLAYBILL ®, a registered
Trademark of PLAYBILL Incorporated, New York, NY.

Program, 1973 *Dracula*. By permission of PLAYBILL ®, a registered Trademark of PLAYBILL Incorporated, New York, NY.

# Chapter 10

# Film Adaptations, 1897-1992

Blood is...the symbol of human passion, the source of all passion....
Blood is the primary metaphor. In *Nosferatu* Murnau saw the connection
between the vampire's diseased blood and plague; people today may see,
as we did, the connection with AIDS. Even if people today don't feel a
sacramental relationship with God, I think they can understand how many
people renounce their blood ties to creation—to the creative spirit, or
whatever it is—and become like living dead. The vampire has lost his soul,
and that can happen to anyone.

—Francis Ford Coppola,
*Bram Stoker's Dracula: The Novel and the Legend*

From 1897 to 1993 there have been at least 600 vampire
movies. Dracula has been portrayed on film at least 130 times, more
often than any other fictional character with the possible exception
of Sherlock Holmes. Clearly this is a subject more vast than the one
I have undertaken, stage vampires, which number around 40 in
English, French, and American plays, and about 100 internationally,
including opera and ballet, from 1820 to the present.

Since my treatment of the subject would be incomplete without
a discussion of at least some of the vampire films, and since
Stoker's novel is my link to the 20th century, the films examined
will be limited to screen adaptations and sequels of *Dracula*, which
indeed dominate the genre. (See Appendix E for a filmography of
*Dracula*.) I have chosen ten films which seem to me to be the most
interesting, both in connection with the stage works which were
their source material, and in terms of artistic achievement. The
selected films are French, German, British, American, and latterly,
of no specific nationality, as movies began to be produced by
international corporations.

Vampires appeared on film almost as soon as the motion picture
was invented; one might almost say *before* that, since the magic
lantern shows in Paris, which began at the turn of the 19th century,
featured vampires among the ghosts and skeletons of the
*Fantasmagorie* spectacles. Nicéphore Niepce and Jacques Mandé

Daguerre were two innovators who experimented with light-and-shadow shows, out of which developed the dioramas, some of which featured spectres and demons which were operated somewhat like Balinese shadow puppets, or were translucent projections. In 1894, Louis and Auguste Lumière made the first practical motion picture projector, and, in partnership with Georges Méliès, a magician, mime, and showman, produced the first vampire film, *Le Manoir du Diable* in 1896, a year prior to the publication of *Dracula*.[1]

Also known as *The Haunted Castle, The Manor of the Devil,* and *The Devil's Manor,* Méliès's film is 195 feet long (three times the length of other films of this period), with a three-minute running time. It features the image of the devil as a vampire bat, and is set in a gothic castle. A bat flies in the window, circles in the air, and is transformed into Mephistopheles, performed by Méliès. He conjures up a cauldron, and out of it come beautiful girls, demons, witches, skeletons and so forth, until a "cavalier" arrives brandishing a crucifix, causing the devil to vanish in smoke. In the *Encyclopedia of Horror Movies*, Phil Hardy remarks, "This is strictly speaking the first vampire movie.... But although the work of Méliès teems with demons, monsters, apparitions and bizarre mutilations, on very rare occasions gruesome in effect...he was too steeped in the pantomime tradition of amusing fantasy to figure in the history of horror" (17).[2]

Theda Bara made a number of "vamp" films in America, and a comedy, *Mutt and Jeff Visit the Vampire*, was made in 1918. Commenting on the sudden explosion of "spooky-house" films in these years, Walter Kendrick writes,

The belated recognition of film's horrid power occurred on a large scale first in the United States, and it came as a by-product of the very works that latter-day mavens disdain, spooky-house comedies. Frequently based on stage plays, they made a direct link between nineteenth-century melodrama and twentieth-century film, the clearest case of continuity in the lurching history of scary entertainment. (207)

In 1922 the German company Prana Film produced one of the best vampire films ever created, F. W. Murnau's *Nosferatu*. Hardy describes it as "an unparalleled masterpiece, scripted by Hans Heinz Ewaers's disciple, Galeen, designed by a spiritualist, Albin Grau, photographed by a virtuoso cinematographer and directed by one of the three undisputed masters of the German cinema [with Lang and Lubitsch]" (29).

"Nosferatu" is the Romanian word for "undead" or "devil" (Florescu and McNally, *Dracula, Prince of Many Faces* 225). Despite the title change, *Nosferatu* was judged to be an unauthorized use of copyrighted material, namely Stoker's *Dracula*, and an English court ordered all copies of the film destroyed. A few pirated copies inevitably surfaced, and widow Florence Stoker's lawyers energetically hunted them down in various law courts while attempting to sell the film rights in Hollywood. Fortunately *Nosferatu* survived, and is an acknowledged masterpiece of German expressionist cinema. Although there are similarities in the characters, in my opinion *Nosferatu* differs so much from *Dracula*, its putative source, in plot, emphasis, and mood, that it is surprising that the lawsuit was successful.

The film has artistic links with *The Golem* (1914, remade 1920), *The Cabinet of Dr. Caligari* (1919), as well as the experiments in stage expressionism of Max Reinhardt. Murnau's vampire, Graf Orlock, is no prince of darkness but rather a human vermin, an embodiment of disease and death by plague, more resembling the descriptions of Varney the Vampire (in the early chapters) than Stoker's Dracula, and matchlessly played by Max Schreck. "Schreck" means "fear" in German, but apparently it was the actor's real name (Skal 53). A member of Reinhardt's company in Berlin, in which he played Death in the *Salzburg Everyman*, Schreck is extraordinary looking—corpse-like, impossibly thin, with dangling arms and strange eyes. He goes though several make-ups in the course of the film, becoming more and more loathsome, with pointed ears and elongated front teeth like a rat. Unlike Dracula, Orlock casts a shadow, used to frightening effect. Donald Glut remarks, "While Stoker's...Dracula was an impressive, strangely handsome and undeniably noble character, Schreck's Orlock was a bald, human rodent, resuscitated from some foul smelling grave, moving stiffly as if impaired by the restrictions of rigor mortis" (103).

Murnau shifts Stoker's London setting to Bremen, from 1893 to 1838, a year in which plague struck the city. Hutter and Nina (Ellen in some versions), representing Stoker's Harker and Mina, are established as ideally happy young newlyweds. The journey into fear toward the vampire castle is beautifully realized, with negative shots, draped horses which seem to run in terror of their lives, and magically opening doors. When Orlock looks at the portrait of Nina, he utters (via the intertitle) the outrageous, unforgettable line, "Is this your wife? What a lovely throat."[3]

Nina is a clairvoyant, mentally linked with her husband, sensing his danger from afar; this differs from Stoker's psychic connection between Mina and Dracula, victim and vampire. She begins to sleepwalk, to have nightmares, and to wait by the shore for her husband's return. The journey home is depicted with rapid cross-cutting between the husband on horseback and the nightmare voyage on board the ghoul-haunted ship. Orlock, now fully evolved as Nosferatu, "the undead," stalks the crew one by one, and in one remarkable shot rears up unnaturally out of his coffin, as Skal comments, "like an obscene jack-in-the-box, an image simultaneously suggesting erection, pestilence, and death" (54). (The effect was achieved by running the shot in reverse, and is reproduced in Coppola's 1992 *Dracula*.) The looming prow of the derelict ship gliding into Wisborg harbor with its cargo of coffins filled with plague-infested rats is one of the most famous sequences in cinema history, copied frame-for-frame in Werner Herzog's *Nosferatu* remake (1979) and also in the Coppola film.

Murnau alters Stoker's theme and story by changing the relationship between the woman and the vampire. Nina understands his true nature and sacrifices her life to save the city. He spends the night in her embrace, is caught in the cleansing light of the morning sun, and disintegrates, the first vampire to be so destroyed. Murnau's innovation has been accepted vampire lore ever since.[4]

Murnau's achievement is to be admired for the formal composition of the shots, the visual poetic metaphors, and a use of shadow and light that is almost abstract. Thematically, the story is shifted away from the misogyny and perceived female depravity of Stoker's novel, to the more traditional view of woman as self-sacrificing nurturer. Greta Schroeder gives a luminous performance in the role of Nina. The feeling of the film is out of any specific time, almost medieval, in contrast with Stoker's attempted scientific modernism.

Contemporary reviews of the film were not very perceptive: "More of a soporific than a thriller...[with actors] like cardboard puppets doing all they can to be horrible in papier-maché settings" (*New York Times*); "Jumbled and confused...[the film] flopped woefully due to inexpert cutting or bad continuity" (*New York Herald Tribune*). Only the *New York Post* recognized the film's greatness:

Not since *Caligari* has this reviewer been so taken with a foreign horror film as with...*Nosferatu the Vampire*...taken from *Dracula*, recently seen on the stage...and infinitely more subtly horrible than the stage edition, Mr. Murnau's is no momentary horror, bringing shrieks from suburban ladies in the balcony, but a pestilential horror coming from a fear of things only rarely seen.[5]

Murnau's treatment of the *Dracula* material foregrounds the plague symbolism of vampirism, the sixth interpretive theme offered in Chapter 9. He minimizes the erotic content and the misogyny by idealizing woman and demonizing (in this case literally making a monster of) the vampire. Aesthetically, it bears a closer relationship to German expressionist drama of the 1920s than to 19th-century melodrama, from which it retains schematic character types of pure good and pure evil.

Werner Herzog's 1979 remake with Klaus Kinski and Isabelle Adjani was generally regarded as a failure, despite the beauty of its cinematography. Leonard Wolf admired the world-weariness which Kinski brings to his vampire (*Connoisseur* 160), but others ridiculed the spotlessly clean and sanitary-looking white rats obviously supplied from a laboratory, the low-voltage acting, the death-march tempo, and the shot-by-shot quotation of many of Murnau's sequences. Hardy writes, "Herzog's version fails to match the original's symphonic mastery of light and rhythm and testifies to a radical incomprehension of Murnau's insights into the fantasy at stake in his masterpiece" (30).

In 1931, the same year that Carl Dreyer made *Vampyr*, a cinematic masterpiece and doubtless the greatest of the vampire films, Hollywood produced its first version of *Dracula*, made for Universal Films by Tod Browning, director of *Freaks* (1932). Browning's *Dracula* is the film most closely dependent on a theatrical source, the Deane/Balderston play of 1927. Many scenes which occur nowhere in the novel are taken directly from the stage play. In fact, the film is so "stagebound" that the staking of Dracula occurs off camera, and the filmmakers eschew the use of technical special effects of which the industry was then capable. For this reason, the film seems static, talky, and uneventful. Also, the play itself is a poor piece of theatre, as discussed in Chapter 9.

Although *Dracula* has to be called a seminal film, since it produced over 130 sequels and remakes, it is generally considered today to have been overpraised. Commenting in general on the period, Kendrick remarks:

Many American films of the late 1920s and the 1930s—especially those produced at Universal—show the influence of Expressionism in their deployment of impossible architecture, warning shadows, and oblique camera angles. But the spooky-house inheritance was not the property of a single school, nor was it strictly European.... In retrospect, *Dracula* looks like a transitional film, stuck between spooky-house comedies and the more singleminded cinematic horrors that would soon follow. (212, 216)

Browning had previously made another vampire movie with Lon Chaney, *London After Midnight*, and had invited the actor to play Dracula for him. But Chaney died suddenly in 1930, and, after considering Conrad Veidt, Joseph Schildkraut, Paul Muni, William Courtenay, and Ian Keith, the producers settled on the Broadway Dracula, Bela Lugosi, whose energetic lobbying for the role gave Universal a bargaining advantage in contract negotiations, and Lugosi was paid the derisive sum of $3500. Edward Van Sloan also repeated his stage role, Van Helsing, and played the role in several sequels.

The filming of *Dracula* is related in admirable detail by David Skal in his 1990 study, *Hollywood Gothic*. He has interviewed everyone still living who worked on the film, and quotes David Manners, who played Harker: "To be quite honest, Tod Browning was always off to the side somewhere. I remember being directed by Karl Freund, the photographer who came from Germany and had a great sense for film. I believe he is the one who is mainly responsible for *Dracula* being watchable today" (130).

Browning adored cobwebs, draping them everywhere, and in a very eccentric touch, insisted on dressing the Castle Dracula set with live armadillos, ludicrously out of place scurrying in and out of the nooks and crannies of the gothic set. The screenwriters—Louis Bromfield, Garrett Ford, and Dudley Murphy all worked on it at various times—decided to tie up the loose strands of the novel by sending Renfield instead of Harker to Transylvania and have him driven insane by his experience there. Almost all film sequels follow this alteration. Stoker never explains why his vampire is psychically attuned to this particular English lunatic.[6] Dwight Frye, also repeating his Broadway role, was so definitive that he was typecast in similar parts ever afterward. Mina's character was rewritten to further cleanse it of any taint of the "New Woman." Helen Chandler, who played the role, remarked, "I played one of those bewildered little girls who go around pale, hollow-eyed and anguished, wondering about things" (126). She had a fragile, if wooden, quality and was very pretty and blonde.

Manners describes Lugosi on the set:

I mainly remember Lugosi standing in front of a full-length mirror between scenes, intoning "I am Dracula." He was mysterious and never really said anything to the other members of the cast except good morning when he arrived and good night when he left. He was polite, but always distant. I never thought he was acting, but being the odd man he was. (qtd. in Skal 132)

Carroll Borland, who appeared in several films with Lugosi, attributed his remote attitude to his poor command of English.

In terms of thematic emphasis, the Browning *Dracula* foregrounds the theme of racism, as discussed in the previous chapter. Lugosi's interpretation, which influenced all the Draculas that followed, is distinctly "human"; that is, unlike Chaney in *London After Midnight*, he used no special make-up, no fangs. As Andrew Tudor, in *Monsters and Mad Scientists: A Cultural History of the Horror Movies*, remarks, "Lugosi...is essentially human in all outward signs, comporting himself as a stereotypically stylized foreign aristocrat. Constantly clothed in full evening dress, only the strange rhythms and accents of his verbal delivery ('I am...Dracula') ...serve as...reminders that he is both malevolent and alien" (163).

The film drew mixed reviews:

Tod Browning directed—although we cannot believe that the same man was responsible for both the first and latter parts of the picture. Had the rest of the picture lived up to the first sequence...*Dracula*...would have been a horror and thrill classic long remembered" (*Hollywood Filmograph*, 4 April 1931)

In spite of pronounced merit the story of human vampires who feast on the blood of living victims is too extreme to provide entertainment.... Plainly a freak picture, it must be accepted as a curiosity devoid of the important element of sympathy that causes the widest appeal. (*Los Angeles Times*, 22 February 1931)

Mr. Browning is fortunate in having in the leading role in this eerie work, Bela Lugosi.... What with Mr. Browning's imaginative direction and Mr. Lugosi's make-up and weird gestures, this picture succeeds to some extent in its grand guignol intentions. This picture can at least boast of being the best of the many mystery films. (*The New York Times*, 13 February 1931)

Most critics agreed that the first two reels, the Transylvanian section of *Dracula*, are the best. Skal believes that the cinematographer,

Karl Freund, who had worked in Berlin with Murnau and Pabst, lost interest in the project after the opening sequence and his realization of what a hack Browning was. Agreeing, William K. Everson in *Classics of the Horror Film*, comments:

[It] was never quite the definitive vampire film that it deserved to be, or that its opening two reels indicate it could have been.... [They are] obviously dominated far more by the pictorial style of cameraman Karl Freund...than by the static and stage-bound style of Browning.... It is stilted, pedestrian, and sadly in need of a musical score to bring some vitality to its many lifeless passages. (194)

Probably because of budget-scrimping, the fate theme from *Swan Lake* was used instead of original music, to disconcerting effect. Skal points out some of the crude errors of the final cut: the subplot involving the discovery and destruction of Lucy is dropped mid-film and never resolved; Renfield attacks the maid, yet she turns up well and hearty a few minutes later (139). Several expensive sets were cut out of the final print. Leonard Wolf, while acknowledging the film's shortcomings, sums up his attitude toward it: "Beyond all this, there is in Browning's film always Lugosi, passing on probably for all time the image of Dracula in white tie and tails moving elegantly from one cool bed to another like a bloody Don Giovanni as he pursues what Universal Pictures, in its advertisement for the film, asserted was 'The Strangest Love a Man Has Ever Known'" (*Dream* 287).

One of Skal's main theses in *Hollywood Gothic* is the superiority of the Spanish-language version of *Dracula*, shot at the same time and on the same set as Browning's. More imaginative cinematography; atmospheric lighting; tighter pacing; better acting, with Carlos Villarias' elegant vampire and especially Lupita Tovar's voluptuous Mina, showing a character progression from innocence to corruption; and much more imaginative direction by George Melford, make the Spanish *Dracula* a favorite among horror film connoisseurs.[7]

Although *Dracula* was overshadowed, both in profits and in critical reception, by Universal's *Frankenstein* released the following year, an era of Dracula sequels was about to commence, which continued through the thirties and forties, including *Dracula's Daughter, Son of Dracula, House of Frankenstein* (featuring Dracula), *House of Dracula* (featuring Frankenstein), and many others listed in Appendix E. Of these the finest is *Dracula's*

*Daughter* (1936), directed by Lambert Hillyer. It has never received much critical attention, possibly because it lacked a recognized name or male star in the vampire role. Countess Marya Zaleska is powerfully portrayed by Gloria Holden, supported by Edward Van Sloan repeating his Van Helsing role, and Otto Kruger as the hero and object of the vampire's desire, a London psychiatrist.

The film has excellent camera work, a good musical score, well-written dialogue, and a well-structured plot (co-written by John L. Balderston). The ritual cremation of Dracula's body by the mysterious black-swathed countess and her lurching, grim-visaged servant, Sandor, is wonderfully realized amid swirls of smoke and shadow. The countess's farewell to her father:

Unto Adoni and Aseroth, into the keeping of the lords of the flame and lower pits, I consign this body, to be for ever more consumed in the purging fire. Let all baleful spirits that threaten the souls of men be banished by the sprinkling of this salt. Be thou exorcised, O Dracula, and thy body, long undead, find destruction throughout eternity in the name of thy dark, unholy master. (qtd. in Glut 126)

Fearing that she is cursed with her father's vampirism, she consults the dashing Dr. Geoffrey Garth, seeking his help in overcoming her addiction to blood. The hint of lesbianism surfaces for the first time in vampire films as the countess lures a young streetwalker to her studio under the pretense of wanting her for a model, but "seduces" her with the aid of a hypnotic ring. The experience sends the girl into a fatal coma. The lust for blood is too strong for the countess's scruples, and she is soon planning to make Dr. Garth one of the undead to join her as an eternal consort. She flees to Transylvania, kidnapping Garth's fiancée to make sure he will follow. But Sandor is jealous, and shoots his mistress with an arrow, a small but fatal wooden stake. Although the film takes a romantic and sympathetic view of the vampire woman, it is a descendant of Blink's *The Vampire Bride* (1834).

The British film industry had imposed a moratorium on horror films in 1937, but they crept slowly back into production, and in 1958 Hammer Films released the first of its vampire series, *The Horror of Dracula*, followed by *The Brides of Dracula* (1960), *Dracula, Prince of Darkness* (1965), *Dracula Has Risen from the Grave* (which won the Queen's Award for Industry, 1968), *Taste the Blood of Dracula* (1969), *The Scars of Dracula* (1970), *Countess Dracula* (1970), *Twins of Dracula* (1971), *Dracula A.D.*

*1972* (1972), *Satanic Rites of Dracula* (1973), and *Dracula and the Seven Golden Vampires* (1973). The Hammer Films house style included rich technicolor photography (previous horror films had been in black-and-white), lavish-looking but actually inexpensive costumes and sets, graphic violence, and beautiful girls in low-cut negligées, and plenty of pointed teeth and spurting blood. A rich palette of blues, purples, and especially reds; glamourous, candelabra-strewn, vaguely 19th-century castles; and an air of grim seriousness are hallmarks of these films.

The first of the series, *Horror of Dracula*, is considered the best. It was directed by Terence Fisher, who made several of the sequels, and gave star billing to Peter Cushing, a fine-boned, ice-cold British actor, but "introduced" Christopher Lee in his first performance as Dracula. Cushing and Lee, previously Frankenstein and monster for Hammer in *The Curse of Frankenstein* (1957), were to become horror film's most famous acting partners.

Lee broke with the Lugosi tradition by speaking with an upper-crust British accent as he welcomes Harker, hired to catalogue his library, into his castle, a bizarrely overdecorated Bavarian hunting lodge. This Dracula has a mania for serpentine columns and stuffed animal heads. After a remarkably graphic impalement of one of Dracula's importunate brides (shot in three different versions for the censors of various countries), the scene shifts to Harker's home. Strangely, considering the British character names and Cockney servants, we discover we are supposed to be in a German city called Krogstad. In yet another realignment of the secondary characters, Harker's fiancée is Lucy, sister to Arthur Holmwood, who is married to Mina. Renfield is eliminated from the plot.

While Cushing gives an overly sanctimonious performance as Van Helsing, full of British mannerisms and phony intensity, Lee is sensational as Dracula, with his "blood-smeared mouth and brutal stride" (Kendrick 236). After the opening sequence, he does not speak at all, but appears as a kind of lurid sex fiend and snarling beast. Unlike the stately Lugosi, Lee could move with speed and violence, and was equipped with fangs. Glut remarks, "Lee's Dracula was a *dynamic* figure, fangs bared and dripping blood, red eyes flaring with Satanic fire. He would toss his victims about like the truly supernaturally strong character that Stoker had described" (158). With Freudian wit, the writers place Dracula's hiding place in the house's cellar, in a white coffin, no less. He is pursued back to his castle, where he is literally disintegrated into dust by Cushing with sunlight and crucifix. Hardy remarks:

Fisher deployed a poetic, subtly ironic realism for this epoch-making movie, which marked the first significantly *British* cinematic interpretation of the myth. His Dracula is the nineteenth-century equivalent of James Bond—a man with all the qualities, power and pleasures the petty bourgeoisie guiltily pines for…. The acting of the most famous horror duo in film history—Cushing and Lee—is impeccable, as is that of the female protagonists. But it is Fisher's uncanny sense of atmosphere, rhythm and colour, his poetic ellipses…which makes this one of the most enthralling films made in Britain. (111-12)

The French film critic Gérard Lenne also gives the film high praise:

*The Nightmare of Dracula* (Terence Fisher 1958), whose public triumph never fails, does not depart from the strict observance of vampire rituals. Its dramatic progression, prodigiously effective, espouses the evolution of the erotic/affective relationship in which Dracula becomes the omnipresent master of ceremonies, always feared and always hoped for. Thus the plastic perfection of *Nightmare* comes to sustain the internal structures of meaning without which it would have the gratuitous value of sheer aestheticism [without context].[8]

Christopher Lee remarked later of the film, "It's the only one that I've done that's ever been any good, in my opinion. It's the only one that remotely resembles the original book" (qtd. in Glut 164).

Lee refused to play Dracula again for eight years, but, like Lugosi before him, eventually resigned himself to the inevitable. He returned to Hammer Films for *Dracula, Prince of Darkness* in 1965, again directed by Terence Fisher, which features a spine-tingling resurrection scene which is a favorite of aficionados of this series:

The Count's servant…revives his master by hanging Alan…upside down over the tomb containing Dracula's ashes and draining the blood from him. The scene is one of hallucinatory beauty as bright colours and swirling mist emphasize the overwhelming physicality of the ritual which allows Tingwell's lifeblood to be released as pure energy making Dracula swell into a blood-gorged body dedicated to the pursuit of sensual pleasure. (Hardy 220)

The film introduced Barbara Shelley, who, along with Barbara Steele, was one of horror's leading women. She is done away with by monks in a scene of particular brutality.

The Hammer *Dracula* series vividly focuses on the misogynistic theme of Stoker's novel. The many female victims are presented for our delectation as so many toothsome morsels, with much cleavage, as though the vampire were fixated on breasts, not throats. The hypocrisy and sexism of the sixties' sexual revolution, or at least as it was commercially exploited, stand revealed in these films, which seem almost designed to illustrate Laura Mulvey's theory of the male gaze.[9] The actresses, mostly interchangeable, unknown (in contrast to the two male stars), and amateurish, appear to have been recruited off Carnaby Street; they wear heavy makeup and transparent nightgowns to bed, contrary to logic, practicality, and realism, which have no place in this world. But since the "girls" are presented so artificially, no emotional involvement is possible, so the fear quotient is lowered. Thus the sexism, in one way, has an adverse effect on the commercial product. We are looking as a predator at these females, but they are presented with such boring predictability that one meal is like the next. Eventually the Hammer Films formula was exhausted and the series ground to a halt in 1973.

As in the 1820s, the scary pieces were followed by a series of comedies and take-offs, beginning with Roman Polanski's *The Fearless Vampire Killers* in 1967, a spoof of the Hammer Films series. Polanski, who co-authored, directed, and starred in the film, brings a feeling of authenticity to the Eastern European locale: the peasants are more loutish and crude than British or American directors would have thought of making them, and everything is covered in deep snow. The vampire, Count von Krolock (cf. Murnau's Orlock), is played in the classic mold by Ferdy Mayne.

The action culminates in a vampire ball attended by ghoulish guests in 18th-century and medieval costumes. The movie's last gag is that the Sharon Tate character is rescued too late by the supreme exertions of the heroes; already a vampire, she puts the bite on Polanski in the film's final frame.

*The Fearless Vampire Killers* has a fine score by Krzysztof Komeda, and very impressive settings, which to my eyes have more a Polish than a Transylvanian feeling. The film was heavily re-edited to suit American taste, and Polanski attempted to remove his name from the final cut. The comedy is heavy-handed, but many horror film chroniclers have praised it:

The film is an astounding cinematic *tour de force* that is funny, chilling, and intensely lyrical at the same time and shows that the generally accepted wisdom that horror shall either be played straight or become a comedy, is false since both jokes and anxiety are rooted in the same soil of unconscious desires and combine to generate the sense of the uncanny. The resulting movie is one of the very few perfectly achieved examples of the uncanny, delicately poised between the familiar and the weird. (Hardy 258)

Everson particularly praises the comic and extremely likable Jewish vampire (Alfie Bass), who laughs with glee at the ineffectual crucifix thrust at him. He points out that this is the first vampire film in which evil is permitted to triumph over good (7).

Andy Warhol, who had previously made a series of "underground" movies, *Dracula* with Naomi Levine, *Batman Dracula* with Jack Smith and Baby Jane Holzer, and *Batman*, again with Smith, which were all released in 1964 through the Film-makers' Cooperative, lent his name to an international commercial release, *Andy Warhol's Dracula* (1973), made at Cinecitta in Rome and written and directed by Paul Morrissey. It starred Udo Kier as an effete invalid who, despite his obvious repugnance for women, requires the blood of "wirgins" to sustain his life. The difficulty is that every *soi-disant* virgin is really a slut, whose tainted blood gives the delicately constituted vampire severe attacks of food poisoning and nausea. Complaining "My body can't take this treatment anymore—the blood of these whores is killing me," he and his sister travel to rural Italy in search of pure unspoiled female flesh, and descend on the villa of impoverished aristocrats. Unfortunately the daughters of the house have been previously debauched by the gardener (Joey D'Allesandro), a socialist and revolutionary. Vittorio de Sica gives an eccentric performance as the pious old father, and Roman Polanski has a cameo as an angry peasant.

This comedy ends in graphically depicted butchery: D'Allesandro chops off the vampire's arms, legs, and penis before impaling him. The film intends to satirize the horror genre by taking the butchery so far as to enter into the realm of the ridiculous, but is done so poorly that it is merely disgusting—the makers would no doubt claim that this was the intention. It also weakly parodies the irrational code of honor of the old European aristocracy. The disgust for and loathing of women that the film displays is so strident that the film is more obnoxious than funny. Others have appreciated it, however; film critic Ginger Strand writes, "There is an incredible beauty in Kier's Count—the beauty of the aesthete who had outlived his own aesthetic" (24).

*Love at First Bite* (Stan Dragoti, 1979) is a funnier spoof, which Leonard Wolf calls "ebullient yet impeccable" (179), with George

Hamilton in an amusing high-comedy send-up of Bela Lugosi. Evicted from his castle by Romanian Communists, he flies (by airplane) to America, accompanied by his trusty assistant, Renfield, and experiences culture shock in the mean streets of New York. Hamilton falls for a crass New York model and liberated woman (Susan St. James), winning her away from her psychiatrist boyfriend (tiresomely played by Richard Benjamin), who fruitlessly tries to exorcise him with the Star of David. As the lovers fly off (as bats) into the night, Benjamin and the cop are left to try on his abandoned vampire cape, a symbol of the elegance and romance our age is lacking.

Universal's 1979 *Dracula* was a lavish and spectacular entry, directed by John Badham and starring Frank Langella repeating his Broadway role as the count; as Van Helsing, Laurence Olivier (who seems to be reprising his mad Nazi dentist from *The Marathon Man*); as Seward, Donald Pleasance; and as Mina, the young and relatively unknown Kate Nelligan, who almost capsizes the film with the intelligence and ferocity of her performance. The film cost $40 million, the largest budget ever for a horror movie, and fairly large for any film of this period. Filmed on location at Tintagel, Cornwall, it is sensual, romantic, and beautiful to look at, and has some brilliant moments. Critics complained that Langella's languid and Byronic Dracula was too much the lover and not at all frightening, and disliked the odd updating of the material to the Edwardian period, which allowed the vampire hunters to pursue their foe in a brigade of antique sports cars. Badham attempted to create a filmic equivalent of the ecstasy of the vampire's kiss with a sort of abstract, psychedelic flame effect. His emphasis is definitely on the erotic nature of the vampire myth, and "the call of the dark stranger." The plot follows the 1927 stage play, with some additions from the novel.

Three big-budget vampire movies were released in 1979— Badham's *Dracula*, Herzog's *Nosferatu*, and *Love at First Bite*— duplicating the trio of Draculas on the New York stage in 1973. Since 1979, the most important vampire film has been Francis Ford Coppola's adaptation, opening 13 November 1992, which he called *Bram Stoker's Dracula*, a title previously used by several films. While I have treated the other films cursorily, I would like to discuss this one in some detail, as it is not only the most recent, but also in my opinion the best film version of Stoker's novel.

While it hews closely to the specifics of the novel, the emphasis on the vampire's supernatural powers, especially of flight, recalls

Dumas's *Le Vampire* (1851). The cinematography emphasizes vertiginous drops and ornately designed dissolves. The director and his son, Roman Coppola, the visual effects director, rather than using modern techniques such as "morphing" and computer imaging, chose to reproduce the "within-the-camera" or "floor" effects of the early days of filmmaking, so that the film contains a series of *hommages* to the classics of the genre: the free play of shadows recalls *Vampyr*; the "falling up" of the perfume in the chamber of the vampire brides, as well as the human arm sconces, the withering of flowers at the approach of the monster, and the conversion of Mina's tears into diamonds, are recreated from Jean Cocteau's *La Belle et le bête*. Running footage in reverse reproduced the eerie and unnatural way in which the vampire rises from his coffin, repeating the scene exactly from Murnau's *Nosferatu*. This effect is used throughout the film. Dracula's dizzying crawl down his castle wall was somewhat disappointing, but the vampire brides (out of Gustav Klimt, one seemingly a Medusa) crawled all over the walls and ceiling to eerie effect. Their magical rising up out of the bed where they attack Harker was an effective and unexpected use of the oldest special effect associated with stage vampires: Planché's vampire trap, first used in 1820, thus linking the film with the first English vampire play, Planché's *The Vampire, or The Bride of the Isles*.

The visual style of the film is such that the emphasis is primarily on the costumes (which won the film's only Academy Award), designed by Eiko Ishioka with a rare combination of imagination and extravagance. I noticed the influence of Gustav Klimt and Gustave Moreau; the picture book commemorating the film's opening also mentions Caspar David Friedrich, Fernand Khnopff, and the entire Symbolist movement (Coppola and Hart 70). The protective gear of the madhouse keepers, the straitjackets resembling the segmented bodies of insects, the correctness of the Victorian period broken by flashes of pure fantasy such as Lucy's bizarre wedding gown and burial dress, lift the costuming beyond the realm of a run-of-the-mill period piece.

The film opens with a pre-title sequence in 15th-century Transylvania, attempting to justify Dracula's war against God. Dracula's perception of Mina as his long-lost bride is a device, not to be found in Stoker, that the screenwriters claim to have drawn from historical sources.[10] It had actually been used before in *Dracula* remakes, including a 1973 film also called *Bram Stoker's Dracula*, directed by Dan Curtis[11] and starring Jack Palance—in this screenplay, by Richard Matheson, Dracula's lost love is Lucy rather than Mina. The device was also used in the 1972 *Blacula* with William Marshall, previous to that in *The Mummy* with Boris Karloff.

After the suicide of his wife, in rage and grief Dracula thrusts his spear into the altar cross, which gushes blood (the iconography of *Parsifal* being played with here). The filmmaker is creating new vampire myth—as long as the cross bleeds, Dracula will be cursed as a drinker of blood. Anthony Hopkins (later Van Helsing) is briefly seen as a priest denying holy burial to the suicide wife, and establishing the Van Helsing family as *dhampires*, or vampire killers—all correct lore, but flashing by too quickly for moviegoers to grasp in one viewing, as does the dimly lit and extraordinarily costumed gypsy woman who hands Harker the protective crucifix and repeats from Bürger's "Lenore" the line "For the dead travel fast." Renfield's connection to Dracula, too, is falsely accounted for—Stoker's madman had never seen Dracula.

The film unfolds using the epistolary narrative device of the novel. What is "rich and strange" about Coppola's treatment of the Castle Dracula section is its touches of comedy—not just macabre humor, but genuine wit, both verbal and visual. This Dracula is a gracious, if creepy, host, and his shadow is as mischievous as Peter Pan's, but far more menacing.

All the major events of the novel are included in this film, including the scene where Mina drinks Dracula's blood, shown very erotically, but here too screenwriter James V. Hart gives it a more romantic reading: Dracula hesitates—he loves her too much to damn her to his eternally cursed existence, and so sates his needs with Lucy. Ironically, the filmmakers are repeating the artificial division between true love and sexual desire which rang so false in the Planché and Moncrieff melodramas of 1820: Ruthven's old division of women into those too good for him (Malvina=Mina), and those "low" enough to be suitable for food (Lovette=Lucy). Another aspect of this scene is that the way in which Dracula's blood-offering is filmed recalls the Christian iconography of the crucifixion. In many medieval and Renaissance paintings blood pours from the spear-wound in Christ's body, sometimes into a cup or grail, where it changes into the sacred wine of the Eucharist: "This is my blood of the new testament" (Matthew 26:28). Dracula's blood offers eternal life-in-death.

The film's best sequence is Mina's encounter with Dracula on the streets of London. They happen to meet outside the Lyceum

Theatre, where a billboard announces that Henry Irving is appearing in *Hamlet*. We can imagine Bram Stoker sitting inside the theatre in his manager's office working on his novel. Mina leads Dracula into a cinematograph, where the show features an approaching train, a reference to Lumière's famous film which panicked its first audience, and a shadow-puppet recreation of Dracula's battle with the Turks (a reference to Georges Méliès, who made the first vampire film in 1896, also a magician and puppeteer). In this dreamlike sequence, Mina, amid crowds of people, is stalked by the escaped wolf, Berserker, functioning as Dracula's double.

Coppola films the end of the novel exactly as written, with the chase over the Borgo Pass, the attack of the vampire brides and the circle of fire, the fight with the gypsies, and the death of Dracula in the snow. According to Leonard Wolf, in over 130 previous film versions of *Dracula*, the original ending of the book had never been used.

The acting is on an operatic scale and, considering the nature of the material, is appropriate. Coppola is known to be "an actor's director," allowing great creative freedom to his actors, whom he regards as collaborative artists. Winona Ryder makes a beautiful, romantic, sensitive Mina; Sadie Frost creates a gorgeous, sensual, innocent but voluptuous Lucy; Tom Waits is a superbly revolting and sympathetic Renfield. Anthony Hopkins has great fun with Van Helsing, offering his thumb with paternal affection to a tiny vampire bat in a lecture to medical students, and capturing the grotesque and often inappropriate sense of humor that Stoker gave the character, a dimension that never enters the performances of less imaginative interpreters like Peter Cushing or Edward Van Sloan.

Gary Oldman, a former member of both the Royal Court Theatre and the Royal Shakespeare Theatre whose previous film work includes brilliant portraits of Sid Vicious, Joe Orton, and Lee Harvey Oswald, portrays Dracula as a tortured, lost soul, a throwback to Nodier's romantic conception of Ruthven: "I saw the features of a young man, only he was pale and appeared to cast his eyes upon me with the most touching expression, seeming to beg for help" (I, iii, 15).[12] Stoker's Dracula was not really looking for a lost love through the centuries, but that was the interpretive thrust of Coppola's vision. The character's aura of tragedy is aided by the script's close appropriation of the last words of Christ for the dying Dracula: "Where is my God? He forsakes me.... It is finished.... Give me peace" (Coppola 163). Oldman's vocal characterization alone is remarkable, and with the aid of special effects he shape-shifts eight times: a 15th-century Wallachian warlord, a 400-year-old man, a young prince, a bat creature (drawn from Sätty's illustrations in *The Annotated Dracula*), a hairy incubus (straight out of Fuseli's "Nightmare"), a wolf, a green mist, and a swarm of rats. Critics who complain that the film was insufficiently frightening missed what Coppola and Oldman were attempting to achieve in their interpretation; Coppola calls his film "a dark, erotic dream."[13]

Although box office returns far exceeded expectations, reviews of the film were mixed. Vincent Canby gave high praise to the film-maker's achievement, calling it

such a dizzy tour of movie-making forces that it comes close to overwhelming all reasonable doubts.... With its gorgeous sets and costumes, its hallucinogenic special effects and mad montages that recall the original grandeur of Abel Gance's *Napoleon*, this *Dracula* transcends camp to become a testimonial to the glories of film making as an end in itself.... After *Apocalypse Now*, everything Mr. Coppola touched seemed a bit puny, either light of weight or more technically innovative than emotionally involving. With *Dracula* it's apparent that Mr. Coppola's talent and exuberance survive. ("Coppola's Dizzying Vision of Dracula," *The New York Times*, 13 November 1992, C: 1, 19)

Others were more negative:

The one thing the movie lacks is headlong narrative, energy and coherence. There is no story we can follow well enough to care about. Coppola seems more concerned with spectacle and set-pieces than storytelling. I enjoyed the movie simply for the way it looked and felt.... [It] is an exercise in feverish excess, and for that if for little else, I enjoyed it. (Roger Ebert, "It's 'Dracula' for Fangsgiving," *New York Daily News*, 13 November 1992, 60)

David Denby, slammed the film as "the Hotel Fontainebleau of vampire movies," concluding that Coppola had lost his way as an artist:

The day Francis Ford Coppola abandoned realism for artifice has to rank among the saddest in modern film history.... His *Bram Stoker's Dracula* is an unholy mess, a bombastic kitschfest of whirling, decomposing photography, writhing women, and spurting blood.... Nothing can replace Bela Lugosi's intimidating theatrical inflections and magnificent hands, but Oldman does have a few giddy moments.... The actresses work themselves up to ecstasies by sucking blood and mating with devil dogs. This *Dracula* is bound to become notorious, but despite such gaudy scenes as Ryder licking the blood on Oldman's chest, it's still among the most boring movies ever made. ("Bad Blood," *New York* 25: 45, 16 November 1992, 72)

The critical opinion most closely agreeing with my own was that of Richard Corliss, who wrote in *Time* (15 November 1992), "Coppola composes movies as Wagner composes operas.... The force of his will is as imposing as the range of his art."

We seem to be in the midst of a new cycle of vampire movies—these titles were released in 1992 alone: *Innocent Blood*; *To Sleep with a Vampire*; *Buffy, the Vampire Slayer*; *Tale of a Vampire*; and *Bram Stoker's Dracula*; and in 1994, *Interview with the Vampire*. The films seem always to have come in clusters—1979 brought three large-budget vampire pictures; a Hammer *Dracula* came out almost every year from 1958 to 1972, and the 1931 *Dracula* spawned a series of sequels, which however did not get under way until 1936. In his study of the genre, *The Celluloid Vampires*, Michael Murphy notes that the period from 1970 to 1975 produced more vampire movies than the entire output from film's beginnings in 1896 to 1970, the great majority produced in the United States (ix).

In a more recent study, Noël Carroll in *The Philosophy of Horror, or Paradoxes of the Heart* attempts to formulate a theory for these surges as symptomatic of cultural anxiety during periods of societal crisis.[14] Carroll writes:

Horror cycles emerge in times of social stress, and...the genre is a means through which the anxieties of an era can be expressed. That the horror genre should be serviceable in this regard comes as no surprise, since its specialty is fear and anxiety. What presumably happens in certain historical circumstances is that the horror genre is capable of incorporating or assimilating general social anxieties into its iconography of fear and distress.

Film history provides several well-known examples of this. The horror films in the style of what is called German Expressionism were produced in the crisis milieu of the Weimar Republic; the Universal cycle of horror classics, in the United States, occurred during the Great Depression; the science fiction/horror cycle of the early fifties, in America, corresponds to the early phase of the Cold War. Moreover, these different cycles tended to use their horrific imagery to express certain anxieties that correlate with the uneasy temper of their times. (207-08)

I would categorize the main cycles of vampire films as follows:

1. 1931-41. The first wave began with the Lugosi *Dracula*, was killed off by too many repetitions, leading to parody, and ending in joint appearances with Frankenstein's monster, Abbott and Costello, and the Bowery Boys. As Kendrick states:

Mired in the Great Depression, audiences may have sought escape into fantasy—though their attraction to fantasies that stood their hairs on end remains hard to account for (perhaps it was homeopathic medicine). The advent of the talkies may have helped horror, since howling wolves and creaking doors could be portrayed, not merely suggested.... Though far from new in inspiration, these films launched an assault on their audiences' nerves that indeed *was* new; they thrilled in double measure for that reason. (219-20)

This cycle was interrupted by World War II. After the war, the cultural demonization of Communists in an atmosphere of witch-hunt, invasion fantasies, and paranoia of the "red menace" led to a wave of science fiction movies with totally unsympathetic aliens, bug-eyed monsters, and giant insects. Often the birth of these creatures is specifically attributed to the use or testing of the atom bomb. It seems that, in the fifties, nuclear anxiety displaced the sexual preoccupations which are more closely connected with vampires.

2. 1958-72. Hammer Films offered more violence and more sex—therefore lots of dead women. While on one level they are a camp recreation of the Victorian horror of female sexuality, they repeat the sadistic acts against women so obsessively that there is little doubt of the sincerity behind the joke. These films were a conservative reaction against the "flower children" of the sixties. This cycle was probably done in by such a glut of Dracula sons, daughters, cousins, aunts, and uncles that the vein became exhausted.

3. 1979-89. Vampires are presented much more sympathetically; some films make us privy to their world. The popularity of Anne Rice's novels may have influenced this new point of view.[15] Also, there have been a number of lesbian vampires, such as Catherine Deneuve in *The Hunger* (1983), indicating more tolerance of "alternative lifestyles." We no longer feel qualified to judge any individual as "damned." The vampire is often seen as a rebel against unjust norms, because he or she transgresses against

the oppressive cultural order; therefore these films are in the emancipatory rather than the reactionary mode.

Also, as Katherine Ramsland speculates in *Psychology Today*, we seem to be in a cycle where we are bored or disenchanted with science and technology, and therefore are turning to the trivial or the arcane—primitive superstitions, for instance. Ramsland quotes the sociologist, priest, and horror novelist Andrew Greeley, who told her in an interview that "Religious imagination [is] the key to life's delight; the vampire cult and similar oddities are drab substitutes, junk food of spirituality" (33).

4. 1992. Why a spate of vampire films today? Why so many books, articles, and so much media attention? It may be part of a general end-of-century malaise and sense of personal vulnerability symptomatic of our era. Another hypothesis is that we are passing from a fairly liberal sexual climate to a more repressive and puritanical one with the rise in power and influence of the religious right, and a return to the contagion theme. There is the sense— wrong, illogical, and cruel—that AIDS is a plague sent to punish sexual transgressors, a plague which attacks the depraved and sexually promiscuous, destroying them through the very act of their transgression. In times of sexual repression, the vampire appears, for he embodies the forbidden: desire but coercion, pleasure which embodies its own punishment—erotic death. In what struck me as a rather bizarre newspaper article, Frank Rich speculated that Francis Ford Coppola had

tapped into a...rampant and...lethal terror running through the public consciousness. *Bram Stoker's Dracula*, a movie that was ridiculed in advance by much of Hollywood and the press as a certain flop, a "Bonfire of the Vampires," was an unexpected sensation in its opening weekend, selling $32 million worth of tickets.... [The movie] both frightens and arouses by playing off the unchecked fear of further AIDs invasions of the national bloodstream.... [It] is an orgy of bloodsucking, bloodletting and blood poisoning. It's beyond Grand Guignol: it's opera for the new blood culture. ("The New Blood Culture," *The New York Times*, 6 December 1992, 9: 1, 11)

I completely disagree with Rich's interpretation of the film's symbolism. Oldman's Dracula is very dissimilar to the personification of plague of Max Schreck's Count Orlock in Murnau's *Nosferatu*, and Coppola has stated in many interviews that, in his film, blood symbolizes passion.[16]

Mass-culture theorists such as Robin Wood and Bernard Hatlen offer a Freudian analysis of horror:

Wood...develop[s] an analysis based on the proposition that patriarchal capitalism demands certain forms of surplus repression (of, for example, sexual energy, bisexuality, female sexuality, and children's sexuality), and that one way in which this is managed is by projecting that which is repressed outward onto the "Other." Horror movies, as collective nightmares, illustrate that process at work; they represent "the return of the repressed." (Tudor, *Monsters* 3)

Such theorizing is probably more valid for film than for theatre, because film's audience is more massive and reflects a broader range of social strata. Because of this, film has attracted the interest of cultural historians, and there have been many studies of the popular film genres as cultural artifacts, attempting to discover what they reveal about the "collective unconscious" of our society. As Tudor notes, "[There are] intractable difficulties in researching past audiences, [but] that hardly justifies an approach which...minimizes their active contribution to constructing and sustaining genre meanings" (4).

All such argument is reductive, however, and others would argue that popular art reflects little of the social history of its time, and is merely a reflection of the taste of its particular audience. Taking this more conservative approach, we can look at the *Dracula* films in a more superficial and traditional way, and note in passing that as our century progresses we have an increasingly free notion of what constitutes "sexiness." The prudish Hays Office production code, which gradually lost its power, may have had more to do with this than changes in audience demands. The best portrayers of Dracula—Bela Lugosi, Christopher Lee, and Gary Oldman—all felt they emphasized the erotic element of the character. Lugosi philosophized on his audiences in an interview in 1931:

Women wrote me letters. Ah, what letters women wrote me! Young girls. Women from seventeen to thirty. Letters of a horrible hunger. Asking me if I cared only for maiden's blood.... And through these letters, couched in terms of shuddering, transparent fear, there ran the hideous note of *hope*. They hoped I was Dracula.... It was the embrace of Death their subconscious was yearning for. Death, the triumphant final lover. It made me know that the women of America are unsatisfied, famished, craving sensation, even though it be the sensation of death draining the red blood of life.[17]

In an interview with Leonard Wolf, Christopher Lee made the following observations:

He had also to have an erotic element about him (and not because he sank his teeth into women).... It's a mysterious matter and has something to do with the physical appeal of the person who's draining your life. It's like being a sexual blood donor.... Women are attracted to men for any of hundreds of reasons. One of them is a response to the demand to give oneself, and what greater evidence of giving is there than your blood flowing literally from your own bloodstream? It's the complete abandonment of a woman to the power of a man. (qtd. in *Dream* 178)

The latest Dracula, Gary Oldman, remarks:

Vampires are fascinating. They are selfish, destructive creatures who half despise what they are doing yet can't avoid doing it. I don't play him as out-and-out evil. It's a delicious cocktail because you know he's like the devil. But I've tried to show the good and bad paralleling one another—there's a dynamic there. The film image I can't get away from is Bela Lugosi. He was really on to something: the way he moved, the way he sounded. I based my voice on his a little. (qtd. in Coppola 162)

In *The Darkling: A Treatise on Slavic Vampirism*, Jan Perkowski comments on the film vampire as an evolving sexual symbol:

More important is the surfacing of an erotic theme, only intimated in Bela Lugosi's interpretations, and its association with attack and violence. Lee's characterization is that of a seducer whose sex appeal is reflected in the willingness of his victims. Rather than a Devil figure, he is a Faustian figure.... The supernatural contexts of these films justified the elements of sexual sadism in the eyes of the censors, but, when censorship was lifted in the mid 70's, vampire films were no longer the main prop for such scenes of sex and violence. The new X-rated films, which are de-personalized, developed along different lines. Thus the second series of Dracula films came to an end by 1974. Starting with Bela Lugosi's Dracula of menacing evil with the sex theme sublimated, we finally come to a focus on explicit, sadistic sex acts themselves, leaving no room for Dracula as a dominating character. (137)

I would like to discuss one other aspect, besides the sexual symbolism, of the vampire on film: what it tells us about our attitude toward death. In a culture completely alienated from aging and death, the special effects department of Hammer Films sensationalized death by again and again showing Dracula being killed, and, in speeded-up motion, rotting, becoming a skeleton, crumbling into dust, and blowing away, all in the space of a few seconds. This, we subliminally understand, happens only to evil monsters, and it isn't permanent for him either—we know he will be back. As Kendrick points out, the entire horror genre could be called "a symptom of Western culture's recoil from mortality." He also makes the striking and probably true observation that "The horror that accompanies portrayals of the trenches of World War I, Nazi extermination camps, and the killing fields of Cambodia has surely been bolstered by the 20th-century sense that the last obscenity is not so much death as it is decay" (261).

In Coppola's film we experience the death of Dracula as tragic loss, a *memento mori* of our own death. Thus his film is revolutionary rather than reactionary: it is in the category of horror which, like *King Kong*, challenges the norms, valorizes the monster, and depicts his defeat and destruction as tragedy.

Why would vampires be so suited to the medium of film that the world market could support 600 of them in 100 years? The standard argument for the superiority of theatre over film is the living presence of the actor, and the exchange of energy between performer and audience, who between them create the evanescent work of art that is live theatre. What film offers, in place of this, is that it can show the impossible—via its tricks of light, it can show us things that could not exist in reality or be created on a stage. Carroll states:

The argument has been that if horror is, in large measure, identified with the manifestation of categorically impossible beings, works of horror, all things being equal, will command our attention, curiosity, and fascination.... Moreover, that fascination with the impossible being outweighs the distress it engenders can be rendered intelligible by what I call the thought theory of our emotional response to fiction, which maintains that audiences know horrific beings are not in their presence, and indeed, that they do not exist, and, therefore, their description or depiction in horror fictions may be a cause for interest rather than either flight or any other prophylactic enterprise. (206)

Implied in this argument is the suggestion that film is better suited to horror than the stage because it is further removed from reality. But surely it is a matter of audience consent, or, as the phrase is, "willing suspension of disbelief," in both cases. When in London in 1820, Ruthven disappeared in a clap of thunder via Planché's vampire trap, the audience was no doubt amazed at the trick, and wondered how it was done, but probably very few were under the illusion that T.P. Cooke had vanished from the face of the earth. When today we view the latest visual marvels of George Lucas's Industrial Light and Magic Company, we may experience a momentary interest in the technique, but the nature of film is to enter into the dream. In the cinema, one is a voyeur, not really participating. As Leonard Wolf puts it:

Film, with its capacity to simulate the fusion of the ordinary with the incredible, is the natural medium for dreams, and it is a particularly happy one for the re-creation of nightmares. The moving frames of celluloid are already a parable of dark and light; and it is hardly surprising that they have, then, lent themselves especially well to the chiaroscuro of the vampire theme. (279)

In a movie theatre the performance is only a pattern of light— daydream or nightmare.

The ten films analyzed in this chapter retain nearly all the elements of 19th-century melodrama iterated in Chapter 3: a powerful villain who is prime mover; schematic characterization of good and evil; elevation of visual over literary elements; mixed genre—artificial fear with a leavening of comedy; musical under-scoring of the action; norms restored (happy ending). Thus the structural and thematic elements of the 19th-century form are still with us, as Kendrick phrases it, like items in an old warehouse where nothing is ever thrown away: "There's nothing new...except the special-effects technology that produces it, and even the technology has precursors in the stagecraft of the Grand Guignol and 19th-century melodrama" (239).

Horror films tend to recycle everything from which profit can be squeezed: there were eight *Friday the Thirteenths* between 1980 and 1990, and six *Nightmare on Elm Street* sequels between 1985 and 1991. After *Psycho* (1960), horror was hard-pressed to keep up with the tidal waves of blood that audiences seemed to demand. Films have moved toward explicit and extreme depiction of bloodshed and mutilation, or "splatter films," showing us a vision of alienation and *anomie* in which "the person is meat" and everything is permitted. *Blood Feast* (1963), leads to *Night of the Living Dead* (1968), *The Texas Chainsaw Massacre* (1976), and eventually to *Snuff* (1976), the alleged filming of an actual murder, thus passing from horror through pornography to the truly obscene, leaving Dracula far behind.

"Fantasmagorie" (c. 1797), *Cinemathèque Française.*

Max Schreck, *Nosferatu*, 1922.

Bela Lugosi, publicity still for *Dracula*, 1931.

Isabelle Adjani and Klaus Kinski, *Nosferatu*, 1979. Photo credit: Photofest, New York, NY.

Winona Ryder and Gary Oldman. Photograph by Ralph Nelson. From *Bram Stoker's Dracula: The Film and the Legend.* Published by Newmarket Press, 18 East 48 Street, New York, NY 10017. Copyright © 1992 Columbia Pictures Industries, Inc. All rights reserved. Reprinted by permission.

# Conclusion

Bridebed, childbed, bed of death, ghost-candled. *Omnis caro ad te veniet.* He comes, pale vampire, through storm in his eyes, his bat sails bloodying the sea, mouth to her mouth's kiss. Here. Put a pin in that chap, will you? My tablets. Mouth to her kiss. No. Must be two of them. Glue em well. Mouth to her mouth's kiss.

—James Joyce, *Ulysses*

A vampire is pure id, a "chthonic doppelgänger" personifying repressed sexual desires and fear of death. The threat to normality posed by the vampire is more ambiguous and threatening than that in other monsters because he is a double of ourselves, a mirror reflection, as Gérard Lenne remarks, "The vampire is of course before everything a double:...The proof is that the vampire, being only the double of a being, is like a shadow or reflection. And this is why it is impossible for him to cast a shadow or to reflect his image in a mirror."[1]

According to Robin Wood's theory (examined in Chapter 10), patriarchal capitalistic culture demands repression of "abnormal" sexuality, which is projected outward onto the "Other" and returns in nightmare form from our unconscious. As Noël Carroll points out, "There really is no deep paradox of horror, for the repulsiveness of its monsters is what makes them attractive for the scheming, circuitous psyche. What appears to be displeasure, and, figuratively speaking, pain...is really the road to pleasure, given the structure of repression" (170).

The vampires of stage and film—Ruthven and Dracula—represent an infantile view of sexual intercourse as wounding and killing, with what is referred to in Freudian theory as "displacement upwards." Lenne, summing up the complex symbolism of the vampire myth, writes:

*Vampirism is manifestly the symbolic representation of eroticism.* No need to be immersed in the subtleties of sexology to recognize what is signified by the kiss-bite, the exchange of blood (vital substance), the phallic

**248**

prominence of the canines, and even the destruction-castration…. Once more, we remark on the psychoanalytic ambivalence of monstrosity here, in the vampiric act itself, which includes at the same time penetration by teeth (rape, aggression, possession) and the sucking of blood (sucking: persistence of a pre-Oedipal state). Like all "fantastic" monsters, the vampire is at once the Father and the Child of Freud, the victim and the executioner.[2]

Christopher Frayling postulates four vampire archetypes in 19th-century literature: 1) the Satanic lord (Polidori to Stoker); 2) the Fatal Woman (Tieck, Hoffmann, Gautier, Baudelaire, Swinburne and Le Fanu); 3) the Unseen Force (de Maupassant, Blackwood, O'Brien); and 4) the folkloric vampire favored by Slavic writers (Gogol, Turgenev, Alexis Tolstoy) (*Vampyres* 62). Of these, only the first, Polidori's Ruthven and his epigones, inhabited the 19th-century stage. The female vampire is represented only by Blink's *The Vampire Bride*; Le Fanu's *Carmilla* (1872), considered by many to be a superior work to *Dracula*, was not dramatized until 1975 (by Wilfred Leach), and so unfortunately lies outside the purview of this study.

Ruthven, this "eidolon of Romantic consciousness" in James Twitchell's phrase, evolves in the theatre from a Romantic anti-hero modeled on Lord Byron in the 1820s, to a Satanic supernature with the added powers of flight, mesmerism, and psychic and astral projection in the 1850s. Supernatural gothic melodrama was driven from the stage by the 1860s with the onslaught of realism, and in the following decades became the butt of satire. With the advent of Dracula at the turn of the century the erotic element is again foremost, with the added themes of racism and fear of contagion, and shifting from Polidori's portrait of Byron to Stoker's portrait of Henry Irving.

As Richard Switzer notes, the more often the Ruthven formula was repeated, the weaker was the resultant work (107-12). Once the character and the pattern of action are set, the material loses its energy, although innovations are possible within the convention. In the 110 years between 1820 and 1930, the 40 or more plays we have examined in this study yield some general patterns:

1. *Eroticism.* First, the erotic symbolism of the vampire, from the first play (Nodier) to the last (Lochhead), is inescapable. Uniquely among gothic monsters, the vampire assumes an intimate physical relationship with his victim, similar to a loving embrace. The vampire does not dismember his victim; the act of blood-

drinking is as delicate as a kiss. The victims, always women, are paralyzed, unable to resist, in a dream state, or willing participants.

2. *Infantilism.* The plays usually come early in the playwrights' careers, often the first major success. It seems to be a young man's subject. Vampire plays may also have provided a rite of passage for male adolescents in the audience, an initiatory peek into the mysteries of adult sexuality, addressing sexual anxiety and aggressive impulses with fantasies of helpless, willing females, and dressed up in the Christian iconography of death and resurrection. As Margaret Carter remarks, the vampire myth reinforces a social paradigm and also a psychological one (*Vampire and the Critics* 114).

3. *Sublimation.* Prudery, which we nowadays consider quintessentially Victorian, was characteristic of the lower classes, not the whole society (a fact which provides Bernard Shaw with a great deal of sport in several of his plays). Therefore lower-class audiences were susceptible to the vampire motif in their entertainment because, like my temperance grandmother with her fondness for rum fruitcake, they didn't know what they were eating. It is a phenomenon of popular culture that, while we react with horror to news stories of gruesome murders, child abuse, and the like, there is a great deal of prurience in the way these stories are played in the popular media. Similarly, the vampire melodrama titillated its audience with erotic images of misogynistic sadism, while the play's ending reassured their sense of righteousness, thus providing a guilt-free form of pornography. Temporary vicarious release from the prohibitions against eating human flesh, wanton killing, ravaging villages, kidnapping, and sexual torture provides a kind of catharsis, and norms are restored with the death of the vampire at the final curtain. Revulsion toward the monster, as discussed earlier, is the way in which the spectator salves his conscience and procures pleasure.

4. *Cult of the star actor.* The plays have been vehicles for charismatic actors who were famous for their good looks, powerful voices, and hypnotic stage presence: Monsieur Philippe, T.P. Cooke, Henry Kemble, Dion Boucicault, and Monsieur Arnault. None of these reached the first ranks of fame in theatre history because they did not measure themselves in the classical repertory. We could compare their popularity to that of today's screen idols or rock stars.

5. *Artificiality.* It is a minor curiosity that so many of these plays were set in Scotland. It is emblematic of the superficiality of the

works that none of them drew from the eldritch lore of Celtic Scotland or Ireland, which was rich with legendary vampire-like creatures. Instead they relied on the ersatz fabrications of Macpherson's *Ossian* as over-embroidered by the French and shipped back to London, doubly removed from any true ethnic source or connection with Freud's "archaic remnants" or Jung's "collective unconscious."

6. *Reactionism*. The vampire plays come in clusters, usually with a grand melodrama in the lead like a stately whale and, attached to it like so many parasitic pilot-fish, farces, satires, vaudevilles, and burlesques. The two major groupings, in the 1820s and 1850s, occurred in times of social stress in both London and Paris. They followed periods of upheaval and revolution, in which ambivalences and repressed social anxieties returned in nightmare form in art and literature. In each period the impetus came from Paris, with British adapters following the French lead, except in the case of *Dracula*.

7. *Evolution*. The two main characteristics of vampirism are revenance and bloodsucking. The earlier plays emphasize the former, with strongest focus on the creature's repeated and unnatural resurrections. Yet he is seductive, more forbidden than deadly, "mad, bad, and dangerous to know," as Caroline Lamb is said to have remarked of Lord Byron.

The dread expressed in the early plays is of being at the mercy of a stranger who, because of *marriage*, can do as he likes—kill one slowly over a year's time. The primary image is of hymeneal blood and of being drained of life and vitality by a husband with absolute rights.

The Ruthven of the 1820s is a melancholy Romantic hero with some semblance of remorse for his innocent prey; Dracula is a foreigner, spreading disease and death, a depraved sexual killer; the important characteristic becomes the blood-drinking. In *Dracula* the evil itself is erotic. He is an anti-Christ with the attractiveness of the uncanny, *mysterium tremendum fascinans et augustum*, speaking deeply to buried psycho-sexual desires.

8. *Misogyny and racism*. All vampire plays follow the standard invasion narrative—the vampire represents an alien race (the "undead") with abnormal, dangerous, yet somehow familiar, sexual practices. In the later versions the concept is introduced that the victim is sullied by the attack and becomes contaminated. In *Dracula* and other late Victorian fiction, the women welcome their violation and are complicit in it. The vampire becomes more

violent, more monstrous and powerful, less sympathetic, as the social climate becomes more sexually repressive.

9. *Anomie*. In the films of the modern era, the vampire, along with his fellow monsters of the horror genre, is an all-powerful embodiment of evil, presenting an iconography of personal vulnerability and individual helplessness (along with graphic depictions of the utter degradation and rending of the human body), in keeping with the tenor of our times.

Walter Kendrick characterizes 19th-century gothic melodrama as follows:

Artificial fear counted as only one among the entertainment industry's many flavors of emotion; at no time did it rank first in popularity.... The typical nineteenth-century theatre product was a heterogeneous article compounded of low comedy, high sentiment, suspense, catchy tunes, perhaps a few dances, and in many cases a graveyard chill or two. Little effort was made to force these diverse, even contradictory elements into any sort of coherence. One piece might emphasize comedy, another thrills, but each took its place in evening-long barrages of entertainment designed to pluck every string of the spectators' hearts, as strongly and often as possible. (132, 124)

While vampires in literature and art are a manifestation of the social construction of the fear of sex and death, there are pitfalls involved in attempting to derive a sexual ideology or social climate from the art produced in another era, or attempting to interpret what meaning an audience of the past read into a cultural object such as a play performance; genre meaning is constructed as much by the expectations of the audience as by the artifacts of which it is composed. Vampire plays span all the genres, from tragedy to burletta, with examples from opera, ballet, farce, burlesque, operetta, extravaganza, and folie-vaudeville, as well as their genre of genesis, melodrama. Do sociological patterns create these shifts of genre or merely reflect them? In either case, they serve as markers and provide a history, if not of social values, at least of popular taste.

Sociologist Leo Lowenthal in *Literature, Popular Culture, and Society* takes the bold position that "By studying the organization, content, and linguistic symbols of the mass media, we learn about typical forms of behavior, attitudes, commonly held beliefs, prejudices, and aspirations of large numbers of people" (vi).

Nineteenth-century theatre is of particular interest in this regard, because the plays themselves have been considered unworthy of interest by literary critics. Melodrama, one of the first forms of mass entertainment, is more likely to reflect the norms of the age than the elitist products of "high culture."

Demographic studies of audiences today are conducted with a great degree of sophistication, advances in this field having been driven by the market place. Projecting a particular mindset onto an audience of the past requires, first, caution, and second, site and object specificity. Audiences for genres and individual theatres were particularized and, in some cases, strongly local. I have expended some effort in this study examining the histories of the theatres where the vampire plays were produced. Each had a distinctive personality, location, clientele, ambience, and genre specialty. The coming together of producing organization, writer, collaborating artists, and specific audience produced the variations in the Ruthven play which we have seen illustrated.

The Porte-Saint-Martin, birthplace of Romanticism and melodrama, was the place of origin. Nodier's *Le Vampire* is an innovative and revolutionary work of blood, poetry, and thunder, seeming to draw its audience from all levels of society—the aristocracy, intelligentsia, and the rough street crowd from the "Boulevard du Crime" which inhabited the "Paradise." The Vaudeville and Variétés treated the material as a springboard for witty farce and buffoonery tailored for their more homogeneous bourgeois audience. The English Opera House, home of English Romanticism if any theatre deserved the name, took Nodier as its base, adding touches of Shakespeare and moonlight, fairies, songs, scenic enchantment, and ethnic comedy. The Adelphi, for its chic, sophisticated audience, transmuted the material into an elegant burletta, with an adorable transvestite fiend in tights who sang charmingly. The Coburg, transpontine haunt of young male ruffians, produced a crude, violent, simplified version which reinforced the code of maleness with violence and chauvinism. The English Opera House (now the Lyceum) provided a spattering of German gore, an opera decked in von Weberian phantasmagoria for its more educated patrons oriented to European culture.

The second wave began in Paris, where the Ambigu-Comique supplied a fresh infusion of French energy and invention, an extravagant "drame féerie" with a flying vampire, ghouls, fairies, five sprawling acts of spectacle and ballet. In London, the elegant and prestigious Princess, patronized by high society and Queen

Victoria herself, matched the Ambigu with an equally elaborate spectacle spanning, instead of three countries, three centuries, with massive technical requirements including dissolving scrims, rising tombs, and falling towers. Meanwhile the Grecian quickly produced a cheap, sensationalized knock-off for its less aristocratic clientele.

In America, from the lavish Wallack's Theatre to humble Liberty Hall in Honesdale, Pennsylvania, Dion Boucicault provided a simplified version of the story, with less plot framework and more physical action and thrills—fistfights, swordfights, and tossings off cliffs—and a vampire melded with the typical villains of American melodrama: the rapacious landlord and the hypocritical voluptuary priest.

The Savoy whipped up a whimsical, light, satirical operetta in which the vampire finds his daily burden of evil deeds rather a dreadful bore. The Gaiety offered a festive extravaganza for Christmas, in which a lovelorn vampire can't hang on to his girlfriend and teams up with Frankenstein's monster to sing and dance.

When Dracula was at last dramatized in the 20s at the Little Theatre in London and the Fulton in New York, the material returned to melodrama, but in a pallid and derivative form. Modern revivals at the Martin Beck and elsewhere have been of a nostalgic flavor, a pastiche of past styles, half tongue-in-cheek, a kind of condescending post-modernism.

Of all these performance places, the Lyceum (English Opera House) was the vampire theatre *par excellence*, presenting Planché's melodrama in 1820, 1823, 1829, and 1839; Marschner's opera in 1829; the staged reading of *Dracula* in 1897; and the *Dracula* revival in 1939 starring Hamilton Deane, with a guest appearance by Bela Lugosi.

Applying the "anxiety model" to the horror fiction of the beginning of this century, Jack Sullivan in "Psychological, Antiquarian and Cosmic Horror" wrote:

The dark apocalyptic quality of...horror fiction is absolutely contiguous with a spirit of restlessness and malaise that some historians, citing the works of Freud, Huysmans, Schoenberg, and others, view as an emotional key to the age and as a premonition of World War I.

Stephen Spender, T.S. Eliot, and many others have written eloquently about the atmosphere of trauma that darkened this period and manifested itself in increasingly bizarre and subjective modes of expression. This was a transitional age characterized by convulsive social changes, ugly repercussions from an unpopular war, economic instability, a sneering cynicism about...the established order, and a fascination with counter-cultures and occult societies. Since this is the cataclysmic climate in which the tale of terror seems to flourish, it is perhaps no accident that the Vietnam and Watergate periods also witnessed a spectacular revival of the genre. (*Horror Literature* 222)

Michael Booth speculates on the reasons for the end of melodrama in this period:

Twentieth-century man does not know where he stands, does not appreciate a simple realm of fantasy governed by a few plain rules, is not sure what is virtue or what is vice or how to distinguish between them. In addition Freud has turned our attention to interior rather than external action, to the probing of psychological motive in the darkest corners of the human mind. To these developments melodrama is irrelevant. (*English Melodrama* 184)

While this is true to an extent in the theatre, melodrama, particularly the horror sub-genre, thrives today in a debased form in commercially oriented slasher movies.

In the conclusion to her book, *The Vampire in Nineteenth-Century Literature*, Carol Senf observes that the vampire came out of folklore, was treated seriously in the literature of the 19th century, and in the 20th century has become a figure of popular culture, so in a sense has returned to folklore (163). The vampire theme has become hackneyed through over-use and abuse, and further trivialized by television and comic books. In the Romantic period, the vampire, along with Don Juan, Prometheus, and the Wandering Jew, was a poetic archetype. Today, he is as tiresomely over-familiar as Sherlock Holmes, Tarzan, James Bond, Mickey Mouse, and Frankenstein's monster. Further, he has been reduced to hucksterdom. David Skal lists these commercial items embellished with the likeness of Bela Lugosi:

Children's phonograph records, plastic toy pencil sharpeners, greeting cards and talking greeting cards, plastic model figures, tee-shirts, sweatshirts and patches, rings and pins, monster old-maid card games, soap and detergent products, Halloween costumes and masks, enlargograph sets and kits, target games, picture puzzles, mechanical walking toys, ink-on transfers, trading cards, Halloween candy and gum, comic books, self-erasing magic slates, cutout paper dolls and books, "monster mansion" vehicles, wax figurines, candy dispensers, transparencies, kites, calendars and prints, sliding square puzzle games, children's and ladies' jewelry, belts and belt buckles, wall plaques, wallets, juvenile luggage, "bike buddies"...animated flip books, lapel buttons, photo printing kits, advertising campaigns, stirring rods and spoons and toy horoscope viewers, junior high school English textbooks, five-cent candy, two-for-one-cent penny taffy candy, hard candy cigarettes, tattoo transfers used on inner wrappers of bubble gum, decals, printed vending-machine gumballs, filmstrips, and hors d'oeuvres accessories. (*Hollywood Gothic* 191-92)[3]

How could any poetic image survive such an assault of trivialization? Hannah Arendt's "banality of evil" comes to mind, but in a sense the creature has been stripped of any connotation of evil by such rampant consumerism.

As for the erotic symbolism, Robin Wood has argued that the time has come to be rid of the vampire, because, as poetic symbol, he is inextricably bound up with the representation of sexuality as evil:

It is time for our culture to abandon Dracula and pass beyond him, relinquishing him to social history. The limits of profitable reinterpretation have been reached.... The Count has served his purpose by insisting that the repressed cannot be kept down.... But we cannot purge him of his connotations of evil—the evil that Victorian society projected onto sexuality, and by which our contemporary notions of sexuality are still contaminated. If the "return of the repressed" is to be welcomed, then we must learn to represent it in forms other than that of an undead vampire-aristocrat. ("Burying" 186)

It may well be that the vampire as a mythopoetic archetype is exhausted. The creature seems to have forgotten its mystery and become hopelessly debased and vulgar. When we think of the vampire today, we are more inclined to snicker than to shudder. We know everything; we have no need of images of sexual sublimation; the trashy take-offs have, vampire-like, sucked out the blood and potency of the original myth until it has finally succumbed, like the dinosaur, to the ultimate insult—it has been made cute.

But the vampire on stage, the black villain of melodrama, had a power to him. He was a primordial nightmare of evil—sinister, soulless, decadent—who could provide a cathartic confrontation with ancient terrors. The vampire myth had a resonance, a depth of symbolism that can still chill the spine and heat up the libido if the creative artist has sufficient skill and imagination, as we see in the Coppola and Lochhead *Draculas*. There is something buried under all the trash that is still compelling: why are we afraid of the dead, and why do we desire them?

The figure turns half round.... It is perfectly white—perfectly bloodless. The eyes look like polished tin...the fearful-looking teeth glaringly white and fanglike.... What was it?—what did it want.... Her bosom heaves.... He advances. God of Heaven! Is it real or some dream...a sudden rush.... Then she screamed.... The bedclothes fell in a heap.... Her beautiful round limbs quivered.... He forces [her head] back by the long hair...he seizes her neck in his fang-like teeth—a gush of blood, and a hideous sucking noise follows. *The girl has swooned, and the vampyre is at his hideous repast!* (*Varney the Vampire* 149-51)

# Appendices

# Appendix A

# List of Dramatizations

1. Year, author
2. Title, genre
3. Composer
4. Theatre, première date
5. Publisher

*French*

1820 Charles Nodier, Pierre Carmouche, Achille Jouffrey d'Abban
LE VAMPIRE (mélodrame 3 a. & prologue)
music by Alexandre Piccini
Porte-Saint-Martin, 13 June 1820
Paris: J.N. Barba, 1820

1820 Eugène Scribe & Mélesville (pseud. Anne Honoré Joseph Duveyrier)
LE VAMPIRE, or LE VAMPIRE AMOUREUX (com.-vaud. 1 a.)
Théâtre de Vaudeville, 15 June 1820
Paris: Guibert, 1820

1820 Nicholas Brazier, Gabriel Lurieu & Armand d'Artois de Bournonville
LES TROIS VAMPIRES OU LE CLAIR DE LA LUNE (folie-vaud. 1 a.)
Théâtre des Variétés, 22 June 1820
Paris: J.N. Barba, 1820

1820 Emile B.L. (pseud. Michel Nicholas Balisson de Rougemont)
ENCORE UN VAMPIRE (farce)

1820 Auguste Rousseau
LES ETRENNES D'UN VAMPIRE

1820 Marc Antoine Madeleine Désaugiers
CADET BUTEUX, VAMPIRE (3 a.)
Paris: Rosa, 1820

1820 LE VAMPIRE (burlesque)
Paris: Martinet

261

1823 François Alexis Blache (& Albertin?)
POLICHINEL VAMPIRE (ballet-pantomime-divertissement en une acte et à
   spectacle)
music by M. Alexandre
Porte-Saint-Martin, 27 May 1823
Paris: Pollet, 1823

1826 Martin Joseph Mengals
LE VAMPIRE (opera-comique, 1 a.)
Ghent, 1 March 1826

1844 Eugène Deligny (& Siraudin & Laloue?)
LE VAMPIRE (com.-vaud.)
Théâtre des Variétés, 11 July 1844

1851 Alexandre Dumas père & Auguste Maquet
LE VAMPIRE (drame fantastique, 5 a.)
Ambigu-Comique, 20 December 1851
Paris: Michel Lévy, *Théâtre Complet*, 1863-74

1855 Albert Masquelier (& M...?)
LE VAMPIRE DE LA RUE CHARLOT (vaud. 1 a.)
Ambigu-Comique, 18 March 1855

1870 Eugène de Richemont & Leon Frank
VAMPIRE ET LOUP GAROU, OU LE VIOLON DE VOYAGE (operetta 1 a.)
music by Blangy
Paris: Auguste Grandjon

1874 Victor Séjour
LE VAMPIRE
L'Ambigu

1879 Emile Durafour (& Louis-Cesar Desormes?)
LE VAMPIRE DE MONTLIGNON (fol.-vaud., 1 a.)
Pepinières, 27 December 1879

1891 Lucien Desgenettes
LE VAMPIRE D'ARGENT (drame, 5 a.)
Folie Voltaire, 15 August 1891

*English*
1820 James Robinson Planché
THE VAMPIRE, OR THE BRIDE OF THE ISLANDS (melodrama, 3 a. & pr.)
music by Joseph Hart
English Opera House, 9 August 1820
London: John Cumberland, 1826

1820 William Thomas Moncrieff
THE VAMPIRE (melodrama, 3 a.)
Royal Coburg Theatre
London: T. Richardson, 1829

1821 James Robinson Planché
GIOVANNI THE VAMPIRE!!! OR HOW SHALL WE GET RID OF HIM? (burletta)
Adelphi Theatre, 15 January 1821
London: John Lowndes, 1821 (prologue & lyrics only)

1821 St. John Dorset (pseud. Hugo John Belfour)
THE VAMPIRE (tragedy, 5 a.)
(not performed)
London: C. & J. Ollier, 1821

1823 E. Ball (pseud. Edward Fitzball)
THALABA THE DESTROYER (melodrama-romance)
Royal Coburg, 18 August 1823

1829 Heinrich Marschner
DER VAMPYR (opera)
libretto by J. R. Planché, adapt. fr. W.A. Wohlbrück
Lyceum, 25 August 1829

1834 George Blink
THE VAMPIRE BRIDE, OR THE TENANT OF THE TOMB
(romantic drama, 2 a.)
London: J. Duncombe, 1834

1852 Dion Boucicault
THE VAMPIRE (melodrama, 3 a.)
Princess Theatre, 14 June 1852
(unpublished) ms. Lincoln Center Library

1859 Augustus Harris
RUTHVEN (drama, 4 a.)
Royal Grecian Theatre, 1859
London: T.H. Lacy, 1859

1872 Robert Reece
THE VAMPIRE (burlesque)
Royal Strand, 18 August 1872
London: E. Roscoe, 1872

1887 Richard Henry (pseud. Richard Butler & Henry Chance Newton)
FRANKENSTEIN, OR THE VAMPIRE'S VICTIM (Christmas burlesque extravaganza)

Gaiety, 24 December 1887
(unpublished) ms. British Museum

1887 W.S. Gilbert & Arthur Sullivan
RUDDYGORE (operetta, 2 a.)
Savoy Theatre, 22 January 1887

1897 Bram Stoker
DRACULA, OR THE UNDEAD (drama, 5 a. & pr.)
staged reading, Royal Lyceum, 18 May 1897
(unpublished, no ms.)

1909 M. Joseph Levy
THE VAMPIRE
Paragon Theatre, 27 September 1909

1924 Hamilton Deane
DRACULA
Grand Theatre, Derby, 5 August 1924
(unpublished) ms. Lord Chamberlain's Manuscript Collection, British Library

1927 Charles Morrell
DRACULA
Royal Court Theatre, Warrington, Sept. 1927
(unpublished) ms. Lord Chamberlain's Manuscript Collection, British Library

*American*

1856 Dion Boucicault
THE PHANTOM (drama, 2 a.)
Philadelphia, 1856; New York: Wallack's Lyceum, 1857
New York: French's Standard Drama, 1857

1862 (Anon., adapt. fr. Boucicault)
VAMPIRE! OR THE SPECTRE OF MT. SNOWDEN [sic]
Liberty Hall, Honesdale, PA, 29 May 1862

1863 E.F. Taylor
BRUNHILDA, OR WAKE NOT THE DEAD
Barnum Museum, September 1863
(unpublished) ms. Lincoln Center Library

1909 Edgar Allan Woolf and George Sylvester Viereck
THE VAMPIRE
Schubert Theatre, Kansas City, 1909

1918 Gerard van Elten
THE VAMPIRE CAT "Japanese Legend of Nabeshima Cat"
Chicago: Dram. Pub. Co., 1918

1927 Hamilton Deane & John Balderston
DRACULA, THE VAMPIRE PLAY
Fulton Theatre, 15 October 1927
New York: Samuel French, 1933

### German

1821 Heinrich Ludvig Ritter
DER VAMPYR, ODER DIE TODTEN BRAUT
(Romantiche Schauspiel in drei Acten)
Karlsruhe, 1 March 1821

1828 Heinrich Marschner
DER VAMPYR (Grosse Romantische Oper, 2 a.)
libretto by Wilhelm August Wohlbrück
Leipzig, 29 March 1828
Leipzig: Friedrich Hofmeister, 1828

1828 Peter Joseph von Lindpainter
DER VAMPYR (Romantische Oper, 3 a.)
libretto by Cäsar Max Heigel
Stuttgart, 2 September 1828
Leipzig: [Peters], 1828

1833
STABERL ALS VAMPYR (comedy)
Wurzburg, 1833

1910 Bock von Wulfingen
EIN VAMPIR UNSERER TAGE (verse, 3 a.)
Dresden: 1910
Dresden: *Die Dramen*, 1910

### Italian

1812 Silvestro de Palma
I VAMPIRI (opera buffa, 1 a.)
Naples, 1812

1825 G.C. Cosenza
IL VAMPIRO (lavoro drammatico)

1827 Angelo Brofferio
IL VAMPIRO (commedia en cinque atti)
Torino, 1835

1857 Paul Taglioni
MORGANO (comédie-ballet en 4 a. et 7 tableaux)
music by J. Hatch
Berlin, 25 May 1857

1861 G. Rotta
IL VAMPIRO (ballet)
music by Paolo Giorza
Milan, 1861

1925 Felice Aggio
IL VAMPIRO (dramma en tre atti)
Florence, 1925
Firenze: Carpigiani e Zipoli, 1925

*Other*

1823-1832 Adam Mickiewicz
FOREFATHERS' EVE (verse drama, trilogy)
(produced in 1901)

1877 Ulrich Franks (pseud. Ulla Wolf)
EIN VAMPYR (farce)
Vienna, 1877

1894 Calixto Navarro
LOS VAMPIROS (zarzuela en 1 a. y en prosa)
Musico de A. Rubio
Madrid: R. Velasco, *El Teatro*, 1894

1904 De N. Oñeca
LOS VAMPIROS DEL PUEBLO (drama)
Madrid, 1904

*Selected Adaptations of Dracula*

1970 Leon Katz
DRACULA SABBAT
New York, Judson Poets Theatre
Pittsburgh: Studio Duplicating Service, 1970

1972 Snoo Wilson
VAMPIRE
New York: Theatre Studio, 1972
Ashover: Amber Lane Press, 1979

1977 Deane & Balderston
DRACULA (Broadway revival)
Martin Beck, 20 October 1977
New York: Samuel French, 1933

1977 Bob Hall & David Richmond
THE PASSION OF DRACULA
Cherry Lane Theatre, September, 1977

1979 Marcel van Kherhoven
THE DRACULA WALTZ
Paris, Théâtre du Marais

1984 Christopher Bond
DRACULA
London, Half Moon Theatre, 23 November 1984

1985 Liz Lochhead
DRACULA
Edinburgh, Royal Lyceum, 14 March 1985
London: Penguin, 1989

# Appendix B

# Plot Outlines and Excerpted Scenes

*Chapter 2: Evolution*

1. *The Vampyre*, by John Polidori.

A self-portrait of Polidori, Aubrey is described as an innocent idealist who "cultivated more his imagination than his judgement. He had, hence, that high romantic feeling of honour and candour.... He thought, in fine, that the dreams of poets were the realities of life." As Polidori did with Lord Byron, Aubrey travels abroad with the depraved but charismatic Lord Ruthven, who little-by-little reveals his vicious character: Ruthven is a sadist and a catalyst for vice in others, a supernaturally successful gambler who enjoys winning only from the poor and desperate, an irresistible and merciless seducer who is attracted only to virtuous women, for the reason that the triumph in destroying them is greater.

They quarrel and separate when Aubrey interferes with Ruthven's plan to debauch a young Italian noblewoman. Aubrey travels alone to Greece and falls in love with a peasant girl, Ianthe, who more resembles a forest sprite than a human girl. She and her parents are terrified of vampires, and her descriptions of them bear a striking resemblance to Lord Ruthven.

Traveling through a dark wood at night against all warnings, in the midst of a terrible storm Aubrey hears fiendish laughter and a woman's screams. He enters a hovel and is attacked in the darkness by some superhuman enemy. He awakes to find Ianthe beside him, murdered and savagely mutilated. A bloody dagger is found nearby, but is not the murder weapon, the wounds being too terrible to have been made by a knife.

Ianthe's parents die of grief, and Aubrey lies ill and delirious for many days. Ruthven arrives from Athens, and nurses him back to health while gloating maliciously at him, almost seeming to be "playing with his food," as one commentator remarks. They then travel through some remote parts of Greece, are set upon by robbers in a mountain pass, and Ruthven receives a mortal gunshot wound. His strength ebbs for two days; at last he forces Aubrey to swear to keep his death secret for one year, and he dies. The robbers have been bribed to place the corpse at the top of the mountain where it will be exposed to the rays of the moon. The next night the body has disappeared, and Aubrey assumes the robbers have stolen it for the rich clothing. Among Ruthven's effects he finds the blood-stained sheath of the strange-looking dagger which had been found by Ianthe's body.

Returning to London after his terrible ordeal, he is reunited with his devoted sister, whose seriousness, modesty, and grave manner have a "melancholy charm." To his horror he encounters Ruthven in a fashionable drawing room, who whispers "Remember your oath!" Aubrey becomes distracted, sees the vampire everywhere, and is confined to bed for months with brain fever. His sister becomes engaged, meanwhile, to an "Earl of Marsden." She shows a miniature of the Earl to Aubrey; of course it is Ruthven. Going into paroxysms of rage, Aubrey is judged to be insane and is confined. He escapes and confronts the vampire, who confounds him with the words, "Remember your oath, and know, if not my bride today, your sister is dishonoured. Women are frail!" Aubrey breaks a blood vessel in his head, loses consciousness, and the marriage is solemnized. Near death when the year of his oath finally expires, he reveals all to his solicitors, and dies. "The guardians hastened to protect Miss Aubrey; but when they arrived, it was too late. Lord Ruthven had disappeared, and Aubrey's sister had glutted the thirst of a VAMPYRE!"

### Chapter 3: Paris, 1820

1. *Le Vampire*, by Charles Nodier, Pierre Carmouche, and Achille Jouffrey.

Before dawn in a terrible storm, Malvina, after becoming separated from her brother Aubray during a hunt, has taken refuge in the Cave of Staffa and has fallen asleep. Oscar, an ancient supernatural bard, tells Ituriel, spirit of the moon, that Malvina is in terrible danger:

ITURIEL: Explique-toi.... Serait-il vrai que d'horribles fantômes viennent quelquefois, sous l'apparence des droits de l'hymen, égorger une vierge timide, et s'abreuver de son sang?

OSCAR: Ces monstres s'appellent les *Vampires*. Une puissance, dont il ne nous est pas permis de scruter les arrêts irrévocales, a permis que certaines âmes funestes, dévouées à des tourmen[t]s que leurs crimes se sont attirés sur la terre, jouissant de ce droit épouvantable qu'elles exercent de préférence sur la couche virginale et sur le berceau. Tantôt elles y descendent, formidables, avec la figure hideuse que la mort leur a donnée. Tantôt, plus privilégiées, parce que leur carrière est plus courte et leur avenir plus effrayant, elles obtiennent de revêtir des formes perdues dans la tombe, et de reparaître à la lumière des vivan[t]s sous l'aspect du corps qu'elles ont animé. (Prologue 4-5)

### English translation:

[ITURIEL: Explain.... Could it be that horrible phantoms come sometimes under the cover of the rites of Hymen to devour a timid virgin and to drink her blood?

OSCAR: These monsters are called *Vampires*. A power, which does not permit us to understand its irrevocable ends, has allowed that certain malefic dead souls, punished for the torments that their crimes on earth have caused, use that terrifying right which they perform for preference in the virgin's bed and the cradle. Sometimes they descend there, formidably, with the hideous features which death has given them. Others, more privileged because their span is shorter and their future more frightful, succeed in regaining the forms they lost in the tomb and reappear under the aspect of the body which they have animated.]

Oscar relates that the vampire Rutwen has carried on his depredations through 20 countries, been killed and resurrected many times, but now must feed again on virgin blood within 36 hours or suffer annihilation: "Le néant! Le plus sévère des châtimen(t)s infligés par le grand esprit" (Prologue 6). [Nothingness! The most severe punishment inflicted by the great spirit.] Then, at the tolling of a bell, pale shades rise from the various graves, and from the tomb of Fingal the spectre of Rutwen rises in the form of a beautiful young man wrapped in a shroud, calling piteously to Malvina. Later she will recall this visitation as a terrifying dream. Oscar protects Malvina and drives off Rutwen with the threat of "Le néant!" Ituriel vanishes in a cloud, and day dawns.

After the Prologue, the play follows the outline of the last part of Polidori's short story. Malvina's brother Sir Aubray relates as narrative the events which took place in Greece: Rutwen's murder there by bandits, and the disappearance of the body. In this version, Aubray's life has been saved by Rutwen. He has never suspected the vampire's real nature, and mourns the loss of his friend so much that he has promised the hand of his sister to Rutwen's younger brother, now Lord Marsden, whom he has never met. Malvina is dutifully acquiescent to her brother's wishes, but troubled by her night in the Cave of Staffa and her disturbing vision there.

To Aubray's amazement and delight, Rutwen himself appears to claim the bride, explaining away his supposed death with various ingenious excuses. Malvina recognizes him as the strange figure of her dream, and nearly faints when he touches her hand: "Quel charme inconcevable agit sur moi?" (I, vii, 25). Malvina's misgivings are no match for Rutwen's ardent and compelling gaze coupled with her brother's earnest entreaties, and she consents to the match.

Rutwen urges Aubray that great haste is necessary—"urgent business in London"—and wishes the marriage to take place immediately, that very night. One of Aubray's servants, Edgar, is to marry Lovette, daughter of Petterson, a farmer on Rutwen's estate (which is nearby, an hour's boat-trip away). As lord of the manor he is invited to the wedding feast, and graciously agrees to attend with Aubray. After they cross the water, another storm blows up, preventing their return and thus delaying the wedding of Rutwen and Malvina.

Act Two takes place at the farm on Rutwen's estate (Château Marsden) which is decorated for the marriage. Rutwen is immediately smitten with the peasant bride, the adorable Lovette. During the celebration Oscar, disguised as "un vieillard dont la tête vénérable inspire le respect" [an old man whose venerable head inspires respect], sings a marriage hymn which contains a mysterious warning to the bride:

> Quand le soleil de ces déserts,
> Des monts ne dore plus le cime,
> Alors les anges des enfers
> Viennent caresser leur victime.
> Si leur douce voix vous endort,
> Reculez!...leur main est glacée!...
> Gardez-vous, jeune fiancée,
> De l'amour qui donne la mort. (II, iv, 36)

[When the sun of these deserted places
No longer gilds the mountain peaks,
Then the angels of hell
Come to caress their victim.
If their sweet voices hypnotize you,
Recoil!...Their hands are icy!
Guard yourself, young bride,
From the love that brings death.]

This is the only song in the melodrama. It is followed by a ballet of wedding guests.

Rutwen is offended by Oscar's song and orders them to throw the old man out. He then attempts to seduce Lovette, pursues her, finally resorting to force, when he is shot (offstage) by her fiancé Edgar. The dying Rutwen extracts Aubray's promise not to divulge his death to Malvina for 12 hours, and to place his body in the moonlight where he may address his last vows to heaven.

Act Three follows Polidori only loosely: Aubray is of course beside himself when Rutwen reappears, but is silenced by Rutwen's "Souviens-toi de ton sermont!" (III, iv, 50) [Remember your oath!]. Aubray is assumed to be mad and is carried off by the servants. As the wedding hour approaches, Aubray escapes from his captors and confronts the vampire again at the altar. Rutwen attempts to stab Aubray; Malvina faints; the hour sounds; and ghosts of his victims rise out of the earth and envelope him as the Exterminating Angel descends in a cloud and a rain of fire.

2. *Le Vampire*, by Eugène Scribe and Mélesville.

Hermance de Mansfred (cf. Byron's "Manfred") is engaged to the Baron de Lourdorff, and their marriage is to be celebrated this very night. She is scolded by her sister Nancy for being untrue to her previous lover, Adolphe de Valberg, a soldier now presumed dead. Nancy is in love with Adolphe herself, but has kept silent out of respect for his courtship of Hermance, who now sings a little song about Hungarian vampires:

Oui, ces paysans respectables
Nous rappellent le bon vieux temps;
Chez eux on croit encor au diable,
Aux vampires, aux revenan(t)s;
On croit a toutes les magies,
Aux amours, aux soins assidus,
Aux grands sorciers, aux grand génies...
Bref, à tout ce qu'on ne voit plus. (i, 4)

[Yes, these respectable country folk
Recall to us the good old days;
At their house one believes again in the devil,
In vampires, walking dead,
One believes in all magic,

In lovers, in paying court,
In great sorcerers, in genies,
In short, in everything one no longer sees.]

Actually Adolphe is far from dead; he has faked his demise to escape the
control of his uncle the field marshall, Comte de Valberg, who opposes his
love affair. Adolphe arrives at the chateau and announces himself, "Je suis
Anglais.... On me nomme Lord Ruthven" (sc. ix, 40) [I'm English.... My
name's Lord Ruthven]. This throws the servants, who take him for a
vampire, into total panic. Learning of the wedding and lamenting
Hermance's faithlessness to him, Adolphe sings that to be dead is a very
good way of finding out how your sweetheart really feels about you:

> Oui, je le vois,
> En homme habile,
> Mourir parfois
> Et fort utile.
> Amant docile,
> Époux facile,
> Mourez souvent,
> C'est très utile
> Et très prudent. (xii, 53)

> [Yes, I see it,
> It suits a man
> To die sometimes;
> It's very useful.
> Docile lover,
> Easy husband,
> Die often;
> It's very useful,
> And very prudent.]

The count arrives in pursuit of his nephew, who again pretends to have
died by bribing his servant Charles to report that he has jumped off a
bridge and drowned. Nancy's reaction to this news reveals to Adolphe her
love for him; the uncle becomes reconciled; and the play ends in a double
wedding:

NANCY (au Public): Chaque Vampire a la puissance
De revenir à l'existence;
Mais la moitié du temps son sort
        Est d'être mort.
Partageons...; qu'en cette demeure,
Chaque matin le nôtre meure,
Pourvu que le soir seulement
        Il soit vivant,
        Bien vivant,
        Long-temps vivant. (xvii, 76)

[Each vampire has the power
To return to existence;
But most of the time his fate
Is to be dead.
Let's agree...; that in this dwelling
Each morning our vampire dies,
As long as in the evening
He should again be living,
Living well and long.]

3. *Les Trois Vampires ou le clair de la lune*, by Nicholas Brazier, Gabriel Lurieu, and Armand d'Artois.
   M. Gobetout, householder of Pantin, is sitting with his wife in their garden which is enclosed by a high wall. They are reading about the plague of vampires in Paris.

M. GOBETOUT: J'ai lu dans le Journal de Paris q'il en a paru un à la Porte-Saint-Martin. Ainsi il n'y a pas des raison pour qu'il n'en vienne pas à Pantin, ils n'ont que le faubourg à monter....
MME.: Mais enfin, de quel pays peuvent-ils venir?...de la Suisse?...de la Russie? de la Cochinchine?
M. GOBETOUT: Les vampires...Ils nous viennent d'Angleterre...C'est encore une gentillesse de ces messieurs...ils nous font de jolis cadeaux! (i, 3, 4)

[GOBETOUT: I've read in the *Paris Journal* that a vampire appeared at the Porte-St.-Martin Theatre. So there is no reason for one not to come to Pantin; they have only to cross the suburbs....
MME.: From what country could they have come? from Switzerland? Russia? Indochina?
GOBETOUT: The vampires...they come to us from England...It's another kindness of these gentlemen...They give us such nice presents!]

Montague Summers recounts that this remark always brought down the house, and was "nightly greeted with a hurricane of applause" (*Kith* 304).
   Thérèse the gardener informs the Gobetouts that three white ghosts appeared in the garden last night and made love to their two daughters, Louisa and Clara. The parents conclude that the girls are under attack by vampires, and hide in the garden to kill them. The three lovers (two gentlemen and their valet) climb over the wall and chat about the delicious supper they have brought to eat with their mistresses: "Amoureux et gourmand! Ah! méchant, comme tu vas l'en donner!" (iii, 16) [Amorous and hungry! Ah! Rascal, how you're going to give it to them!]. As they sing about this jolly supper, the Gobetouts overhear and think they plan to devour the girls. "Les vampires qui soupent avec mes filles!" [Vampires feasting on my daughters!] the father cries, while the lovers sing:

LAROSE: Quel plaisir!
       Ils vont donc mourir.
LEDOUX: C'est que ces deux jeunes filles
       Sont très appétissantes.

GOBETOUT: Les monstres! (Il leve son fusil in tremblant. Larose et Ledoux tombent par terre.) (iii, 16)

> [LAROSE: What pleasure!
>      They're going to die.
> LEDOUX: These two young girls
>      Are very appetizing.
> GOBETOUT: The monsters! (Trembling, he raises his gun. Larose and Ledoux fall down.)]

There follows a love scene in which Larose calls himself the Vampire of Love:

> Des vampires, pleins de furie
> Ici vous font trembler déjà
> Mais nous sommes, ma douce amie,
> D'une autre espèce que ceux-la....
> Enfin nous sommes
> Des vampires d'amour. (iv, 18)

> [Some vampires, full of fury,
> Have already made you tremble.
> But, sweetheart, we belong to
> Another species than they....
> In a word we are
> Vampires of love.]

Villagers arrive, misunderstandings clear up, and the play ends in a triple wedding (the valet gets the female gardener) and another song:

> Un vampire, l'effroi des femmes
> Aux boulevards fait trembler et courir
> Mais avec les nôtres, mesdames,
> Vous n'avez pas le plaisir de fremir.
> Fils du vampire, ils n'ont ni sa colere
> Ni son spectacle, ni son bruit....
> Et s'ils ne montrent pas d'esprit,
> C'est pour ressembler à leur père. (v, 20)

> [A vampire, terror of women,
> On the boulevards makes everybody tremble and run.
> But with ours, dear ladies,
> You don't have the pleasure of shivering.
> Sons of the vampire, they have neither the fury
> Nor the spectacle, nor the noise...
> And if they are not witty,
> That's because they're like their father.]

4. *Polichinel vampire*, by François Alexis Blache.

Polichinel is a brave Sicilian, servant of Juliano. Juliano falls in love with Léontina, daughter of Prince Huberto, governor of the Isle of Mutes. Dandini, lord of the neighboring isle, also loves Léontina, and challenges Juliano to prove his royal birth. Since his native island is far away, Juliano sends Polichinel on the mission to obtain the proof, since he possesses a hot air balloon. Dandini's servant Merlin, disguised as a necromancer, tells the villagers that a vampire is on the loose and shows them the portrait of Polichinel. All the men swear to kill him on sight. Polichinel's balloon (returning?) is caught in a storm, and he is forced to bail out into the sea. He crawls onto the shore and collapses. The moon rises, and he begins to revive (à la Ruthven). "Le bruit s'est bientôt répandu que le vampire, prédit par l'enchanteur, est descendu sur l'île. On aperçoit des soldats et des paysans armés faisant des recherches exactes et se préparant à faire la chasses au monstre qui vient porter la mort parmi les jeunes filles, espérance du royaume des Muets" (vii, 6). [The rumor is quickly spread that the vampire, as predicted by the sorcerer, has landed on the island. One perceives soldiers and armed farmers making thorough searches and preparing to hunt the monster who comes to bring death to young girls, the hope of the Kingdom of the Mutes.] Polichinel hides in the branches of the oak, jumps down and frightens the village girls, and flirts with them. There is a bit more similar nonsense, then the villains are exposed, Juliano marries Léontina, and Polichinel is awarded the shepherdess Isabella. "Fête générale et tableau."

## Chapter 4: London, 1820

1. *The Vampire, or the Bride of the Isles*, by James Robinson Planché.
The expository material on vampires is delivered as follows:

ARIEL: Aye, they must wed some fair and virtuous maiden,
    Whom they do after kill, and from her veins
    Drain eagerly the purple stream of life;
    Which horrid draught alone hath pow'r to save them
    From swift extermination.
UNDA:                   Yes; that state
    Of nothingness—total annihilation!
    The most tremendous punishment of heaven.
    Their torture then being without resource,
    They do enjoy all power in the present.
    Death binds them not—from form to form they fleet,
    And though the cheek be pale, and glaz'd the eye,
    Such is their wondrous art, the hapless victim
    Blindly adores, and drops into their grasp,
    Like birds when gaz'd on by the basilisk. (Prologue 15)

The entire prologue is written in blank verse, ending in a "charm" in trochaic quadrameter.

In Act One, the drunkard henchman McSwill relates a story to his wife Bridget and Robert, the steward, similar to that of Polidori's Ianthe:

MCSWILL: Once upon a time there lived a lady named Blanch, in this very castle, and she was betrothed to a rich Scotch nobleman; all the preparations for the wedding were finished, when, on the evening before it was to take place, the lovers strolled into the forest.

BRIDGET: Alone?

MCSWILL: No: together, to be sure.

BRIDGET: Well, sot, I mean that; and I think it was highly improper.

MCSWILL: They never came out again.

ROBERT: Bravo! an excellent story!

MCSWILL: But that isn't all. The next morning the body of the lady was found covered with blood, and the marks of human teeth on her throat, but no trace of the nobleman could be discovered, and from that time to this he has never been heard of. (I, i, 18)

The scene between Margaret and Bridget follows Nodier closely, as does the following scene with Lord Ronald. The disastrous adventure in Greece now occurs between Ruthven and Ronald's son, who has died there, killed by bandits despite Ruthven's devoted nursing. Lord Ronald, traveling to Greece to retrieve the body of his son, continues the journey with Ruthven, and the rest of the story conforms to Nodier:

RONALD: I threw myself into the arms of my expiring friend—he pressed my hand—"Lord Ronald," said he, "I have saved your life—I die content—my only regret is that fate has prevented me from becoming your son." Gallant unfortunate Ruthven! what a destiny was thine, to fall in a foreign land, in the flower of thy youth, deprived of sepulchre.

MARGARET: How! deprived of sepulchre! (I, i, 23)

Ruthven's romantic transports at the sight of Margaret are cut back, but her aside, "Heavens! how strange a thrill runs through my frame," is followed by an aside for Ruthven, "Then she's mine!"

The servants' wedding (I, iii), is placed in the garden of Ruthven's castle with the sea in the distance, and the arrival of the noble guests is visible (probably done in miniature), accompanied by a boat song to the tune of "Ye Banks and Braes," followed by the first aria of Effie, Robert's bride. The scene then follows Nodier line for line, but at the climactic moment, Ruthven carries Effie off by force, not to ravish but to marry her:

RUTHVEN: You weep; those tears are for me.

EFFIE: No, no; indeed, my lord—

RUTHVEN: This instant let me bear thee to the priest.

EFFIE: My lord, for pity's sake—

RUTHVEN: You plead in vain: Effie, thou art mine for ever! (I, iii, 31)

Reversing Nodier's stage directions, in which Ruthven follows Lovette off, then runs onstage pursued by Edgar to be shot, the English vampire carries off the bride and is shot offstage (by Robert), staggering back to die. Ruthven asks Ronald to cast his ring into the sea (cf. Byron's short story, "Fragment of a Novel") and extracts the vow: "Conceal my death from every human being till yonder moon, which now sails in her full splendor, shall be set this night.... Remember your oath. The lamp of night is descending the blue heavens; when I am dead, let its sweet light shine on me. Farewell! Remember your oath" (I, iii, 31).

Act Two begins with an entirely new scene, set, like the prologue, in the Cave of Staffa by moonlight, where Ronald, accompanied by Effie, has come to carry out the ritual disposing of the ring, and where Robert has hidden from his pursuers. Again we see the approach and landing of the boat. While Ronald and his attendants search the cave, Effie and Robert have a moment for a farewell duet. She departs, and Ronald returns, throws the ring into the waves, and voices his awakening suspicions in soliloquy:

By heaven, my soul, that lately mock'd at superstition, is so subdued by circumstances, that I could almost bring myself to give faith to every legend I have scorn'd as idle. Here is the ring—what am I about to do—what horrible suspicion flashes across my brain! Ruthven! Mysterious being! what mean these ceremonies? Before, when I supposed him dying, he bade me place his body in the light of the moon; and now again. And wherefore make me swear to conceal his death until the moon be set?—But let me not reflect or pause. Unhappy Ruthven! thy friend performs his promise. (II, i, 33-34)

Ronald and Robert fight; Robert is thrown into the sea and left for dead, but is seen clinging to the rocks as the curtain falls.

In II, ii, Margaret, looking out her tower window, sees Ruthven approaching by moonlight. He instructs her to descend and immediately begin the marriage ceremony. Ronald, returning from the cave, is aghast at the sight of the living Ruthven: "Horror overwhelms me! I know not what thou art; but terrible conviction flashes on my mind, that thou art nothing human. A mist seems clearing from my sight; and I behold thee now—oh, horror! horror!—a monster of the grave—a—a—Vam—" (II, ii, 36). Margaret faints a second time, into Ruthven's arms, as Ronald is dragged off by his own servants. Ruthven now places the ring on Margaret's finger, binding her to him:

RUTHVEN: Receive this ring, and let it be a sacred pledge between us. (Kisses the ring, and places it on her finger.)
MARGARET: Ha!
RUTHVEN: (Aside, smiling.) Her fate is sealed.—She cannot now retract. (Aloud.) You shudder—what ails my love?
MARGARET: A strange sensation runs throughout my frame; tears fill my eyes, and my heart beats as though 'twould burst my bosom. Methinks my father's voice still rings in mine ears, "Wed not before the moon shall set." (II, ii, 37)

Now Effie, Robert, and McSwill assemble themselves for the rescue, but not before another Scottish love ballad from Effie and a drunk scene for McSwill:

My master's gone mad—there's a pretty job.... Old mother Bridget never lets me drink in quiet at home, so I carry a pocket pistol about with me. (Pulls out a flask.)...It's a great consolation on a night excursion to one who has so respectful a belief in bogies and warlocks, as I have. Whiskey is the only spirit I feel a wish to be intimately acquainted with. (II, iii, 39)

The scene ends with another lengthy drinking song.

The last scene is in the chapel, and, in a fine touch, through a large Gothic window the moon is seen sinking into the sea. Many supernumeraries (priests and vassals) are assembled to witness the nuptials, and Ruthven speaks a bit of blank verse, in which he speaks of Satan as his enemy:

> All is prepared; o'er the great fiend once more
> I triumph! Ere yon orb shall kiss the wave,
> The tributary victim shall be paid.
> Bow, ye less subtle spirits—bow abashed
> Before your master. Margaret!
> 'Tis Ruthven calls thee. Hasten, sweet, and crown
> Thy lover's happiness. (II, iv, 40-41)

Margaret weakly resists going forward with the ceremony, and when Ronald bursts in raving, she faints a third time. Finally Robert arrives, saves Ronald's life, and prepares to kill Ruthven a second time, but is prevented by the timely setting of the moon:

RUTHVEN: Nay, then, thus I seal thy lips, and seize my bride. (Ruthven draws his poniard, and rushes on Ronald—Lady Margaret shrieks; when Robert throws himself between Ruthven and Ronald, and wrenches the dagger from his grasp.)
MARGARET: Hold! Hold!—I am thine;—the moon has set.
RUTHVEN: And I am lost! (A terrific peal of thunder is heard—Unda and Ariel appear—a thunder-bolt strikes Ruthven, who immediately vanishes through the ground—general picture.) (II, iv, 42)

### Chapter 5: London, 1820-23

1. *The Vampire*, by W.T. Moncrieff.

The play opens in the Cave of Fingal on the Isle of Staffa, with a chorus of singing vampires:

> Vampires—rejoice! rejoice!
> Though spell-bound in our grave we lay,
> We feel the coming of our prey!
> Vampires—rejoice! rejoice!
> Lur'd to this fatal spot,
> Death is the maiden's lot.
> We'll burst our graves,
> Like pent up waves,
> And drink the rich flood
> Of her crimson blood!
> When rises the moon, and the bell beats ONE,
> Vampires—rejoice! rejoice! (Introduction, 9)

The next scene opens, not with a drinking song, but with a chorus of vassals singing a lament for Malvina's disappearance. The story of the murdered heiress, now called Ida (from Planché but not in Nodier) is repeated. A new scene follows between Malvina and her sweetheart Edgar—she tells him of her terrible dream (similar wording in all three versions), and jilts Edgar in favor of the mysterious stranger:

EDGAR: This is indeed a frightful dream.
MALVINA: I would, yet dare not, tell my brother;—Sir Malcolm is so incredulous;—he comes, away, dear Edgar.
EDGAR: Away, indeed!—why should I tarry here and feed a hope that never can be realized?—farewell, dear lady—had it been my lot to—what would I say? Pardon this presumption—I—I—humbly take by leave. (Exit, F.E.P.S [First Entrance, Prompter Side, meaning downstage left])
MALVINA: Poor Edgar! I think—I know he loves me, but am I not betrothed unto another—Count Marsden?—young, powerful, and accomplished—the favourite of kings, and— (I, i, 16)

Sir Malcolm enters with his henchman, Mac Dirk. Malcolm and his sister repeat the identical scene as in the two earlier plays. Edgar already suspects the vampire and, in order to entrap him, invites him to the wedding of Sandy and Jeannie. Ruthwold insultingly offers Edgar a purse as a reward, which is rejected. The act ends in an interesting dumbshow:

(Mac Dirk leads the way; Sir Malcolm takes the hand of Lord Ruthwold; Edgar steals on with Sandy—motions him in pantomime to beware of Lord Ruthwold, and follows him; Lord Ruthwold turns suddenly round—sees Edgar and Sandy—looks furiously—they bow, but when he has departed, follow him threateningly. End of Act One.) (I, i, 22)

At the wedding in Act Two, Edgar assumes the plot function of Oscar in Nodier's drama: he disguises himself as a blind bard, and, accompanying himself on the harp, sings to the bride:

> Maiden of Staffa, list, beware
>   Of smiles that beam but to betray,
> For many a bright but fatal snare,
>   Will steal thy life and peace away.
> Thy veins' rich flow is pure and sweet,
> But ah! too quickly may it fleet;
> Tremble lest, my wild lay spurning,
> With unholy passion burning,
> Maiden of Staffa, be warn'd and save
> Thyself from ruin and the grave. (II, i, 26)

As he leaves he repeats the warning, "Beware the Hour of One."
In the seduction scene with Jeannie, this vampire behaves in a highly confused manner: he attempts to seduce the girl, then threatens to stab her with his dagger, tries to force a wedding ring on her finger, and finally attempts to carry her off when he is interrupted by Sandy and Edgar.

While the couple flees, Edgar confronts the vampire ("Leave me to combat the seducer!—now, cannibal, yield!"), and he and Ruthwold have a sword fight in which Ruthwold is killed, but not for long.

Act Three follows Planché's addition of the second cave scene, but it is Mac Dirk who pursues Edgar. There is another sword fight, and Mac Dirk is killed. Lord Malcolm enters—the business of the ring is omitted—and, satisfied that Edgar is dead and Ruthwold avenged, he returns to the castle. Edgar, in his disguise as the old minstrel, warns Margaret (the maid in this version) of Malvina's danger; then for no apparent reason the servant Davie sings a comic song about the loquaciousness of old women.

Moncrieff now closely follows Planché's sequence, with a nice bit of heightened dialogue for the vampire and victim. (In this and most plays published in this period, the stage directions *follow* the lines they refer to, rather than preceding them, which is the modern practice.)

RUTHWOLD: She's mine!—she's mine! (Embraces her—she shudders.) you tremble—what do you fear? (Sternly.)
MALVINA: Alas, I know not. How cold!—it seemed the kiss of death—an unknown dread pervades my soul!—The vision of the cave of Fingal!—my brother's mysterious words—all should be revealed when the castle bell tolls One.
RUTHWOLD: Should it strike! I'm lost. (Aside.) It wants but a few moments.... Come, Malvina, come, and complete my felicity;—all then will be secure—Edgar no longer lives—Sir Malcolm is confined—Malvina is my own. The Invisible shall have his tribute, and Ruthwold for another term be free. (III, iii, 39)

The ending shows some slight variations:

SIR MALCOLM: Strike! If I cannot save Malvina, I will perish with her!
RUTHWOLD: Then perish both!
EDGAR: Never! (Attempts to stab Edgar. The bell tolls One—Malvina faints in Edgar's arms. Thunder. The stage darkens. The Invisible exclaims, "Ruthwold thou'rt lost for ever!—I wait for thee—come, come!")
RUTHWOLD: Ah! the hour passed—the moon risen, and no victim!—lost! lost! lost! The Invisible! I come! (Phantoms...rise from the different traps in fire, which throws a red light on all. Ruthwold drops his dagger and attempts to fly; they pursue and force him down the grave trap. Soft music. The painted window opens at the back of the altar. Lunaria and Terra descend in clouds.—Picture.—Curtain Falls.) (III, iii, 40)

2. *The Vampire*, by St. John Dorset.
In addition to the protagonist, Abdalla the Persian, there are six stock characters in the style of French neoclassicism: Samer, juvenile; his sister Astarte, ingenue; Benassar, their old father; Nourayah, the lustful and wicked queen; a pair of *confidants*, Moabdar and Osman; and assorted non-speaking Alexandrians, conspirators, and soldiers. The play is written in blank verse, occasionally strained but with some effective passages, as in this soliloquy and confrontation between Abdalla and Samer:

ABDALLA: There is a shade upon my soul:
                    (striking his breast) thou barren
Desolate spot, the beauteous spoiler smote thee;
But revenge came swiftly: poison'd on that eve
of sinful wedlock! I am damn'd for that.
. . . . . . . . . . . . . . . . . . . . . . . . . . . . . . . . . . . .
SAMER: Foul-feeding demon, that with moisten'd lip
Dost glut on blood and happiness, and crawl
About the world to charm thy human prey,
In form as brilliant as the scaled snake,
Thou fiend of evil eye and rav'nous heart,
Death to thy vampire soul, thou fell destroyer!
ABDALLA: Hence!
SAMER:              Refuse of Persia, no: here will I rest,
And foot to foot, and face to face till dooms-day. (IV, i, 64-65)

At the denouement, Abdalla kills Samer, Nourayah kills Astarte, Abdalla throws Nourayah from a precipice into the sea and walks off into the storm.

3. *Giovanni the Vampire!!! or How Shall We Get Rid of Him?* by James Robinson Planché.
       Since only the prologue and lyrics were published, the plot of this burletta must be surmised from the character descriptions in the cast list: Giovanni, "an old acquaintance considered in a new light"; Leporello, "his Valet of all Work"; other characters from Mozart's opera are the Ghost of the Commandant; Donna Anna, "Daughter of the Commandant, looking as well as can be expected." Others are "Miss Bellamira Bustle, Daughter to the Manager, a Young Lady of great Musical Abilities, and very much in love"; the Bride, "a Spinster"; and the Bridegroom, "a Bachelor." We can infer the drift of Planché's humor, if not the specifics of it, from the presence in the cast of three playwrights—Cabbage, Cribb, and Fudge—and Tragedy and Comedy, "Melancholy representatives of two Species of composition nearly obsolete." The work seems to be a debate on genre and commercialism. The cast is rounded out by Giovanni's slaves, Europe, Asia, Africa, and America, played by Messrs. White, Brown, Black, and Red.
       The prologue in the Cave of Staffa, with which we are so fulsomely familiar, takes place between the Genius of Imagination and the Spirit of Burlesque. A comparison of the opening lines of Planché's 1820 melodrama and his 1821 burletta proves that, if you want pointed satire of your writing, it may be necessary to do the job yourself.

*The Vampire*:
          UNDA: Spirit! Spirit of the Air!
          Hear and heed my spell of power;
          On the night breeze swift repair
          Hither from thy starry bower.
          CHORUS: (Without, L.) Appear! Appear!
. . . . . . . . . . . . . . . . . . . . . . . . . . . . .

QUARTETTO:
By the charm of might and word of fear,
Which must never be breath'd to mortal ear,
Spirit! Spirit of the Air,
Hither at my call repair!

. . . . . . . . . . . . . . . . . . . . . . . . . . . . . . . .

ARIEL: Why, how now, sister? wherefore am I summoned? (*The Vampire*,
Introductory Vision, 1)

*Giovanni the Vampire*:
IMAGINATION: Spirit! Spirit of Burlesque!
Hear and heed my spell of pow'r;
Hasten in thy shape grotesque,
Hither from thy laughing bower.
CHORUS: Appear! Appear!
QUARTETTO: (Without.)
By the charm of might and the word of fear,
Which must ne'er be breath'd to mortal ear;
Spirit!—Spirit of Burlesque!
Hasten in thy shape grotesque.

. . . . . . . . . . . . . . . . . . . . . . . . . . . . . . . .

BURLESQUE: Why how now Maggie! wherefore all this clatter?
What, in the name of Momus, is the matter? (*Giovanni*, Introductory
Vision, 2)

They debate in rhymed couplets over the prostrate form, not of Malvina-
Margaret, but the Manager of the Adelphi, Mr. R.H. Bustle, asleep in his
armchair. Imagination tells Burlesque that an author has brought in a new
play and vowed to resurrect the vampire at the Adelphi.

IMAGINATION: Aye, Burlesque!—that many-
Liv'd Libertine!—that monster!—Don Giovanni:
At every house in turn he rears his head;
In vain, alas! you think him damn'd and dead.
When first the Opera Italian burn'd him,
Into a pantomime some author turn'd him;
At Covent Garden, and at Drury Lane,
The cry was "Curse him! there he is again!"
Across the water, driven in a hurry,
Up starts the endless rascal at the Surrey;
Astley's, the Royalty, and Sadler's Wells,
Fry'd him in vain in all their separate hells!
Not e'en the devil could from flight withhold him,
At the Olympic, Presto! you behold him
Alive and kicking.—At the Coburg next!
He changes climate, and costume, and text;
And now in spite of reason or of rhythm,
I'faith! they threaten the Adelphi with him!
BURLESQUE: What's be done? The town, I'm sure is sated.
IMAGINATION: Why, let the Vampire be annihilated.

But first let's warn this Managerial wight,
And raise a vision to his sleeping sight. (Int. Vision, 4)

They conjure the fiend to appear, using the tune of the Incantation from *The Vampire*. As they sing "Appear! Appear!" the vampire, a breeches role, rises out of the lumber chest, saying, "I would appear at the Adelphi."

The songs include a trio of playwrights pushing their Giovanni plays, several arias for the Don, including one to the tune of "Ye Banks and Braes" (previously used in the Planché *Vampire* as a rowing song). The borrowed tunes are an eclectic and playful collection: "He is dead and gone, lady," from Ophelia's mad scene in *Hamlet* (IV, vii), is appropriated for Miss Bustle, and the three playwrights and Leporello sing to "What shall he have that killed the Deer?" from *As You Like It*. "My Love is like a red, red rose," is a ballad to Leporello's drunkard wife. Two tunes are actually taken from Mozart's *Don Giovanni*: "Vedrai carino" for Miss Bustle, and the Zerlina-Giovanni duet, "La ci darem la mano," for Miss Bustle and Giovanni. Oddly, both Mozart tunes are used for a passionate discussion about preparing some toasted cheese, perhaps an important plot point, but one which must remain forever lost. The grand finale is to the tune of "Rob Roy Macgregor, O!:"

> Gentles, we've got rid at last,
>   Of Don Giovanni, O!
> Surely now the freaks are past,
>   Of Don, & c.
>
> But if pens of greater pow'r,
> Can still revive him for an hour,
> Be it so;—but don't damn our
>   Vampire Giovanni, O! (Songs, Duets, Glees, & c. 15)

### Chapter 6: German Influence

1. *Der Vampyr* by Heinrich Marschner; libretto by Wilhelm August Wohlbrück.

Act One: At a witches' sabbath by moonlight, Rutwen bargains for extended life with the Vampire Master (a non-singing role):

> VAMPYRMEISTER (spricht): Dieser hier, des schon verfallen
> Unsrem Dienste ist.
> Wünscht Noch eine kurze Frist
> Unter den freien Menschen zu wallen.
> Sein Begehren sei bewilligt,
> Wenn er seinen Schwur erfüllt,
> Wenn er bis Mitternacht
> Drei Opfer für uns gebracht:
> Für drei Bräute, zart und rein
> Soll dem Vampyr ein Jahr bewilligt sein.
> LORD RUTWEN: Bei der Urkraft alles Bösen
> Schwör'ich euch, mein Wort zu lösen.

Doch fliehet diesen Aufenthalt
Denn eins der Opfer naht sich bald.
(Der Meister verschwindet, der Mond scheint wieder.)
CHOR DER HEXEN UND GEISTER: Leise, leis' beim Mondenschein
Husch in die Erde, husch hinein.
Tausend Spalten, tausend Ritzen
Dienen uns zum Aufenthalt.
Lasst uns brütend unten sitzen
Bis die Mitternacht erschallt. (I, no. 2)

[MASTER VAMPIRE (spoken): This creature here is already
One of our slaves.
He wishes for a short time
To be among free men.
His desire will be granted
When he fulfills his vow:
Before midnight to bring
Three sacrifices before us.
For three brides delicate and pure,
A year shall be given to the vampire.
RUTWEN: By all-powerful evil
I swear to keep my word.
But fly this place,
Because the first of the sacrifices
Will soon be here.
(The master disappears, then moon shines again.)
WITCHES AND SPIRITS: Lightly, lightly, the moonbeams shine,
Quickly into the earth, quickly inside
A thousand gaps, a thousand fissures
Serving as our dwelling place.
Let us sit down there, brooding
Until midnight sounds.]

Act Two: Emmy's seeming foreknowledge of Rutwen's nature,
indicated in her *Ballade*, is not enough to save her:

Sieh, Mutter, dort den bleichen Mann
Mit seelenlosem Blick!
Kind, sieh den bleichen Mann nicht an,
Sonst ist es bald um dich getan,
Weich schnell von ihm zurück!
Schon manches Mägdlein jung und schön
Tät ihm zu tief ins Auge sehn,
Musst' es mit bittern Qualen
Und seinem Blut bezahlen,
Denn still und heimlich sag ich dir:
Der bleiche Mann ist ein Vampyr!
Bewahr'uns Gott auf Erden,
Ihm jemals gleich zu werden. (II, no. 12)

[See, Mother, over there, the pale man
With his soulless gaze!
Child, do not look upon that pale man,
Because he will destroy you.
Stay away from him!
Many a beautiful young maiden
Looked too deeply into his eyes
And had to pay with bitter anguish
And her life blood,
Because, secretly and softly I tell you:
The pale man is a vampire!
God save all of us on earth
From ever becoming like him!]

At the opera's climax Aubry exposes the vampire, breaking his vow at risk
of his own life:

AUBRY: Nicht zag'ich vor des Ew'gen Grimme,
Laut ruf'ich es mit Donnerstimme,
Dies Scheusal hier...
RUTWEN: Zermalmung bebt durch meine Glieder
Gottes Donner wirft mich nieder
Wehe mir! (Es schlängt Eins.)
AUBRY (mit höchster Kraft): Dies Scheusal hier
Ist ein Vampyr!
ALLE: Weh! (Der Blitz zerchmettert Ruthven; aus der Erde
schlagen Flammen, er versinkt in die Erde. Alle stürzen betäubt nieder.)
CHOR: Ha, was war das, was ist geschehen hier?
DAVENAUT: Gott! Mein Kind, welch' Unglück drohte dir!
MALWINE: Wer Gottesfurcht in frommen Herzen trägt,
Im treuen Busen reine Leibe hegt...(II, no. 20, Finale)

[AUBRY: I do not fear the wrath of the eternal one.
Loudly I cry and with a voice of thunder,
This hideous monster...
RUTWEN: All my body parts are ground to pieces.
God's thunder strikes me down.
Ah, woe! (The clock strikes one.)
AUBRY (with greatest force): This hideous monster
Is a vampire!
ALL: Woe! (Lightning strikes Rutwen; flames leap from the earth.
He sinks into the floor; all fall to their knees and are struck dumb.)
CHORUS: What was that? What has happened here?
DAVENAUT: God! My child, with what misfortune have you been
threatened?
MALWINE: Whoever reveres God with a pure heart,
And who preserves love in a faithful bosom...]

Aubry is rewarded with the hand of Malwine.

*2. The Vampire Bride, or the Tenant of the Tomb,* by George Blink.

Conversing with his friend Werl, Lord Walter laments the loss of his wife, and resists the reasonable advice not to neglect his living wife and children. His undying love of Brunhilda is viewed by Werl, the *raisonneur*, as a character weakness, an unbreakable but destructive addiction. Walter departs and there is some flirtation between Werl and Annetta, the maid. Two comic servants, Kibitz and Jansen, enter, and all three vie for her attentions.

Scene three is set in a dark cypress grove, "a magnificent tomb—the moon rising," Walter is discovered lying on Brunhilda's grave. The Sorcerer rises up out of the earth. He can resurrect Brunhilda, but there are certain conditions:

SORCERER: But once with thee
She must remain, e'en till thy day of doom.
However she appall thee by her acts,
However she may then be loath'd by thee,
However thy affections turn to hate—
Unless thou bathe thy hands—aye, in her blood—
The blood of her you idolize.—Pause ere
You make the rash resolve—wake not the dead!
LORD WALTER: Only release her from the bonds of death—
Restore her for me to gaze on—to adore—
To worship—as I did when first we loved;
And thou shalt have, if riches be thy god,
Enough to pave thy subterranean dwelling,
Were it as spacious as the realm above us.

. . . . . . . . . . . . . . . . . . . . . . . . . . . . . . . . . . . . . . . .

SORCERER: Once more I warn thee, Wake not the dead! But if thou dost insist—it shall be even as thou wishest. Step aside. (Solemn music—The Sorcerer draws a blue fire circle with his wand round the Tomb—the moon becomes suddenly obscured—a storm begins to howl—owls and other birds of night flap their wings and utter their low cries of omen—with a crash the tomb flies apart, leaving a passage for Brunhilda to rise through—the Sorcerer scatters into the yawning earth, roots and herbs of magic power—the wind becomes more boisterous—thunder peals louder—the clouds divide—the moon bursts forth with all her power, and her beams are scattered on the fragments of rock that composed the tomb.)
Awake! spirit, awake!
Receive again thy breath—
Awake, spirit, awake!
Shake off that sleep of death.
CHORUS: Arise, spirit, arise!
Thy bridegroom waits for thee;
Arise, spirit, arise!
Henceforth a mortal be!
SORCERER (looking into the vault):
Yes, thy heart again beats with life, thine eye
Again is opened.—Arise from the tomb!

(She rises slowly through the trap— the sorcerer takes her by the hand—leads her to Lord Walter—who stands as if rooted to the ground with amazement. The storm ceases.) (I, iii, 8-9)

In the next scene we learn from the gossiping servants that Brunhilda has supplanted Swanhilda in the household. Kibitz, now appointed constable, comments, "Secrets that are worth keeping, are worth telling, that's my motto.... Swanhilda is to be divorced from Lord Walter, and returned like a package to her friends—and the new lady, 'tis whispered, is his bride already" (I, iv, 10).

Werl suspects the new bride's true identity:

If I am not mistaken she is the same Brunhilda I saw safely laid in the grave five years ago—her pallid cheek and sunken-eye, whose glance is any thing but human, strike me with conviction. I met but now a woman wailing her infant's death—I saw another, who, with a frightful shriek, exclaimed, "I am lost—where, Oh! where is my child?"...Close to Brunhilda sat the children of Lord Walter, on whom she glared, as they looked up and smiled on her. (I, iv, 11)

Kibitz has a comedy routine reminiscent of the incompetent ditherings of Dogberry: "If I was not a constable, I would be off—I tell you what, I'll apprehend her, if my authority goes so far. But, if she really be a vampire and preys on innocence, I stand but a poor chance. Did you ever hear of a vampire swallowing a constable? I should make a very dainty mouthful if I did not *stick*" (I, iv, 12).

The children are indeed in danger, as Brunhilda soliloquizes:

> Already have the whispers gone abroad
> That I
> Do cause these midnight horrors, which have blanch'd
> The cheeks of every menial here, who shrink
> From me, and mutter curses as they hurry by me.
> Children pass from life into eternity.
> Pale, bloodless, and emaciated, they
> Have died, and no visible sign hath yet
> Denoted what has been the cause of the
> Dire malady. The village I have thinned
> Of its young inmates, and but two remain,
> Gifted with youth and beauty, and they are—
> Lord Walter's children—they or I must perish—
> And then the father—but he comes, he comes! (I, v, 12)

Brunhilda's true nature is revealed to Walter, but even the terrible truth is not enough to repulse him or break his obsession: "Absent from me, I think but of her deeds;/Present, her beauty binds me like a spell" (I, v, 16). Now the Sorcerer comes to his aid, and Walter, almost unable to perform the deed, at last stabs the sleeping Brunhilda with an enchanted dagger. She awakes, shrieks "I curse thee—the vampire curses thee!" and dies.

Now Walter is safe, or so he thinks. He has vowed never to think of the vampire with love, but of this he is incapable, and is soon regretting his decisive act. The moon rises over the scene, and (since Brunhilda is of the same species as Ruthven), we know she will rise again and avenge herself.

In Act Two, scene five, a terrible storm has the servants all aflutter. Kibitz is sulking about being dismissed by Walter for tippling from the wine cellar, and a drinking and scolding scene ensues. Werl enters with the surprising news that Kibitz has just been appointed guardian over Brunhilda's tomb:

KIBITZ: I don't admire the office.
WERL: You will find it an agreeable one—plenty of trees to shelter you.
KIBITZ: I dare say there are; but as I don't admire the office, Brunhilda may be the officer—pop from the ground, and down upon me like an extinguisher....
WERL: You don't want courage, Kibitz?
KIBITZ: Neither will I show my want of it.... I'll be no vampire-watcher—But are you sure she is dead? (II, v, 21)

The other servant, Jansen, now relates that Walter has encountered a fair Stranger who remarkably resembles Brunhilda. (In Ludvig Tieck's story, the resemblance was to Swanhilda.) "Mystery on mystery!" exclaims Werl, and Kibitz is left to soliloquize and sing:

If I stay here, I may become a vampire. I should not mind that if vampires lived on wine; but curse me if I could stomach anything else....
    If I were wedded, and who knows
        But what I may soon be;
    I wonder if, were I to die,
        My wife would grieve for me?
    She'd groan and squall, there is no doubt,
        To think of Kibitz dead,
    But could she for a vampire wish,
        This flesh and blood instead? (II, v, 22)

Kibitz and Annetta agree to marry; he resigns himself with "Hey for the nuptial noose, and lots of little Kibitz."

The final scene is in "a magnificent Banquetting [sic] Hall," the Stranger attired as a huntress. All the guests are in a festive mood. Lord Walter is elated, full of wine and sexual anticipation, oblivious to the dreadful events which have just befallen him and his family, and clearly being set up for the terrible denouement. Walter and the Stranger toast each other:

WALTER: Give me a bowl of wine—here's to our fair guest. (Shouting and laughter.)
This is a pregnant hour with every joy—
Give it a welcome, friends. And let wine stream
Abundance! till your hearts, like mine, are drown'd
In the ruby flood.

STRANGER: Lord Walter, here's to thee, in wine as red
As that which circulates within thy veins.
WALTER: This is our nuptial hour—and surely thou
Art no less beautiful than the queen moon,
When young Endymion, ravished with her charms,
Lay in her light and worshipped her.
Who would not sigh to have so fair a dame
Honour his house and heart?
STRANGER:                              I am no stranger.
We have met before—we've banquetted [sic] together,
And we have loved.

. . . . . . . . . . . . . . . . . . . . . . . . . . . . . . . . . . . . .

WALTER (in a frenzied manner): Who art thou?
STRANGER: And knowst thou not? There was a time, when but
A glance at me, your answer would have been,
Who was't the Sorcerer summon'd from the grave?
WALTER: It cannot be—
STRANGER:                          It is Brunhilda!
(A violent noise runs through the apartment and the SCENE changes to...The
Cave of Death. Loud shouting, & c.—They all rush out, excepting LORD WALTER,
BRUNHILDA, and her ATTENDANTS.)
BRUNHILDA: You stabb'd me to the heart—you buried me;—
But when the rite was done—mark'd you the moon?
Her light restored me—but to be revenged!
Come to my arms!—Brunhilda's arms!
                              (clasping him) Now then,
Our doom is seal'd—Brunhilda's wrongs revenged.
Come, to the grave—the grave—"Wake not the dead!"
(The fabric falls with a crash, LORD WALTER and BRUNHILDA
descend in a shower of fire.) (II, vi & vii, 25-27)

## Chapter 7: Paris, London, and America, 1851-62

1. *Le Vampire*, by Alexandre Dumas père.
     The first act is set in Spain, in the courtyard of an inn, where the marriage
of the innkeeper's daughter is being celebrated. It begins with a peasant ballet
and chorus. A young noblewoman, Juana, has run away from a convent to
meet her lover, Don Luis de Figeuroa, and is seeking a guide to the ruined
Castle of Tormenar, but no one is willing to go there—the castle is known to
be haunted. Soon a party of nobles arrives, led by the romantic hero, Gilbert
de Tiffauges. Because of the wedding the inn cannot accommodate them as
guests; so Gilbert, scorning all warnings, proposes to spend the night at
Tormenar, and offers to accompany Juana there, taking her under his
protection in the name of his beloved sister Hélène. Before departing the inn,
he finds himself attracted to a mysterious Moorish woman. She is La Goule, a
vampire in love with Gilbert, who shadows his life without his knowledge.
Overhearing Juana's remark that Don Luis is alone at Tormenar, she
whispers to herself, "Il te faut deux heures pour aller trouver ton beau
fiancé.... Je l'aurai joint dans trois minutes!" (I, vii, 420). [It will take you two
hours to find your handsome fiancé.... I will join him in three minutes!]

The second act is set in an old ruined banquet hall at Tormenar, "une vaste salle composée de colonnes encore solides, de grands fenêtres ruinées, par lesquelles on peut apercevoir l'orage qui commence à gronder....Vieux portraits avec cadres vermoulus. Ameublement gothique, immense cheminée, que surmontent des armoiries sculptées" (II, Deuxieme Tableau, 420). [A vast room composed of still-sturdy columns, great ruined windows through which one can see the storm beginning to rage.... Old portraits with gilded frames, Gothic furnishings, immense fireplace, decorated with sculpted coats-of-arms.] As the clock strikes eleven, La Goule emerges from a darkened side room where she has killed Don Luis, exclaiming, "Il était jeune! Il était beau!... Me voilà redevenue jeune et belle!.... A l'an prochain, Gilbert!" (II, i, 420). [He was young! He was handsome! I shall be young and beautiful again! Until next year, Gilbert!] She disappears as the travelers arrive. They spread out their picnic and proceed to regale each other with ghost stories. The subject of vampires is mentioned, and at the stroke of midnight, Ruthwen appears:

Oh! pardon, cent fois pardon, mesdames!...Excusez-moi, messieurs!...Vous me demandez qui je suis? Je suis un voyageur renvoyé, comme vous.... Ce que je veux? Mais, puisque vous avez trouvé ici un bon gite, je désire tout simplement que vous daigniez m'admettre parmi vous. J'apporte mes provisions et mes armes. Je suis Lord Ruthwen, pair d'Angleterre, votre bien dévoué serviteur. Remettez votre épée au fourreau, messieurs; et vous, mesdames, pardonnez-moi de ne point m'être fait annoncer; mais je n'ai trouvé personne dans l'antichambre. (II, iii, 431)

[Oh pardon, a hundred pardons, ladies!...Excuse me, sirs!...You ask who I am? I am a returning traveler, like yourselves. What do I wish? I simply desire, since you have found a good resting place here, that you deign to admit me among you. I carry my own provisions and weapons. I am Lord Ruthven, English peer, your very devoted servant. Return your swords to their sheaths, gentlemen; and you, ladies, pardon me for not having had myself announced, but I found no one in the antechamber.]

The comic servant Lazare, just fired from the inn for flirting with the bride, is now the vampire's valet with the happy assignment of carrying Ruthwen's purse. Lazare relates the history of the castle, of a fratricide who killed his two older brothers. No traveler who tries to spend the night in the deserted ruins survives till morning. Just as it is revealed that Don Luis is the heir of Tormenar, his dead body is discovered in the next room (killed by La Goule). Then Juana screams for help, and she too is found dead (killed by Ruthwen). Gilbert confronts Ruthwen running from the chamber and mortally stabs him. Ruthwen explains that he, too, was in pursuit of the murderer, who escaped through the window. Gilbert is beside himself with remorse. Ruthwen exacts the usual promise not to bury his body. Dumas provides a striking version of the vampire's resurrection in the final scene of the second act:

Troisième Tableau: Le penchant d'une colline hérissée de roches nues.—Nuit profonde. Vaste horizon sombre.... Gilbert arrive lentement, avec le cadavre de

Ruthwen sur ses épaules. Il le dépose sur une roche saillante, le visage tourné à l'occident; puis il s'agenouille un instant auprès du corps, et redescend le sentier.—Dès qu'il a disparu, la lune transparait derrière les nuages; un coin de son disque argente les saillies des rocs et les pitons de la montagne; la clarté grandit it envahit peu à peu le cadavre et finit par monter jusqu'à son visage.—a peine la face est-elle baignée de cette lumière, que les yeux du cadavre s'ouvrent tout grands; sa bouche sourit lugubrement. Lord Ruthwen se met sur son séant, puis se lève tout à fait, et, après avoir secoué ses cheveux au vent, il déploie de grandes ailes et s'envole.

RUTHWEN: Tu as tenu parole...Merci, Gilbert! (II, Scène Unique 448).

[Third tableau: The slope of a hill studded with bare rocks. Very dark night. Horizon vast and somber.... Gilbert arrives slowly, with the corpse of Ruthwen on his shoulders. He places it on a jutting boulder, the face turned to the west; then he kneels an instant near the body, and climbs back down again. As soon as he has disappeared, the moon appears behind the clouds; a corner of its disc silvers the projections of the rocks and mountain peaks; the light grows, and little by little creeps over the corpse and at last mounts up to its face—at the point when the face is bathed in this light, the eyes of the corpse open very wide; the mouth smiles lugubriously. Lord Ruthwen sits up, then rises completely, and, after shaking out his hair in the wind, he unfurls gigantic wings and flies away.

RUTHWEN: You have kept your word...Thanks, Gilbert!]

Act Three takes place a year later in Brittany, at the Château de Tiffauges, where Hélène awaits her brother Gilbert's return. The bones of the Polidori/Nodier/Planché plot begin to emerge, as we learn that she has thrown over her childhood sweetheart in favor of the Baron Georges de Marsden. Gilbert arrives, accompanied by Lazare (now in Gilbert's employ, still holding Ruthwen's money). Gilbert has been wandering about Europe trying to forget the terrible accident at Tormenar, and has become engaged to a beautiful Dalmatian girl, Antonia.

Gilbert is astonished to find Ruthwen alive and engaged to his sister, but is reassured by Ruthwen's clever explanations. La Goule, now disguised as a gypsy, whispers to Gilbert to sleep in the room with the tapestry of the fairy Mélusine and her court. That night, in a kind of dream ballet, the tapestry comes to life, and he is warned of the danger to his sister.

The next scene begins with a comic monologue for Lazare, suborned again by vampire gold, but struggling with his conscience. When Gilbert accuses the vampire of the murder of Juana as revealed to him by Mélusine, Lazare supports Ruthwen's alibi, and Gilbert is taken to be insane for insisting, among other horrors, that he has already killed Ruthwen, who is a revenant. Deducing that someone has revealed his secrets, Ruthwen calls upon his supernatural enemy, La Goule, to appear, and the two vampires confront each other. She warns him to stay away from Gilbert, whom she loves; he threatens her with loss of her eternal life if she violates the law against betraying their own kind.

Ruthwen has 12 hours left to secure a virgin's blood or die. He courts Hélène, assuring her that her brother is mad, and begging her to remain true to him. As she prays to her dead mother for guidance, Lazare, switching allegiance once again, reveals the truth to her. Then, vampire and victim are face to face:

RUTHWEN: Comme vous êtes pâle!

HÉLÈNE: Moins que vous, milord.

RUTHWEN: Moins que moi? Vous savez, Hélène, que cette pâleur m'est habituelle, et c'est tout simple: j'ai perdu tant de sang le jour où votre frère a failli me tuer.

HÉLÈNE: Cette pâleur, escusez moi, Georges, mais c'est celle d'un mort, et non celle d'un vivant.

RUTHWEN: Que voulez-vous dire, Hélène?

HÉLÈNE: Je veux dire, milord, que je suis d'une race vaillante; je veux dire que je n'ai jamais eu peur, je veux dire que vous m'épouvantez!

RUTHWEN: Et vous aussi, Hélène?...Ah! voilà ce que c'est que de vous avoir laissée seule; la solitude, le silence, les ténèbres ont agi sur votre imagination. Les ténèbres...Mais j'avais laissé des lumières dans cette chambre, cependant?

HÉLÈNE: En votre absence, elles se sont éteintes.

RUTHWEN: Oh! c'est étrange!...toutes seules?

HÉLÈNE: Toutes seules!

RUTHWEN: Vous tremblez, Hélène.

HÉLÈNE: Je vous l'ai dit: j'ai peur! j'ai peur!

RUTHWEN: Votre main, ma bien-aimée! (Il lui prend la main.)

HÉLÈNE: Froide comme celle d'un cadavre!

RUTHWEN: Oui, froide, Hélène; car votre doute me glace...Oh! viens, viens, ma fiancée! viens, mon épouse! viens contre ma poitrine! viens contre mon coeur!

HÉLÈNE: Oh! laissez-moi! Il me semble que votre poitrine n'est pas vivante, il me semble que votre coeur ne bat pas! (IV, v, 507-08)

[RUTHWEN: How pale you are!

HÉLÈNE: Less than you, milord.

RUTHWEN: Less than I? You know, Hélène, that this pallor is habitual to me, and it's simply because I lost so much blood the day your brother tried to kill me.

HÉLÈNE: Excuse me, Georges, but such pallor is more like that of a corpse than a living person.

RUTHWEN: What are you trying to say, Hélène?

HÉLÈNE: I am saying that I am of a valiant race; I say that I have never been afraid; I say that you horrify me!

RUTHWEN: You too, Hélène? Ah, this is what comes of having left you alone; the solitude, the silence, the darkness have excited your imagination. The darkness...But I left lights in this chamber, did I not?

HÉLÈNE: In your absence they went out.

RUTHWEN: Ah, how strange!...All by themselves?

HÉLÈNE: By themselves!

RUTHWEN: You are trembling, Hélène.

HÉLÈNE: I've told you! I'm afraid! I'm afraid!

RUTHWEN: Your hand, my beloved. (He takes her hand.)

HÉLÈNE: Cold as a corpse!

RUTHWEN: Yes, cold, Hélène, because your doubt freezes me...Oh come, come my betrothed! Come, come, my wife! Come to my breast, come to my heart!

HÉLÈNE: Ah, leave me! It seems to me your breast is not alive, that your heart does not beat!]

He kills Hélène offstage just as midnight strikes, as Gilbert and Lazare break down the door. Ruthwen and Gilbert struggle, and the vampire is hurled through the window to the precipice below. The men naively assume he is dead for good:

(Ruthwen, au fond du précipice, brisé par la chute; Gilbert, descendant à travers les rochers, une torche à la main. Gilbert arrive jusqu'à Ruthwen et l'examine à l'aide de la torche.)
GILBERT: Ah! cette fois, le monstre est bien mort! (Il remonte quelques pas, puis se retourne.) N'importe!.... (Il pousse un rocher que se détache et roule sur Ruthwen.) Oh! ma soeur! ma soeur! je n'ai donc pu que te venger? (IV, Huitième Tableau, Scène Unique, 510)

[(Ruthwen, at the bottom of the precipice, broken by the fall; Gilbert, descending across the rocks, a torch in his hand. Gilbert approaches Ruthwen and examines him with the aid of the torch.)
GILBERT: Ah! This time, the monster is truly dead! (He climbs a few steps, then looks back.) It doesn't matter. (He pushes a rock, which detaches itself and rolls on Ruthwen.) O my sister! My sister! All I could do was to avenge you!]

The fifth act is set in a palace in Circassia, with a view of the sea, where Gilbert has fled with his beloved Antonia from the pursuing vampire, with the help of La Goule, now known as Ziska. She reveals herself to him, and offers to save him from the vengeful Ruthwen and give him eternal life if he will renounce Antonia. He refuses, and instead asks her for a poison so that he and Antonia may be joined forever in death. Meanwhile, the vampire reappears in a wonderfully eerie scene:

LAZARE: Le navire s'est brisé! les malheureux vont périr.... Allez, mes amis, allez! tâchez d'en sauver quelques-uns...Exposez-vous, mes amis! exposez-vous!...(Les Pêcheurs partent.) Moi, je ne le puis: ma responsibilité m'attache au rivage...Ah! mon Dieu! voilà encore une chaloupe qui sombre, le dernier espoir de ces pauvres gens!...Oui, nagez, c'est comme si vous ne nagiez pas!...Ah çà! mais, Lazare, vous êtes un coquin, vous êtes un lâche! Quoi! vous laisserez périr des malheureux sans essayer d'en sauver au moins un.... Attends! attends! je vais faire aussi une bonne action, moi je vais me racheter quelques péchés. (Il ramasse une corde.) Voyons! (Il la jette par-dessus le parapet de la terrasse.) Bien! voilà que ça mord, ça mord ferme! (Il tire.) Hein! hein!...pauvre homme, va!... Tous les hommes sont frères.... Hein!... Viens, mon frère, viens mon semblable! viens! (Il aperçoit la tête pâle de Ruthwen, qui apparait à la hauteur de la sienne.) Ah!...(Le Vampire s'est cramponné à la terrasse; Lazare prend son élan et le culbute dans la mer; puis, tremblant, il chancelle et balbutie.) Au secours! au secours! (V, vii, 523)

[LAZARE: The boat is foundering! The wretches will drown.... Come on, my friends, try to save some of them. Exert yourselves, friends!...(The fishermen go.) Me, I can't help, my responsibility glues me to the shore. Oh my God, there's another rowboat sinking, the last hope of those poor people. Yes, swim, it's as if you weren't swimming! Oh there! But Lazare, you are a rogue, you're a coward! What! You'll let those poor wretches drown without trying to save even one!... Wait! Wait! I too am going to do one good deed, I'm going to redeem some of my sins.

(He uncoils a rope.) Look! (He throws it from the parapet of the terrace.) Good! There's a bite, a strong bite! (He pulls.) Hey! Hey!... Poor man, come on!... All men are brothers.... Hey!... Come on, my brother, come, my fellow creature! Come! (He sees the pale head of Ruthven, which appears at an equal height.) Ah!...(The vampire clings to the terrace, Lazare takes a leap and pushes him into the sea; then, trembling, he staggers and stammers.) Help! Help!]

Antonia and Gilbert are about to take poison when Ziska, sacrificing her immortality, reveals that the vampire can be annihilated with a consecrated sword. She vanishes in flames: "Adieu pour ce monde! Adieu pour l'autre! Adieu pour l'éternité!" The last scene:

Un cimetière.—Tombes, cyprès. Fond sinistre et fantastique; neige sur la terre; lune rouge au ciel.
GILBERT: (acculant Ruthwen à une tombe ouverte): Pour la dernière fois, adore Dieu!
RUTHWEN: Non.
GILBERT: Alors, désespère et meurs! (Il lui enfonce l'épée dans le coeur. Ruthven tombe dans la fosse ouverte en poussant un cri. Le couvercle de pierre retombe de lui-même et l'enferme.) Au nom du Seigneur, Ruthwen, je te scelle dans cette tombe pour l'éternité!
(Il trace sur la pierre une croix qui devient lumineuse. En ce moment, le ciel se peuple d'Anges.—Hélène et Juana se détachent d'un groupe et viennent chercher Ziska, qui sort de terre, les mains étendues vers le ciel.—Antonia parait, et se précipite dans les bras de Gilbert.)
HÉLÈNE (à Gilbert): Frère, sois heureux!
JUANA (à Antonia): Soeur, sois hereuse! (V, Scène Unique, 535)

[A cemetery.—Tombs, cypresses. Background sinister and fantastic; snow on the earth, red moon in the sky.
GILBERT (throwing Ruthwen into an open grave): For the last time, worship God!
RUTHWEN: No!
GILBERT: Then, despair and die! (He forces a sword into his heart. Ruthwen falls into the open hole and gives a cry. The stone slab falls of itself and encloses him.) In the name of God, Ruthwen, I seal you in this tomb for eternity! (He traces on the stone a cross which becomes luminous. At that moment the sky is filled with angels. Hélène and Juana detach themselves from a group and come to fetch Ziska, who rises from the earth, her hands extended to heaven. Antonia appears, and falls into Gilbert's arms.)
HÉLÈNE: (to Gilbert): Brother, be happy!
JUANA (to Antonia): Sister, be happy!]

2. *The Vampire*, by Dion Boucicault (from the handwritten promptbook, Lincoln Center Library).
The First Drama is set in the Welsh village of Raby Peveryl on August 15, 1660. Boucicault sets the family conflict between brothers from Dumas's play in the context of England's Civil War. The play opens, as does the French play, in the courtyard of an inn, with singing and dancing peasants. Instead of wedding preparations, there is talk of the war, and news is brought of Cromwell's death. Lucy Peveryl (Dumas's Juana) is

attempting to reach Raby Castle (Tormenar) to meet her Royalist fiancé, her cousin Roland Peveryl (Don Luis). The party of nobles arrives, led by Lord Arthur Clavering (Gilbert). He explains why the castle is haunted: "Alan Raby, the youngest of the family espoused the cause of Cromwell. Twas he who after the battle pursued the shattered regiments of his brothers when they retreated to Raby Castle. The place was carried by assault, and it is said that the Puritan looked on while his myrmidons butchered his two brothers on the threshold" (I, i, 5).

Watkyn Rhys, a local huntsman and guide, reluctantly agrees to lead the group up the dangerous passes of Mount Snowdon to the castle. The second scene is in the ruined turret chamber of Raby Castle. In the manuscript promptbook the diagram for this set shows the vampire trap to be set in the stage-right wall. The company soon falls to telling ghost stories, giving the vampire his cue to enter, dressed in the garb of a Roundhead:

LORD C: Who art thou?
ALAN: I am a stranger, benighted in the storm. I heard that a noble company had sought shelter here—I came to claim your hospitality.
ALL: A Puritan!
ALAN: Aye, a Puritan—one who has been your foe. (Thunder and lightning). But on a night like this, may we not be at peace?
LORD D: You are welcome, sir. (Alan advances.)
SIR G: What a strange figure!
NEVIL: Do you remark the unnatural pallor of this countenance!
LORD C: May we ask whom we have the honor to entertain?
ALAN: My name is Gervase Rookwood, a poor gentleman, and a stranger to these mountains—in the darkness of the storm, I lost the path, and thus became a suppliant to your courtesy. (I, ii, 19)

(These are the first lines from this play to be retained in Boucicault's 1856 *Phantom*.) An important plot point is that one of the women makes a drawing of the vampire during this conversation. Watkin recognizes Raby as the fratricide who was killed 15 years earlier by being hurled out the window to the immense precipice below. The action then proceeds in parallel with the Dumas play, with the discovery of the murdered fiancé (killed by Raby, as the Ghoul has been eliminated), the murder of Lucy, the killing of Raby by Lord Arthur, the oath, and the revival of Raby by moonlight: "Fountain of my life! once more thy rays restore me. Death!—I defy thee!" (I, iii, 25). The promptbook specifies limelight for the moon effect.

The Second Drama (Act Two), 15 August 1760, takes place in the same room, the turret chamber of Raby Castle, now restored. The promptbook shows this was ingeniously accomplished by using a scrim over the first set, on which were hung portraits of the murder victims of 1660—Roland and Lucy Peveryl, the two murdered brothers, and one portrait covered with "black curtain in draw," which turns out to be a painting of the vampire taken from the sketch made in Act One, but which no one has looked at in living memory.

The room is set with elegant furniture; a minuet plays; there is laughter and flirtation. The act contains echoes of Planché and Dumas, but differs in details. Alice Peveryl, with her mother and guests, is awaiting the return of her brother Edgar on his birthday. He has written home praising his mysterious traveling companion, Mr. Gervase Rookwood. The vampire's entrance is staged identically to his appearance in Act One, but "now in costume of the period of George III." Very effectively, he remains silent for three pages. With wonderful dramatic irony, the new guest is told the history of the castle, and informed that he is now standing in Alan Raby's bedchamber, and shown the portraits of all his murder victims. Watly Rys, the descendant of Watkin Rhys of Act One, now the traveling valet of Edgar, sees through the vampire as his forefather did, and warns Lady Peveryl: "He is no Englishman. No food or drink has passed his lips. That ain't English. He never gave his hand to anyone—that ain't English! He ain't an Englishman, he's a foreigneering Beelzebub" (II, i, 44).

Dinner is served, and the vampire and Alice are left alone for an ardent love scene:

ALAN: I have heard your name ever allied to terms of endearment, never uttered but in the tones of love. Yes, I, the thirsting student, the stoic who had foresworn the world, surrounded by the great spirits of the past, living, I might say, with the dead, your image seemed to beckon me back to life. In sorrow I dreamed that from your swimming eyes, I quenched my thirst for knowledge in a deep draught of love. In sickness, I dreamed that from your heart there flowed a stream in which I could revive my life.
ALICE: Forbear, Sir. Oh, forebear. (xLH [cross to left-hand side]) I know not how to answer you.
ALAN: The truth that trembled on your lip, my spirit has preceded me. Unknown, I have watched you, and you were long since marked for mine, you have confessed it. Alice, I am no stranger here. (II, i, 47-48)

Alice is left alone and falls asleep. By a change of lighting, the scrim fades and we are in the ruined chamber of Act One. The portraits come to life to warn her of her danger. She awakens and undrapes the portrait of Raby, concludes she must be mad or dreaming still, when Raby suddenly materializes through the vampire trap:

ALAN: Why dost recoil from me?...
ALICE: Because that breast on which you press me seems to be the bosom of a corpse, because from the heart within, I feel no throb of life. (He starts, she recoils)....
ALAN: Thy heart has yielded to me, it is mine.
ALICE: (x around to RH back to audience) Away Phantom, demon. I know thee now. (Retreats into next room, pursued by Alan.) (II, i, 53-54)

Raby kills Alice while the turret clock chimes midnight. Edgar bursts in crying, "Demon, where is my sister? Ah, she is dead! Fiend, back to thy native hell!"

(He draws his sword, Alan steps behind him and places his hand on his head. Edgar stretches out his arms, the sword escapes from his hand, he utters a groan and falls as if the hand had struck death into his brain. Alan steps onto balcony.)

ALAN: Once more my cup of life is full, a hundred years of respite from perdition, ye fated halls of Raby, fare ye well.
(The moon shews full upon him, as Act drop descends.) (II, i, 55)

The Third Drama is set one hundred years later in the inn courtyard of Act One; the village has become a town; there is a railroad; and the inn is now the private residence of Walter Rees, Esq., attorney at law, descendant of Watly Rys. Captain Charles Peveryl, who has been abroad in "Burmah," is in search of his cousin, the delicate and spiritual Ada. Rees informs him that she and her mother are under the influence of "a serious friend," a sinister faith healer, Mr. Gervase Rookwood: "She is shut up, secluded they call it, they have darkened the child's mind and made her believe that the world is a snare of the devil's and everybody in it his imps in disguise—they have frozen the smile on her lips.... Mrs. Raby has got religion, given up backgammon and toddy!" (III, i, 61-62).

The next scene is in the turret chamber, now decorated in modern style. The portrait of the vampire is gone, replaced by one of Alice Perveril. (The manuscript copyist changes spelling halfway through.)

Rookwood (Raby) has a Svengali-like power over Ada. She seems to be in a hypnotic trance. She begs for Charles's help and then rejects him: "When he is away, I determine to resist his power, but then he comes, his influence like a shadow creeps over me, and I am helpless" (III, ii, 72). The vampire convinces Charles that Ada is mad, and that her scheduled trip abroad is actually to an insane asylum.

Act Three, scene two is a long soliloquy for Rees, evolved into the clever helper of stock melodrama, in which he uncovers some old manuscripts and deeds in the locked-up and abandoned Raby Castle, and discovers Rookwood's signature is identical to that on the old documents. He also finds a book of vampire lore, revealing that the vampire must claim a victim every hundred years by midnight of August 15. Rees sets the hands of the turret clock back one hour, "so that when they think tis but eleven, it will be midnight." He reveals his discoveries to Charles and Mrs. Raby, and all charge to the rescue. The last scene is in a graveyard:

(The stage is occupied by a platform which was part of the ancient defenses of Raby Castle.... The clock tower, a ruin, is an object in the scene. The arch for the dial is [indecipherable] and the back of the tower having crumbled away. The sky is seen through the orifice of the dial. A huge sarcophagus tomb C, on which in nearly effaced letters is engraved, "To the memory of Lucy Peveril who departed this life on 15th of August, 1660." The stage represents green knowles [sic] and uneven sward with half-buried tombstones so as to convey the idea of a very ancient disused cemetry [sic]. On the platform Alan Raby is discovered descending slowly with Ada in his arms. He places her on the ground.)
ALAN: Again I triumph—she is in my power. At midnight ends my demon life. At midnight—a hundred years once more have lapsed and once again a pure untainted life drawn into mine, will yield to me a century. Ada—arise. (III, iv, 85)

Ada resists and summons the ghosts of Alice and Lucy to aid her. The tombs rise up out of the earth:

ALAN: Invoke their aid, for none human can avail thee now. (Pull below to raise C Tomb and discover RH Tomb.)
ADA: Avoid thee, demon.
ALAN: My life, my life ebbs fast. (Bell) Ha! the hour is come—Ah!—malediction. Mercy! Mercy!
(The lid of Lucy Peveril's tomb flies open. The bottom of the tomb rises with Lucy on it. She stretches forth her arm, and places her hand on Alan's shoulder. He utters a cry, staggers back, and a ruined tower (RH) falls and buries him in the ruins. On the last stroke of 12 the tower LH falls. Thunder. Crashes LH. Ruins fall. At the time that Lucy's tomb opens, Alice appeared in ruined tomb RH. They both sink again and their tombs close up.)
PEVERIL: (without, R) Ada! (rushes down platform, catches fainting Ada in his arms. End.) (III, iv, 87)

3. *The Phantom*, by Dion Boucicault.
The first scene is set in the interior of a Welch inn, but instead of a singing and dancing crowd of peasants, in this stripped-down version we have a newlywed couple, Davy and Janet, the innkeepers. After a few henpecking jokes and light sexual badinage, Lucy Peveril, as before, arrives in search of her Puritan fiancé; then Lord Clavering and his party appear. Davy is given the exposition of the dangers of Raby Castle, and again, the group elects to go there immediately to spend the night. Scene two is an added, "A rocky path leading to Raby Castle" (I, ii, 6), where we see the party climbing the mountain, with many jokes from the superstitious and terrified Davy, about how he is spending his honeymoon:

DAVY: The bridge gone! then how am I to get home on my wedding night?
NEVIL: You must pass it along with us in Raby Castle—I am sorry for the charming maiden, your bride.
DAVY: No, I'm the charming maiden in this case, she was married before. (I, ii, 7)

Scene three is in the ruined chapel of the castle, where Lucy, much more than in the previous version, has prescience of some dreadful fate. She is frozen with fear, unable to eat or speak. The vampire's entrance is identical to the first version, and the first speech is retained. His costume is described as follows:

A Puritan's suit of black serge, bound with black velvet—cloak and breeches to match—black belt and buckle—black gauntlets—shirt collar thrown back so as to show the throat bare—black stockings—black velvet shoes with strap across the instep—black sugar-loaf hat and broad riband and steel buckle—phosphoric livid countenance—slightly bald head—long black lank hair combed behind the ears—bushy black eyebrows and heavy black mustache.

He is immediately recognized by Davy as the Puritan Alan Raby, who ten years previously killed his Cavalier brother Owen, and was later thrown from the window to his death when the castle was retaken by Royalist forces: (DAVY: Throw him out the window—do, sir. CLAVERING: Are you mad, fellow? DAVY: He's used to it, sir [I, iii, 11]). The action then proceeds identically, with the addition of another climbing scene with the guests descending Snowdon in terror of their lives.

Act Two is set in a hall of Raby Castle, with an entirely new set of characters. Some time elapses before Boucicault lets us know the period by the news of the Battle of Blenheim (1704), a time lapse of 44 years; but elsewhere the time is indicated to be much later, probably contemporary, that is, 1856. Another reference indicates 1755. Boucicault's second costume was "Black dress coat and overcoat of the same colour—black trousers—black waistcoat—black kid gloves, white wristbands over them—white cravat and black German hat—all modern, and such as would be worn by a gentleman at the present time."

Low comic relief is offered by Stump, a soldier, and Jenny, the maid:

STUMP: That's my way of doing it—off hand—without any ceremony.
JENNY: Without any ceremony! Oh, you villain, dare you offer to marry me without a ceremony!
STUMP: My dear little Welsh angel—you shall have it all complete—bell—marrow-bones—cleavers and all the poetic mind could desire.
JENNY: I'm an innocent and helpless girl, but if you take advantage of my feelings.... I should break your back with a chopper!
STUMP: Moderate your virtue, my dear Jenny—and subdue its indignant blazes; come along, and rely on me, the honor of a British soldier is a matter of history.
JENNY: Yes, but my virtue is a matter of fact. And a girl is a fool, who relies on her lover, before she has lost all reliance on herself. (II, i, 16)

Ada is a neurasthenic invalid, who, given the false news that her sweetheart Edgar has been killed in the war, has fallen down dead and lain for five nights in her coffin, before being revived by the mysterious faith healer, Alan Rookwood. Ada has a father rather than a mother in this version, Colonel Raby, heir to Raby Castle. His friend, Dr. Rees, the physician attending Ada (who somewhat confusingly refers to Ada as his child), is suspicious of the priest:

REES: A brain fever struck my dearest child, and my darling Ada died in my arms.... As I live she was dead! for five days I watched, and for five nights I prayed by her bedside;—it was the night before her funeral when a carriage drove into the castle.—A stranger alighted.... He came to see Ada.... He waived [sic] me aside, and...finding his way to her chamber, as if every avenue in the castle were known to him.... We stood by her bedside; he gazed long upon her, and then placed his hand on her forehead; his brow contracted; his eyes seemed to glow with fire. Long time he stood thus, until I started with horror: a shudder quivered through her frame; she moved. The stranger smiled; he stooped down and pressed his lips to hers.... I fear this man deals in witchcraft, and I believe there is something in him supernatural.
COLONEL: Because he cured my child when you had given her up?
REES: No, because I have watched him, and he never eats, drinks, or sleeps. At night he wanders from the castle into the mountains: and one bright moonlight night, from the high turret window, I followed his track with my telescope. (II, ii, 17)

Ada is reunited with her former sweetheart Edgar, but he finds her very changed. She is enthralled by the vampire's personality in some way she cannot explain. Rookwood now presents a deed under which he claims Raby Castle through his descent from Gervase Rookwood, leaving Ada and the Colonel penniless. Asked by her father to choose between Edgar and Rookwood, Ada has no will of her own:

ADA: What power is this which oppresses me?
ALAN: It is my will; mine eyes fix upon thy heart as if with fangs, while my soul like a serpent entwines thee within its folds, and crushes thee to my will. Ada, thou art mine!
ADA: Yes, thou art my master; I cannot oppose thee.
EDGAR: She turns away from me. Not one look, Ada—Ada, will you not speak to me? (II, ii, 21)

Rees discovers an old book with recipes for killing vampires with fire, water, and bullets, and he and Stump plan their attack. Rees also finds Rookwood's will, dated 1645, on paper with a watermark of 1750. (The period of the second act is very inconsistently maintained: "This paper is barely five years old!") When Rookwood signs the marriage contract, the signature is discovered to be the same. With nice dramatic irony, the vampire is accused of forging his own genuine signature. He challenges Edgar to a duel on the peak of Snowdon.

Ada struggles to awaken from the vampire's power, and Dr. Rees defends her with a pistol. The vampire sets out for Snowdon, determining to make Edgar the victim instead of Ada, with Stump and Rees in pursuit. Scene six, on the mountain, discovers Edgar and the vampire on a narrow ledge, where he perfidiously attacks Edgar with a dagger, since there is no room to draw swords:

ALAN: Take it in thy throat, and let me slake my thirst in thy life-blood!
(A shot is heard outside—Alan falls back with a cry—Edgar rises.)
STUMP (entering with Rees): I say, Doctor, I rung the bell, didn't I? (II, v, 27)

The moon rises as they stand around the body, and watch with amazement as it begins to revive, but Dr. Rees knows how to prevent another resuscitation:

REES (reads): "After death, his body must therefore be preserved from the moonlight, lest, by virtue of its rays, he might revive." See—watch his heaving form—already the life comes back to him, limb by limb!
COLONEL: Hold! what would you do?
REES: Exterminate the phantom—into this black chasm, where the light of heaven never visited, I cast his body!—may his dark spirit sink as low into eternal perdition! (Casts the body of Alan into the abyss. Curtain.) (II, v, 28)

4. *Ruthven*, by Augustus Harris.
The plot is identical to Dumas's *Le Vampire* (1852). The last scene, in a graveyard, is more rough-and-tumble, but much less grand:

(Music—he advances towards Antonia to take her in his arms, when he suddenly starts, and seems driven back by a supernatural power.)

RUTHWEN: What fiend of hell has done this? She bears an amulet, which annihilates my power. Who has done this? I am betrayed—she is beyond my reach! Curses on this infatuated feeling of revenge, which made me neglect my own safety. I will hence—some other victim must be found ere the hour strikes, or I am lost for ever....

GILBERT: Fiend, repent! for your hour is at hand!

RUTHWEN: Never—let me pass! or this moment is your last!

(Bell begins to strike twelve—Ruthven presents pistol, but on hearing the clock, starts—Gilbert takes advantage of this movement, and with his sword, strikes the pistol from his hand—he then rushes on Ruthven, gets him down, and presents sword to his chest—Enter Lazare L.)

GILBERT: Repent ere it be too late!

RUTHWEN (Struggling for life): Never! Curses on you all! Idiot that I have been! Ziska has betrayed me—but she has paid the forfeit! What forms are these around drawing me back? Mercy! Back!

(All this is spoken while the clock is striking—on the last stroke of twelve, a thunderbolt strikes Ruthven to the ground—a flame and smoke issue from the earth where he falls, and when it clears off, no signs are seen of him, except a flat mass of rags.... Music changes.—The chapel disappears, and discovers: The Heavens, in which is [sic] seen Helene and Juanna, clad in white, with their arms extended towards the Ghoule, who, in the act of prayer, is seen gradually ascending toward them. The Tableau is illuminated by celestial rays. Curtain. (IV, ii, 52)

### Chapter 8: Satire and Misogyny, 1872-88

1. *The Vampire*, by Robert Reece.

A party of two lady novelists, Ada Raby and Lady Audley Moonstone, and their sweethearts, Edgar and Lord Alfred Clavering (breeches roles), are having a picnic in the ruins of Raby Castle, when they encounter Alan Raby, a spinner of penny-dreadful gothic horror novels. He attempts to steal the ladies' notebooks which contain their plot outlines. Claiming to be the real author of Tennyson's "Maud" and "Idylls of the King" and Swinburne's "Songs Before Sunrise," Raby is recognized by Edgar as his cousin, the Irish plagiarist:

ALAN: I'm someone else, sir.

EDGAR:                           No, no, that won't do!
You're Alan Raby, sir, my blackguard cousin!
I'll swear to it; you're some excuse preparing.

ALAN: Tho' I'm your *cussin*, you need not be *swearing*!

EDGAR: And why speak Irish?

ALAN:                           Sir, the biggest rogue,
Can claim forgiveness, if he's got the brogue;
A look, that in another would be "sly,"
Is called the "Irish twinkle" in *his* eye!
I've been an Englishman for half my days,
But now I'm Irish—and for why?—it pays! (Ray 1st, 10-11)

The two men challenge the vampire to a duel on the peak of Snowdon, where they apply the vampire-slaying device of issuing a warning proclamation to all publishers. Alan drops dead, but begins to revive, so they order the stagehands to turn off the limelight. Yelling that now he's done for, Alan throws himself off the mountainside, and as all are peering over the cliff's edge, he pops back up behind them through the vampire trap:

ALL: Gone! (Alan rolls through vampire C. into stage)
ALAN:         No! I've done ye by a vampire trap!
Accustomed to this sort of thing I am,
I played Claude Frollo, sir, in "Notre Dame!"
ALFRED: Yield!
EDGAR:          And get out!
COLONEL:                    Being kind to superfluity
I'll let you henceforth have a small annuity!
But change your name! (Ray 3rd, 25)

The play ends with an exhortation to the audience not to be ashamed of having enjoyed the piece, arguing that the satire was morally superior to the original:

ADA: Pray overlook this nonsense for a season,
Our ray of moonshine, with no ray of reason!
And say, some little fun you think you can see,
Out of this twisting of Lord Byron's fancy,
Remembering that this stuff, whate'er its name,
Is healthier than the idea whence it came!
ALAN: We're at the Strand, incorrigible folk,
So treat the whole affair, please, as a joke! (Ray 3rd, 26)

### 2. *Ruddygore*, by Gilbert and Sullivan (original version).

The premise of the plot is a family curse: many generations previously, a witch being burnt at the stake (cf. *Il Trovatore*) has decreed that each Baronet of Ruddygore must commit at least one wicked deed per day or die in horrible agony. Part of the comic conceit is that villainy is an exhausting occupation to which very few are temperamentally suited. The current heir, Ruthven, last of the Murgatroyds, has run away from such dreadful chores and hidden in the fishing village of Rederring, Cornwall, under the assumed name of Robin Oakapple. He has fallen in love with Rose Maybud, who is bound in every action and reaction by a book of etiquette, and never allows herself to have a natural or honest response to anything.

Ruthven's younger brother, Sir Despard Murgatroyd, has assumed the baronetcy and driven Mad Margaret insane with his evil deeds and neglect of her. She has a Donizettian mad scene accompanied by solo flute, followed by a lovely and sad song, "To a garden full of posies." Ruthven also has a foster-brother, Richard Dauntless, a typical British jolly jack tar who dances a hornpipe (in homage to T.P. Cooke, perhaps), and reveals Ruthven's true identity to Despard, in order to win Rose Maybud for himself. Despard naturally feels the older brother should resume the title and the curse.

In Act Two, Robin and his servant Adam Goodheart have assumed the names and wicked personas of Sir Ruthven Murgatroyd and Gideon Crawle. They are finding the daily quota of evil deeds a heavy burden. Ruthven tries some villain-ese on his sweetheart, Rose, but is foiled by her new boyfriend, his brother Richard, who repulses him with a Union Jack instead of a cross:

ROBIN: Soho! pretty one—in my power at last, eh? Know ye not that I have within my call who, at my lightest bidding, would immure ye in an uncomfortable dungeon where ye would linger out a lonesome lifetime, in sad and silent solitude? (Calling) What ho! within there!
RICHARD: Hold—we are prepared for this (producing a Union Jack). Here is a flag that none dare defy (all kneel), and while this glorious rag floats over Rose Maybud's head, the man does not live who would dare to lay unlicensed hand upon her!
ROBIN: Foiled—and by a Union Jack! (II, 294)

Ruthven, in soliloquy, begs for relief from the portraits of his ancestors:

ROBIN (addressing pictures): Oh, my forefathers, wallowers in blood, there came at last a day when, sick of crime, you, each and every, vowed to sin no more, and so, in agony, called welcome Death to free you from your cloying guiltiness. Let the sweet psalm of that repentant hour soften your long-dead hearts, and tune your souls to mercy on your poor posterity! (Kneeling) (The stage darkens for a moment. It becomes light again, and the Pictures are seen to have become animated.)
CHORUS OF FAMILY PORTRAITS: Painted emblems of a race,
    All accurst in days of yore,
Each from his accustomed place
    Steps into the world once more!
(The Pictures step from their frames and march round the stage.)
Baronet of Ruddygore
    Last of our accursèd line,
Down upon the oaken floor—
    Down upon those knees of thine!
        Coward, poltroon, shaker, squeamer,
        Blockhead, sluggard, dullard, dreamer,
        Shirker, shuffler, crawler, creeper,
        Sniffler, snuffler, wailer, weeper,
        Earthworm, maggot, tadpole, weevil!
        Set upon thy course of evil
        Lest the king of Spectre-Land
        Set on thee his grisly hand! (II, 295)

The twenty-first Baronet of Ruddygore, Sir Roderic, sings an aria which is a salute to the gothic genre:

When the night wind howls in the chimney cowls, and the bat in the moonlight flies,
And inky clouds , like funeral shrouds, sail over the midnight skies,
When the footpads quail at the night-bird's wail, and black dogs bay the moon,
Then is the spectres' holiday—then is the ghosts' high-noon! (II, 296)

Ruthven agrees to try to do better at being bad, and sends Gideon Crawle out to abduct a woman—any woman. Meanwhile Despard has been reunited with Mad Margaret: both have reformed the wild excesses of their first-act behavior, and become almost respectable. Gideon Crawle returns, dragging in his unlikely kidnap victim, a spry old crone who spits defiance at her reluctant ravisher, Ruthven, and turns out to be Sir Roderic's long-lost love, Hannah. He proposes marriage, but she points out that marriage to a ghost automatically makes a woman a widow, which would force her to marry someone else immediately.

The plot is resolved when it occurs to Ruthven that, since a Baronet of Ruddygore can only die by refusing to commit a crime, the refusal is suicide, which is itself a crime; therefore none of the Murgatroyd ghosts have violated the terms of the curse, and therefore ought still to be living. They descend again from their frames, and marry the chorus of professional bridesmaids.

4. *The Vampire's Victim*, by Richard Henry.

As in Shelley's novel, Dr. Frankenstein's Monster demands a mate. Mary Ann is the candidate, but, since she is a vampire, she is frustrated by the fact that the Monster is made of clay (taken to mean pottery), and has no circulatory system. Her lover, Visconti, also a vampire, becomes jealous. In a reference to the 1885 Lyceum *Faust*, "assuming the attitude of Irving as Mephistopheles," he sings, apparently accompanied by business with a trick wig:

VISCONTI: Since Mary Ann's flown from her owniest own
I'm a Vampire who can't keep his hair on.
CHORUS: Ha! ha! ho! Ha! ha! ho! ho! It's really so!
I'm a Vampire who can't keep his hair on
Ho, ho, ho, ho, ho, ho!

An antic abduction scene closes the act, when the Monster rejects Mary Ann for Tartina, Frankenstein's fiancée. Act Three opens at the Vampire Club, where the Monster has gone to escape his vampire wife and plot with Frankenstein against Visconti. The vampire secretary and Frankenstein serenade him with another song, "One of the Boys." In the last scene, the whole motley assortment descends on a pirate ship trapped in an ice floe near the North Pole. The Sun Goddess descends, and all is resolved.

*Chapter 9: Stage Adaptations: 1897-1985*

1. *Dracula*, by Bram Stoker.

Jonathan Harker, a young British lawyer, travels to Transylvania with the deed to an English estate, Carfax, which Count Dracula wishes to purchase. Dracula imprisons Harker and gives him to his vampire harem to feed on while he travels by ship to England, where he mentally enslaves the madman Renfield and makes a vampire of the young aristocratic Lucy Westenra. Lucy has three suitors—a psychiatric doctor (and Renfield's keeper), Dr. Seward; a young aristocrat, Arthur Holmwood (later Lord Godalming); and an American cowboy, Quincey Morris. They summon the Dutch doctor, Abraham Van Helsing, to save the life of Lucy, who they believe is dying of anemia. Lucy dies, but walks by night, seducing and preying on young children. The men open her tomb, impale her and behead her corpse.

Harker is found alive, having escaped Castle Dracula, and marries Lucy's friend, Mina Murray. She is besieged in turn by Dracula, who forces her to drink his blood, forming a psychic link with the vampire, which the men then use to trace Dracula's flight back to Transylvania, where is he destroyed at the climax of the novel, and Mina is redeemed.

2. *Vampire*, by Snoo Wilson.

Wilson's play is a commentary on the Dracula theme, with three disconnected acts: first, a Victorian family is preyed upon by a traditional vampire; second, a female "succubus" takes the life of a shell-shocked soldier in the period of World War I; the third act deals with political exploitation—politicians as bloodsuckers of the people. Charles Dickens appears as a character; passages from St. Theresa are recited; Jung and Freud disrupt a Nativity scene and Jung puts Freud in a coffin and impales him with a vampire stake. Sample dialogue:

[Virgin] MARY (kittenish): Is there anyone there?
FREUD (in a voice like granite and ashes): My name is Sigmund Freud. Originally, all of the dead were vampires. They had a grudge against the living and sought to injure them and rob them of their lives. We fear the dead because we fear death still and wish to put off what must be the gravest misfortune. (He paces uneasily.) Our bodies, however, are destined to decay and cannot dispense with anxiety and pain as warning signals. There is no escape. We are told that—
MARY: Can't you just *imagine* you're happy? (II, 60)

3. *Dracula*, Liz Lochhead.

Lochhead follows the plot of Stoker's novel, but the characters are fleshed out, filtered through a modern sensibility, and supplied with heightened poetic dialogue. A sample passage:

(A howling of wolves.)
DRACULA: Listen. Listen to the children of the night. What music they make.
JONATHAN: Mus-ic?
DRACULA: Ah yes, music. Not a true soul but knows its melody. By heart. The first time he hears it.

JONATHAN: They curdle my blood.

DRACULA: Come, come, Mr. Harker, blood is not so easily curdled. In milksop kindergartens perhaps, tales of the Big Bad Wolf might—what do you say—scare the pretty children witless? But a man whose heart has wintered enough for him to be worth something, he hears the wolf sing to the moon his own sometime desolation and it quickens the hunter in him so in his mind he runs with the grey pack in the night. Can't you see them, flowing like a ragged wind over Russia, pouring lower than the blown grasses over the steppes? Outside, in that black forest, their eyes are more than the stars and twice as secret.

(It is as if Jonathan is hypnotized into this next.)

JONATHAN: They ringed our coach—the horses screamed and plunged and stopped stock still, and I looked out and saw them in the full moonlight. White teeth. Red tongues. Shaggy hair.

DRACULA: The dogs of nature.

JONATHAN: The other passengers were frightened. There was a girl there, she was terrified. I could feel her shiver under her thin shawl. So I held her close. For human comfort you understand, to calm her as one would a child! She taught me words. *Ordog, Pokol, Stregioca, vrolok, vlkoslak*. She said...werewolf. (Dracula has been murmuring translations.)

DRACULA: "Satan," "hell," "vampire"...Ah, my friend, girlish superstition. I am sure your reason tells you so? I can assure you: these outside you hear howling are real wolves. All animal. Were-wolves, are-wolves, and ever-more-shall-be-wolves. (Pause.) Ah, Jonathan, I make a joke. Is good. No? (I, vii, 94-95)

# Appendix C

# Biographical Material

*Chapter 3: Paris, 1820*

1. *Charles Nodier* (1780-1844) was a "novelist, scholar, bibliophile, naturalist, master of style and slave of paradox...at once the earliest pioneer of Romanticism and the keenest critic of its extravagances" (Davidson 48). Before writing *Le Vampire* 1820 he had published two Romantic novels: *Jean Sbogar* (1818), and *Thérèse Aubert* (1819); works of literary analysis: *Dictionaire des onomotopées* (1808), *Questions de littéraire légal* (1812); commentary on the works of La Fontaine, Cyrano de Bergerac, and Bonaventure des Périers; travel books: *Voyages pittoresques et romantiques dans l'ancienne France* (1820), and *Promenade de Dieppe aux montagnes d'Ecosse* (1821). In his "Scottish period" (which might be said to include *Le Vampire*), he wrote *Trilby, ou le lutin d'Argail*, and *La Legende de Saint-Oran*. The preceding list is merely a sampling of his output prior to 1820, still early in his career. He wrote regularly for the *Journal des Débats, le Temps, la Quotidienne*, and *la Revue de Paris*, and was an influential theatre critic. His biographer Francis Lacassin, in the preface to his edition of *Les Démons de la nuit*, calls 1820-22 Nodier's "frenetique" period, in which he published *Smarra*, a vampire novella (mentioned in Chapter 2); contributed pieces to the anthology *Infernalia*; played some role in the writing of *Lord Ruthven ou les vampires*; and co-authored two plays: *Le Vampire*, adapted from Polidori, and *Le Château de Saint-Aldobrand*, adapted from Charles Maturin's *Bertram*. Lacassin writes: "Nodier apparaît comme le patriarche bienveillant du movement romantique. On serait tenté de dire, par référence à sa culture débordante, à sa personnalité tournoyante et à sa fonction non officielle de Conservateur du Pays des Songes: Charles Nodier, le mage du Romantisme." [Nodier appeared as the benevolent patriarch of the Romantic movement. One is tempted to say, in reference to his overflowing culture, his whirling personality, his unofficial function as conservator of the Land of Dreams: Charles Nodier, the magus of Romanticism] (12).

2. *Pierre-Luc-Charles Ciceri.* Rivaled only by Daguerre, Ciceri was one of the foremost artists of the Romantic revolution, the most important stage innovator of the period, and the chief designer at the Porte-Saint-Martin. He began his career as a landscape artist, having studied classical art at the Académie des Beaux Artes. He held the position of court painter and designer for the court theatres at the Tuileries and Saint-Cloud. His designs for l'Opéra and the Porte-Saint-Martin were renowned for their exquisitely realized romantic landscapes, desolate ruins, and ghostly and nostalgic

historical settings. Ciceri created the first independent scene studio in Paris in 1822, where many specialized artists produced scenery for all the major theatres. His students continued to dominate French scene design for the rest of the century.

3. *Monsieur Aumer* was ballet master at the Porte-Saint-Martin. In 1821 he and Ciceri moved to l'Opéra, which was newly equipped with the innovations of gas lighting and a water system for fountains, continuing their collaboration with a series of ballets and operas. Aumer was among the first to develop pointe-work, the foundation of classical ballet.

4. *Alexandre Piccini* (1779-1850), composer, was nephew to Niccolò Piccini, the rival of Gluck. He was a very prolific composer for melodrama, in which, besides the set pieces (songs and ballets), much of the action was underscored by music; he also wrote comic operas and romances. He was long a popular favorite, and died an octogenarian.

5. *Monsieur Philippe* [Emmanuel de la Villenie, d. 1824] was the actor who first played Nodier's Rutwen. Paul Ginesty writes, "Philippe, c'était le grand premier rôle fatal, et sa création du *Vampire* l'avait entouré d'un singulier prestige. C'était un fort bel homme 'manquant souvent de sagesse dans son jeu, rarement d'intelligence.'" [Philippe was the first great star in fatal roles, and his creation of the Vampire had given him exceptional prestige. He was a splendid man, 'often lacking wisdom when he acted, but never intelligence.'] (207). Ginesty quotes a "Countess Dash" in *Mémoires des Autres*, "Le Vampire, où Philippe était si beau: je dis si beau dans toute l'acception physique du mot; il avait un visage pâle, admirable avec ses vêtements noirs." [The *Vampire*, in which Philippe was so beautiful: I say beautiful in the full physical meaning of that word; he had a pale face, admirable in his black costume] (207). Alexandre Dumas père, who also saw *Le Vampire*, described him as follows: "Quant à Philippe, qui l'écrasait, à cette epoque, de la dignité de son pas et la majesté de son geste, c'était la représentation du mélodrame pur sang Pixérécourt et Caignez.... Nul ne portait comme Philippe la botte jaune, la tunique chamois bordée de noir, la toque à plume et l'épée à poignée en croix." [As to Philippe, who overwhelmed us in that epoch with the dignity of his gait and the majesty of his gesture, he was the representation of the pure-blooded melodrama of Pixérécourt and Caignez. No one carried like Philippe the yellow boot, the leather tunic bordered in black, the plumed hat, and the sword with cross-shaped hilt] (*Mémoires* III: xxvii). Among Philippe's other memorable leading roles were Salvator in Scribe's *Les Frères Invisibles*, Wallace in Pixérécourt's *Les Chefs écossais* (1819), and François in Boirie's *Les Deux Forçats* (1822).

He was still very young when he was found dead in his bed of an attack of apoplexy on 16 October 1824. The curé at Saint-Laurent refused to give him religious obsequies, and the actors of Paris, infuriated, caused a near riot at his funeral at Père Lachaise, which was attended by three thousand people. Dumas wrote, "Sa mort fit presque autant de bruit que sa vie" [His death was almost as famous as his life], and Ginesty, "Le corps de l'acteur fut accompagné au cimitière par un escadron de gendarmerie, sabre au claire. L'ombre de Philippe vit sans doute sans déplaisir cet imposant déploiment de forces autour de son cercueil, et le prit peut-être pour un hommage." [The body of the actor was accompanied to the cemetery by a squadron of gendarmes, sabres drawn. The ghost of Philippe doubtless saw without displeasure this imposing deployment of forces around his coffin, and perhaps he took it for an homage] (207).

6. *Marie Dorval* (Marie Delaunay, 1798-1849) was the first Malvina. Dorval, Pierre Bocage, and Frédérick Lemaître were the leading interpreters of French Romantic drama. The daughter of itinerant players, she was rejected by the Conservatoire, played for a while in the provinces, joined the Porte-Saint-Martin in 1818 and debuted in *Pamela*. She played opposite Philippe in *Les Chefs écossais* and *Les Deux Forçats* before starring with him, at the age of 22, in *Le Vampire*, a sensational success for both of them. Later she triumphed as Kitty Bell at the Comédie Française in Alfred de Vigny's *Chatterton*, in Victor Hugo's *Marion Delorme*, as Adèle opposite Bocage in Dumas père's *Antony*, and many others. Jules Janin, a leading critic, reviewing her performance opposite Frédérick Lemaître in Ducange's *Trente Ans ou la Vie d'un jouer*, wrote: "The budding Mme. Dorval had a personality to justify the strongest sympathies. She was frail, imploring, timid; she wept amazingly, with desolation, with agonies, with an overwhelming delirium" (qtd. in Collins 295). Théophile Gautier wrote that her art

...in which temperament was all in all, fitted her as completely for the boulevard theatre, as it unfitted her for the classic stage. [She was] helpless in characters which she could not build up round her own personality.... Her art was accordingly a thing of fits and starts, intuitive, eruptive, uncalculated and incalculable.... She had within her range screams so piercingly true, sobs that seemed so to tear the bosom, intonations so natural, tears so heartfelt and helpless, that the stage was forgotten, and it was impossible to believe that this was but a simulated sorrow. (qtd. in Duerr 297)

Gautier commented elsewhere that her talent was "all impassioned; not that she neglected art, but her art came from inspiration. She did not calculate her playing gesture by gesture, or plan out her entrances and exits with a pencil on paper; she put herself into the situation of her role, wed it completely, became it, and acted as the character herself would act" (qtd. in Carlson, *French Stage* 69). Her style, summed up, seems to have been marked by simplicity and truth—real tears, sighs and blushes, lack of pretension, vulnerability, and complete empathy with the role.

Le Grande Larousse Encyclopedique (197) states that she was married at 16 to an actor, Allan, called "Dorval," who died in Russia. With two daughters to support, she made a second marriage in 1829 to a journalist named Merle, and later became the mistress of Alfred de Vigny (who wrote about their affair in *Le Colère de Samson*) and of Alexandre Dumas père. Her career faded with the passing of Romanticism, and she died in obscurity in 1849, two years before Dumas wrote his vampire play.

7. *Jenny Vertpré*, who played the soubrette role of Lovette, later became a leading actress for Scribe at the Gymnase. Apparently she was very short. The critic Harel, writing of her debut in *La Pie Voleuse*, called her "la plus petite actrice par la taille, la plus grande par le talent, après Mlle. Mars" [the smallest actress by height, and the largest for talent, after Mademoiselle Mars] (qtd. in Ginesty 135). According to Ginisty, Vertpré was married to Pierre Carmouche, one of the three authors of *Le Vampire*. After 1820, both moved away from melodrama and toward light comedy in their work:

Carmouche était...d'humeur plus gaie: après avoir sacrifié au genre larmoyant et même fantastique, comme avec *Le Vampire*, il fut plus à l'aise dans le vaudeville et dans la fantaisie: il lui arrive même, lui qui en avait fait, de parodier les mélodrames. Sa femme, Jenny Vertpré, comédienne charmante...cette petite femme si vivre et si fine...avait passé, elle aussi, [de] drame à comédie. [Carmouche had a happier personality; after having paid tribute to the tearful, even fantastic genre, as with *Le Vampire*, he was more at ease in vaudeville and fantasy; he even came to the practice of parodying melodrama, even though he had written them himself. His wife, Jenny Vertpré, that charming comedienne, that little woman so lively and delicate, had also moved from drama to comedy.] (168, 208)

8. *Eugène Scribe* (1791-1861). Shortly after writing *Le Vampire*, Scribe signed an exclusive contract with the Théâtre du Gymnase. Between 1820-30 he wrote more than one hundred plays for the Gymnase, establishing for himself a dominant position in French boulevard theatre, from which "he was besieged by directors soliciting new plays, by composers requesting libretti, by artists aspiring to favorable roles, by dramatists begging the privilege of collaborating with him" (Arvin 15).

All this activity was still early in his career. He continued to write another 200 plays, 23 of which were produced at the Comédie Française, and branched out into opera and serious drama. Most important, he developed the structure of the "pièce bien-fait," which emphasizes logical plot and cause-to-effect development, the basic structure (though not Scribe's light subject matter) adopted by the movement of Realism.

### Chapter 4: London, 1820

1. *James Robinson Planché* (1796-1880). There is a humorous and affectionate portrait of Planché in the preface to *Personal Reminiscences by Chorley, Planché and Young* by Richard Henry Stoddard, published in 1874, just prior to Planché's death. Stoddard states that Planché's parents, who were cousins, were the children of French Huguenot refugees and that the household was bilingual. His mother died when he was nine, his father, a watch-maker, when he was 20. According to Stoddard, he studied painting, then writing.

[Then] he developed a propensity common to young men, the belief that he was an actor, and...turned amateur, and at various private theatres murdered sundry great personages to his entire satisfaction, in company with other juvenile aspirants, who afterwards rose to eminence on the stage. Finding nothing in Shakespeare or Sheridan worthy of his abilities, he resolved to write a play himself. (xvi-xvii)

This was a burletta in the style of Rhodes's *Bombastes Furioso* (1816) called *Amoroso, King of Little Britain*, "A Serio-Comick, Bombastic Operatick Interlude." By what seems to have been an extraordinary piece of luck, it fell into the hands of John Harley, then manager of Drury Lane (later to act McSwill in *The Vampire*), who produced it on 21 April 1818. With the encouragement of Harley, Robert Elliston, and Stephen Kemble, Planché decided he had found his vocation.

A selection of play titles gives an idea of his metier: *A Hit If You Like It*, *The Merchant's Wedding*, *Charles the Twelfth*, *The Brigand*, *Olympic Revels*, *Olympic Devils*, *The Romance of a Day*, *The Love Charm*, *The Student of Jena*, *Gustavus the Third*, *The Red Mask*, *The Two Figaros*, *Blue Beard*, *Faint Heart Never Won Fair Lady*, *Fortunio*, *The Loan of a Lover*, *The Yellow Dwarf*, *The King of the Peacocks*, *Abdullah*, *Maid Marion*, *The Paphian Bower*, *The Deep Deep Sea*, *Telemachus*, *Puss in Boots*, *The Sleeping Beauty in the Wood*, *Beauty and the Beast*, *The White Cat*, *The Fair One with the Golden Locks*, *Theseus and Ariadne*, *The Golden Fleece*, *The Prince of the Happy Land*, *Mr. Buckstone's Ascent of Parnassus*, *Orpheus in the Haymarket*, and at least 150 others. In addition to his enormous output of plays, like Charles Nodier he wrote travel books: *Lays and Legends of the Rhine* (1827), *Shere Afkun, A Legend of Hindoostan* (1823); also poetry, translations of German and French fairy tales, plus the original libretto for Weber's *Oberon*, and English versions of Mozart's *The Magic Flute*, Rossini's *William Tell* and *The Siege of Corinth*, Bellini's *Norma*, Halévy's *La Juive*, and Donizetti's *L'elisir d'amore*.

Planché also stage-managed ("directed" is the modern term), and was the manager (artistic director) of the Adelphi, Vauxhall Gardens, and second-in-command to Eliza Vestris at the Olympic, where he also wrote, designed, and directed. He testified for and actively supported Bulwer-Lytton's Dramatic Author's Act of 1833 and the Theatre Regulation Act of 1843.

He was a designer of sets and costumes, and made important and early contributions to accuracy in period costuming with his designs for Charles Kemble's production of *King John* (1823) at Covent Garden, which, despite the hostility of the actors and management through the rehearsal period, received great acclaim. Out of his research for this production grew his *History of British Costume* (1834), long a standard reference, which in turn gave impetus to the antiquarian movement and fostered historically accurate productions, especially of Shakespeare.

Planché was often consulted by leading painters for authenticity of historic detail in dress, armor, and architecture, and he was a founding member of the British Archaeological Association. In 1854 he was appointed to the College of Arms as Rouge Croix Pursuivant, and in 1867 he received the honor of being named Somerset Herald, accompanying the Garter missions to Portugal, Austria, and Italy; his stage expertise in royal ceremonials thus crossing over into real life.

According to Martin Meisel, Planché crossed paths with Ciceri, designer of the Paris *Vampire*: "For a *Pageant of the Coronation of Charles X* (1825), J.R. Planché was dispatched to Rheims to sketch the full particulars of costume and decoration. The result at Covent Garden eclipsed a rival production at Drury Lane, though perhaps not the ceremony at Rheims, which had been staged by the master scene designer of the Paris Opera, P.L.C. Ciceri" (34).

2. *T.P. Cooke* (Thomas Potter Cooke, 1786-1864) was the first English Ruthven and the most prominent actor of melodrama of this period. His stage career lasted 56 years. The son of a London doctor, he was orphaned young and joined the Royal Navy at the age of ten. He took part in several naval battles against the French under the command of the Earl of St. Vincent, serving on H.M.S. *Raven* and H.M.S. *Prince of Wales*. He was commended for gallantry and survived shipwreck. He left the navy at age 18 after the Peace of Amiens, and acted at the Royalty, Surrey, Drury Lane, Covent Garden, and Adelphi. On the recommendation of Robert Elliston, manager of Drury Lane, he took over the management of the Surrey, and later of the Coburg.

William Oxberry, a fellow actor who took to writing keyhole memoirs of his colleagues, has great admiration for Cooke, and also for Samuel Arnold, manager of the English Opera House. The association of the two was mutually beneficial: "Mr. Cooke, in common with many, has much to thank Mr. Arnold for. On his boards, and under his management, Mr. Cooke had opportunities for a full development of his extraordinary powers...[but] Mr. Cooke is so *notoriously* a talented creature, that every managerial speculator is anxious to 'have a taste of his quality,' in his own domain" (*Dramatic Biography and Green Room Spy* I: 255-56). As for his talent as an actor, Oxberry finds him extraordinary, but not without his limits:

Mr. Cooke has done almost every individual part he has appeared in, better than any other actor whom we are acquainted with could have done it.... His sailors are more steady than Munden's.... His melo-dramatic performances equal those of Wallack; and in serious pantomime, no one (save Obi Smith) can stand one moment in competition with him.... In a word, Mr. T.P. Cooke is, in most parts of the drama, a surprising performer. Whether he would have succeeded in the first characters of tragedy, is matter of doubt. There is a want of flexibility in his features and tones, for higher assumptions; and his expressive face, that so well depicts the strong workings of intense passions, might not so easily pourtray [sic] the nicer shades of minute ones.... He is married to a very amiable lady, and enjoys the regard of a highly respectable circle of acquaintance. Mr. T.P. Cooke is five feet eleven inches in height, and of a dark complexion. (I: 251, 259-60)

Cooke was one of the first English actors to appear in Paris. On 10 June 1826 he acted at the Porte-Saint-Martin in the mime role of the monster in *Le Monstre et le magicien* (Nodier, Carmouche, Merle, 1826), which ran 80 performances. In *British Entertainers in France* Victor Leathers states that the manager, J.T. Merle, engaged Cooke for the summer season of 1826 after the success of his performance as the monster in Peake's *Presumption, or the Fate of Frankenstein* at the Lyceum in 1823. The implication is that Merle saw the English production, and, as one of the French adaptation's three authors, created the Frankenstein piece as a vehicle for Cooke. This was "a three-act *mélodrame féerie à grand spectacle* complete with a ballet and concluding with an impressive catastrophe in the form of a tempest" (Leathers 55).

Wischhusen (168) and Sherson (160) both state that Cooke performed Rutwen in French in Nodier's *Le Vampire* at the Porte-Saint-Martin. Summers manages to confuse the issue thoroughly as he writes, "In 1825 T.P. Cooke visited Paris and appeared as Le Monstre in Planché's melodrama which proved a remarkable success, running for no less than eighty nights" (*Kith* 308). Both date and playwright are incorrect. Summers is not the source of Sherson's confusion, however, since Sherson's book was published three years earlier. It is indisputable that the role of Rutwen was created and performed by the French actor M. Philippe, both in the original 1820 production and in the 1823 revival, but he died suddenly in 1824, and it is *barely* possible that Cooke gave a special performance of Nodier's Rutwen in the summer of 1826, while he was acting at the Porte-Saint-Martin.

Planché, also in Paris in 1826 to hire singers, reports that the actor was struggling against illness to fulfill his acting obligations on both sides of the channel:

T.P. Cooke and his wife were at this moment in Paris, he having accepted an engagement to perform at the Porte-St.-Martin in a French version of Peake's melodrama, "Frankenstein, or the Modern Prometheus" [sic; *Presumption, or the Fate of Frankenstein*], his original part of the monster, which he, rather than Prometheus, had created at the Lyceum Theatre in London.... I made my way to Cooke's lodging, where, cruel as it seemed, I could scarcely forbear laughing to find him laid up with the gout. The monster, who was to frighten all the fair Parisians into fits, moping in an armchair, with his foot enveloped in flannel...in a state of hopeless inactivity! There was something exceedingly ludicrous in the position; but it was no laughing matter to him, poor fellow. There he was, literally tied by the leg, unable even to attend rehearsals, and uncertain whether he would be well enough to make his appearance before the expiration of his *congé* from Mr. Arnold. He never had the gout before, and attributed the attack to the acidity of French wines. Fortunately it was as short as it was sharp, and his success was so great that "monstre bleu," the color he painted himself, became the fashion of the day in Paris. (*Recollections* I: 89-90)

Leathers (56) and Forrey (34) both state that Cooke also performed in a vaudeville revue, *Les filets de Vulcain, ou le lendemain d'un succès* on 15 July 1826, contributing a scene in English from *The Pilot*; a ballet-pantomime, *Le Déserteur*; and a vaudeville, *Le Monstre*, in which he spoke French. *Le Journal des Débats* (18 July 1826) commented:

M. Cooke a paru dans cette pièce sous costume bourgeois, et l'on a vu avec plaisir que le monstre si effrayant avec sa peau verte et sa perruque à la conseillière, avait de très-bonnes manières.... L'étrangeté de son accent, et ses efforts pour prononcer le français, avaient une sorte de charme qu'augmentait encore la modestie avec laquelle il s'est présenté. [Mr. Cooke appeared in that play in ordinary clothes, and one saw with pleasure that the monster, so frightening with his green skin and counselor's wig, had very nice manners.... The oddness of his accent, and his attempts at pronouncing French, had a kind of charm still more augmented by the modesty with which he presented himself.] (qtd. in Forrey 34)

In "The Acting of Thomas Potter Cooke," Harold J. Nichols compares Cooke's phenomenal popularity to that of today's film stars, and cites the ratings of popular actors of the *Theatrical Chronicle and Dramatic Review* of 1842, which lists Charles Kean's popularity as "great," Ben Webster's as "middling," Madame Vestris as "great at wit," but Thomas Cooke's as "wonderful" (73). Nichols surmises that Cooke's two years in minor roles at the Drury Lane gave him the opportunity to observe and play opposite Edmund Kean, whose passionate intensity and flamboyant, energetic style Cooke may have absorbed. Nichols writes, although it would be difficult to prove that Kean influenced Cooke, it seems significant that the tragedian "was especially noted for his use of 'accent, look, and gesture,' features which were to be important in the mature Cooke's performances" (75). Cooke was noted for the energy, physicality, and sharp transitions of his acting, characteristics of the new romantic style popularized by Kean, and he made a sensation with his powerful performance in *The Vampire*, and in the mime roles of Frankenstein's monster, billed "*****," in Peake's *Presumption, or the Fate of Frankenstein*, and as Vanderdecken in Fitzball's *The Flying Dutchman*.

His early triumphs in gothic melodrama were eclipsed by his long series of sailor roles. In *English Melodrama* Michael Booth writes:

After *The Shipwreck of the Medusa* [Cooke] was known and idolized for his nautical parts, which he performed by the dozen.... Some idea of the popularity of the best nautical plays and the ceaseless activity of Cooke himself is revealed by the fact that during an acting span of about twenty-five years he played Harry Hallyard in *My Poll and My Partner Joe* 269 times, Long John Coffin in *The Pilot* 562 times, and William in *Black-Eyed Susan* no less than 765 times. (*Illustrated London News*, Oct. 15, 1853.) In Cooke, whose stage heroism and virtue and loyalty to his country remained massively unshaken for a generation of nautical drama, English audiences found a symbol of nautical glories simply enshrined in the large heart and manly soul of one of their own kind. (108-09)

Cooke last played Sweet William and danced the hornpipe in 1860 at the age of 74, and died four years later.

3. *Mrs. W.S. Chatterley*, sometimes spelled Chatterly, born Louisa Simeon (1797-1866), was the first Margaret. Daughter of a milliner, she was raised in a Liverpool convent, a Bath boarding school, and a London seminary, where she developed an interest in theatre. She married the actor William Simmonds Chatterley, debuted as Juliet in Bath in 1814, and in 1816 joined the English Opera House. In the winter of 1820 (after *The Vampire*), Mr. and Mrs. Chatterley performed at the Surrey, after which she joined the Olympic. Some of her roles were Kate Hardcastle, Letitia Hardy, and Lady Teazle. Oxberry quickly disposes of the husband:

"Poor Chatterley was more attached to his bottle than his profession.... He was one of the best actors that have appeared within the last quarter of a century; but dissipation made a dreadful havoc upon his constitution, and he expired at Lynn, in the year 1822, a victim to evil habits" (*Dramatic Biography and Historic Anecdotes* V: 274).

Oxberry is much troubled by irregularities in Mrs. Chatterley's private life, which, with the age-old technique of the gossip-monger, he exposes and exploits while pretending to defend her. Of more interest, however, is his damning assessment of her acting:

The acting of Mrs. Chatterley is in the French school—chastened and sobered down by observation of English manners. She is a cold and artificial actress, though a fascinating one...who has an archness—a coquetry of expression— completely *a-la-mode de Paris*, and quite removed from any thing of the luxurious or the sensual. Mrs. Chatterley never appears to us to be in earnest—her heart never seems engaged—her eyes sparkle, but it is not with the fire of love, but the consciousness of internal power—rather with the pleasure of self-contemplation, than the rapture of contemplating any other object. Mrs. Chatterley's acting, though in a different line, is of the Siddonian school, and excludes all impulsive effort.... She is above the common height; with expressive and intelligent blue eyes; her face is too flat to be called beautiful, but it is certainly what is termed pretty. (280-82)

According to W. Davenport Adams's *Dictionary of the Drama* (277), in 1830 she remarried, briefly retired from the stage, but then joined Wigam's company at the Olympic. Her last appearance was at the Adelphi in 1858.

4. *John Pritt Harley* (b. 1790), the first McSwill, was the son of a silk merchant. After touring extensively in the provinces, he joined the English Opera House in July 1815 and in September moved on to Drury Lane, becoming the senior comedian there. He and Oxberry became friends while still amateurs, so Oxberry knew and revealed that his friend lied about his age and had tried several times to marry but never succeeded. He excelled at comic singing:

He possesses...that great gift of nature—animal spirits;...he is always bustling; this is sufficient to make him moderately popular.... Mr. Harley never inspires us with any strong touch of nature, and but seldom with any markings of character, though he frequently extorts our laughter, at the expence [sic] of our sense of propriety, by his eccentricity. In fact, he is an excellent farce actor, but in comedy he is beyond his depth; and though he may keep his head above water by paddling, he can never breast the billows.... He is, like most of our comedians, a decided mannerist. (*Dramatic Biography and Historic Anecdotes* I: 76-77)

As manager of Drury Lane, Harley befriended Planché and helped him with his first play.

5. *George Bartley* (1782-1858) was the first Lord Ronald. Planché wrote of him:

[Bartley] was a sensible, unaffected actor, without any pretension to genius, but thoroughly dependable to the extent of his ability. He was also a courteous, discreet gentlemen, well calculated to fill the position he so long sustained, under various lessees, of stage manager. Of the intelligence of the British public his opinion was not flattering. "Sir," he would say to me, "you must first tell them you are going to do so and so; you must then tell them you are doing it; and then that you have done it; and then, by G-d" (with a slap on his thigh), "*perhaps they will understand you!*" British public, on your honor, as ladies and gentlemen, is this true? (Planché, *Recollections* I: 145)

In 1800 Bartley played Orlando in Bath, attracting the attention of Mrs. Jordan, who recommended him to the Drury Lane, and then to the Haymarket and Covent Garden, where he became a well-known Falstaff, a role he played at the Park Theatre in New York in 1818. He became famous for his "veteran" roles: Sir Toby Belch, Polonius, Sir Peter Teazle, Sir Anthony Absolute, Sir David Dunder, Old Mirabel, and others. Oxberry praises his acting:

For tragic assumptions, Nature has given Mr. Bartley few endowments. Even in his youth he was too dwarfish for the serious scene; and now, when years have thrown upon him a comfortable covering of flesh, he is still less fitted for the representative of woe.... The few faults observable in Mr. Bartley are easily enumerated. One is a proneness to laughing onstage...and the other, a straining of his voice in his old men, to an unnatural and disagreeable height. Mr. Bartley is about five feet three inches in height; very stoutly made; with light hair and blue eyes. In his youth he bore some resemblance to Master Betty. (*Dramatic Biography and Historic Anecdotes* V: 228-30)

William Hazlitt, the critic, did not care for him: "There is a thinness in his voice, and a plumpness in his person, neither of which is to our taste" (qtd. in Adams 119).

Bartley managed the English Opera House in 1818.

### Chapter 5: London, 1820-23

1. *W.T. Moncrieff* (1794-1857) was a playwright whose career closely paralleled the first stage of Planché's—the two seem to have been in close commercial competition. Moncrieff's first play was a burletta, *The Diamond Arrow; or the Postmaster's Wife and the Major's Daughter*, produced at the Olympic in December 1815. He then wrote for the Coburg, the Adelphi, the Surrey, Sadler's Wells, and Drury Lane. His *Giovanni in London; or the Libertine Reclaimed*, at the Olympic in 1817, gave Eliza Vestris one of her first great successes in breeches parts, and was one of a string of Don Giovanni plays to which Planché contributed his vampire piece in 1821. Among his other great successes were *Tom and Jerry; or, Life in London* (1821), *The Spectre Bridegroom; or A Ghost in Spite of Himself* (1826), and *Eugene Aram* (1832).

2. *Henry Stephen Kemble* (1789-1836), the first Ruthwold, led an adventurous life, even as related by William Oxberry, who seems to have despised him:

> The subject of this Memoir stood precisely in the predicament of one of these colts of famous pedigree, when he first sought metropolitan favour. With John and Charles Kemble for his uncles—Mrs. Siddons, his aunt—his mother, an admirable actress—and his father, a performer of great judgement at least,—it was warmly anticipated that he would inherit the talent of the family. But genius is not hereditary. (*Dramatic Biography and Green Room Spy* I: 146)

He attended Trinity College, Cambridge, for two years, then joined his father's company which was then on tour. He fell in love with one of the actresses, a Miss Freize, and over the objections of his parents eloped with her, for which both were dismissed from the company. He was hired at Drury Lane at the behest of his father, and debuted in 1818 as Romeo:

> The most decided failure...it was ever our misfortune to behold...HARRY's roaring, in the banishment scene, we never shall forget. S—— is reported to have said, that KEMBLE "*had promised to let his Bath friends hear*.... Dustmen stopped their ears, in the galleries.... A punchy gentlemen in that region...said..."WHAT A WOICE!" (Oxberry, *Dramatic Biography and Green Room Spy* I: 149-50)

Other roles at Drury Lane were Macduff, George Barnwell, Douglas, and Biron. Oxberry states he was then fired, while his wife made a successful debut at the English Opera House as Polly Peachum. He moved on to the Surrey and the Coburg, playing tyrants and villains, where he gained a reputation for being quarrelsome with managers and other actors, but was a favorite with the galleries because of his penchant for rant, vulgarity, loudness, and being drunk onstage to the great amusement of the spectators. Oxberry quotes a long extract from an anonymous pamphlet and offers some advice:

> "H. KEMBLE has, from year to year, become lamentably degraded in the scale of actors.... [He] was looked upon, as...a person who, by the accident of good connexions [sic], was placed before the public, without one jot of talent; possessed of nothing but a name, from which he borrowed everything, without returning anything;—he was a speculator on the title of Kemble.... We hear H. KEMBLE is a gentleman of education: from whatever causes he embarked in the minor drama, it would have well accorded with his education and name, to have cultivated that drama—to have forwarded its respectability and moral enlightenment. Instead of this...[he] made a school for himself—was speedily identified with the rant, the rhodomontade, and the vulgar and disgraceful squabbles which the mismanagement of the Surrey rendered so prolific.... As a minor actor, Mr. H. KEMBLE possesses the strongest lungs and weakest judgement, of any performer in his station; all his efforts are to make passion, feeling, scorn, every motive and every sensation, subservient to sound—to make the windpipe the only communication to the heart—we regard his opened mouth and a distended bagpipe with equal horror. When this actor attempts quiet sentiment, his words fall

as if from the lips of a drunkard, when language is broken by hiccups; when he makes love, it is in the half-vulgar, half-buckish tone of an amateur buckster. He has neither grace, passion, nor feeling; but he proffers in their stead a nautical swagger, extended mouth, and a sound like the rippings of a hundred yards of linen." ....Whenever *his* judgement tempts him to rant, let him be quiet...let him check his love of stamping, and remember, that success in acting depends on the head, not the heel. (*Green Room Spy* I: 151-54)

Off the stage, he was known to stagger unshaven though the public streets in a state of undress, to consort with gangs of ruffians, to sleep in gutters, and to have abused his health:

H. KEMBLE is not yet thirty-eight years old, yet his hair is as white as snow—his brow furrowed—and he says he cannot walk without the assistance of a stick: and this is a man who was naturally of a robust constitution.... We have heard, that, on a late occasion, when he went to C. Kemble, to arrange the terms on which he would engage at Covent Garden, he visited his uncle in a state of intoxication. If this be true, advice will be wasted upon him. (*Green Room Spy* I: 153)

After so much disapprobation, Oxberry makes a passing reference to his good qualities, which goes a way to counterbalance the negative impression: "It is due to him to state, that he is as notorious for being a warm-hearted generous man, as he is for being a reckless one.... Mr. H. KEMBLE is about five feet eleven inches in height; his face is expressive, but has not so much of the family *contour* as has been stated; his eye is peculiarly expressive" (*Green Room Spy* I: 154-55).

Although one cannot avoid the impression that Kemble's Ruthwold was in most ways as inferior to T.P. Cooke's as Moncrieff's script is to Planché's, one can also imagine it had flashes of brilliance. A reckless man with expressive eyes who married for love, unusually well-educated, open-hearted—perhaps Henry Kemble would have been more to our taste than Oxberry's.

3. *Mrs. Waylett* (b. 1800), who played Giovanni the Vampire, was one of the actresses most admired by William Oxberry. She was born in Bath, daughter of a upholsterer named Cooke. The beauty of her singing voice brought her into the theatre, and she debuted in Bath in 1816, and stayed in the provinces. In 1818 she became very ill and almost died. While playing in Coventry in 1819, she made a terrible marriage with an actor named Waylett. Oxberry's account of her ordeal with this parasite is reminiscent of the famous misalliance of Susanna Arne and Theophilus Cibber in the 18th century.

In 1820 she made her London debut at the Adelphi and quickly made herself indispensable to the management. In Birmingham, where the couple were both engaged, Waylett was fired for incompetence, and in 1821 they separated. In 1824 she appeared under Elliston's management at Drury Lane, where her husband resurfaced to attach her salary. Struggling against financial difficulties and calumnious attacks in pamphlets instigated by her husband, she tried her fortune in Dublin and had a triumph there, which brings us up to the publication date of Oxberry's memoir. Oxberry felt that her career was ruined by being tied to a man unworthy of her, and that she sometimes displayed a lack of self-confidence, perhaps as a result of her personal difficulties:

Her requisites for the stage consist of a remarkably sweet voice, and probably more science in music than, with one or two exceptions, any lady before the public; her acting is extremely vivacious, and there is a *naiveté* in her manner, which is quite captivating. But we cannot help thinking that MRS. WAYLETT's performances would be even more effective than they are, if she trusted a little more to her own powers—in plainer terms, if she was more confident. As a *soubrette*, she may be considered the best we have—because, as an actress, she is equal to, and as a singer, superior to, any lady undertaking the same line of business. (*Dramatic Biography and Green Room Spy* I: 63)

There is more material on Mrs. Waylett in Mrs. C. Baron Wilson's *Our Actresses, or Glances at Stage Favorites, Past and Present* (1844). In the florid style typical of the period she informs us that the actress was known as "Queen of the Ballad Singers," and had "one of the sweetest voices for light or plaintive music that woman had ever been gifted with" (I: 97). She leased a theatre in Chester, which failed. Waylett died in 1841, and she returned to the English Opera House in 1843, where she reprised most of her favorite characters and sang "Kitty Kearney," her signature song. She retired to her home town of Bath.

4. *Edward Fitzball* (1792-1873). Some examples of Fitzball's oeuvre are *The Floating Beacon* (1824), *The Pilot* (1825), *The Innkeeper of Abbeville* (1826), *The Flying Dutchman* (1827, one of several versions), *Nelson, or the Life of a Sailor* (1827), *The Earthquake, or the Spectre of the Nile* (1829), *The Inchcape Bell* (1828), *The Red Rover* (1829), and *Jonathan Bradford, or the Murder at the Roadside Inn* (1833). He also dramatized many of Walter Scott's works. Fitzball spent most of his career with the minor theatres, but wrote under Osbaldiston's management at Covent Garden, and at Drury Lane he was the librettist for Bunn's operettas.

### Chapter 6: German Influence, 1829-34

1. *Heinrich Marschner* (1795-1861). Born in Zittau, the son of Bohemian artisans, Marschner became a chorister at the Zittau Gymnasium in 1804, left when his voice broke in 1808, and began to write his first songs. He traveled to Leipzig with the intention of studying law, but was soon diverted to music. In 1817 he made the first of four marriages, to Emilie von Cerva, who died within a year; in 1820 he married the pianist Franziska Jaeggi, who died in 1825. He wrote a festival overture on folk themes, and incidental theatre music for the Leipzig production of Kleist's *Prinz Friedrich von Homburg* (1821), Kind's *Schön Ella* (1823), and T. Hell's *Ali Baba oder 40 Räuber* (1823), all three playing in both Leipzig and Dresden. He gained access to Ludvig Tieck and his circle, and joined their call for a national German opera.

In 1824 Marschner was appointed *Musikdirector* of the Dresden Opera, the most important center (after Vienna) of German music, replacing Francesco Morlacchi. Morlacchi had been a champion of Italian opera (forbidding the performance in Dresden of any German piece but *Fidelio*), a policy which Marschner changed; Weber's *Der Freischütz* and *Euryanthe* were quickly produced (Carlson, *German Stage* 88). However, Volkmar Köhler states that this appointment was against Weber's wishes, and that "after Weber's death Marschner was not appointed to succeed him [as *Kantor*] and therefore terminated his contract" (*New Grove* [1980 ed.] XI: 707).

In 1825 Marschner married the soprano Marianne Wohlbrück, for whom the role of Malwine in *Der Vampyr* was written. He traveled to Berlin, becoming friends with Mendelssohn, and received a post at the Leipzig Stadttheater. There he produced his *Der Vampyr* (1828), and *Der Templar und die Jüden* (1829, a version of Walter Scott's *Ivanhoe*). In 1830 he became conductor of the Hanover Hoftheater, where he composed and produced his masterpiece, *Hans Heiling* (1831-32), which projected him to the forefront of young German composers. He was awarded an honorary doctorate from the University of Leipzig in 1834.

He renewed his commitment to a national German opera free of foreign influence, positioning himself against Spontini (then in Berlin) and Meyerbeer on this question.

Marianne Wohlbrück died in 1854, and Marschner remarried (his fourth time), to Therese Janda in 1855. His late operas, *Das Schloss am Atna* (1836), *Kaiser Adolph von Nassau* (1845), *Austen* (1850), and *Sangekönig Hiarne* (1857), were less successful than those of his middle period.

Marschner completed thirteen operas, two Singspiels, three pageants, a ballet and incidental music to six plays. The high esteem in which he was held by Mendelssohn and Schumann, and later by Bülow, Hanslick, Spitta, and Pfitzer, was due mainly to his operas; beside them his other stage works are insignificant. Marschner regarded himself as a creator of "Romantic operas," and sought a form "in which the music springs directly from the poetry as its inevitable consequence." (E.T.A. Hoffmann) (*New Grove* [1980] XI: 701)

In his last years he was overshadowed by Meyerbeer and Wagner. There have been no major revivals of Marschner's operas in this century, and many of his manuscripts were destroyed in World War II.

2. *Peter Josef von Lindpainter* (1791-1856) was a student of the violin at a Jesuit school in Augsburg. He studied under Peter Winter in Munich, and in 1812 became the *Musikdirector* of the newly opened Isarton Theater. In 1819 he became *Kapellmeister* of the Royal Stuttgart Orchestra, where he remained until his death. A guest conductor for the New Philharmonic Society of London in the 1850s, he received many honors and was a member of many European musical societies. In 1835 Mendelssohn wrote of him, "Lindpainter is the best conductor in Germany; it is as if he played the whole orchestra with his baton alone" (qtd. in *New Grove* [1980 ed.] XI: 5). Berlioz also admired his conducting,

although he felt he took most pieces too fast, in common with many German conductors. Jennifer Spencer, author of the Lindpainter essay in the *New Grove Dictionary of Opera*, sums up: "A technically skilled but unoriginal composer, his greatest gifts were for attractive melody and occasional striking dramatic effects" (*Grove* [1980] XI: 5).

In addition to oratorios, three ballets, cantatas, masses, concerti, songs, and overtures, he wrote 28 operas, the most successful being *Der Bergkönig* (1825) and *Der Vampyr* (1828).

### Chapter 7: Paris, London, and America, 1851-62

1. *Alexandre Dumas père* (1802-1870). Among his early influences, Dumas mentions Shakespeare, Goethe, Schiller, Byron, Fenimore Cooper, and Walter Scott—particularly *Ivanhoe* (Davidson 5). He was an admirer of the English style in acting, and an avid devotee of Macready, Kean, Kemble, and Harriet Smithson (Stowe 23).

In the five years prior to *Le Vampire* (approximately his seventieth play), he teamed with Albert Maquet, his most frequent collaborator, in a series of Romantic historical dramas for the Théâtre Historique: *La Reine Margot* (1847), *Intrigue et Amour* (1847, adaptation of Schiller), *Le Chevalier de Maison-Rouge* (1847), *Monte-Cristo*, Parts I and II (1848), *Catalina* (1848), *La Jeunesse des mousquetaires* (1849), *Le Chevalier d'Harmental* (1849), *La Guerre des femmes* (1849), *Urbain Grandier* (1850), and *La Chasse au chastre* (1850). Other collaborators during this period were Paul Maurice, on *Hamlet* (1847, Théâtre Historique); Jules Lacroix, *Le Testament de César* (1849, Comédie Française); Eugène Nus, *Le Cachemire vert* (1849, Gymnase); and four plays with Eugène Grangé and Xavier de Montépin: *Le Connétable de Bourbon* (1849, Porte-Saint-Martin); and *Pauline* (1850), *Les Chevaliers du Lansquenet* (1850), and *Les Frères corses* (1850), all for the Théâtre Historique. *Les Frères corses* became an international success in Dion Boucicault's adaptation, *The Corsican Brothers*. The last play before *Le Vampire* was another collaboration with Maquet, *Le Comte de Morcerf*, premiering at the Ambigu-Comique on 1 April 1851.

The division of labor between the two writers is subject to dispute; Maquet sued to establish his co-authorship of the plays and novels. The consensus of Dumas scholars is that Maquet contributed the plots and historical research, and Dumas wrote the dialogue, and added polish and theatricality. He is known to have taken an active role in the staging of his plays. Carlson writes:

*Le Chevalier de Maison-Rouge*...was an even greater success, running for an unheard-of 134 consecutive evenings. A mob of *sans-culottes* was needed and Dumas' regisseur Achille hired hundreds of extras for each performance. Dumas himself supervised their costume and herded them onto the stage to create what were hailed as the most imposing and delirious mob scenes ever witnessed in the theatre. There were even rumors later that many of the workers who took part in the rebellion of 1848 had learned techniques of mob violence under the direction of Dumas at the Théâtre-Historique. (*French Stage* 114)

2. *François Alphonse Arnault* (1819-60), who played Dumas's Ruthwen, began his adult life in commerce, but soon left it for theatre, winning the second prize for tragic acting upon graduating from the Conservatoire in 1845. He debuted at the Odéon and married a company member, Gabrielle Geneviève Naptal. The couple went to Brussels, where they built their reputations. Returning to Paris, they joined the Ambigu-Comique and remained for six years, where Arnault played many roles and began to dabble in playwriting. In 1852 they moved on to the Gaité, where he played in his own *Oeuvres du démon*, *l'Ane mort*, and *Cossaques*, on the subject of the Crimean War. In 1854 they joined the Porte-Saint-Martin, and remained until they were engaged by the Théâtre Français de Saint Pétersbourg. Arnault died in Russia after four years, and his wife is also believed to have died there. His brother, Lucien Arnault, was the builder and director of the Paris Hippodrome in the Place d'Etoile. (This rather dry account is taken from *La Grande Encyclopédie* [II: 1064], which lists none of his roles. The titles of his plays suggest they may have been gothic melodramas.)

3. *Jane Essler* (1836-92), who played Hélène, was born Jane Faessler; eventually her stage name became simply Jane. She began her career at the Théâtre Historique, moved on with Dumas and Maquet to the Ambigu-Comique, and later performed at the Odéon, Porte-Saint-Martin, Gaité, and Chatelet. She played the leads in *La Reine Margot*, *Mathilde*, *Les Beaux Messieurs de Bois-Doré*, and *Les Misérables*. A chest ailment forced her to retire at an early age, and she died in Antibes. The *Nouveau Larousse Encyclopédie*, comments, "C'était une actrice très intelligente, incomparable dans les rôles òu elle pouvait donner libre carriere à sa grâce fantastique" [She was a very intelligent actress, incomparable in the roles where she could give free rein to her fantastic grace.] (IV: 304).

4. *Joseph Laurent* (1822-1903), who played Lazare, was one of the favorite comic actors of the boulevard theatres, "grâce à sa ronde gaieté, à sa bonhomie et à la sobrieté de son jeu" [thanks to his open gaiety, his friendliness, and the restraint of his acting] (*Grande Encyclopédie* XXI: 1899). He played over one hundred roles at the Ambigu-Comique, Gaité, and Porte-Saint-Martin, specializing in the comedy parts in "drames et feéries."

5. *Dion Boucicault* (1820-90), born Dionysus Lardner Boursiquot in Dublin, had a truly international career and was the most commercially successful playwright of the last half of the 19th century. He ran away from the grammar school of the University of London and joined Charles Hill's company in Cheltenham. Acting under the name of Lee Moreton, he produced his first play, *A Legend of the Devil's Dyke*, in Brighton in 1838, and came to London in his own *Lodgings to Let* in 1839. After his great success with *London Assurance* in 1841, he stopped acting and produced 18 plays under his own name between 1842 and 1844. He spent four years in France (1844-48), where he collected the plots and mastered the techniques of French melodrama. To this base he added Irish wit and sentimentality, a flair for creating local color, and masterful use of sensationalism.

A particular characteristic of Boucicault's "sensation plays" was the use of catastrophes—fires, snowstorms, explosions—and the incorporation of the latest scientific inventions—telegraphs and cameras—as important plot elements. Major works are *The Corsican Brothers* (1852, adaptation from Dumas), *The Poor of New York* (1857, adaptation from Brisebarre and Nus), *The Octoroon* (1859), and the Irish plays, probably his best work: *The Colleen Bawn* (1860), *Arrah-na-Pogue* (1864), and *The Shaughraun* (1874). Also an innovative producer, he introduced the out-of-town tryout, and the run-of-the-play contract for actors. He is said to be the first playwright to effectively collect royalties based on a percentage of the play's receipts, and he was the major influence in creating the first international copyright law.

6. *Agnes Robertson*. Born in 1833 in Edinburgh, she was the protegée and ward of Charles Kean and Ellen Tree. A child actress and singer, she debuted at the Theatre Royal, Aberdeen, at the age of ten, acted with the Terry family at Hull, and sang in Dublin at Judd's Music Hall. She went on to Glasgow, Manchester, and Liverpool, where she met and acted with the Keans and was invited to join the company. She first appeared in London at the Princess in 1850 at the age of 17. She played Nerissa in *The Merchant of Venice*, and a number of light comedy roles, before teaming with Boucicault on *The Vampire*.

"It was at the Princess's," she later told a journalist, "I met my fate. Dion Boucicault was then writing plays for the Keans and was, indeed, the regular author of the house." Boucicault, who enjoyed the company of women, was immediately taken by her charms and good looks, and became her constant companion, taking her for long rides in his carriage. In the summer of 1852, unknown to the Keans, they became lovers, and Agnes spent more time with Boucicault in his Soho apartments than she did with the Keans. Boucicault showered her with gifts and gave her money to supplement the paltry wage...she was receiving from Kean. (Fawkes 75)

According to Townsend Walsh, she refused the Earl of Hopetown for Boucicault. Robert Hogan writes, "There is no record of where or when Boucicault married Agnes, and in the last years of his life, he both admitted the marriage and denied it. If we are to believe Boucicault that his mother opposed his return to acting until she learned that he had married an actress, then the marriage must have occurred before the production of *The Vampire*" (34-35).

They had six children. In 1885 while touring Australia, Boucicault married Louise Thorndyke, a member of the company, denying he had ever been married to Agnes. In 1888 Agnes was granted a divorce in England. He remarried Louise, and died in 1890.

*Chapter 8: Satire and Misogyny, 1872-88*

1. *William Schwenk Gilbert* (1836-1911) attended London University and worked as a clerk in the Office of the Privy Council, meanwhile writing satirical verses which would be published as the *Bab Ballads*. Encouraged

by T.W. Robertson to take up playwriting, he wrote some 40 plays, a few of which—*Pygmalion and Galatea* (1871) and *Engaged* (1877)—were quite successful. He married Lucy Turner in 1867, and though they had no children, an American-born singer, Nancy MacIntosh, lived with the couple as an adopted daughter beginning in 1893. Bernard Shaw, with perhaps a tinge of competitiveness, assesses Gilbert's gift for language and cleverness:

Mr. Gilbert's paradoxical wit, astonishing to the ordinary Englishman, is nothing to me. Nature has cursed me with a facility for the same trick; and I could paradox Mr. Gilbert's head off were I not convinced that such trifling is morally unjustifiable.... [The Savoy Theatre needed] relief from Mr. Gilbert, whose great fault was that he began and ended with himself, and gave no really congenial opportunities to the management and the composer. He exploited their unrivalled *savoir faire* to his heart's content; but he starved their genius, possibly because he did not give them credit for possessing any. (qtd. in Allen xiii)

2. *Arthur Seymour Sullivan* (1842-1900) was the son of an Irish military bandmaster and a musically gifted Italian mother. He won the Mendelssohn Scholarship in Music and studied in Leipzig. Always an aspirant to "serious" artistic achievement, he wrote cantatas, songs, and hymns, including "Onward Christian Soldiers" (1872). His early work is characterized by heaviness, sentimentality, and a solemn ecclesiasticism. He was appointed director of the National Training School of Music (which later became the Royal College of Music) in 1876, and was awarded an honorary doctorate in music by Cambridge University. He never married, but his nephew, Herbert Sullivan, lived with him from 1877 as his adopted son. Bernard Shaw comments:

Sir Arthur Sullivan made his reputation as a composer of comic operas by...a personal and social talent...which had been cultivated musically by a thorough technical training in the elegant and fastidious school of Mendelssohn, and by twenty years' work in composing for the drawing room, the church, the festival, and the concert room.... When he plunged into the banalities and trivialities of Savoy opera he carried his old training with him.... He taught the public to understand orchestral fun; but his instrumental jokes, which he never carried too far, were always in good taste; and his workmanship was unfailingly skillful and refined, even when the material was of the cheapest. (qtd. in Allen xiv)

Sullivan was knighted by Queen Victoria in 1883, and Gilbert by Edward VII in 1906.

### Chapter 9: Stage Adaptations, 1897-1985

1. *Bram Stoker* (1847-1912), born in Dublin, was a child invalid, and did not walk until the age of seven. He had a congenital crippling condition, perhaps of psychosomatic origin, which suddenly disappeared. At Trinity College he was remembered as an outgoing, robust, athletic, red-bearded giant who majored in mathematics and admired the poetry of Walt Whitman, defending his poetry at the college debating society.

Stoker's mother Charlotte was the dominant personality in the family, a dynamic woman who was involved in social work and attempting to improve the condition of women in Ireland. His interest in the theatre came from his father, Abraham, a devotee of Charles Kean.

After college, Stoker joined the Irish civil service. His first published work was *The Duties of Clerks of Petty Sessions in Ireland* (1878). He also took a position as an unpaid drama critic for the *Dublin Mail*, started his own literary magazine, and began to write short stories. The first was "The Chain of Destiny."

After meeting Henry Irving in 1876, Stoker followed the actor to England and was invited to become Irving's business manager. He married Florence Balcombe in 1878, whom George du Maurier called the most beautiful woman in England, who had previously been engaged to Oscar Wilde. The marriage was unhappy; after the birth of a son, Noel, in 1879, conjugal relations were broken off. Daniel Farson, Stoker's nephew, states that Stoker died of syphilis (*Man Who Wrote Dracula* 233-35).

Stoker joined an occult society, the Hermetic Order of the Golden Dawn, which preached a kind of Rosicrucianism, and whose members included Swinburne, Yeats, and Aleister Crowley. Some have found traces of this society's mystical beliefs in Stoker's writings.

The most important relationship in Stoker's life was with Henry Irving, whose business affairs he managed for 27 years. In 1906-07, after Irving's death, Stoker wrote the two-volume *Personal Reminiscences of Henry Irving*, a very adulatory memoir containing almost nothing of a personal nature, with no mention of Oscar Wilde, Bernard Shaw, Florence Stoker, or *Dracula*.

In 1906 he returned to Cruden Bay in Scotland, where he had begun the work on *Dracula*. Although he continued to publish novels, his physical condition deteriorated in the last six years of his life, with blindness and finally paralysis. Stoker's major works include *Under the Sunset* (1882), *The Snake's Pass* (1890), *The Mystery of the Sea* (1902), *The Jewel of the Seven Stars* (1904), *Famous Impostors* (1910, a non-fictional account of historical female transvestites), *The Lair of the White Worm* (1911), and a number of short stories including the posthumous "Dracula's Guest," which Florence Stoker stated was a chapter of *Dracula* which was omitted by the publisher because of undue length. *Dracula* towers above everything else Stoker wrote in terms of writing skill, inspiration, and far-reaching influence.

2. *Hamilton Deane* was a bank clerk who made his acting debut in 1899 with the Henry Irving Vacation Company, a touring branch of the Lyceum. He had known Bram Stoker previous to this business association, having been born in Ireland and grown up on a neighboring estate. Their fathers, Colonel Deane and Abraham Stoker, were friends, and Bram had a close friendship with Deane's mother (*Dracula Scrapbook* 53). Deane claimed that he and Bram grew up believing in vampires, "a well-known Irish superstition."

He formed his own company, the Hamilton Deane Company, in the early 1920s, and became a popular provincial actor. He conceived the idea of dramatizing his old manager's novel, but could not interest any playwright in the idea, and finally made the adaptation himself at the suggestion of Dora May Patrick, his leading lady and future wife, who took the role of Mina. He wrote, "Fortunately, I then developed a severe cold, for it put me to bed and, idly at first, I began to write a draft of the play. I then became so immersed in it that on obtaining Mrs. Bram Stoker's permission, I went ahead with the script and did not stop until I had completed it four weeks later" (qtd. in Glut 80).

3. *Bela Lugosi* (1882-1956) was born Béla Blaskó in Lugos, Hungary (now in Romania). In his twenties he changed his name to Lugossy and later to Lugosi. His early years were the subject of mythologizing by Hollywood press agents and by Lugosi himself, but his biographer, Arthur Lennig, researched the actor in the Hungarian National Archives, and found that Lugosi's father was not a count but a baker, the son of a farmer, who died when Lugosi was in his late teens.

Lugosi worked as a locksmith, then decided to try acting. He joined the Franz Joseph Theatre of Temesvár and began appearing in operettas and supporting roles in classical plays. One early role was Christ in a passion play. Critics described him as "handsome and intelligent and having a rich, melancholy voice, a velvety voice that spoke straight to the audience's hearts" (Lennig 33).

He arrived in Budapest in 1911, debuted as Vronsky at the Magyar Szinház, and enrolled at the Rákosi Szidi Acting School soon after that. In 1913 he was hired by the Nemzeti Szinház, the National Theatre of Hungary, and there performed approximately 34 small roles between 1913 and 1916. In 1914 he joined the 43rd Royal Hungarian Infantry and saw action in Serbia and Russia. Wounded in 1916, he left the army and returned to the National Theatre, playing the role of Fortinbras.

In 1917 he married Ilona Szmik and made his first film, *A Leopárd* (now lost). He made more than a dozen Hungarian films, none of which survive, and became a popular leading man. In 1918, a revolution overthrew the Hungarian government and placed Béla Kun in power. Lugosi took part in organizing the actors and artists behind the new regime. When the Kun government collapsed in 1919, Lugosi was forced to flee, as were fellow refugees Alexander Korda and Paul Lukas. He went first to Vienna and then to Berlin, where he appeared in German films, including F. W. Murnau's *Der Januskopf* (now lost), which starred Conrad Veidt and was photographed by Karl Freund (who filmed *Dracula* in 1931).

His wife went back to Budapest and divorced him, and he arrived in New York without papers in 1921, where, without knowing English, he landed the role of Fernando in *The Red Poppy*. According to Boris Karloff, Lugosi never did completely master English, learning his roles syllabically. In 1923 made his first American film, playing a villain in *The Silent Command*, followed by *The Rejected Woman*, *The Midnight Girl*, and *Daughters Who Pay*. In 1925 he was on Broadway again in *Arabesque*, designed and directed by Norman Bel Geddes. He became an American citizen in 1930.

After his success in *Dracula*, he was not at first offered the film role, which would have gone to Lon Chaney, Sr., but for his untimely death before filming began. The role eventually fell to Lugosi. A rival production with Conrad Veidt did not materialize because of the death of the producer.

Lugosi refused the role of Frankenstein's monster, believing it had too few lines, and this was the beginning of a lifelong rivalry with Boris Karloff, with whom he acted in *The Black Cat*, *The Invisible Ray*, *Black Friday*, *Son of Frankenstein*, and *Curse of Frankenstein*. Lugosi tried a number of times to break out of the horror genre, but always fell back into it, playing Dracula and other vampires, ghouls, wolf-men, and demented scientists. He had a cameo in *Ninotchka* in which he acquitted himself well. He was never able to cash in financially on his fame despite the money he made for his producers. He made over 100 films, but never a great one, although he performed for such directors as Tod Browning, Raoul Walsh, Mervyn Le Roy, William Dieterle, Ernst Lubitsch, William Beaudine, and Robert Wise. Lugosi married five times.

In 1955 he was committed to a state mental hospital, telling the court he was destitute and had been heavily addicted to heroin for twenty years. The last years of his life were sad ones: his film and stage appearances had descended to self-parody, and he became involved with the execrable director Edward D. Wood, appearing in *Glen or Glenda?* and *Plan 9 from Outer Space*, his last (posthumous) film. One highlight in the last part of his life was a stage revival of the American *Dracula* in London.

He had a fatal heart attack in 1956 and, as he had requested, was buried in his vampire cape. Carroll Borland, who played his daughter Luna in *Mark of the Vampire* (1935), remarked, "It was strange, for I have seen Bela lying in his coffin so often that it was a familiar sight" (qtd. in Lennig 317).

# Appendix D

# Cast Lists

## Chapter 3: Paris, 1820

*Le Vampire*, by Nodier, Carmouche, and Jouffrey.
(Théâtre de la Porte-Saint-Martin, 13 June 1820.)

Lord Rutwen, M. Philippe; Sir Aubray, M. Perrin ou Thérigny; Malrina [sic], Mad. Dorval; Brigitte, Mad. St.-Armand; Edgar, M. Edmon; Scop, M. Pierson; Petterson, M. Dugy; Lovette, Mlle. J. Vertpré; Oscar (génie des Mariages), M. Moessard; Ituriel (ange de la lune), Mlle. Descotte. Vampires, Fantômes, Domestiques, Villageois.

*Le Vampire*, by Scribe and Mélesville.
(Théâtre de Vaudeville, 15 June 1820.)

Adolphe, M. Isambert; Nancy, Mlle. Lucie; Saussmann, M. Hippolyte.

*Les Trois Vampires ou le clair de la lune*, by Brazier, Lurieu, and d'Artois.
(Théâtre des Variétés, 22 June 1820.)

M. Turcelin and M. Blondin alternated in the role of Gobetout, and the singing vampires were played by Mssrs. Odry and Arnal.

## Chapter 4: London, 1820

*The Vampire, or the Bride of the Isles*, by Planché.
(English Opera House, 9 August 1820)

Unda (Spirit of the Flood), Miss Love; Ariel (Spirit of the Air), Miss Worgman; The Vampire, T.P. Cooke; Lady Margaret, Mrs. Chatterley; Ronald (Baron of the Isles), Mr. Bartley; Robert (an English attendant of the Baron), Mr. Pearman; McSwill (the Baron's henchman), Mr. Harley; Andrew (steward to Ruthven), Mr. Minton; Father Francis, Mr. Shaw; Effie (daughter of Andrew), Miss Carew; Bridget (Lord Ronald's Housekeeper), Mrs. Grove. Retainers, Peasants, Bargemen, etc.

(Park Theatre, New York, 1820)

Ruthven, Mr. Simpson; Margaret, Mrs. Barnes; McSwill, Mr. Barnes; Ronald, Mr. Maywood; Robert, Mr. Moreland; Effie, Mrs. Johnson.

(Revival, English Opera House, 1829)

Unda, Miss Phillips; Ariel, Mrs. East; The Vampire, Mr. J. Vining; Margaret, Miss Gray; Ronald, Mr. F. Mathhews; Robert, Mr. Thorne; McSwill, Mr. G. Penson; Andrew, Mr. Minton; Father Francis, Mr. Shaw; Effie, Mrs. Keeley; Bridget, Mrs. C. Jones.

**328**

## Chapter 5: London, 1820-23

*The Vampire*, by W.T. Moncrieff.
(Royal Coburg Theatre, 1820.)
The Vampire, Mr. Kemble; Terra, Mr. Higman; Sir Malcolm, Mr. Cordell; Edgar, Mr. Blanchard; Sandy, Mr. Cowell; Mucklegear, Mr. Howell; Davie, Mr. Davidge; Mac Dirk, Mr. Bradley; Friar, Mr. Hobbs; Malvina, Miss Watson; Lunaria, Miss Goodwin; Margaret, Miss Holland; Jeannie, Mrs. LeClerq.

*Giovanni the Vampire!!! or How Shall We Get Rid of Him?* by J.R. Planché.
(Adelphi Theatre, 15 January 1821.)
Spirit of Burlesque, Mr. Simpson; Genius of Imagination, Miss Yeats; Giovanni the Vampire, Mrs. Waylett; P.S. Bustle (Manager of the Adelphi), Mr. Cowell; Leporello (Valet of All Work), Mr. Wilkinson; Three Authors, Messrs. Jones, Callahan, and Dennis; Miss Bellamira Bustle, Mrs. Tennant; Ghost of the Commandant, Mr. J. Shaw; Donna Anna, Miss Strait; The Bride (a Spinster), Miss Strait; The Bridegroom (a Bachelor), Mr. St. Alban; Tragedy, Miss Strutt; Comedy, Miss Blink. Europe, Asia, Africa, and America, Slaves to Giovanni.

*Thalaba the Destroyer*, by Edward Fitzball.
(Royal Coburg Theatre, 1823.)
Thalaba, Mr. Stanley; Hamed (the usurping sultan), Mr. Bengough; Oneiza, Miss Edmiston; Zeinah, Mrs. Bradley; Moath, Mr. Harwood. "Grand Asiatic Pas de Deux," Monsieur and Madame Le Clerq.

## Chapter 6: German Influence, 1829-34

*Der Vampyr* by Heinrich Marschner
(Leipzig, 29 March 1828)
Rutwen, E. Genast; Malwine, W. Streit [and Marianne Wohlbrück?]; Aubry, W. Höfler; Davenaut, Köckert; Dibdin, Vogt; Emmy, D. Devrient; Suse, Mme. Köckert; Blunt, F. Fisher; demons, witches, hobgoblins and other creatures from the underworld; hunters and servants of Berkley and Davenaut; peasants...ladies and gentlemen of the nobility.

*The Vampire Bride, or the Tenant of the Tomb*, by George Blink.
(London, 1834.)
Walter, Mr. Campbell; Werl (his friend), Mr. Johnson; Kibitz, Mr. W.H. Williams; Sorcerer, Mr. Villiers; Jansen (a Servant), Mr. Mathews; Brunhilda (the Vampire Bride), Mrs. Wilkinson; Annetta (a waiting Maid), Mrs. Young; Swanhilda, Miss Reckie. Hunters, Dancers, Ghosts of Swanhilda and her two children.

### Chapter 7: Paris, London, and America, 1851-62

*Le Vampire*, by Dumas père.
(Ambigu-Comique, 20 December 1851.)

Lord Ruthwen, M. Arnault; Gilbert de Tiffauges, M. Goujet; Lazare, M. Laurent; La Goule, Mme. Lucie Mabire; Juana, Mlle. Marie Clarisse; Antonia, Mlle. Daroux; Hélène, Mlle. Jane Essler; Mélusine, Mlle. Isabelle Constant.

*The Vampire*, by Boucicault.
(Princess Theatre, 14 June 1852.)

Alan Raby, Dion Boucicault; Lord Arthur, George Everett; Rhys, John Chester; Lucy, Carlotta Leclerq; Alice, Agnes Robertson; Rees, John Pritt Harley; Ada, Miss Desborough.

*The Phantom*, by Boucicault.
(Wallack's Lyceum, 1857.)

Alan Rookwood, Dion Boucicault; Lucy and Ada, Agnes Robertson; Lord Albert Clavering, Mr. J.B. Howe; Davy, Mr. T.B. Johnstone; Janet, Mrs. H.P. Grattan; Colonel Raby, Mr. Ralton; Edgar, Mr. J.B. Howe; Dr. Rees, Mr. Burnett; Jenny, Mrs. L.H. Allen.

*Ruthven*, by Harris.
(Royal Grecian Theatre, 1859.)

Gilbert de Tiffauges, Mr. Sinclair; Ruthven, Mr. T. Mead; Lazare, Mr. Manning; The Unknown or Ghoule, Miss Jane Coveney; Juanna, Miss H. Correy; Helene, Miss A. Conquest; Antonia, Miss E. Hale.

### Chapter 8: Satire and Misogyny, 1872-88

*The Vampire*, by Reece.
(Royal Strand Theatre, 18 August 1872.)

Colonel Cadwallader Raby (a retired Veteran), Mr. Harry Cox; Edgar (a Soldier and Poet), Miss Topsy Venn; Lord Alfred Clavering (the Colonel's guest, in love with Ada), Miss Bella Goodall; Doctor Horace Cope (the Family Physician—a reader of Necromancy), Mr. H.J. Turner; Alan Raby (the Vampire), Mr. Edward Terry; Ada Raby (the Colonel's Daughter), Miss Emily Pitt; Lady Audley Moonstone (his guest, a fashionable novelist), Mrs. Raymond. Picturesque Peasants: Ceder Idris, Tal y Llyn, Badd Gellert, Aberystwith, and Llangollen.

*Ruddygore*, by Gilbert and Sullivan.
(Savoy Theatre, 22 January 1887.)

Robin Oakapple (a Young Farmer), Mr. George Grossmith; Richard Dauntless (his foster-brother—a Man-o'-War's Man), Mr. Durward Lely; Sir Despard Murgatroyd (of Ruddygore—a wicked Baronet), Mr. Rutland Barrington; Rose Maybud (a Village Maiden), Miss Leonora Braham; Mad Margaret, Miss Jessie Bond; Dame Hannah, Miss Rosina Brandron; Sir Roderic Murgatroyd (the twenty-first Baronet), Mr. Richard Temple.

*Ruddy George, or Robin Redbreast*, by H.G.F. Taylor.
(Toole's Theatre, 19 March 1887.)

Robin Redbreast, Mr. E.D. Ward; Dick Leward, Mr. C. Wilson; Sir Jaspard Rougegorge, Mr. G. Shelton; Old Daddy Longlegs, Mr. W. Brunton; Rosy, Miss Marie Linden; Old Chloe, Miss J. Wise; Sir Gilbert Rougegorge, Mr. C.M. Lowne; Sir Arthur Rougegorge, Mr. G. De Pledge; Sir Doyley Rougegorge, Mr. J.B. Catell.

*The Vampire's Victim*, by Richard Henry.
(Gaiety, 24 December 1887.)

Dr. Frankenstein (a German medical student), Miss Nellie Farren; Tartina (his Swiss sweetheart), Miss Marion Hood; Mary Ann (a Maid of Mystery), Miss Maria Jones; Il Capitano Marachino (of the Italian Guards), Miss Jenny Rogers; Tamburina (Goddess of the Sun), Miss Sylvia Grey; Caramella, Miss Emma Gwynne; Vanilla, Miss Sybil Grey; The Monster (Frankenstein's Invention), Mr. Fred Leslie; Visconti (a Vampire Viscount), Mr. E.J. Lonnen. Bandits, guards, soldiers, villagers, and vampires.

## Chapter 9: Stage Adaptations, 1897-1985

*Dracula or the Un-dead*, by Bram Stoker
(Lyceum Theatre [staged reading], 18 May 1897.)

Count Dracula, Mr. Jones; Jonathan Harker, Mr. Passmore; John Seward, Mr. Rivington; Professor Van Helsing, Mr. T. Reynolds; Quincey P. Morris, Mr. Widdicombe; Hon. Arthur Holmwood, Mr. Innes; M.F. Renfield, Mr. Howard; Captain Swales, Mr. Gurney; Coastguard, Mr. Simpson; Attendant at Asylum, Mr. Porter; Mrs. Westenra, Miss Gurney; Lucy Westenra, Miss Foster; Mina Murray, Miss Craig; Servant, Miss Cornford; Vampire Woman, Mrs. Daly.

*Dracula, the Vampire Play*, by Hamilton Deane
(Little Theatre, 14 February 1927.)

Count Dracula, Raymond Huntley; Abraham Van Helsing, Hamilton Deane; Doctor Seward, Stuart Lomath; Jonathan Harker, Bernard Guest; Quincey P. Morris, Frieda Hearn; Lord Godalming, Peter Jackson; R.M. Renfield, Bernard Jukes; The Warder, Jack Howarth; The Parlormaid, Kilda Macleod; The Housemaid, Betty Murgatroyd; Mina, Dora Mary Patrick.

*Dracula*, by Deane and Balderston
(Fulton Theatre, 5 October 1927.)

Count Dracula, Bela Lugosi; Wells, Nedda Harrigan; Jonathan Harker, Terrence Neill; Doctor Seward, Herbert Bunston; Abraham Van Helsing, Edward Van Sloan; R.M. Renfield, Bernard Jukes; Butterworth, Alfred Frith; Lucy Harker, Dorothy Peterson.

(Revival, Martin Beck Theatre, 15 October 1977.)

Lucy Seward, Ann Sachs; Miss Wells (maid), Gretchen Oehler; Jonathan Harker, Alan Coates; Dr. Seward, Dillon Evans; Abraham Van Helsing, Jerome Dempsey; R.M. Renfield, Richard Kavanaugh; Butterworth, Baxter Harris; Count Dracula, Frank Langella.

# Selected Filmography

This list, limited to adaptations and sequels of *Dracula*, includes the film versions of the novel mentioned in Chapter 10 and a few others, including some made for television and some documentaries which admirers of the novel may find of interest.

There are over 600 vampire films, 130 of which are about Dracula.The story of Ruthven, who dominated 19th-century melodrama, has never been filmed.

1. Title
2. Alternate Titles
3. Director
4. Studio, Country
5. Leading Players

### 1922

*Nosferatu; Eine Symphonie des Grauens*
    *Nosferatu—A Symphony of Horror; Nosferatu the Vampire; Terror of Dracula; Dracula; Nosferatu—A Symphony of Terror; The Twelfth Hour; Die Zwoelfte Stunde; Eine Nacht des Grauens*
F.W. Murnau
Prana; Germany
Max Schreck, Gustav von Wangenheim, Greta Schroeder

### 1931

*Dracula*
Tod Browning
Universal; U.S.
Bela Lugosi, Helen Chandler, Edward Van Sloan, Dwight Frye

*Dracula* (Spanish language version)
George Melford
Universal; U.S.
Carlos Villarias, Lupita Tovar, Pablo Alvarez Rubio

### 1936

*Dracula's Daughter*
Lambert Hillyer
Universal; U.S.
Gloria Holden, Otto Kruger, Edward Van Sloan

*1943*

*Son of Dracula*
Robert Siodmak
Universal; U.S.
Lon Chaney, Jr., Louise Albritton, Edward Bromberg

*1944*

*House of Frankenstein*
Erle C. Kenton
Columbia; U.S.
Lon Chaney, Jr., Boris Karloff, John Carradine (as Dracula)

*Return of the Vampire*
Lew Landers
Columbia; U.S.
Bela Lugosi, Nina Foch

*1945*

*House of Dracula*
Erle C. Kenton
Columbia, U.S.
Lon Chaney, Jr., Onslow Stevens, John Carradine (as Dracula)

*1948*

*Abbott and Costello Meet Frankenstein*
Charles T. Barton
Universal; U.S.
Bud Abbott, Lou Costello, Lon Chaney, Jr., Bela Lugosi (as Dracula)

*1958*

*Dracula*
    *Horror of Dracula*
Terence Fisher
Hammer; U.K.
Christopher Lee, Peter Cushing

*Blood of the Vampire*
Henry Cass
Tempean; U.K.
Sir Donald Wolfit, Vincent Ball, Barbara Shelley

*1960*

*The Brides of Dracula*
Terence Fisher
Hammer; U.K.
David Peel, Peter Cushing, Martita Hunt

*1965*

*Billy the Kid vs Dracula*
William Beaudine

Circle; U.S.
John Carradine, Chuck Courtney, Melinda Plowman

*Dracula, Prince of Darkness*
    *Disciple of Dracula; The Revenge of Dracula; The Bloody*
Terence Fisher
Hammer; U.K
Christopher Lee, Andrew Keir, Barbara Shelley

*1967*

*The Fearless Vampire Killers*
    *Dance of the Vampires; The Vampire Killers; Your Teeth in My*
    *Neck; Pardon Me But Your Teeth Are in My Neck*
Roman Polanski
Cadre/M.G.M/Filmways; France, U.S., U.K.
Jack McGowran, Roman Polanski, Sharon Tate, Ferdy Mayne

*1968*

*Dracula Has Risen from the Grave*
    *Dracula's Revenge*
Freddie Francis
Hammer; U.K.
Christopher Lee, Rupert Davies, Veronica Carlson

*1969*

*Blood of Dracula's Castle*
    *Dracula's Castle*
Al Adamson, Jean Hewitt
A & E Film Corp.; U.S.
John Carradine, Ray Young, Paula Raymond, Lon Chaney, Jr.

*Taste the Blood of Dracula*
Peter Sasdy
Hammer; U.K.
Christopher Lee, Linda Hayden, Isla Blair

*Dracula*
Patrick Dromgoole
British ABC Television; U.K.
Denholm Elliott, Corin Redgrave, Suzanne Neve

*1970*

*The Scars of Dracula*
Roy Ward Baker
Hammer; U.K.
Christopher Lee, Jenny Hanley

*Count Dracula*
    *El Conde Dracula; Nachts Wenn Dracula Erwacht; Il Conte*
    *Dracula; Bram Stoker's Count Dracula; Dracula '71; The Nights of*
    *Dracula*

Jesus Franco
Fenix Films/Corona Filmproduktion/Filmar Compagnia/Cinema-
tografica/Towers of London; Spain, Italy, West Germany
Christopher Lee, Herbert Lom, Klaus Kinski

### 1971

*Dracula A.D. 1972*
  *Dracula Chelsea '72; Dracula Chases the Mini Girls; Dracula
  Today*
Alan Gibson
Hammer; U.K.
Christopher Lee, Peter Cushing, Christopher Neame

*Twins of Dracula*
  *Twins of Evil; The Gemini Twins*
John Hough
Hammer; U.K.
Peter Cushing, Madeleine and Mary Collinson

*In Search of Dracula* (documentary)
Calvin Floyd and Tony Forsberg
Sweden
Christopher Lee (as narrator and Vlad Tepes)

### 1972

*Blacula*
William Crain
American International; U.S.
William Marshall, Charles McCauley, Vonette McGee

### 1973

*Satanic Rites of Dracula*
  *Count Dracula and his Vampire Bride; Dracula Is Dead...and Well
  and Living in London*
Alan Gibson
Hammer; U.K.
Christopher Lee, Peter Cushing, Joanna Lumley

*Dracula*
Jack Nixon Brown
Canadian Television Network; Canada
Norman Welsh, Blair Brown

*Dracula*
  *Bram Stoker's Dracula*
Dan Curtis
Dan Curtis Productions/Universal; U.S.
Jack Palance, Simon Ward, Nigel Davenport, Fiona Lewis, Pamela Brown

*Andy Warhol's Dracula*
   *Dracula Cerca Sangue di Vergine e...Mori di Sete; Dracula Vuole*
   *Vivere; Cerca Sangue di Vergine; Blood for Dracula; Andy*
   *Warhol's Young Dracula*
Anthony Dawson (Antonio Margheriti)
CC Champion/Jean Yanne-Jean Pierre Rassan Productions; Italy, France
Udo Keir, Vittorio de Sica, Joe Dallesandro

*The Legend of the Seven Golden Vampires*
   *Dracula and the Seven Golden Vampires; The Seven Brothers*
   *Meet Dracula*
Roy Ward Baker
Hammer/Shaw Brothers; U.K., Hong Kong
Peter Cushing, David Chiang, Julie Edge, Shih Szu

### 1974

*The Dracula Business* (documentary)
Anthony de Latbiniere
BBC; U.K.
—

*Daughters of Dracula*
   *Vampyres; Vampyres—Daughters of Darkness; The Vampyre Orgy*
Joseph (José) Larraz
Essay Films; U.K.
Marianne Morris, Anulka, Murray Brown

### 1976

*The Historical Dracula, Facts Behind the Fiction* (documentary)
Ion Boston
U.S., Romania
—

### 1977

*Zoltan, Hound of Dracula*
   *Dracula's Dog*
Albert Band
VIC; U.S.
José Ferrer, Michael Pataki, Reggie Nalder

### 1978

*Count Dracula*
Phillip Saville
BBC Televison; U.K.
Louis Jordan, Frank Finlay

### 1979

*Dracula*
John Badham
Mirisch/U; U.K.
Frank Langella, Laurence Olivier, Kate Nelligan, Donald Pleasance

*Nosferatu: Phantom der Nacht*
   *Nosferatu the Vampire*
Werner Herzog
Werner Herzog/Gaumont; West Germany, France
Klaus Kinski, Isabelle Adjani, Bruno Ganz


*Love at First Bite*
Stan Dragoti
Simon Productions; U.S.
George Hamilton, Susan Saint James, Richard Benjamin

### 1992

*Bram Stoker's Dracula*
Francis Ford Coppola
Columbia/American Zoetrope/Osirus; U.S.
Gary Oldman, Anthony Hopkins, Winona Ryder, Tom Waits, Keanu Reeves

# Notes

### Introduction

[1] An early version of this chapter appeared as "The Eroticism of Evil: Vampires in Nineteenth-Century Melodrama," *Themes in Drama* 14, ed. James Redmond. London: Cambridge University Press, 1992.

[2] Montague Summers (1880-1947) is an interesting and controversial figure in the field of theatre history as well as vampires. According to Brocard Sewell in the preface to the 1961 edition of *The Vampire in Europe*, Summers was a scholar of Restoration theatre whose works include *The Playhouse of Pepys* (1935), *The Restoration Theatre* (1934), and respected editions of Aphra Behn, Congreve, Dryden, Shadwell, Otway, and Wycherley, as well as the first modern edition of John Downes's *Roscius Anglicanus*. He was a founder, producer, and director of the Phoenix Society, a theatre company that revived many Restoration plays in London in the 1920s. He was also an authority on Gothic novels. He edited Horace Walpole's *The Castle of Otranto*, Flamenberg's *The Necromancer*, and others, and wrote the critical study *The Gothic Quest*.

Summers's other interest, however, was witchcraft, and his series of books on this subject are famous: *The History of Witchcraft and Demonology* (1926), *The Geography of Witchcraft* (1927), and the English edition of *Malleus Maleficarum* (1484), a treatise on demonology written during the Inquisition.

The colorful and eccentric aspects of Summers's career—his researches into the occult and his public advocacy of re-instituting the death penalty for witchcraft, as well as his habit of masquerading as a priest in a costume of his own design although he was never ordained (or perhaps irregularly)—cast doubt on his reliability as an authority, at least on the subject of vampires, the reality of whose existence he fervently believed. Despite this, his dual interest in theatre and vampirology makes him a fruitful source for this study.

### Chapter 1

[1] Leonard Wolf considers Varma unreliable. See Wolf, *A Dream of Dracula*, 181-82.

[2] One of Twitchell's main emphases is "psychic vampirism:" Bertha Rochester in *Jane Eyre*, Heathcliff in *Wuthering Heights*, works by Poe, Wilde, D.H. Lawrence, Henry James, even Fitzgerald's *Tender is the Night*, display aspects of vampirism (142-92).

## Chapter 2

[1] This was very surprising to Montague Summers, who commented, "Until we come to Polidori's novel...nowhere do we meet with the Vampire in the realm of gothic fancy.... I hesitate sweepingly to assert that this theme was entirely unexploited. There may be some romance which I have not had the good fortune to find where a hideous vampire swoops down on his victims" (*Kith* 278). This oddity is so striking that the above comment is quoted by James Twitchell (*Living Dead* 30), and by Devendra Varma, who adds, "One should not assert too emphatically that this theme was entirely unexploited. Perhaps in an obscure, dusty library the Vampire even now stalks unseen through the dark pages of some neglected volumes" (*Gothic Flame* 159-69).

[2] This and all other translations from French and German are my own, except where noted. The original texts appear in endnotes, or, for short passages, in brackets. Féval:

C'était un homme d'une trentaine d'années, au moins en apparence, d'une taille haute, élégante et de modèle aristocratique.... Quant à son visage, il offrait un remarquable type de beauté; son front haut, large, et sans ride, mais traversé de haut en bas par une légère cicatrice presque imperceptible quand sa physionomie était au repos, s'encadrait d'une magnifique chevelure noire. On ne pouvait voir ses yeux; mais, sous sa paupière baissée, on devinait leur puissance.... Le front du rêveur était pâle et uni comme celui d'un enfant.... Les jeunes femmes le voyaient en songe avec un oeil rêveur, un front ravagé, un nez d'aigle et un sourire infernal, mais divin. Ses cheveux, bouclés naturellement, groupaient au hasard leurs mèches gracieusement ondées.... "Je sais que vous êtes puissant, milord," répondit la comtesse..."puissant pour le mal comme l'ange déchu" (qtd. in Praz 78-79).

[3] Mein liebes Mägdchen glaubet
Beständing steif und feste,
An die gegebnen Lehren
Der immer Frommen Mutter;
Als Völker an der Theyse
An tödtliche Vampiere
Heyduckisch feste glauben,
Nun warte nur Christianchen
Du willst mich gar nich lieben;
Ich will mich an dir rächen
Und heute in Tockayer
Zu einem Vampyr trinken.
Und wenn du sanfte schlummerst,
Von deinen schönen Wangen
Den frischen Purpur saugen.
Alsdenn wirst du erschrecken,
Wenn ich dich werde küssen
Und als ein Vampir küssen:
Wenn du dann recht erzitterst
Und matt in meine Arme,
Gleich einer Todten sinkest

Alsdenn will ich dich fragen,
Sind meine Lehren besser,
Als deiner guten Mutter?
—Heinrich August Ossenfelder, *Der Naturforscher* (Leipzig: Achtundvierzigstes Stück, 1748).

[4] See James B. Twitchell, "Shelley's Use of Vampirism in *The Cenci*," *Tennessee Studies in Literature* 24 (1979): 120-33.

[5] Tr. Helen Kurz Roberts, *Anthology of German Poetry*.

Aus dem Grabe werd' ich ausgetrieben,
Noch zu suchen das vermißte Gut,
Noch den schon verlornen Mann zu lieben
Und zu saugen seines Herzens Blut.
Ist's um den geschehn,
Muß nach andern gehn,
Und das junge Volk erliegt der Wut.
—Johann Wolfgang von Goethe, "Die Braut von Korinth," *Werke* (Leipzig: 1797).

[6] This scene is described by several witnesses. See John Polidori, "Extracts of a Letter to the Editor from Geneva," repr. in *Three Gothic Novels* 260.

[7] According to Leonard Wolf, Monk Lewis was also part of the group. See *Annotated Dracula* xi; also Twitchell, *Living Dead* 80.

[8] *Fantasmagoriana; ou Recuil d'Histoires d'Apparitions, de Spectres, Revenans, Fantomes, et cie.* Traduit de l'Allemand par un Amateur [Jean Baptiste Benoît Eyriès]. Paris: 1812.

[9] Mary Shelley, "Introduction to the Third Edition of *Frankenstein*," *Frankenstein, or the Modern Prometheus* (1818) 225. These events have been written about by several of the participants. Christopher Frayling casts doubt on Mary Shelley's version (see Frayling, *Vampyres* 13-18).

[10] See Frayling, "Introduction," *The Vampyre; A Bedside Companion* 17.

[11] For a selection of reviews of *The Vampyre*, see MacDonald, *Poor Polidori* 188-89.

[12] Ayez horreur de cette littérature de cannibales, qui se repaît de lambeaux de chair humaine et s'abreuve du sang des femmes et des enfants; elle ferait calomnier votre coeur, sans donner une meilleure idée de votre esprit. Ayez horreur, avant tout, de cette poésie misanthropique, ou plutôt infernale, qui semble avoir reçu sa mission de Satan même. (P.S. Auger, lecture at the Institut de France [1824] quoted in Edmond Estève, *Byron et le romantisme français* [130].)

### Chapter 3

[1] Le *Vampire* épouvantera, de son horrible amour, les songes de toutes les femmes; et bientôt, sans doute, ce monstre, encore exhumé prêtera son masque immobile, sa voix sépulcrale, "son oeil d'un gris mort"…Il offrira, dis-je, tout cet attirail de mélodrame à la Melpomène des boulevards; et quel succès alors ne lui est pas réservé!

[2] Il est temps d'intéresser un peuple et de faire couler ses larmes sur un événment tel qu'on le suppose véritable et passé sous ses yeux, entre des citoyens; il ne manquerait jamais de produire de l'émotion. (Pierre-

Augustin Caron de Beaumarchais, "Preface" to *Eugénie*, quoted in Edmond Estève, *Byron et le romantisme français* 31.)

[3] The Moscow Decree enfranchised only four major houses: the Comédie Française for tragedy and comedy; the Odéon for lighter fare; the Opéra-Comique for operetta, and the Opéra for opera and ballet. Four minor theatres, the Vaudeville, Variétés, Gâité, and the Ambigu-Comique, were allowed to produce the "lower forms" of drama.

[4] For a full account of these events, see Victor L. Leathers, *British Entertainers in France* 47-68.

[5] La Porte-Saint-Martin était en ce temps-là un théâtre fortuné. Mais elle méritait bien le préférence flatteuse, déjà ancienne et soutenue, que lui témoignaient toutes les classes de la société, même la famille royale. Cette faveur, elle la devait à l'intelligence de ses directeurs, au talent d'acteurs qui s'appelaient alors Frédérick Lemaître, Bocage, et Mme. Dorval, à son amour des nouveautés, a ses inventions audacieuses, à de gros sacrifices d'argent allègrement supportés, aux efforts enfin qu'elle multiplait pour réunir chez elle toutes sortes d'intérêt disséminées sur les autres scènes (308-09).

[6] Jouffrey wrote histories of France, Portugal, inventions, the steamboat, and a dictionary of social errors.

[7] Examples: Carmouche/Mélesville/Brazier, *Le Viellard et la jeune fille*, Th. de Variétés, 1824; Carmouche/Brazier, *Tony, ou Cinq ans en deux heures*, Variétés, 1827; Carmouche/Merle/Brazier, *Sans tambour ni trompette*, Variétés, 1822 (*Parisian Stage* I). Like the Jacobean playwrights, they all seem to have been very friendly.

[8] *The Parisian Stage* lists him as the co-author with Taylor[?] of *Le Délateur par vertu*, Panorama Dramatique, 1821; with Béraud and Merle of *Faust*, Porte-Saint-Martin, 1828; possibly with Merle, Béraud and Croznier of *Le Monstre et le magicien*, Porte-Saint-Martin, 1826; and of *Le Vampire. Le Chateau de Saint-Aldobrand* is not listed. Possibly it was not produced. Ginette Picat-Guinoiseau in *Nodier et le théâtre* identifies him as the pseudonymous author of all five plays.

[9] Malvina was one of the most popular names for high-class Parisian prostitutes in this period, along with other English names such as Emily, Pamela, Fanny, and Clara (Mayhew II: 208). The names seem to have been taken from English novels.

[10] O mon ami! comme tout mon être s'est reanimé à sa vue! tu le sais, flétri par les malheurs, isolé sur le terre, tu me vis toujours pret à quitter sans regrêt le néant qui m'entourait pour chercher un néant inconnu encore. Cet ange, cet ange seul peut m'attacher à l'existence, c'est d'elle que j'attends une nouvelle vie: il me semble déjà que je la puise dans ses regards. Oh! Malvina! que votre bouche confirme un espoir si doux. (Nodier, Carmouche and Jouffrey, *Le Vampire* [Paris: J.N. Barba, 1820]. Quoted passages are from this edition, except as otherwise noted.)

[11] La courte nouvelle de Polidori a fourni au *Vampire* quelques données: personalité des protagonistes, rappel des moeurs des vampires, événements hallucinants de caractère prémonitoire, "mort" passée du Vampire, exigence du serment, enfin intrusion de la folie. De ce peu de matière les auteurs ont fait oeuvre forte par un dosage savant du tragique, du dramatique et du mélodramatique ("Introduction," *Charles Nodier: Oeuvres Dramatiques I: Le Vampire et Le Délateur* 21).

¹² Au lever de la toile, le ciel est obscur, et tous les objets confus. Il s'éclaircit peu à peu. La scène se passe dans une grotte basaltique, dont les longs prismes se terminent à angles inégaux vers le ciel. Le ceintre est découvert. L'enceinte de la grotte est semée de tombeaux de formes diverses, des colonnes, des pyramides, des cubes d'un travail brut et grossier. Sur une tombe de l'avant-scène, on voit une jeune fille couchée, et plongée dans le plus profond sommeil. Sa tête est appuyée sur un de ses bras, et recouverte de son voile et de ses cheveux.... La lumière s'est augmentée progressivement. L'ange de la lune, en robe blanche flottante, s'adresse à Oscar.

¹³ Le néant! Le néant! (Il laisse tomber son poignard et cherche à s'enfuir, des ombres sortent de la terre et l'entraînent avec elles; l'Ange exterminateur paraît dans un nuage, la foudre éclate et les Ombres s'engloutissent avec Rutwen. Pluie de feu.) TABLEAU GENERAL.

¹⁴ Son bras qui était levé retombe. La foudre gronde.... Le fond du théâtre s'ouvre et l'on voit paraître les ombres des victimes du vampire. Ce sont des jeunes femmes couvertes de voiles, elles le poursuivent en lui montrant leur sein déchiré d'où le sang coule encore. Au moment où l'ange des amours traverse le théâtre sur un char lumineux).

TOUS (saisis d'effroi): O ciel! (Le tonnere gronde plus fort et tombe sur le vampire qui est englouti.) FIN

¹⁵ Of Pixérécourt's 120 plays, only one, *Valentine*, had an unhappy ending.

¹⁶ Piccini, grand spécialiste du genre, sait composer...les ponctuations de l'action évocatrices et pathétique, les chants de solistes ou de choeurs; enfin danse, sous la forme d'un ballet, qui illustre l'harmonie du monde, tandis que les événements adverses sont déjà engrenés.... La musique peut être descriptive, "peindre" ou "exprimer" une tempête ou un orage; elle peut souligner des paroles; elle peut servir de fond à toute une scène...Les indications scéniques évoquent une sorte de musique de film. La musique poétise l'action (Picat-Guinoiseau 15, 23).

¹⁷ Le théâtre de Nodier se situe à cette limite mal définie entre mélodrame et littérature. Le (mélo)drame a été pour lui un jeu dont il s'est applique à bien suivre les règles, mais en jouant, il s'exprime. On peut s'interroger devant certains tics de langage, ce théâtre n'en constitue pas moins une oeuvre originale et prenante, dont le pouvoir de séduction dépasse le simple pathétique pour toucher aux profondeurs qu'explore et magnifie la littérature (Picat-Guinoiseau 19).

¹⁸ Le mélodrame ne devenait-il pas l'ecole de la désobéissance?.... Quel jargon parlait le mélodrame! Avec quelles libertés il dénaturait l'histoire! De quelles erreurs il nourrissait le public "en brouillant les époques et les faits"! Quelles idées fausses [sic] il répandait! Comment, alors qu'il faisait tant de vacarme, entendre encore des oeuvres aimables et discrétes? Que devenait, avec lui, le culte des gloires littéraires? On courait à un abîme. Cette caricature du commencement du siècle, montrant Melpomène et Thalie mises en fuite par le mélodrame, brandissant un poignard et suivi d'une bande de brigands, n'avait-elle été que trop prophétique? (Paraphrased in Ginisty, *Le Mélodrame* 182-83).

¹⁹ Désaugiers's parodies follow the act structure of their originals; for instance, there are five acts in his surprisingly detailed version of *Paria*

(1822), *Cadet Buteux à la première représentation du Paria, ou récit véridique de cette tragédie, écrit sous la dictée de l'Historien du Gros Caillou, par son Secrétaire intime, Désaugiers.* Previously in 1818, he had written *Cadet Buteux sortant de la représentation des Danaïdes, potpourri.* "Buteux" resembles the French word for "stubborn" (buté), or "stumble" (buter). "Gros Caillou" seems to mean "the Big Pebble" or (colloquial) "Great Embarrassment." Buteux may be modeled on Cadet Roussel, an earlier continuing character used in parodies. There are at least eight of these, one by Désaugiers: *Cadet Roussel, esturgeon* (folie-parade en deux actes, melée de vaudevilles), which played at the Variétés in 1818. In 1823 Désaugiers and Auguste Rousseau, who had each written a satire of *Le Vampire,* wrote a play together, *La Juif* (anecdotique de 2 a. melé de couplets) which was presented by the Porte-Saint-Martin, and in 1827 they collaborated on *L'amour et la peur* (comédie-vaudeville, one-act).

[20] Lisant pour un sou d'politique
Plac' Royale, sur un banc,
J'tombe, le tour est diabolique,
A' point nommé, sur l'Drapeau blanc.
J'prends un billet, non pas pour parterre,
Ces places sont réservées aux amis,
Sans secours de l'abbé Saint-Pierre,
Avec treiz sous j'monte au paradis.
Au dernier banc, paix, qu'chacun s'taise!
A'bas la gueule on crie du premier rang,
L'rideau s'lève et quoique très mal à l'aise,
Le croirez-vous, j'vois le Père Lachaise,
Du dernier banc. (qtd. in Summers, *Kith* 309)

This play was published (Paris: Martinet, 1820), but there is no record of its being performed.

[21] Carlson lists Aumer in this position (*The French Stage*, 40) but no doubt one succeeded the other.

[22] A printer's error labels the last scene as scene iv.

[23] Summers mentions another vampire play, *Le fils Vampire* by Paul Féval. His evidence is the title page of an English play, *The Loves of Paris* by John Wilson Ross (London: Vickers, 1846), which states that it is "translated from the French of Paul Féval, author of 'The Vampire.'" Summers states that the Féval play is also mentioned in Jean Larat's *La Tradition et l'Exotisime dans l'oeuvre de Charles Nodier* (1923) (*Kith* 303). In my opinion, there is no such play. There is no listing of it in *The Parisian Stage, Enciclopedia dello Spettacolo*, or the *National Union Catalogue*. Féval's *Le Ville Vampire* (repr. *Nos Grands Auteurs* [Paris: Dentu, 1891]) is a novel (which he passed off as a translation of a work by Ann Radcliffe). His play, *Le Fils du Diable*, is about pirates, not vampires. Féval's play is also mentioned in Donald Glut, *The Dracula Book* (41), but his source is Summers; he shows no familiarity with the plays beyond what Summers states, and errs in many details.

[24] L'épidemie de vampires, qui s'abat sur la France au moment où les *Meditations poétiques* donnent une tout autre image du romantisme.... [était] le domaine de Nodier. Mais celui-ci a senti que l'attrait du vampirisme n'était pas sans rapport avec ce qui se passes dans le psychisme de l'homme

endormi, c'est-a-dire avec ce que nous appelons l'inconscient: "Les inductions ne manquent pas," écrit-il, "pour prouver que certaines des plus épouvantables aberrations de l'homme: la sorcellerie, la lycanthropie, le vampirisme, sont des maladies de l'homme endormi, comme le somnambulisme et le cauchemar." Le fantasme d'une aggression sexuelle à la fois délicieuse et mortelle constitue l'arme absolue de ce "Lovelace des tombeaux," comme l'appelle un critique de l'époque (i, iii).

### Chapter 4

¹ A facsimile of what seems to be the second John Cumberland edition (1830) is printed in The Hour of One: Six Gothic Melodramas, ed. Stephen Wischhusen, and an abridged version in The Golden Age of Melodrama, ed. Michael Kilgarrïff. Michael R. Booth, an authority on this period, considers Wischhusen and Kilgariff to be unreliable: "The texts are facsimiles of early acting editions, and in all three collections [the above mentioned plus Victorian Melodramas, ed. James L. Smith (1976)] little or no actual editing of texts seems to have been done. All three contain short general introductions which can only be described as superficial, inadequate, and inaccurate" (Michael R. Booth, Prefaces to Nineteenth-Century Theatre 217). I agree with Booth: Kilgarrïff erroneously attributes William Hazlitt's review of The Vampire to Leigh Hunt (87-88), and Wischhusen erroneously states that T.P. Cooke performed in Paris in Nodier's Le Vampire (168). He writes interestingly about the theatres of this era, however.

² This should not be confused with what we call the poverty rate today in this country, which hovers around 25 percent. To be a pauper meant to have absolutely nothing; in other words, what we now call a homeless person.

³ Most of the English Romantic poets attempted to write for the stage; none were successful. Some examples are Wordsworth's The Borderers (1795), Coleridge's Remorse (1813), Keats's Otho the Great (1819), Shelley's The Cenci (1819), conceived for Edmund Kean, and Prometheus Unbound, obviously a closet drama. Byron, more familiar with the theatre through Richard Brinsley Sheridan and his connection with Covent Garden, nevertheless had only Marino Faliero (1821) produced in his lifetime. Sardanapalus (1821) later became a vehicle for Charles Kean, and Werner (acted 1830) for Charles Macready. The poets professed that they wrote for the mind, not the playhouse; further, financial remuneration was poor for playwrights, who were held in low esteem. (See Michael R. Booth's essay in The Revels History of the Drama in English, Vol. 6.) Romantic drama failed in England largely because of the dominance of melodrama; it fared much better in France.

⁴ Ernest Bradlee Watson in Sheridan to Robertson: A Study of the Nineteenth-Century Stage lists 15 theatres in London in 1820. Three legitimate: Drury Lane, Covent Garden, the Haymarket (summer only until 1840); one opera house, the Italian Opera; and eleven minor houses: Sadler's Wells, Astley's, Surrey, Royalty, Sans Souci, Olympic, Adelphi, Queen's, Coburg, the Lyceum (summer only), and the Argyll Rooms.

⁵ Madame Tussaud gave her first London exhibition here.

⁶ New incidental music for the production was composed by Joseph Hart (1794-1844).

[7] Victoria ascended the throne in 1837.

[8] Even more sensational, the Corsican trap, invented by Boucicault for *The Corsican Brothers* (1852), was used for characters rising up out of the stage and moving forward at the same time.

[9] William Hazlitt, *Criticisms and Dramatic Essays of the English Stage* (London, 1851), 138, quoted in Harold J. Nichols, "The Acting of Thomas Potter Cooke," *Nineteenth Century Theatre Research* 5.2 (Autumn 1977), 75.

[10] Ici...nous rencontrons les noms les plus illustres du romantisme. Mettant à part la gloire toute contemporaine du Vampire Philippe aussi fameux en France que le Vampire Cooke en Angleterre, Cooke qui interpréta aussi glorieusement le Monstre des deux côtés de la Manche, nous trouvons Frédérick Lemaître pour Mephisto, et, pour presque toutes les héroïnes, de Malvina à Marguerite, la grand Marie Dorval ("Introduction," *Le Vampire/Le Délateur* 25).

## Chapter 5

[1] The play, the first of several, related the events of an actual shipwreck and recreated in tableau the famous painting by Géricault.

[2] This argument is essentially correct. Montague Summers in *The Vampire in Europe* states that belief in vampires began in Scotland around the 12th century. He lists many case histories and quotes a number of historical sources. See his Chapter II, "The Vampire in England, and Ireland, and Some Latin Lands" (78-131 *passim*). See also Carol Senf, *The Vampire in Nineteenth Century Literature* (19-20), and Anthony Masters, *The Natural History of the Vampire* (139-40).

[3] The glass curtain was removed soon afterward because its five-ton weight put too much strain on the building's structure. For an analysis of the social statements of the Coburg architecture, its separate entrances, changing facade and interior, with illustrations, see Marvin Carlson, "The Old Vic: A Semiotic Analysis," *Semiotica* 71-3/4 (1988): 187-212.

[4] Wischhusen takes the title of his anthology, *The Hour of One*, from Moncrieff's *Vampire*, but, oddly, does not include it or even mention it in his introductory remarks.

[5] Frayling adds, "He couldn't have been wider of the mark if he had tried."

[6] The Giovanni series includes Thomas Didbin's *Don Giovanni; or A Specter on Horseback*, "a Comic, Heroic, Operatic, Tragic, Pantomimic Burletta-Spectacular Extravaganza in two acts," which played the Royal Circus and Surrey Theatre in 1818; W.T. Moncrieff's *Giovanni in the Country; or The Rake Husband* at the Royal Coburg in 1819 (with Henry Stephen Kemble, Moncrieff's Ruthwold, as Giovanni); W. Barrymore's *Giovanni in the Country, or A Gallop to Gretna Green*, "a New Comic, Melodramatic Hippodrame" at Astley's Royal Amphitheatre in 1820; and Moncrieff's *Giovanni in London; or the Libertine Reclaimed*, "the New Broad Comic Extravaganza Entertainment" at Drury Lane in 1820.

[7] For the theory of the "male gaze," see Laura Mulvey, "Visual Pleasure and Narrative Cinema," *Narrative, Apparatus, Ideology*, ed. Philip Rosen (New York: Columbia University Press, 1986), 198-207; E. Ann Kaplan, "Is the Gaze Male?" *Women and Film: Both Sides of the*

*Camera* (New York: Methuen, 1983), 25-35. Among others who have applied this theory to theatre, Jill Dolan, *The Feminist Spectator as Critic* (Ann Arbor: University of Michigan Press, 1988).

## Chapter 6

[1] Tr. Hal Draper, *Complete Poems of Heinrich Heine* 390.
> Du hast mich beschworen aus dem Grab
> Durch deinen Zauberwillen,
> Belebtest mich mit Wollustglut—
>
> Jetzt kannst du die Glut nicht stillen.
> Press deinen Mund an meinen Mund,
> Der Menschen Odem ist göttlich!
> Ich trinke deine Seele aus,
> Die Toten sind unersättlich.

[2] The story was published circa 1800, but not attributed to Tieck until 1820. See Blieler, "Introduction," *Three Gothic Novels* and Frayling, *Vampyres* 165.

[3] W.A. Wohlbrück, *Der Vampyr, Grosse Romantische Oper* by Heinrich Marschner (Leipzig: Friedrich Hofmeister, 1828). Vocal Score with piano. All quoted passages are from the score in the Music Division of Lincoln Center Library for the Performing Arts.

There was an earlier opera on the theme of vampires: Silvestro di Palma's *I Vampiri* (opera buffa in one act, 1812, Teatro San Carlo, Naples) which is now lost. The opera was based on Giuseppe Davanzati's treatise, *Dissertazione sopra i Vampiri di Giuseppe Davanzati Patrizio Fiorentino e Tranese, Arcivescivo di Trani, e Patriarca d'Alessandria* (Napoli: Presso Filippo Raimondi, 1789) (Summers, *Kith* 311). Summers gives the date of the opera as 1800; The *Enciclopedia dello Spettaculo* gives it as 1812. Di Palma also wrote *Gli amanti della dote*, dramma giacoso per musica (1791, Florence), and *L'erede senza eredita, o sia, Il fantasma immaginario* (1811), libretto di G. Palomba.

Other Italian works in this period include G.C. Cosenza, *Il Vampiro* (lavoro drammatico, 1825); Angelo Broffiero, *Il Vampiro* (commedia en cinque atti, 1827), both mentioned in the *Enciclopedia dello Spettaculo*.

[4] Ha, welche Lust aus schönen Augen
> An blühender Brust neues Leben
> In wonnigem Beben
> Mit einen Kusse in sich zu saugen.
> Ha, welche Lust in liebendem Kosen
> Mit lüsternem Mut
> Das süsseste Blut
> Wie Saft der Rosen
> Von purpurnen Lippen
> Schmeichelnd zu nippen!
> Und wenn der brennende Durst sich stillt,
> Und wenn das Blut dem Herzen entquillt,
> Und wenn sie stöhnen, voll Entsetzen,
> Ha, ha, welch'Ergötzen,

Welche Lust!
Mit neuem Mut
Ihr Todesbeben
Ist frisches Leben.
Armes Liebchen, bleich wie Schnee,
Tat dir wohl im Herzen weh.
Ach, einst fühlt' ich selbst die Schmerzen
Ihrer Angst im warmen Herzen,
Das der Himmel fühlend schuf.
Mahnt mich nicht in diesen Tönen,
Die den Himmel frech verhöhnen.
Ich verstehe euern Ruf!
Ha, welche Lust.

[5] It is interesting to note that Marschner himself was married four times. All four wives died of natural causes.

[6] The 1992 edition of *The New Grove Dictionary of the Opera* replaces the Köhler entry on Marschner with one by A. Dean Palmer. The comments on *Der Vampyr* are much briefer, and, in my opinion, less insightful. Some of his additional points:

"Marschner employed additional dramatic techniques to support the generally sombre ambience of his romantic operas. One was melodrama.... Speaking or acting against orchestral accompaniment had proved an effective means of heightening dramatic tension. Mozart, Beethoven and Weber had all used it, and in Marschner it became particularly important. Instances include the passage in which the light of the moon revives the murdered vampire.... On the other hand, comic relief is necessary to keep operas of this sort from becoming overwhelming. [Examples]...are the drinking-song and the antics of Suse Blunt, who jumps on to a table to castigate her husband and his cronies for drunkenness." (III: 226)

Palmer is also the author of *Heinrich Marschner (1795-1861): His Life and Stage Works*. His analysis of *Der Vampyr* is marred by his inability to obtain a text of Nodier's *Le Vampire*, leading him to many erroneous conclusions. He attributes the borrowings from the French original, differing from Ritter's adaptation, to inventions by Wohlbrück.

[7] For those readers interested in hearing this rarely performed work for themselves, excerpts from the opera were recently released on compact disc on the Memories label (HR 4466/67). This is a digitally remastered recording of a live performance in Vienna, on 9 April 1951, of the Tonkünstlerchor and Grosses Weiner Rundfunkorchester, conducted by Kurt Tenner. The cast includes Liane Synek as Malwine; Gisela Rathauscher as Janthe; Traute Skladal as Emmy; Georg Oeggl as Ruthwen; Fritz Sperlbauer as Edgar Aubry; Leo Heppe as Sir Humprey; and Wolfgang Weise as the Vampyrmeister.

[8] Montague Summers states that some authorities give the opening date as 25 August 1829 (*Kith* 311), but this is impossible if the other dates are correct.

[9] C.M. Heigel, *Der Vampyr*. Romantiche Oper in drei Aufzügen nach Byrons Dichtung von C.M. Heigel; Musik von P.V. Lindpainter (Leipzig: [Peters], 1828).

[10] I have been unable to locate a recording of any of the Lindpainter *Vampyr*.

[11] The play is mentioned in E.F. Bleiler's "John Polidori and the Vampire," which introduces the Polidori short story in *Three Gothic Novels* (xxxix). Margaret L. Carter lists the play in her bibliography, *The Vampire in Literature*, incorrectly estimating the date as circa 1820 and giving the reference in the Bleiler preface as her source.

Although he seems unaware of Blink's play, Montague Summers mentions a ballad called "The Vampire Bride" by the Hon. Henry Liddell, published in 1833. It concerns a knight who places a ring on the finger of a statue of Venus "whilst he is a quoiting." The ring cannot be removed and that night a phantom, the spirit which inhabited the statue, claims him for a husband. "With difficulty he is freed from the thrall of the succubus" (*Kith* 331). Prosper Mérimée's short story, "Venus de Lille," employs a similar plot. However it is the German story which is the source of Blink's melodrama.

### Chapter 7

[1] The case of Sergeant Bertrand is recounted in detail in Epaulard's *Le Vampirisme*, Huysmans's *Souvenirs*, and all the standard vampire studies by Tony Faivre, Anthony Masters, Montague Summers, Leonard Wolf, and Ornella Volta.

[2] "Mais, quand on en vint au tombeau de Kisilova—c'était le nom du vieillard,—on le trouva les yeux ouverts, la bouche vermeille, respirant à pleins poumons, et cependant immobile, comme mort. On lui enfonça un pieu dans le coeur; il jeta un grand cri, et rendit le sang par le bouche; puis on le mit sur un bûcher, on le réduisit en cendre, et l'on jeta la cendre au vent.... Quelque temps après, je quittait le pays; de sorte que je ne pus savoir si son fils était devenu vampire comme lui."

"Pourquoi serait-il devenu vampire comme lui?" demandais-je.

"Ah! parce que c'est l'habitude, que les personnes qui meurent du vampirism deviennent vampires."

"En vérité, vous dites cela comme si c'était un fait avéré."

"Mais c'est qu'aussi c'est un fait avéré, connu, enregistré!" (II, 129)

[3] L'Ambigu monte toutes ses machines [sic] de manière attirer la foule qui se porte avec empressement vers ce théâtre: décorations pittoresques et très bien servies, costumes frais et parfaitment adaptés aux circonstances, ballets joliment dessinés et éxecutés par des danseurs qui valent presque ceux de l'Opera, évolutions militaires, combats, rien n'est négligé pour satisfaire les spectateurs.

[4] From the title page in *Théâtre Complet* (XI: 399). Gorman and Davidson give the opening date as December 30.

[5] There is some discussion of vampires in *The Count of Monte Cristo* (1845) also. At a performance of *Parisina* at the Theatre Argento in Rome, Haidée, Countess of G——, remarks of a cadaverous-looking person in the box opposite, "Why, he is no other than Lord Ruthven himself in a living frame.... I'll tell you...Byron had the most perfect belief in the existence of vampires, and even assured me he had seen some. The description he gave me perfectly corresponds with the features and character of the man before us.... The coal-black hair, large, bright,

glittering eyes, in which a wild, unearthly fire seems burning,—the same ghastly paleness!" (I: 466-68).

Dumas's short story "The Pale-Faced Lady" (1848) also features a vampire, Count Kostaki, and is set in the Carpathian Mountains of Moldavia.

[6] Mélusine was played by "sweet, pale Isabelle Constant." She became Dumas's mistress, and was dropped nine years later for "slim, boyish Emilie Cordier" (Gorman 373, 389).

[7] Mélusine: Sachez quel est cet homme à la figure sombre,
       Quelle trame il ourdit.
Cet homme, ainsi que nous, est un enfant de l'ombre,
       Mais un enfant maudit.
Même pour nos regards, sa nuit est trop profonde.
       Dans quel morne dessein
Le Seigneur permet-il qu'il demeure en ce monde,
       Immortel assassin?
Nul ne le sait; Dieu met ses plus blanches colombes
       Dans sa fatale main,
Et l'on retrouverait sa trace par les tombes
       Qu'il sème en son chemin.
              (Gilbert s'agite douloureusement)
Nulle vierge n'échappe aux meurtres qu'il entasse;
       Le hideux oppresseur
Brave les éléments et commande à l'espace...
Gilbert: Ô ma soeur! ô ma soeur!
Mélusine: Juana, sa victime, à peine est expirée,
       Le spectre ravisseur,
Envolé du tombeau, retourne à la curée...
Gilbert: Ô ma soeur! ô ma soeur!
Mélusine: Hier il voulut tuer notre fils dans la plaine
       Car de son défenseur
La sanglant fiancé comptait priver Hélène...
Gilbert: Ô ma soeur! ô ma soeur!
Mélusine: Prions, pour qu'à Gilbert Dieu tout-puissant inspire
       Un généreux effort.
Ruthwen est un démon, Ruthwen est un vampire;
       Son amour, c'est la mort!

[8] *The Parisian Stage* (very reliable) lists as Albert Marguelier (1851-75: 225).

[9] After its initial runaway success, *Varney* rapidly passed into obscurity and the book became unprocurable. Gothic bibliophile Montague Summers offered large sums of money in the 1920s to secure a copy, but was unsuccessful (*Kith* 333). Reawakened interest in vampire literature in the 1960s prompted Dover to reprint the text of a rare surviving copy, with a preface by E.F. Bleiler. There are now several modern editions.

[10] Authorship is disputed: "Montague Summers (and other vampirologists from the 1920s onwards) thought that *Varney the Vampyre* was the work of Thomas Preskett Prest.... But in 1963 Louis James established beyond any doubt that Varney was the work of the Scotsman James Malcolm Rymer—the evidence being two of Rymer's own scrapbooks" (Frayling, *Vampyres* 145).

[11] Frayling writes, "*The Feast of Blood* was so successful that a play was rushed on to the London stage while the penny parts were still coming out: in it, the first plot cycle was expanded to fill a whole evening" (*Vampyres* 40). I can find no mention of this play in *Victorian Plays: A Record of Significant Productions on the London Stage, 1837-1901, Enciclopedia dello Spettacolo, National Union Catalogue, British Museum General Catalogue of Printed Books*, or in any study of vampire literature I consulted.

[12] For Rymer's true opinion, see quote at beginning of chapter.

[13] Rymer was very *au courant* to set this scene at Vesuvius: the first Pompeii excavations were begun in 1815.

[14] In addition, during this period he wrote *The Queen of Spades* (1851, adaptation of Scribe) for Drury Lane, and *Sixtus V; or, The Broken Promise* (1851, also called *The Pope of Rome*) for the Olympic.

[15] Henry Morley, *The Journal of a London Playgoer, from 1851 to 1866* 45-46. Richard Pascoe, in *Our Actors and Actresses: The Dramatic List* (1880), states that this review appeared in the *Examiner* 19 June 1852. Unattributed excerpts from it also occur in Walsh 45-46.

[16] *The Dictionary of Historic American Theatres* lists a theatre called Liberty Hall as still standing in Honesdale, Pennsylvania. It opened in 1860 and offered drama, vaudeville, burlesque, opera, boxing and wrestling matches, and political rallies. Originally the Masonic Hall, its name was changed when it became the site of Abolitionist rallies during the Civil War. The theatre closed in 1875, and is now in use as an office building (224).

[17] Play bill in the Billy Rose Collection at Lincoln Center Library of the Performing Arts, New York.

[18] *Brunhilda*, at the Barnum Museum, was in 1862.

### Chapter 8

[1] For a comprehensive study of demonic women in late 19th-century literature, see Bram Dijkstra, *Idols of Perversity: Fantasies of Evil in Fin-de-Siècle Culture.*

[2] *The Parisian Stage* lists Louis-César Desormes as a possible co-author.

[3] I am indebted to Marc Levy, whose unpublished paper, "The Influence of Melodrama on Gilbert and Sullivan's Comic Operas," I have drawn on.

[4] It was later the home of Harley Granville Barker's Stage Society, whose Shakespeare season in 1912 is considered to have laid the foundation for a national theatre. It burned down in 1990, carrying with it irreplaceable Gilbert and Sullivan memorabilia stored in the basement.

[5] Gilbert was impatient at the delay, which was caused by Sullivan's engagement in composing a cantata, *The Golden Legend*, for the 1886 Leeds Festival. Their dislike of each other is well documented.

[6] A performance of the original version of *Ruddygore*, certainly the preferable one from the point of view of this study, has been released on compact discs (MCA Classics MCAD2-11010) with the New Sadler's Wells Opera Chorus and Orchestra conducted by Simon Phipps. This is a recording of the 1987 centenary production directed by Ian Judge. The cast includes Gordon Sandison as Ruthven Murgatroyd; Marilyn Hill Smith as Rose Maybud; David Hillman as Richard Dauntless. According to the

jacket notes prepared by David Russell Hulme, the performance includes previously unpublished music, discovered in Sullivan's autograph score, which had not been heard in 100 years. Another classic performance is Sir Malcolm Sargent's, with the Glyndebourne Festival Chorus and Pro Arte Orchestra (EMI CDS7 47787-8). This is the complete revised version without dialogue. For even more stringent purists, the D'Oyly Carte Opera Company version, under the direction of Dame Bridget D'Oyly Carte, issued by London Records in the 1970s, is definitive.

*Chapter 9*

[1] This and all quoted passages are from Leonard Wolf, *The Annotated Dracula* (New York: Clarkson N. Potter, 1975). This edition, considered definitive but now out of print, has been extensively revised and reissued as *The Essential Dracula* (New York: Plume, 1993). I served as researcher and associate editor for this revision. It is not to be confused with Florescu and McNally's *The Essential Dracula* (New York: Mayflower Books, 1977), also out of print.

[2] This interpretation makes sense of one of the novel's most cryptic and fascinating passages, an exchange between Dracula and his vampire harem: "'You yourself never loved; you never love!' On this the other women joined, and such a mirthless, hard, soulless laughter rang through the room that it almost made me faint to hear; it seemed the pleasure of fiends. Then the Count turned, after looking at my face attentively, and said in a soft whisper:—'Yes, I too can love; you yourselves can tell it from the past. Is it not so? Well, now I promise you that when I am done with him you shall kiss him at your will. Now go! go!'" (41). It seems Dracula's sexual conquests become his daughters, and thus lose their erotic attraction for him.

[3] Ironically, such transfusions, if the wrong blood type, would have killed her.

[4] Van Helsing's mention of Charcot's recent and sudden death pinpoints the time of the novel's action as 1893, a point which has eluded some critics.

[5] Elaine Showalter, in *Sexual Anarchy: Gender and Culture at the Fin de Siècle*, places *Dracula* in a genre she calls "male romances," a surprising number of which involve fantasies of alternate methods of reproduction which avoid contact with female genitals: cloning in Robert Louis Stevenson's *The Strange Case of Dr. Jekyll and Mr. Hyde* (1886); reincarnation in H. Ryder Haggard's *She* (1886); "aesthetic duplication" in Oscar Wilde's *The Picture of Dorian Gray* (1890); vivisection of animals in H.G. Wells's *The Island of Dr. Moreau* (1895); and transfusion in *Dracula* (1897) (78). In a way, the parent of them all is Mary Shelley's *Frankenstein* (1818) involving laboratory creation. This list of course comprises most of the 19th-century masterpieces of horror fiction. While this is beside Showalter's main argument, it seems it would be a fruitful area of exploration.

[6] All three essays are reprinted in *Dracula: The Vampire and the Critics*, ed. Margaret L. Carter.

[7] Many biographies and critical studies argue that Stoker did not know what his book was about. For example, suggested interpretations have included Dracula as a symbol of decadent capitalism—Stoker would have been amazed to hear himself labeled a Marxist.

[8] The connection between this melodrama and the vampire works of Dion Boucicault and Heinrich Marschner has been mentioned in Chapters 6 and 7. Irving's terrifying portrayal of the Dutchman (which was also one of T.P. Cooke's most famous roles) prefigured his Mephistopheles, and through that, influenced Stoker's Dracula.

[9] Terry's soft, feminine, sympathetic Lady Macbeth broke with the traditional, "monumental" interpretation handed down from Sarah Siddons at the beginning of the century. It was considered by many to be Terry's greatest role. In "Escaping the Vampire Trap," Nina Auerbach suggests a link between Stoker's vampire women and Mrs. Patrick Campbell, another great actress of this period.

[10] Another name parallel: Joseph Harker (1855-1920) was a set designer for the Lyceum who worked on *Macbeth*; Jonathan Harker is a character in *Dracula*.

[11] In the same year, the Grand Guignol Theatre, which curiously omitted vampires from its repertory of the gruesome and the macabre, opened in Paris.

[12] Unidentified newspaper clipping, 20 February 1927, collection of the Theatre Museum, London (qtd. in Skal 74).

[13] Deane and Balderston, *Dracula, the Vampire Play* (New York: Samuel French, Inc., 1927). All quoted passages are from this edition.

[14] One of Anne Rice's amusing notions in her vampire novels is that only those vampires who were devout Catholics during their mortal lives are frightened by the cross and other religious paraphernalia.

[15] Also, in its previous incarnation as the English Opera House, the "house of Ruthven" in the 1820s.

[16] Skal relates the story of the conversion of *Dracula* from novel to stage to film in complete and interesting detail, with particular attention to the financial and legal battles among the various parties, and the many eccentric personalities involved.

[17] National Recording Co., DF9060 (1970). Excerpts from Welles's script are printed in Glut 282-85.

[18] Another repeated pattern is the confluence of both the Ruthven and the Dracula plays with *Frankenstein*. Frankenstein's monster and Ruthven were both played by T.P. Cooke in the 1820s; Bela Lugosi and Boris Karloff also each played Dracula and Frankenstein's monster on film. We also note the compulsion of hack writers to feature joint appearances of both monsters: *Frankenstein, or the Vampire's Victim* (1887) by Richard Reece, and the film *House of Frankenstein* (1944) and many others.

## Chapter 10

[1] My source for this brief survey of the evolution of film is Michael J. Murphy, *The Celluloid Vampires* 1-3.

[2] Several lost vampire films follow: *The Secrets of House Number Five* (1912), a Russian film; *In the Grip of the Vampires* (Guam Film Company, no date); and the Danish film *De Dodes O* (*Isle of the Dead*, 1913). A number of horror films made in Denmark peripherally concerned vampires: *The Necklace of the Dead* (1910, lost); and *The Vampire's Trail* (1914), directed by R.G. Vignola. In 1915 a French film with the promising title *Les Vampires* was made by Louis Feuillade, but turns out

to concern a gang of street criminals and their enigmatic "moll," Musidora.

³ This showing of the woman's portrait, which occurs in nearly every version of *Dracula*, plays an essential part in the story. The Hindu taboo against showing a picture of one's wife to anyone, lest it invite misfortune, has a similar cautionary resonance. A kind of folkloric hubris, it invites the lust of the monster and brings calamity into the marriage.

⁴ Some critics have complained that Murnau violated his own logic by showing the vampire in broad daylight in some scenes, but perhaps they are unaware that before day-for-night filters were developed, it was standard practice to print night scenes on blue-tinted film stock, thus eliminating the imagined logical discrepancy.

⁵ Reviews of *Nosferatu* qtd. in Skal 101.

⁶ Wolf believes that Renfield, a life-obsessed lunatic incarcerated near Carfax, was a plausible choice of victim.

⁷ Skal had to travel to Cuba against State Department interdiction in order to view a print in 1989. Probably due in large part to his praise of it in *Hollywood Gothic*, the Spanish *Dracula* has recently been restored, subtitled, and released in videocassette by MCA/Universal Classics.

⁸ *Le Cauchemar de Dracula* (Terence Fisher, 1958), dont le triomphe public ne s'est jamais démenti, ne s'écarte pas de la stricte observance du rituel vampirique. Sa progression dramatique, d'une prodigieuse efficacité, épouse l'évolution des rapports érotiques/affectifs dont Dracula se fait l'ordonnateur omniprésent, toujours craint et toujours espéré. La perfection plastique du *Cauchemar* vient ainsi soutenir les structures internes d'un *sens* sans lequel elle aurait la gratuité de l'esthétisme (*Le Cinéma "Fantastique"* 104).

⁹ See Laura Mulvey, "Visual Pleasure and Narrative Cinema," in *Narrative, Apparatus, Ideology*.

¹⁰ Dracula's mistress is mentioned as having committed suicide by jumping out a window in Florescu and McNally, *Dracula, Prince of Many Faces* 154-55.

¹¹ Curtis also directed television's vampire serial, *Dark Shadows*, in the seventies.

¹² Je vis le traits d'un jeune homme...seulement il était pâle et paraissait souffrant ses yeux sur moi avec l'expression la plus touchante, semblaient me demander de secours.

¹³ Coppola, television interview, "Closeup: *Bram Stoker's Dracula*," Entertainment Channel, November 1992.

¹⁴ Michael R. Booth points out, in a different context, that the artistic reflection of a historical event becomes manifest in the period *after* the event, *e.g.*, the glorification of the English tar on the British stage in the 1820s occurred after the important naval wars early in the century, as nostalgic recalling of former glory; and the melodramas of Pixérécourt became popular in Paris only after the Reign of Terror (*English Melodrama* 104).

¹⁵ Anne Rice's vampire tetralogy is a pleasure for theatre historians because she writes lovingly and often about the theatre. In *Interview with the Vampire*, an American vampire comes to Paris in search of his roots, and discovers the Théâtre des Vampires, whose performances (the descriptions of which are among the most brilliant passages in the book)

are reminiscent of the Grand Guignol (1897-1962, heyday circa 1915), with the difference that the vampire-actors are really dispatching the victims, which the human audience passes off as clever illusion. But Rice seems to have set the Grand Guignol at least 40 years too early, in the age of Napoleon III.

In the *Vampire Lestat*, partly set in the late 18th century, the protagonist Lestat, while still mortal, becomes an actor in the commedia dell'arte company in Paris whose wonderfully described performances resemble those of the Théâtre des Italiens, although she sets the theatre on the Boulevard due Temple, making the Porte-Saint-Martin an obvious candidate. After becoming a vampire, Lestat becomes the romantic idol of the city (as did Monsieur Philippe, the star of Nodier's *Le Vampire*; see Appendix C). He comes to own the theatre and leaves it to a coven of vampires, whose productions, as the Théâtre des Vampires, would obviously be the hot center of the vampire craze of 1820-30. Again, Rice's dating is off: Marie Antoinette and Louis XVI are still reigning during the novel's action, so the setting must be prior to 1789, at least 30 years too early for historical accuracy.

The third book, *Queen of the Damned*, is set mainly in the present and strikes me as inferior to the first two. Lestat is still in show business, now performing as a heavy-metal rock star. The fourth, *Tale of the Body Thief*, is weaker still.

The most interesting character in the series, the child-vampire Claudia (said to be based on Rice's own daughter, who died of leukemia), is killed in the first book. The difficulty of casting the role, a five-year-old body housing the mind of a mature woman, has probably contributed to the problem of filming this novel, which was optioned a number of times prior to its release in 1994.

Rice's vampires feed on blood to live, and create other vampires by sharing their own blood (which must be done only rarely and judiciously). They become stronger with age and can sense each other's presence from a distance. All vampires are related, all descended from Isis and Osiris (Akasha and Enkil), the Mother and Father. The revenants of Transylvania are a kind of Neanderthal offshoot of the vampire race, more like mindless animals than the godlike main characters.

The tragedy of immortality, as Rice sees it, is that vampires, like mortals, are creatures of their age, and as time passes, they become outsiders, left behind in the mindset of their own centuries, and eventually despair and commit suicide, or are killed by other vampires. Only the resilient minds can ride the tide of times and stay open to new ideas; these vampires over the centuries lose their need for human blood and become gods—Baldar, Pandora, and so forth. The books are steeped in eroticism, the act of blood-drinking described as superhuman ecstasy. Rice's homo-erotic scenes are more vivid than her heterosexual ones, but she makes a valiant effort to include a little of everything.

[16] See quotation at the beginning of this chapter.

[17] Qtd. in Gladys Fall, "The Feminine Love of Horror," *Motion Picture Classic*, January 1931. The quote sounds suspiciously as though it were dreamed up by someone in Universal's publicity department.

### Conclusion

[1] Le vampire est donc avant tout un double:...La preuve en est bien que la vampire, n'etant que le double d'un être, en est comme une ombre ou un reflet. Et c'est pourquoi il lui est impossible de projeter lui-même une ombre, ou de se réfléchir dans un miroir (99).

[2] *Le vampirisme est manifestement la représentation symbolique de l'érotisme.* Nul besoin d'être rompu aux subtilités de la sexologie pour reconnaître ce que signifient le baiser-morsure, l'échange du sang (substance vitale), la proéminence phallique des canines et jusqu'à la destruction-castration.... Une fois de plus, nous remarquons ici l'ambivalence psychanalytique de la monstruosité, dans l'acte vampirique lui-même: lequel comprend en même temps pénétration des dents (viol/agression/possession) et l'aspiration de sang (succion: persistance d'un stade pré-oedipien). Comme tous les monstres "fantastiques," le vampire est à la fois le Père et l'Enfant de Freud, la victime et le bourreau (101).

[3] Qtd. from a lawsuit. Lugosi received no remuneration for the use of his likeness, and his heirs lost their case.

# Bibliography

Listings for the manuscripts and first editions of the plays are to be found in Appendix A.

Abel, Richard. *French Cinema: The First Wave, 1915-1929*. Princeton: Princeton UP, 1984.

Adams, W. Davenport. *Dictionary of the Drama*. 1904. New York: Burt Franklin, 1968.

Albert, Maurice. *Les Théâtres des boulevards (1789-1848)*. Paris: Société Française, 1902.

Aldridge, A. Owen. "The Vampire Theme: Dumas père and the English Stage." *Revue des Langues Vivants* 39 (1973-74): 312-24.

Allen, Reginald. *The First Night Gilbert and Sullivan*. London: Chappell and Co., Ltd., 1961.

Ansorge, Peter. *Disrupting the Spectacle: Five Years of Experimental and Fringe Theatre in Britain*. London: Pitman, 1985.

*Anthology of German Poetry Through the Nineteenth Century*. Eds. Alexander Gode and Frederick Ungar. New York: Frederick Ungar, 1964.

Arata, Stephen D. "The Occidental Tourist: 'Dracula' and the Anxiety of Reverse Colonization." *Victorian Studies* 33.4 (Summer 1990): 621-46.

Ariès, Philippe. *The Hour of Our Death*. Trans. Helen Weaver. New York: Vintage, 1982.

Arvin, Neil Cole. *Eugène Scribe and the French Theatre, 1815-1860*. New York: B. Blom, 1967.

Astle, Richard. "Dracula as Totemic Monster: Lacan, Freud, Oedipus and History." *Sub-stance* 25 (1980): 98-105.

Auerbach, Nina. *Ellen Terry: Player in Her Time*. New York: W.W. Norton, 1987.

____. "Escaping the Vampire Trap." Paper presented at the Victorian Theatre and Theatricality Conference of the Victorian Committee of the Doctoral Program in English, City University of New York, 8 May 1992.

____. *Private Theatricals: The Lives of the Victorians*. Cambridge: Harvard UP, 1980.

____. *Woman and the Demon: The Life of a Victorian Myth*. Cambridge: Harvard UP, 1982.

Axton, William. *Circle of Fire*. Lexington: U of Kentucky P, 1966.

Babener, Liahna Klenman. "Predators of the Spirit: The Vampire Theme in Nineteenth-Century Literature." Ph.D. diss., U of California, 1975.

Bailey, J.O. *Plays of the Nineteenth Century.* New York: Odyssey, 1966.

Baker, Michael. *The Rise of The Victorian Actor.* London: Croon Helm, 1978.

Barber, Paul. "The Real Vampire." *Natural History* Oct. 1990: 79-106.

_____. *Vampires, Burial and Death: Folklore and Reality.* New Haven: Yale UP, 1990.

Barker, Clive. "A Theatre for Poor People." *Essays on Nineteenth Century British Theatre.* Ed. Kenneth Richards and Peter Thomson. London: Methuen and Co., 1971.

Bayer-Berenbaum, Linda. *The Gothic Imagination.* London: Associated UP, 1982.

Beaulieu, H. *Les Théâtres du Boulevard du Crime.* Paris: H. Daragon, 1904.

Bell, A. Craig. *Alexandre Dumas: A Biography and Study.* Incl. "Spurious Works and Works of Doubtful Authenticity." London: Cassell, 1950.

Bentley, Christopher. "The Monster in the Bedroom: Sexual Symbolism in Bram Stoker's *Dracula.*" *Literature and Psychology* 22.1 (1972): 27-34.

Bentley, Eric. *The Life of the Drama.* New York: Atheneum, 1967.

Bérard, Cyprien. *Lord Ruthven ou les vampires.* Paris: Ladvocat, 1820.

Bernhardt-Kabisch, Ernest. *Robert Southey.* Boston: Twayne, 1977.

Bierman, Joseph. "*Dracula*: Prolonged Childhood Illness and the Oral Triad." *American Imago* 29 (1972): 186-98.

Birkhead, Edith. *The Tale of Terror.* London: Constable, 1921.

Bleiler, E.F, ed. "John Polidori and the Vampire." *Three Gothic Novels.* New York: Dover, 1966.

Bodkin, Maud. *Archetypal Patterns in Poetry.* New York: Vintage, 1958.

*The Book of Dracula.* Ed. Leslie Shepard. New York: Wings, 1991.

Bojarski, Richard. *The Films of Bela Lugosi.* Secaucus, NJ: Citadel, 1980.

Booth, Michael R. "The Acting of Melodrama." *University of Toronto Quarterly* 34 (1964): 31-48.

_____. "East End Melodrama." *Theatre Survey* 17 (1976): 57-67.

_____. *English Melodrama.* London: Herbert Jenkins, 1965.

_____. *Hiss the Villain.* New York: B. Blom, 1964.

_____. *Prefaces to Nineteenth-Century Theatre.* Manchester: Manchester UP, 1981.

_____. *Victorian Spectacular Theatre 1850-1910.* London: Routledge and Kegan Paul, 1981.

Boyd, Alice Katherine. *The Interchange of Plays Between London and New York 1911-1939.* New York: King's Crown, 1948.

Boyle, Thomas. *Black Swine in the Sewers of Hampstead.* New York: Viking, 1989.

Broeske, Pat H. "Hollywood Goes Batty for Vampires." *The New York Times* 26 May 1992, Arts and Leisure: 1.

Brooks, Peter. "Une ésthetique de l'étonnement: le mélodrame." *Poétique* 19 (1974).

Byron, George Gordon, Lord. "Fragment of a Novel." 1816. *Three Gothic Novels.* Ed. E.F. Bleiler. New York: Dover, 1966.

Caillois, Roger. "De la féerie à la science-fiction." *Oblique.* Paris: Stock, 1975.

Carlson, M.M. "What Stoker Saw: An Introduction to the History of the Literary Vampire." *Folklore Forum* 10.2 (1977): 26-32.

Carlson, Marvin. *The French Stage in the Nineteenth Century.* Metuchen, NJ: Scarecrow, 1972.

____. *The German Stage in the Nineteenth Century.* Metuchen, NJ: Scarecrow, 1972.

____. "The Old Vic: A Semiotic Analysis." *Semiotica* 71-3/4 (1988): 187-212.

____. "Theatre Audiences and the Reading of Performance." *Interpreting the Theatrical Past.* Ed. Thomas Postlewait and Bruce A. McConachie. Iowa City: U of Iowa P, 1989.

____. *Theories of the Theatre.* Ithaca: Cornell UP, 1984.

Carney, Raymond. *Speaking the Language of Desire: The Films of Carl Dreyer.* Cambridge: Cambridge UP, 1989.

Carroll, Noël. *The Philosophy of Horror: Paradoxes of the Heart.* London: Routledge, 1990.

Carter, Margaret L. *Dracula: The Vampire and the Critics.* Ann Arbor: UMI Research, 1988.

____. *Specter or Delusion: The Supernatural in Gothic Fiction.* Ann Arbor: UMI Research, 1989.

____. *The Vampire in Literature.* Ann Arbor: UMI Research, 1989.

Cavendish, Richard. *The Black Arts.* New York: Capricorn, 1967.

Cawelti, John G. *Adventure, Mystery and Romance: Formula Stories as Art and Popular Culture.* Chicago: U of Chicago P, 1973.

Chorley, Henry Fothergill. *Personal Reminiscences by Çhorley, Planché and Young.* Ed. Richard Henry Stoddard. New York: Scribner, Armstrong, 1875.

Collins, Charles W. *Great Love Stories of the Theatre.* New York: Duffield and Co., 1911.

Clarens, Carlos. *An Illustrated History of the Horror Films.* New York: Putnam's, 1967.

Copper, Basil. *The Vampire in Legend, Fact, and Art.* London: Hale, 1973.

Coppola, Francis Ford, and James V. Hart. *Bram Stoker's Dracula: The Film and the Legend.* New York: Newmarket, 1992.

Craft, Christopher. "Kiss Me With Those Red Lips: Gender and Inversion in Bram Stoker's *Dracula.*" *Speaking of Gender.* Ed. Elaine Showalter. New York: Routledge, 1989.

Craig, Edward Gordon. *Henry Irving.* London: Dent, 1930.

Danforth, Loring M. *The Death Rituals of Rural Greece.* Princeton: Princeton UP, 1982.

Darnton, Robert. *Mesmerism and the End of the Enlightenment in France.* Cambridge: Harvard UP, 1968.

Davidson, Arthur E. *Alexandre Dumas: His Life and Works.* London: Archibald Constable, 1902.

Davies, Robertson. *The Mirror of Nature.* Toronto: U of Toronto P, 1982.

De Quincey, Thomas. *Confessions of an English Opium Eater and Other Writings.* Ed. Aileen Ward. New York: New Atheneum Library, 1966.

Dickens, Charles, Jr. "Vampires and Ghouls." *All the Year Round.* 20 May 1871. *The Dracula Scrapbook.* Ed. Peter Haining. New York: Bramhill House, 1976.

*Dictionnaire des comédiens français.* 2 vols. Ed. Henry Lyonnet. Genève: Revue Universelle Internationale Illustré, 1911.

*Dictionnaire des figures et des personnages.* Ed. Cl. Aziza, Cl. Olivieri, and R. Sctrick. Paris: Editions Garnier frères, 1981.

Dijkstra, Bram. *Idols of Perversity: Fantasies of Evil in Fin-de-Siècle Culture.* New York: Oxford UP, 1986.

Dimic, Milan V. "Vampiromania in the Eighteenth Century: The Other Side of Enlightenment." *Man and Nature/L'Homme et la Nature: Proceedings of the Canadian Society for Eighteenth-Century Studies* 3. Ed. R.J. Merrett. Edmonton: The Society, 1984.

Dircks, Phillis T. "James Robinson Planché and the English Burletta Tradition." *Theatre Survey* 17 (1976): 68-81.

*Directory of Historic American Theatres.* Ed. John W. Frick and Carlton Ward. New York: Greenwood, 1987.

*The Dolmen Boucicault.* Ed. David Krause. Maas, Leinster, Rep. of Ireland: Dufour, 1963.

Donohue, Joseph. *Theatre in the Age of Kean.* Totowa, NJ: Rowman and Littlefield, 1975.

Downer, Alan S. "Players and the Painted Stage: Nineteenth-Century Acting." *PMLA* 61 (1946): 537-38.

*The Dracula Scrapbook.* Ed. Peter Haining. New York: Bramhill House, 1976.

Dreyer, Carl Theodor. "Vampyr." *Four Screenplays.* Bloomington: Indiana UP, 1970.

Duerr, Edwin. *The Length and Depth of Acting.* New York: Holt, Rinehart and Winston, 1962.

Dumas, père, Alexandre. *Mes Mémoires.* 1863. Paris: Gallimard, 1958.

Dunhill, Thomas F. *Sullivan's Comic Operas: A Critical Appreciation.* London: E. Arnold, 1928. New York: Da Capo Press, 1981.

Dworkin, Andrea. *Sexual Intercourse.* New York: Free Press, 1987.

Eisner, Lotte H. *The Haunted Screen: Expressionism in the German Cinema and the Influence of Max Reinhardt.* Berkeley: U of California P, 1969.

____. *Murnau.* Berkeley: U of California P, 1973.

*Enciclopedia dello Spettacolo.* Ed. Silvio D'Amico. Roma: Unione Editoriale, 1968.

*Encyclopedia of Horror Movies.* Ed. Phil Hardy. Cambridge: Harper and Row, 1986.

Estève, Edmond. *Byron et le Romantisme Français.* Paris: Boivin, 1929.

Evans, Bertrand. *Gothic Drama from Walpole to Shelley.* Berkeley: U of California P, 1947.

Everson, William K. *Classics of the Horror Film.* New York: Citadel, 1992.

Faivre, Tony. *Les Vampires.* Paris: Eric Losfield, 1962.

Farson, Daniel. *The Man Who Wrote Dracula: A Biography of Bram Stoker.* New York: St. Martin's, 1975.

____. *Vampires, Zombies, and Monster Men.* New York: Aldus, 1975.

Fawkes, Richard. *Dion Boucicault: A Biography.* London: Quartet Books, 1979.

Finné, Jacques. *La Bibliographie de Dracula.* Paris: L'Age d'Homme, 1986.

Fitz-gerald, S.J. Adair. *The Story of the Savoy Opera in the Days of Gilbert and Sullivan.* 1925. New York: Da Capo, 1979.

*The Flesh Is Frail: Byron Letters and Journals.* Ed. Leslie A. Marchand. Cambridge: Harvard UP, 1976.

Florescu, Radu, and Raymond McNally. *Dracula, Prince of Many Faces.* New York: Little, Brown, and Co., 1989.

____. *The Essential Dracula.* New York: Mayflower, 1977.

____. *In Search of Dracula.* New York: Little, Brown, and Co., 1972.

Forrey, Steven Earl. *Hideous Progenies: Dramatizations of Frankenstein from Mary Shelley to the Present.* Philadelphia: U of Pennsylvania P, 1990.

Foust, R.E. "Monstrous Image: Theory of Fantasy Antagonists." *Genre* 13 (1980): 441-53.

Frayling, Christopher, ed. *The Vampire: Lord Ruthven to Count Dracula.* London: Gollanz, 1978.

____. *Vampyres: Lord Byron to Count Dracula.* London: Faber and Faber, 1991.

Freud, Sigmund. *Complete Works.* Ed. James Strachey. London: Hogarth, 1955.

____. *The Freud Reader.* Ed. Peter Gay. New York: W.W. Norton, 1989.

Frost, Brian J. *The Monster with a Thousand Faces: Guises of the Vampire in Myth and Literature.* Bowling Green, OH: Bowling Green State University Popular Press, 1989.

Gerould, Daniel, trans. "From Adam Mickiewicz's Lectures on Slavic Literature given at the College de France: Lesson 16—'Slavic Drama' 4 April 1843." *The Drama Review* 30.3 (Fall 1986): 91-97.

____, ed. *Melodrama.* New York: New York Literary Forum, 1980.

Gilmer, Walter. *Horace Liveright, Publisher of the Twenties.* New York: David Lewis, 1970.

Ginisty, Paul. *Le Mélodrame.* Paris: Louis-Michaud, Bibliothèque Théatrale Illustré, 1910.

Glut, Donald F. *The Dracula Book.* Metuchen NJ: Scarecrow, 1975.

Goethe, Johann Wolfgang von. "Die Braut von Korinth." *Werke.* Leipzig: 1797.

Gorman, Herbert Sherman. *The Incredible Marquis, Alexandre Dumas.* New York: Farrar and Rinehart, 1929.

*La Grande Encyclopédie.* Paris: H. Lamirault, 1899.

*La Grande Larousse Encyclopédique.* Paris: Larousse, 1961.

Granville-Barker, Harley. "Exit Planché—Enter Gilbert." *London Mercury* 25 (1931): 457-66, 558-73.

Gray, Jonathan M. "A Historical Examination of Vampires in 1820s Paris Boulevard Theater." Paper presented at the annual conference of the Popular Culture Association, Louisville, KY, Mar. 1992.

Green, Martyn. *Martyn Green's Treasury of Gilbert and Sullivan.* New York: Simon and Schuster, 1961.

Griffin, Gail. "'Your Girls That You All Love Are Mine': Dracula and the Victorian Male Imagination." *International Journal of Women's Studies* 3 (1980).

Grimsted, David. *Melodrama Unveiled.* Chicago: U of Chicago P, 1968.

Grout, Donald Jay. *A Short History of the Opera*. New York: Columbia UP, 1947.

Hardy, Phil, ed. *Encyclopedia of Horror Movies*. Cambridge: Harper and Rowe, 1986.

Hatlin, Bernard. "The Return of the Repressed/Oppressed." *Minnesota Review* 15 (1980).

Heilman, Robert B. *Tragedy and Melodrama*. Seattle: U of Washington P, 1968.

Heine, Heinrich. *Complete Poems*. Trans. Hal Draper. Boston: Suhrkamp/ Insel, 1982.

Hibbert, Christopher. *Gilbert and Sullivan and Their Victorian World*. New York: American Heritage, 1976.

Hock, Stefan. *Die Vampyrsagen und ihre Verwertung in der deutschen Literatur*. Berlin: A. Duncker, 1900.

Hogan, Robert Goode. *Dion Boucicault*. Boston: Twayne, 1969.

Hollinger, Veronica. "The Vampire and the Alien: Variations on the Outsider." *Science Fiction Studies* 16.2 (July 1989): 145.

Horn, Patrice. "The Vampire Next Door." *Psychology Today* Aug. 1972: 89-92.

Howarth, W.D. *Sublime and Grotesque: A Study of French Romantic Drama*. London: Harrap, 1975.

Hoyt, Olga. *Lust for Blood: The Consuming Story of Vampires*. New York: Stern and Day, 1984.

Huss, Roy, and T.J. Ross. *Focus on the Horror Film*. Englewood Cliffs, NJ: Prentice-Hall, 1972.

*Interpreting the Theatrical Past*. Ed. Thomas Postlewait and Bruce A. McConachie. Iowa City: U of Iowa P, 1989.

Ireland, Joseph N. *Records of the New York Stage 1750-1860*. 2 vols. New York: Burt Franklin, 1968.

Irvin, Eric. "Dracula's Friends and Forerunners." *Quadrant* 135 (1978): 42-44.

Irving, Laurence. *Henry Irving: The Actor and His World*. London: Faber and Faber, 1951.

Johnson, Alan P. "'Dual Life': The Status of Women in Stoker's *Dracula*." *Sexuality and Victorian Literature, Tennessee Studies in Literature*. vol. 27. Ed. Don Richard Cox. Knoxville: U of Tennessee P, 1984: 20-39.

Jones, Ernest. *On the Nightmare*. London: Hogarth, 1949.

Juin, Hubert. *Charles Nodier*. Paris: Editions Pierre Seghers, 1970.

Jung, C.G. *Man and His Symbols*. Garden City: Doubleday, 1964.

Kayton, Lawrence. "The Relationship of the Vampire Legend to Schizophrenia." *Journal of Youth and Adolescence* 1.4 (1972): 303-14.

Kearns, Martha E. "Vampires' Victims: A Feminist Perspective." Paper presented at the annual conference of the Popular Culture Association, Louisville, KY, Mar. 1992.

Kendrick, Walter. *The Thrill of Fear: 250 Years of Scary Entertainment*. New York: Grove Weidenfeld, 1991.

Kiessling, Nicholas. "Grendal: A New Aspect." *Modern Philology* 65 (Feb. 1968): 191-201.

Kilgarriff, Michael, ed. *The Golden Age of Melodrama: Twelve 19th Century Melodramas.* London: Wolfe, 1974.

Köhler, V. "Rezitativ, Szene und Melodram in Heinrich Marschners Opern." *GfMKB.* Bonn, 1970: 461-64.

Koon, Helene, and Richard Switzer. *Eugène Scribe.* Boston: Twayne, 1980.

Lamb, Caroline. *Glenarvon.* London: Colburn, 1816.

Leatherdale, Clive. *Dracula, the Novel and the Legend: A Study of Bram Stoker's Gothic Masterpiece.* Wellingborough, Northamptonshire: Aquarian, 1986.

____. *The Origins of Dracula.* London: William Kimber, 1987.

Leathers, Victor L. *British Entertainers in France.* Toronto: U of Toronto P, 1959.

Lenne, Gérard. *Le Cinéma "Fantastique" et ses Mythologies, 1895-1970.* Paris: Henri Veyrier, n.d.

Lennig, Arthur. *The Count: The Life and Films of Bela "Dracula" Lugosi.* New York: Putnam's, 1974.

Levine, Lawrence W. *Highbrow/Lowbrow: The Emergence of Cultural Heritage in America.* Cambridge: Harvard UP, 1988.

Levy, Marc. "The Influence of Melodrama in Gilbert and Sullivan's Comic Operas." Unpublished paper, Department of Theatre, Graduate Center, City University of New York, 5 June 1990.

Liddell, Henry. *The Wizard of the North, The Vampire Bride, and Other Poems.* Edinburgh: Blackwood, 1833.

London, Rose. *Zombie: The Living Dead.* New York: Bounty, 1976.

Lowenthal, Leo. *Literature, Popular Culture, and Society.* Palo Alto, CA: Pacific, 1968.

Lucas-Dubreton, Jean. *The Fourth Musketeer: The Life of Alexandre Dumas.* Trans. Maida Castelheim Darton. New York: Coward McCann, 1928.

Ludlam, Harry. *A Biography of Bram Stoker, Creator of Dracula.* London: W. Foulsham, 1962.

MacDonald, D.L. *Poor Polidori: A Critical Biography of the Author of "The Vampyre."* Toronto: U of Toronto P, 1991.

Macfie, Sian. "Vampire Women: They Suck Us Dry." *Subjectivity in Literature: From the Romantics to the Present Day.* Ed. Philip Shaw and Peter Stockwell. London and New York: Pinter, 1991.

Macpherson, James. *The Poems of Ossian.* Edinburgh: James Thin, 1871.

Marchand, Leslie A. *Byron: A Portrait.* Chicago: U of Chicago P, 1970.

Markale, Jean. *L'Enigme des vampires.* Paris: Pygmalion, 1991.

Martin, Timothy P. "Joyce and Wagner's Pale Vampire." *James Joyce Quarterly* 23 (Summer 1986): 491-96.

Masters, Anthony. *The Natural History of the Vampire.* London: Hart Davis, 1972.

Maurois, Andre. *The Titans: A Three-Generation Biography of the Dumas.* Trans. Gerard Hopkins. New York: Harper, 1957.

Mayer, David, and Andrew Scott. *Four Bars of 'Agit': Incidental Music for Victorian and Edwardian Melodrama.* London: Samuel French and the Victoria and Albert Theatre Museum, 1983.

Mayer, David. *Henry Irving and The Bells*. Manchester: U of Manchester, 1980.

Mayhew, Henry. *London Labour and the London Poor*. 1861-62. 4 vols. New York: Dover, 1968.

McBride, William Thomas. "Dracula and Mephistopheles: Shyster Vampires." *Literature-Film Quarterly* 18.2 (Apr. 1990): 116.

McConachie, Bruce. *Melodramatic Formations: American Theatre and Society, 1820-1870*. Iowa City: U of Iowa P, 1992.

McFarland, Ronald. "The Vampire on Stage: A Study in Adaptations." *Comparative Drama* 21.1 (Spring 1987): 19-32.

Meisel, Martin. *Realizations: Narrative, Pictorial, and Theatrical Arts of the 19th Century*. Princeton: Princeton UP, 1983.

Mickiewicz, Adam. *Forefathers' Eve. Polish Romantic Drama: Three Plays in English Translation*. Ed. Harold B. Segal. Ithaca: Cornell UP, 1977.

___. *Les Slaves*. Course I. Lectures on Slavic literature given at the Collège de France, Paris. Lesson 16, "Slavic Drama," 4 Apr. 1843. Trans. Daniel Gerould. *The Drama Review* 30.3 (Fall 1986): 91-97.

Mitry, Jean. "Esthetique et psychologie du cinéma." *L'Histoire du Cinéma*. Vol. 1. Paris: Editions universitaires, 1963.

*Monster Fantasy*. "The Vampire Book." Ed. Florence V. Brown and Gary Gerani. 1.1 (Apr. 1975).

*The Monster Times*. "All Dracula Issue." Ed. Joe Kane and Harlan Williamson. 1.46 (Mar. 1976).

Moriarty, J. "Exhuming a Vampire." *Opera Journal* xiv/4 (1981): 4-12.

Morley, Henry. *The Journal of a London Playgoer*. 1866. Old Woking, Surrey: U of Leicester P, 1974.

Moynet, M.J. *French Theatrical Production in the Nineteenth Century*. New York: State U of New York at Binghamton, 1976.

Mulvey, Laura. "Visual Pleasure and Narrative Cinema." *Narrative, Apparatus, Ideology*. Ed. Philip Rosen. New York: Columbia UP, 1986.

Murphy, Brian. "The Nightmare of the Dark: The Gothic Legacy of Count Dracula." *Odyssey* 1, 2 (1976): 9-15.

Murphy, Michael J. *The Celluloid Vampires: A History and Filmography, 1897-1979*. Ann Arbor: Pierian, 1979.

Musser, Charles. *The Emergence of Cinema*. Vol. 1. *History of the American Cinema*. New York: Charles Scribner's Sons, 1991.

Nelson, Hilda. *Charles Nodier*. New York: Twayne, 1972.

Nelson, Lowry, Jr. "Night Thoughts on the Gothic Novel." *Yale Review* 52 (1963): 236-57.

"New Englanders 'Killed' Corpses, Experts Say." *The New York Times* (31 Oct. 1993): A36.

*New Grove Dictionary of Opera*. Ed. Stanley Sadie. London: Macmillan, 1992.

*New Grove Dictionary of Opera*. Ed. Stanley Sadie. New York: Macmillan, 1980.

*New Oxford Dictionary of Music*. Ed. Gerald Abraham. London: Oxford UP, 1982.

Nichols, Harold J. "The Acting of Thomas Potter Cooke." *Nineteenth Century Theatre Research* 5.2 (Autumn 1977): 73-84.

Nicoll, Allardyce. *A History of English Drama 1660-1900*. 6 vols. Cambridge: Cambridge UP, 1955.

Nodier, Charles. *Contes, avec des textes et des documents inédits*. Paris: Garnier, 1961.

____. *Les Démons de la nuit*. Ed. Francis Lacassin. Paris: Union Générale d'Editions, 1980.

____. et al. *Infernalia*. Paris: Samson, 1822. Hubert Juin, Paris: Belford, 1966.

____. *Lord Ruthven ou les vampires*. Ed. Max Milner. Marseilles: Laffitte Reprints, 1978.

____. *Oeuvres*. 12 vols. Genève: Slatkine, 1968.

____. *Le Vampire/Le Delateur, Oeuvres dramatiques*. Ed. Ginette Picat-Guinoiseau. Geneva: Droz, 1990.

*Nouveau Larousse Encyclopédie Illustré*. Paris: Librarie Larousse, n.d.

Odell, George C. *Annals of the New York Stage*. New York: Columbia UP, 1927, repr. AMS Press, 1977.

Oliver, Alfred Richard. *Charles Nodier, Pilot of Romanticism*. Syracuse: Syracuse UP, 1964.

"On Vampires and Vampirism." *New Monthly Magazine and Universal Register* 14. London (1820): 548-52.

"On Vampirism." *New Monthly Magazine and Literary Journal* 7. London (1823): 140-49.

Ossenfelder, Heinrich August. *Der Naturforscher*. Leipzig: Achtundvierzigstes, 1748.

Otto, Rudolf. *Das Heilige*. 1917. Rpt. as *The Idea of the Holy*. Trans. John W. Harvey. New York: Oxford UP, 1958.

Oxberry, William. *Oxberry's Dramatic Biography and Green Room Spy*. New Series. Vol. 1. London: George Virtue, 1827.

____. *Oxberry's Dramatic Biography and Historic Anecdotes*. 6 vols. London: George Virtue, 1825-26.

*The Oxford Companion to the American Theatre*. Ed. Gerald Bordman. New York: Oxford UP, 1984.

Palmer, A. Dean. *Heinrich August Marschner (1795-1861): His Life and Works*. Ann Arbor: UMI Research, 1980.

*The Parisian Stage*. 5 vols. Ed. Charles Beaumont Wicks. University, AL: U of Alabama P, 1973.

Pascoe, Charles E. *Our Actors and Actresses: The Dramatic List*. 1880. London: B. Blom, 1969.

Paulin, Roger. *Ludvig Tieck: A Literary Biography*. Oxford: Clarendon, 1985.

Pearson, Hesketh. *Gilbert and Sullivan; A Biography*. New York: Harper and Bros., 1935.

Perkowski, Jan L. *The Darkling: A Treatise on Slavic Vampires*. Columbus, OH: Slavica, 1989.

Pfitzer, H. "Marschners Vampyr." *Neue Musik Zeitung* 15 (1924): 134.

Picat-Guinoiseau, Ginette. *Nodier et le théâtre*. Paris: Honoré Champion, 1990.

Pirie, David. *A Heritage of Horror: The English Gothic Cinema, 1946-1977*. New York: Avon, 1977.

____. *The Vampire Cinema*. New York: Crescent, 1977.

Planché, James Robinson. *Plays*. Ed. Donald Roy. Cambridge: Cambridge UP, 1986.

____. *Recollections and Reflections: A Professional Autobiography*. 2 vols. London: Tinsley Brothers, 1872.

____. *The Vampire, or the Bride of the Isles*. London: Cumberland, 1830.

Polidori, John. *The Vampyre and Ernestus Berchtold, or The Modern Oedipus: Collected Fiction of John William Polidori*. Ed. D.L. Macdonald and Kathleen Scherf. Toronto: U of Toronto P, 1994.

Pollitzer, Marcel. *Trois Reines de théâtre*. Paris: La Columbe, 1958.

Prawer, S.S. *Caligari's Children: The Film as Tale of Terror*. Oxford: Oxford UP, 1980.

Praz, Mario. *The Romantic Agony*. 1930. Trans. Angus Davidson. London: Oxford UP, 1970.

Prendergast, Christopher. *Balzac, Fiction and Melodrama*. London: Edward Arnold, Ltd., 1978.

Quakenbush, Robert. *Movie Monsters and Their Masters: The Birth of the Horror Film*. Chicago: Whitman, 1980.

Radcliffe, Ann. *The Italian*. 1797. London: Oxford UP, 1968.

Rahill, Frank. *The World of Melodrama*. University Park: Pennsylvania State UP, 1967.

Railo, Eino. *The Haunted Castle: A Study of the Elements of English Romanticism*. London: George Routledge and Sons, 1927.

Ramsland, Katherine. "Hunger for the Marvelous: The Vampire Craze in the Computer Age." *Psychology Today* Nov. 1989: 31-36.

Reed, Donald. *The Vampire on the Screen*. Inglewood, CA: Wagon and Star, 1980.

*The Revels History of Drama in English, VI, 1750-1880*. Ed. Michael R. Booth, Richard Southern, Frederick Marker, Lise-Lone Marker, and Robertson Davies. London: Methuen, 1975.

Reynolds, Ernest. *Early Victorian Drama 1830-1870*. New York: B. Blom, 1936.

Riccardo, Martin. "Satanism, Christianity, and Blood Mania." *Journal of Vampirism* 1.2 (Nov. 1977-Jan. 1978): 16.

____. "The Vampire as a Psychic Archetype." *TAT Journal* 2.3 (Summer 1979): 16-23.

____. *Vampires Unearthed: The Complete Multi-Media Vampire and Dracula Bibliography*. New York: Garland, 1983.

Rice, Anne. *Interview with the Vampire*. New York: Alfred A. Knopf, 1976.

____. *The Vampire Lestat*. New York: Alfred A. Knopf, 1985.

Richardson, Maurice. "The Psychoanalysis of Ghost Stories." *Twentieth Century* 166 (1959): 419-31.

____. "The Psychology of Dracula." *Vampyres: Lord Ruthven to Count Dracula*. Ed. Christopher Frayling. London: Faber and Faber, 1991.

*The Rivals of Dracula: A Century of Vampire Fiction*. Ed. Michel Parry. London: Corgi, 1977.

Rogers, Brian. *Charles Nodier et la tentation de la folie*. Genéve: Editions Slatkine, 1985.

Roth, Phyllis A. *Bram Stoker*. Boston: Twayne, 1982.

____. "Suddenly Sexual Women in Bram Stoker's *Dracula*." *Literature and Psychology* 27 (1977): 113-21.

Rowell, George. *The Victorian Theatre, A Survey*. London: Oxford UP, 1956.

Roy, Donald, ed. *Plays by James Robinson Planché*. Cambridge: Cambridge UP, 1986.

Royer, Alphonse. "Le Mélodrame et ses transformations." *Histoire universelle du Théâtre*. Vol. 5. "Histoire du Théâtre contemporain en France et a l'étranger depuis 1800 jusqu'a 1975." Paris: Paul Ollendorf, 1978: 350-431.

Rymer, James Malcolm. *Varney the Vampire, or The Feast of Blood*. c. 1847. New York: Dover, 1970.

Saxon, A.H. *P.T. Barnum, The Legend and the Man*. New York: Columbia UP, 1989.

Senf, Carol A. *The Vampire in Nineteenth Century Literature*. Bowling Green, OH: Bowling Green State University Popular Press, 1988.

Senn, Harry A. *Were-Wolf and Vampire in Romania*. New York: Columbia UP, 1982.

Sherson, Errol. *London's Lost Theatres of the Nineteenth Century*. London: John Lane, 1925.

Showalter, Elaine. *Sexual Anarchy: Gender and Culture at the Fin-de-Siècle*. New York: Bloomsbury, 1991.

Silver, Alain, and James Ursini. *The Vampire Film*. Cranbury, NJ: A.S. Barnes and Co., 1975.

*The Simon and Schuster Book of the Opera*. Ed. Arnoldo Mondadori. New York: Simon and Schuster, 1977.

Skal, David J. *Hollywood Gothic*. New York: W.W. Norton, 1990.

____. *The Monster Show: A Cultural History of Horror*. New York: W.W. Norton, 1993.

Skarda, Patricia L. "Vampirism and Plagiarism: Byron's Influence and Polidori's Practice ('The Vampyre: A Tale')." *Studies in Romanticism* 28.2 (Summer 1989): 249.

Sorescu, Marin, Paul Russell-Geben, and Ioana Russell Gebben. "Vampires and Vampirology." *Times Literary Supplement* 11 Jan. 1991: 12.

*A Sourcebook in Theatrical History*. Ed. A.M. Nagler. New York: Dover, 1952.

Southern, Richard. *The Victorian Theatre*. Newton Abbott, Devon: David and Charles, 1970.

*Southey: The Critical Heritage*. Ed. Lionel Madden. London: Routledge and Kegan Paul, 1972.

Southey, Robert. *Poems of Robert Southey*. London: Oxford UP, 1909.

Staël, Germaine de. *De L'Allemagne*. Vol II. 1814. Paris: Librarie Hachette, 1958.

Stevenson, John Allen. "The Vampire in the Mirror: The Sexuality of *Dracula*." *PMLA* 103. 2 (Mar. 1988): 139-49.

Stoker, Bram. *Dracula*. Westminster: Constable, 1897.

___. *Personal Reminiscences of Henry Irving.* 2 vols. London: Heineman, 1906.

Stowe, Richard S. *Alexandre Dumas, père.* Boston: Twayne, 1976.

Strand, Ginger. "A Concise History of Blood-Sucking, Vampyrmania and Voyeurism." *Downtown* 306 (18 Nov. 1992): 14, 24, 29.

Sullivan, Jack. "Psychological, Antiquarian and Cosmic Horror, 1872-1919." *Horror Literature: A Core Collection and Reference Guide.* Ed. Marshall B. Tymm. New York: R.R. Company, 1981.

Summers, Montague. *The Gothic Imagination.* 1937. New York: Russell, 1964.

___. *The Vampire: His Kith and Kin.* 1928. New Hyde Park: New York University Books, 1960.

___. *The Vampire in Europe.* 1929. New Hyde Park: New York University Books, 1961.

Svehla, Gary J. "Forgotten Vampires of the Cinema." *The Monster Times* Oct. 1973: 3-5, 29.

Switzer, Richard. "Lord Ruthven and the Vampires." *French Review* 29 (1955): 107-12.

Taylor, Deems, ed. "Ruddigore or The Witch's Curse." *A Treasury of Gilbert and Sullivan.* New York: Simon and Schuster, 1941.

Thorslev, Peter L. *The Byronic Hero.* Minneapolis: U of Minnesota P, 1962.

Thorp, Willard. "The Stage Adventures of Some Gothic Novels." *PMLA* 43 (1928): 467-86.

Trussler, Simon. "A Chronology of Early Melodrama." *Theatre Quarterly* 1.4 (Fall 1971): 19-21.

Tudor, Andrew. *Monsters and Mad Scientists: A Cultural History of the Horror Movies.* Oxford: Blackwell, 1989.

Twitchell, James B. *Dreadful Pleasures: An Anatomy of Modern Horror.* New York: Oxford UP, 1985.

___. *The Living Dead: A Study of the Vampire in Romantic Literature.* Durham, NC: Duke UP, 1981.

___. "Shelley's Use of Vampirism in *The Cenci.*" *Tennessee Studies in Literature* 24 (1979): 120-33.

___. "The Vampire Myth." *American Imago* 37 (1980): 83-92.

*Vampires de Paris.* Ed. Francis Lacassin. Paris: Messageries du livre, n.d.

*Vampires: Two Centuries of Great Vampire Stories.* Ed. Alan Ryan. Garden City: Doubleday, 1987.

Varma, Devendra. *The Gothic Flame: Being a History of the Gothic Novel in England.* London: Barker, 1957.

___. "The Vampire in Legend, Lore, and Literature." Introduction to *Varney the Vampire; or, The Feast of Blood.* New York: Arno, 1970.

Varnado, S.L. *Haunted Presence: The Numinous in Gothic Fiction.* Tuscaloosa: U of Alabama P, 1987.

*Victorian Dramatic Criticism.* Ed. George Rowell. London: Methuen, 1971.

*Victorian Plays: A Record of Significant Productions on the London Stage, 1837-1901.* Comp. Donald Mullin. New York: Greenwood, 1987.

Villenueve, Roland. *Le Diable: érotologie de Satan.* Paris: J.J. Pauvert, 1963.

____. *Loup-garous et vampires*. Paris and Geneva: La Palantine, 1963.

Volta, Ornella. *The Vampire*. Trans. Raymond Rudorff. London: Tandem, 1965.

Waller, Gregory. *American Horrors: Essays on the Modern American Horror Film*. Urbana: U of Illinois P, 1987.

____. *The Living and the Undead: From Stoker's Dracula to Romero's Dawn of the Dead*. Urbana: U of Illinois P, 1986.

Walsh, Townsend. *The Career of Dion Boucicault*. New York: B. Blom, 1967.

Watson, Ernest Bradlee. *Sheridan to Robertson: A Study of the 19th Century Stage*. New York: B. Blom, 1926.

Watt, William W. *Shilling Shockers of the Gothic School; A Study of Chapbook Gothic Romances*. Cambridge, MA: Harvard UP, 1932.

Weissman, Judith. "Women as Vampires: *Dracula* as a Victorian Novel." *Midwest Quarterly* 18 (1977): 392-405.

West, Paul. *Lord Byron's Doctor*. Chicago: U of Chicago P, 1990.

White, P.C. "Two Vampires of 1828." *Opera Quarterly* 1 (1987): 22-57.

Wilson, Mrs. C. Baron. *Our Actresses, or Glances at Stage Favorites, Past and Present*. 2 vols. London: Smith, Elder, and Co., 1844.

Wilson, Katharina M. "The History of the Word Vampire." *Journal of the History of Ideas* 34.46 (Oct./Dec 1985): 577-83.

Winter, Marian Hannah. *The Theatre of Marvels*. New York: B. Blom, 1964.

Wischhusen, Stephen, ed. *The Hour of One: Six Gothic Melodramas*. London: Gordon Fraser, 1975.

Wolf, Leonard. *The Annotated Dracula*. New York: Clarkson N. Potter, 1975.

____. *A Dream of Dracula: In Search of the Living Dead*. Boston: Little, Brown, 1972.

____. *The Essential Dracula*. New York: Plume, 1993.

____. *Horror: A Connoisseur's Guide to Literature and Film*. New York: Facts on File, 1989.

Wood, Robin. "Burying the Undead: The Use and Obsolescence of Count Dracula." *Mosaic* 16 (Winter-Spring 1983): 175-87.

____. "The Dark Mirror: Murnau's *Nosferatu*." *The American Nightmare: Essays on the Horror Film*. Ed. Richard Lieppe and Robin Wood. Toronto: Festival of Festivals, c. 1979.

____. "The Return of the Repressed." *Film Comment* 14 (July 1978): 24-32.

Wright, Dudley. *Vampires and Vampirism*. London: William Rider and Son, 1914.

Young, William C. *Famous American Playhouses*. Vol. 1. *Documents in American Theatre History*. Chicago: American Library Association, 1973.

# Index of Proper Names

*Numbers in italics refer to illustrations.*